African Pentecostalism

African Pentecostalism

An Introduction

OGBU KALU

UNIVERSITY PRESS

2008

OXFORD

UNIVERSITY PRESS

Oxford University Press, Inc., publishes works that further
Oxford University's objective of excellence
in research, scholarship, and education.

Oxford   New York
Auckland   Cape Town   Dar es Salaam   Hong Kong   Karachi
Kuala Lumpur   Madrid   Melbourne   Mexico City   Nairobi
New Delhi   Shanghai   Taipei   Toronto

With offices in
Argentina   Austria   Brazil   Chile   Czech Republic   France   Greece
Guatemala   Hungary   Italy   Japan   Poland   Portugal   Singapore
South Korea   Switzerland   Thailand   Turkey   Ukraine   Vietnam

Published by Oxford University Press, Inc.
198 Madison Avenue, New York, New York 10016

www.oup.com

Oxford is a registered trademark of Oxford University Press

Library of Congress Cataloging-in-Publication Data
Kalu, Ogbu.
African Pentecostalism : an introduction / Ogbu Kalu.
p. cm.
Includes bibliographical references and index.
ISBN 978-0-19-534000-6; 978-0-19-533999-4 (pbk.)
1. Pentecostalism—Africa—History.   2. Africa—Church history—20th
century.   I. Title.
BR1644.5.A35K34 2008
276'.082—dc22   2007029025

9 8 7 6 5 4 3 2 1

Printed in the United States of America
on acid-free paper

To all the grandchildren of my mother,
Maggie Uzumma Uchendu (1905–2005)
Remember the rock from whence you are hewn

Preface

In the past five years, I have team taught a course on global Pentecostalism with Professor David Daniels III. It has been a wonderful experience teaching on Pentecostal historiography and its manifestations in Africa and Asia while Daniels teaches on Pentecostalism in North America and Latin America, and Pentecostal theology. He continually challenged me to write a textbook for the African component. This work is designed to introduce and guide the reader through the literature on African Pentecostalism, to trace the background under the colonial canopy and the contours of Pentecostal Christianity in the postindependence period. The Pentecostal story must be woven into the broader tapestry of Christian presence and African responses. Contemporary scholarship tends to focus on the present manifestations of the Pentecostal movement, and without a long view misses much of the significance of the movement in the Africans' encounters with the gospel. With a keen eye on space/context, time/periodization, significant themes, changing patterns, and underpinning ideology, the historiography brings together many voices, especially the African voices that have not been heard because those who own the printing press dominate the conversation.

I hope to achieve certain goals: to weave the African story into the global and Western historiography and revisit the debate on the genealogy/origins and development of Pentecostalism. The relationship between Western Pentecostal evangelists and Africa differs from the pattern of the old missionary Christianity. One may need a foreign missionary to hear the gospel for the first time, but not necessarily for experiencing the baptism of the Spirit. Yet some scholars write about African Pentecostalism as if they were recounting the saga of nineteenth-century missionaries. The Pentecostal experience broke out without missionaries or any foreigners and often to the consternation of missionaries who deployed the colonial government's clout to contain the flares. In many cases, the indigenes invited the foreigners. This means that we should pay attention to periodization because the patterns of relationship changed through time. African Pentecostalism did not originate from Azusa Street and is not an extension of the American electronic church. We should analyze the relationship with external change agents carefully to show that the movement emanated from the missionary churches and evangelical spirituality. It is one of the ways that Africans responded to the missionary structures and appropriated the message. The Yorubas of southeastern Nigeria have a historiographical tradition called *oriki*. It was performed by women chanting the historical genealogy and identity moorings of the community, because a people who do not know where the rain met them could not possibly know where they are going. This inspires the beginning of this story about where and how the waves of the Pentecostal movement met Africans and how they responded.

The *arokin*, the storyteller, must start somewhere. Here, I choose to start from the first African response to Christian missionaries, namely, the Ethiopianism movement. Many scholars perceive followers of Ethiopianism as cultural nationalists and hardly connect them with Pentecostalism. A detailed and closer look shows that when Mensah Otabil, a Ghanaian Pentecostal, wrote his book *Beyond the Rivers of Ethiopia* in 1992, he was recelebrating the ideals of an older generation for our contemporary period. The battle at that time was the recovery of African identity through religious power. We could hear the echoes in the sermons of Nicholas Benghu of South Africa and in the motivational eloquence of Ezekiel Guti in Zimbabwe. The battle has continued unabated in spite of political independence in various countries of Africa. As Oginga Odinga, the Kenyan politician, declared our frustration, "It is not yet *uhuru!*" Indeed, the African condition has worsened because of failed leadership and the collapse of economies and infrastructure. Ethiopianism was a muscular movement that operated with a certain theodicy claiming that God has not deserted Africans to their humiliations but has raised a people to restore Africa's lost glory. Countering the white man's burden with an assertion of an ideology built around the black man's burden, the Ethiopian movement believed that Africa could be redeemed through Christianity. It carried within it the seeds of the early African American evangelization of Africa who arrived in West Africa in 1792 with a charismatic spirituality, a spirit of antistructure, resistance to colonial Christianity, and a vibrant black nationalism. This stamped African Christianity with recurring themes that would engage and energize African Pentecostalism in the twentieth and twenty-first centuries.

Ethiopian responses to colonialism splintered into a spectrum as some showed loyalty to the colonial missionary structures while others gave voice to African discontent, and others would exit from missionary institutions to found "native" African churches. These informed the responses of the future. The battle cry will echo through the centuries from theirs to our own that Africans must evangelize Africa; the sphinx must solve its own riddle! This message resounds like an echo throughout hollowed conch of African church history traceable in the messages of notable African Pentecostals such as Nicholas Benghu, Ezekiel Guti, Mensah Otabil, and especially Barrister Emeka Nwankpa and the Intercessors for Africa who have documented prophetic messages about God's design for Africa. This message inspired Pentecostal cultural policy that recognized the powers in the African world and crafted a theology of salvation that honed the cleansing and witchcraft eradication strategies of the ancient days. These Pentecostals creatively wove the Christ figure into the African universe as the person who could rescue, the *agyenkwa, as the Akans would say*. Keith Ferdinando entitled his book, *The Triumph of Christ in African Perspective* (1999) to demonstrate that Pentecostalism disagreed with the missionaries that the gods are nothing. Rather, Pentecostals argued from an intense reliance on the Bible that Christ redeems from demons and inimical spiritual forces. From this perspective, the discourse on externality is a Western attempt to impose a foreign interpretation on the African story resulting from the fact that when we fail to tell our story, other people will tell us a tale from their own vested interests. It is germane, therefore, to separate the background and early charismatic movements in the colonial period from the developments in the postindependence period, especially those occurring from the 1970s onward. The nature, goals, tools, strategies, and leadership of the battle for identity through religious power changed under new circumstances, but the goal remained the same.

More cogently, the character of modern African Pentecostalism changed in every generation, indeed, in every decade. We follow clearly the emphasis within the movement in the decades of 1970s, 1980s, 1990s, and thereafter. The diversity in the movement befuddles easy labeling. This compels attention to methodologies, biases, ideologies, and locations of the interpreters. The reflection here follows the new African historiography that is attentive to contextuality. Africa is a vast continent. Pentecostalism responded differently to various ecosystems. Therefore, we adopt a comparative perspective that nuances generalizations and examines the presence of charismatic and Pentecostal movements in various regions of the continent with thick description. The goal is to bring together into a composite image the resources of many monographs and articles devoted to specific regions. I acknowledge the scholarship of many scholars.

At the background is our ability to explain the rapid growth of the movement and the trauma of growth. We avoid the cardinal sin of monocausality and apply four explanatory discourses: the historical, cultural, instrumentalist and religious. The historical discourse avoids the crass form of providential history and traces the roots of the movement in preceding charismatic flares, which we described as a trail of ferments. We identify five types of *bakufuzu*, the Luganda word for revival movements in Africa throughout the period. The first part of the book, therefore, traces the typology of the revivals and the quest for spiritual power and identity in Africa between the years 1900 through 1960.

These prophets tilled the soil on which modern Pentecostalism thrives. They were closer to the grain of African culture in their responses to the gospel and so felt the resonance between the charismatic indigenous world-views and the equally charismatic biblical worldview. In 1910, the year that European missionary leaders gathered in a conference on The Mound, Edinburgh, to map the future of mission in Africa and the rest of the world, Wade Harris trekked from Grebo Island through the Ivory Coast to the Gold Coast, baptizing, healing, teaching new choruses, and charismatizing the religious landscape. The charismatic fire that he lit became more important for the future of Christianity in Africa than the grand Edinburgh Conference of 1910 that shut out African voices.

Then, the world wars came and scattered missionary infrastructure, giving rise to a new vista of African religious initiative. But the wars brought new social and political forces as Europeans consolidated their hold on African lands and economic resources and exploited and abused the African labor force. African response included subversive rumors, nascent political mobilization, and a plethora of radical religious movements predominantly bearing the marks of charismatic spirituality. The seeds that Wade Harris and other African prophets sowed sprouted in the interwar years into the roots of the modern Pentecostal movements. We capture their quest for identity through religious power in a chapter entitled *Moya*. This immediately raises the debate about the relationship between the modern African Pentecostalism and the African Instituted Churches (AICs) that veritably constituted the second African Christian challenge to colonial Christianity. Are they Pentecostals? The Pentecostals demonize them. The Shona of Zimbabwe refer among themselves to the AICs as *mademoni*. Although we will examine the many sides of the debate, I decided that for the sake of analytical clarity, as well as my lacking a view from insiders' perspectives, to leave AICs out of the study.

Because the historical discourse draws a clear line between the precedents and the charismatic movement that emerged in the 1970s, the ironic became clear in that this movement emerged from young people groomed in the missionary churches, Protestant and Catholic. While the force became stronger in the 1980s, it is amazing that the charismatic movement as a whole started among smaller, student-led charismatic movements in many African countries within the same period. A regional profile is adopted to illustrate the rise of the young puritan preachers, dubbed *aliliki* in Malawi. From the historical discourse, it can be demonstrated that the movement in Africa did not start from Azusa Street, therefore, we should pay attention to the case of southern Africa. Zionism did not originate or derive its name from Zion City, Illinois, as we have been made to believe. I conclude that a charismatic wind blew through the African continent in the postindependence period that first hit the youth and women, and later overawed the resistance of the mainline churches. In each country, certain socioeconomic and political factors determined the pattern of the early concerns. But the various strands connected across national boundaries.

All forms of religious expression use the resources of the indigenous cultures. People appropriate the gospel from their cultural worldviews. Therefore, the cultural discourse foregrounds the fit of the Pentecostal movement into the indigenous worldviews as an explanation for the attraction and growth of Pentecostalism, imaged as a religious response to the three publics—the indigenous "village" public, the emergent and urban culture, and the intruding Western public. Each public purveys certain values. It is argued that scholars have tended to start from and end the study of African Pentecostalism with contemporary, urban emergent cultures of Africa and have lost sight of the vitality of the movement as it engages the village public (where most Africans live and have their being) and later, in a reverse flow, the Western public. The starting point and ambience of a study is crucial in one's interpretation of the data. This explains the wrong emphasis on externality in some social scientific interpretations. We give space to emic perspectives and give voice to the African Pentecostal believers and African scholars without losing sight of the missionary enterprises of Western Classical Pentecostals or to critical voices, however hostile. The organic nature of the church as *soma*, body, demands that it should be the story of the whole people of God as agents and participants in what God has done in Christ through the power of the Holy Spirit. This is what church history is about. Adopting as our mascot the bird that the Twi call *sankofa*, we look back like *sankofa* to examine the Pentecostal roots in African heritage and how today's Pentecostals creatively respond to this heritage.

The 1980s were heady years. External Pentecostal and evangelical forces swamped Africa. Access to mass media became increasingly easy, thus allowing these media to serve as fascinating instruments for evangelization. Media can be resources and challenges to Christianity; they may empower evangelism, but they have a culture and spirit of their own. Sometimes Christians think that they are using the new electronic media when the opposite is the case. We will examine how the Pentecostals have used media and thereby became implicated in popular culture of the emergent public, which resulted in media reshaping the image of ministries and their leaders and valorizing Pentecostal missionary capacity. Leaders become the big men of the

big God. The commerciality and glitz of media raise questions of whether
Pentecostals package and sell religious products while their leaders perform
as movie stars and virtuoso healers.

Still, the strongest card of Pentecostals remains their vibrant evangelization. Using Donald McGavran's typology of mission (based on Acts 1:8), we
explore the changing features of Pentecostal missionary engagement from the
congregation, through the national boundaries to other African countries. In a
chapter called "Elijah's Mantle," we focus on the goal of reevangelizing Africa
through tertiary education, mission to the unreached peoples, and mission to
other African countries. Ministerial formation is core to the Pentecostal insurgence. The Pentecostal strategy has scrambled the missionary models of
theological education and reflects one of the traumas of growth, as bulging
numbers inundate all facilities. How do they fund and organize mission?
What has been the implication on their shifting polities and gender ideology?
The chapter also examines its missionary motif, shifting polities, funding
strategies, the theology of money, malpractice, and the problem of accountability. Money, power, and the role of women are like contrary winds that
scatter many ministries. But the role and critical mass of women in the
Pentecostal movement is so strong that women's roles, theology, and the
ambivalent gender ideology within the movement are examined in a chapter
entitled *Gendered Charisma*.

The instrumentalist discourse that has been a staple diet of the social
sciences has many uses. It enables the historian to examine in a scientific
manner the function, impact, and implication of Pentecostalism for the socioeconomic, political, and geopolitical development of the continent. At the
level of public ethics, it queries whether there are any inbuilt ideologies and
values within the movement that could enable the state to achieve democratic
and sustainable development. How does the movement contribute toward a
viable solution of the urgent needs of the people in a terrain fraught with
innumerable problems, especially poverty? Crucial in this regard are the debates on the public roles of Pentecostalism: its political practice, its attitude to
other religious faiths, especially the lack of a theology of interfaith dialogue,
and, therefore, the challenge of doing a holistic mission. Does Pentecostalism
bring *tembisa*, hope, in the Sotho language, in the midst of social suffering?
The discourse demonstrates that, in spite of secularism, religion has remained a force in the modern public space; that religion shapes the society
and it is, in turn, reshaped by cultural forces. But equally crucial is the need to
enlarge the purview of the political and to examine the religious substratum of
the modern public space in Africa. This substratum informs Pentecostal response. But the plurality of the public space exposes the lack of a theology of
dialogue in Pentecostal theology. I illustrate this by examining the demonization of Islam as the child of the bondwoman.

Pentecostalism is often treated as a social movement, and it certainly fits the characteristics. The religious discourse reaffirms that Pentecostalism is a preeminently religious movement and should be studied as such. The nature of its presence, self-understanding, what it says, does, and how it witnesses are important. People are attracted by its message and by its hermeneutics of trust, its certitudes and claim to stand on the word. Therefore, we should study its theology and practices. The discourse enables the brethren to reclaim voice. This does not ignore the critics because self-criticism is important and attention to "what men say" could be helpful as long as the evangelist is not distracted from doing what God says! Certain themes have attracted much attention such as the meaning of salvation; the gospel of prosperity, deliverance, and spiritual warfare; health and healing—theological themes that make the opponents jittery. Each is rooted in the Bible and in the indigenous theory of knowledge and goal of life.

The Akan concept of *nkwa*, the Igbo *nka na nzere*, all describe the goal of abundant life that the Pentecostal message interprets from the Scriptures. The religious discourse counters the instrumentalist emphasis on deprivation, pathology, pessimism, and externality and recasts the story with Christian idiom of hope, optimism, participation in Christ's victory, intercultural theology, antistructure, racial nationalism, and muscular evangelism. At the root of all these are how Pentecostals *interpret* and *preach* the Bible. Pentecostal hermeneutics should be paid attention as a specific lens for reading the Bible differently. Admittedly, it was not until the 1980s that Pentecostals shifted from bumper sticker hermeneutics to pay attention to the scholarly dimension. Still there is a rejection of the scholarly gymnastics in philosophical and liberal biblical interpretation. The homiletics may use colorful language and hyperbole but deploys charismatic resources to craft the tools of hope in daily living. Can African Pentecostalism be branded with the brush of fundamentalism, the characteristic that Philip Jenkins applied to the Christianity of the entire global south?

The reflection ends with the anatomy of reverse flow as African Pentecostalism builds new sanctuaries in the whole wide world. Coincidentally, the concept of reverse flow emerged from the passive revolution that missionaries devised during the decolonization of the church in Africa. It was a cry heard in the fiery debate on moratorium. The debate taught Africans certain lessons: To build a viable cross-cultural missionary enterprise would require a theology of mission, an ecclesiastical self-understanding, attention to sustainable logistics, and the guts or passion that drives the engine. We trace the contours to the contemporary explosion of immigrant Christianity in the global north as African Pentecostalism shows that it has come of age and built the requisites for reversing the flow of the missionary enterprise. We recall that the moratorium call resonated prominently with the ideals of Ethiopianism.

When African Christians returned to Alexandria in 1972 it reminded many of the effect a similar trip had on Wilmot Blyden in 1866. He predicted that the promise to Ethiopia (Africa) in the Psalms would come to pass. In his speech to the American Colonization Society in 1886, he mused that one day, when European materialism and secularism may have dampened its spiritual sensibility, Europe will turn to Africa to rekindle it. We must introduce African Pentecostalism from this perspective. Yet we are aware that immigrant churches have their hands full with the problems faced by immigrant communities not just in the global north but in the Islamized south and in the Holy Land. African Pentecostal churches still face the task of doing mission in the whole world.

In contemporary Christianity, Pentecostalism has become a major force constituting about a quarter of the world's two billion Christians, and the number of Pentecostals has grown by stressing an intimate and joyous relationship with God, adapting to local cultures—especially groups that have strong beliefs in the spirit world—and by focusing on healing, prophecy, and God's direct intervention in the material well-being of his people. The effort will be made to retell the story of African Pentecostalism by paying attention to space, time, themes, and various scholarly discourses, especially African voices.

Contents

PART I

Precedents in Early Charismatic Movements, 1900–1960s

I

Oriki

Genealogy and Identity in Pentecostal Historiography

1. Introduction: A Charismatic Identity

Among the Yoruba of southwestern Nigeria, the *oriki* tradition performed the task of historiography. It dealt with the core matters of genealogy and identity. But it did not merely perform the story of the past, it included a discourse on the significance of the history and how other performers have handled the story. Indeed, the performers, *arokin*, often expounded on how they inherited the tradition and faithfully maintained it. They were like the *griots* among the Mande of Senegal, Mali, and Guinea, also known as *belen Tigui*, respected wise men with deep knowledge of the course and meaning behind events. The Ikwerre of the Niger Delta described such people as having the python's eyes, noted for their penetrating and embracing vision. The goal here is to tell the story of African Pentecostalism as embodying Africans' quest for power and identity through religion. It is the insider's account that preserves the indigenous voice. But this chapter begins by embedding that story within the contours of global Pentecostal historiography that has focused on the concerns of Westerners and has tended to absorb the African story. The African religious achievement is often dismissed by emphasizing the external influences, and the African voice is imaged as an echo lacking the strength of the *arokin* and the *griots*. Our goal is to review the shape and flow of Africa's experience of the Pentecost with the eyes of the python, because of the salience of the Pentecostal movement in African historiography.

In 1996, Presbyterian pastors in Nigeria had a retreat. I was invited with a senior pastor to address the nagging problem of an insurgent charismatic movement. The older pastor spoke first. He castigated the movement that intruded from the United States. I was dismayed but could not contradict him because of cultural protocol about deference to older people. Instead, I told a story about Pastor Asonye whose village lies a stone's throw from the conference location. He was one of the five young men who spoke in tongues in 1934 without a missionary and contrary to their church's belief. They were kicked out from the Faith Tabernacle, formed the Church of Jesus Christ, and in 1939 invited the Assemblies of God (AOG) to take them over. Pastor Asonye served his church in various positions through many years to consolidate the AOG. Happily, the audience was fascinated by the human-interest story that happened near them.

The reflection here is foregrounded on two dimensions of African church historiography. First, Africans have lost their own story and absorbed another people's story. An enduring theme in African history is how to exorcise the humiliations from contacts with the Western world: the battered self-image, distorted identity, and challenges to the cultures and religions. The new studies of African religion and church history serve as the religious tools in the recovery of lost voice, identity, and power. Second, the rapid growth of African Pentecostalism is especially important as a dimension of Africans' allure to the pneumatic ingredients of the gospel that resonate with the power theme in indigenous religions, the power that sustained the cosmos, the socioeconomic and political structures, the power that gave meaning to life's journey from birth through death, and the sojourn in the ancestral world to reincarnated return to the human world. So pervasive was the sacralization of life's journey that religion and identity of persons and communities were ineluctably bound. Contemporary Pentecostalism, rooted in older religious revivals, is another phase of the quest for power and identity in Africa.

In non-Western contexts, traditionalism, an ideology that seeks to encrust traditions inherited from missionaries, turned missionary-founded churches into great opponents of religious radicalism of any color. A strain of anti-intellectualism within the Pentecostal movement worsened matters because it made little effort to develop counter-apologetics or examine its own affirmations. As one of their preachers proudly declared, "I believe in the Bible from Genesis to the index!" The class content of its membership in the early period, its confident diatribes against other religious forms, and the capacity to steal some sheep from the mainline churches created much conflict. Within various regions of the world, the Pentecostal movement seems to have burst onto the scene challenging the temper of Christian practice, doctrinal bastions, revered polities, liturgies, and muted or liberalized dimensions of Christian ethics. But Pentecostalism is a movement of diverse colors. Some have suggested that we should speak of "pentecostalisms." With growth has been a further blurring of the identity of this complex brand of Christianity.

As the background of the analytical reconstruction of African Pentecostalism, this chapter sets out to examine how the identity, origins, and character of the movement have been discussed in the literature. Recent scholarship grappled with the misreading in yesteryears because the contemporary growth of the movement appears unstoppable and globally significant. Beyond caricatures, questions abound about its socioeconomic and political significance, gender ideology, and ecumenical temper precisely because of its aggressive evangelism and nondialogical, deliberate endeavor to reshape many religious landscapes. Indeed, the first question is about Pentecostalism's actual size: Is it really growing, or merely splintering in a noisy, boisterous style? Statistical estimates abound but are usually vitiated by classification, typologies, inaccurate methods of gathering data in some non-Western contexts, and by the lack of reliable census figures in regions where communities do not share the fad of statistics. This difficulty is compounded by Pentecostalism's tendency to splinter, a fragility that is usually dubbed as "setting up new altars" arising from intramural conflicts over doctrine, theological rifts, moral lapses, personality clashes, competing ambition, or financial crises. The durability of a group may depend on the capacity to maintain a moral code that disciplines the body, speech, and sexuality of both leaders and followers. The life span of many groups in the movement could be very short. Within the atmosphere of rapid growth, we often lose sight of the fact that many Pentecostal groups fade as quickly as they started, decimated by schism, power failure, or funding constraints. They also age quickly; the charisma becomes routinized as the institution is bureaucratized. There is also a strong urban-rural divide in understanding this tendency because many churches in the rural areas tend to be poorer and smaller. Rural areas also exhibit a stronger level of competition for turf.

The astonishing growth in Africa must be understood within the larger perspective that all religious forms are growing; much of the population has not been bitten by the charismatic bug. Some of the figures include the African Instituted Churches (AICs). The Roman Catholic Church remains the largest Christian body in most of Africa. With these caveats in mind, statistical estimates are that in 2000, about 20 percent of the population in Zimbabwe, Tanzania, and Malawi were Pentecostal; 14 percent in Kenya; 11 percent in Nigeria; 10 percent in Ghana and Zambia; 8 percent in Democratic Republic of the Congo and South Africa; and 4 percent in Uganda. In absolute figures, these numbers are large. But it was the relative period of rapid and continuous growth that attracted attention and concern. Indeed, the growth of the movement in Africa, for instance, can be measured by nonquantitative indexes, and assessed by the vitality of practice, high visibility in the public space, and the intensity of the debate caused by its diatribe against traditional religion, cultural practices, and the alleged compromises by other forms of Christianity. The force of charismatism is often felt like a wind within the hallowed temples of opponents. As Cephas Omenyo entitled his book, there has been a pentecost outside Pentecostalism.[1]

Paul Gifford labeled it "a paradigm shift" amid the new developments in African Christianity. He noted that though the mainline churches remain significant in Ghana, "nevertheless, in two decades (1979–2000), they have in many ways been eclipsed by something quite new, the charismatic sector.... Nobody in Ghana is unaware of the shift. Everyone is aware of charismatic prayer centers, their all-night services, their crusades, conventions, and Bible schools, their new buildings (or the schools, cinemas and halls they rent), their car bumper stickers and banners, and particularly the posters that everywhere advertise an enormous range of forthcoming activities. Everyone is aware of their media efforts. Above all everyone knows of the new religious superstars."[2]

The shared doctrines, liturgical styles, devotional practices, and fundraising strategies between this movement and other churches indicate that the movement's impact on the religious landscape is significant beyond the tale of the tapes. It could be conjectured that the growth of the Pentecostal movement has even stemmed the growth of the AICs in West Africa and explains its declining numbers. The salience of the Pentecostal movement cannot be ignored as former critics have responded with encapsulation strategies that broadened the space for charismatic activities within their own institutions.

Yet its multiplicity and amoebic character may have created a complex movement that is full of ironies. For instance, scholars have argued that instead of lacking a theology, the movement is defined by its theology that privileges a personal spiritual encounter with God. The theology of mainline churches argues that when one's faith accepts Jesus Christ as Lord, grace and the power of the Spirit underpin the person's salvation. Pentecostals hone the process further by imaging faith as a person's way of receiving grace. *Charis* creates the backdrop for accessing *charisma* as the power freely given to achieve self-discipline, sobriety, holiness, and righteousness. That is, beyond the acceptance of Christ as a savior (conversion-regeneration) is another or second stage, an experience of a new birth (Spirit baptism), the accession of the charismatic power, a transforming experience that changes the relationship with the triune God. The experience and the relationship consolidated in new ethics constitute the core aspects of a new Christian identity.

As Donald Dayton argued, Pentecostal identity is revivalist, emphasizing charisma, conversion, and sanctification. It has a strong Christology because it is an experience of a new relationship with Christ as savior, healer, sanctifier (who baptizes with the Holy Spirit), and the sustainer of the hope of glory. He is the soon-coming-king.[3] Holiness, healing, and premillenial eschatology are woven into a theology that profiles the mainline churches as benchwarmers who have lost the power of the gospel that was very real in the early Jesus movement. This comes out clearly in the diary of Peter Anim (1890–1984), an early apostle of the movement in Ghana: "I was faced with the necessity of contending for a deeper faith and greater spiritual power than what my primary religious experience was able to afford, and I began to seek with such trepidation to know more about the Holy Ghost."[4]

But some Pentecostal scholars have recently questioned the justification of a two-stage understanding from the New Testament.[5] William Faupel and Edith Blumhofer emphasize the restorationist dimension in Pentecostal identity built on a deep recognition of the presence and power of the Holy Spirit, and rooted in the event on the Day of Pentecost. The event was not isolated but linked with the powerful ministry of Jesus that was connected to the fulfillment of God's interventions in the life of Israel in the Old Testament. The old pietists called the born-again experience one of experiencing "a Pentecostal day," and John Wesley believed that every day should be a day of Pentecost for believers as they walk in the Spirit and live a life of holiness. The *Apostolic Herald* (published in Seattle, Washington) declared in 1901 that "instead of this visitation being a reform, or strictly a movement, it is rather a breaking forth of centuries of overdue power, the praying down of heaven's Pentecost."[6] The Pentecost event included the transfer of the baton to the disciples whose ministries were continued in the early church. Naturally, early Pentecostals traced their genealogy to a recovery of the character of the early church.

Contrary to what critics allege, the movement did not lack a historical perspective, heritage, or traditional mooring. It reconnects with the early church of the New Testament. It asserts that there was rain, followed by a drought caused by apostasy, and that a restoration has come just as Joel prophesied. From this perspective, it is primitivist in the sense of returning to the origins, to the Apostolic Faith or continuity with the apostles.[7] The apostleship enunciated in the Pauline letters continues into the contemporary period. At this point another mark of identity becomes palpable as the Pentecostals emphasize the experience and manifestation of a number of *charismata*, spirit gifts or grace gifts. These enable the agents to perform certain services or ministries beyond human ability. Indeed, the polity comprising apostles, prophets, teachers, and evangelists represents charismatic gifts for performing certain roles within the body of Christ. Recently, there has been a scholarly resurgence of interest in pneumatology that could be helpful, for instance, Velli-Matti Karkkainen's contribution that surveyed a wide range of authors.[8] A biblical pneumatological approach would emphasize the reappropriation of the event that occurred on the Day of Pentecost as a defining identity marker.

In doing fieldwork on African Pentecostalism, many researchers have encountered the lack of interest shown by the leadership in their local histories.

Some attribute this to humility, a desire to avoid taking God's glory, but David Maxwell observed that in Zimbabwe, "the new Pentecostal movement's lack of interest in history has a number of explanations. One is a characteristic of all Pentecostal churches, namely a desire to jump back over history to New Testament times in order to bolster their claims to be truly apostolic."[9]

This approach names Pentecostalism by rooting it in the indigenous and contemporary religious experiences of individuals and communities and in the signs of the pneumatic explosions in the lives of transformed individuals who begin to walk and talk like the saved. The manifestation of the *charismata* in the lives of believers defines the devotees of the new religious movement. They were perceived as new because the old Evangelicals believed that these *charismata* had ceased. This means that in studying worldwide Pentecostalism, effort should be made to distinguish the Pentecostals from other forms of Protestant Christianity, just as the insiders do. Of course, Pentecostalism "set to work" the core message of evangelical Protestantism and may be the old evangelicalism writ large, but they are not necessarily the same. Pentecostals emphasize different teachings and have different histories. This explains why older forms of Christianity have been more virulently against Pentecostalism—perceived by both groups as intimate enemies—than unbelievers and secularists.

At this point, some Pentecostals insist that a crucial grace gift that serves as an "initial evidence" of being born again is glossolalia (from two Greek words for tongue and speaking). Believers acquire the power to speak in known or unknown tongues. The Constitution of the Church of Pentecost, one of the largest Pentecostal churches in West Africa, declares that "all believers in Jesus Christ are entitled to receive, and should earnestly seek the Baptism of the Holy Ghost and fire according to the command of our Lord. . . . This is the normal experience of the early Church. With this experience comes power to preach and bestowment of the gifts of speaking in tongues as the Spirit of God gives utterance. This is accompanied by a burning desire and supernatural power to witness to others about God's salvation and power."[10] Others demur about the initial evidence; still others privilege repentance, confession, and lifestyle ("walking the walk, and talking the talk"). But all affirm that appropriating the pneumatic resources of the gospel and recovering the full gospel are the markers of Pentecostal identity. Recent Pentecostal scholarship has revisited the contentious matter of speaking in tongues as an initial evidence of Holy Spirit baptism.[11] This is what Luke Ndubuisi achieved by a linguistic exegesis of Paul's concept of the charisma in 1 Corinthians 11–14.

Admittedly, Pentecostal identity changed through time, showing different characteristics in various regions, but sharing many others. Therefore, attention to periodization and context are crucial in constructing Pentecostal identity. For example, one could recapture how early Pentecostals perceived and described what was happening by using the very first edition of the

Apostolic Faith newsletter published by the Apostolic Faith Mission (AFM), 312 Azusa Street, Los Angeles, in September 1906, as an insider source in the early story of the movement. Asserting that the AFM stood for the "restoration of the faith once delivered unto the saints, camp meetings, revivals, missions, street and prison work and Christian unity," it identified the core characteristic of the salvation story around the concept of power: It claimed that people felt the power of God, became converted, sanctified, and baptized with the Holy Spirit. At the back page, under the heading "Precious Atonement" it clarified the stages in accessing salvation: atonement/forgiveness of sin, sanctification through the blood of Jesus, healing of our bodies as a result of atonement, and baptism with the Holy Ghost and fire upon the sanctified life. W. J. Seymour concludes the contribution by urging that "we that are the messengers of this precious atonement ought to preach all of it, justification, sanctification, healing, the baptism of with the Holy Ghost, and signs following."

It quickly linked glossolalia to mission by claiming that "the gift of languages is given with the commission, 'Go ye into all the world and preach the Gospel to every creature.'" The phenomenon short-circuited the study of foreign languages and enhanced missions. Later issues of the magazine would have, perhaps, corrected the impression after many missionaries failed to communicate in other languages without study. But the newsletter floundered within two years when Florence Crawford took away the subscription list in 1908. Feature articles in the early edition harped upon calls to both home and foreign mission fields, reclaiming backsliders, and signs of forgiveness from sin. Many brief entries dealt with the experience of charismatic gifts such as prophecies, gift of singing, playing instruments, healing, deliverance from demon power, and the miraculous collapse of opposition. The presence of the Spirit became the evidence, as well as the guarantee that the reign of God was being experienced in its full power, that the events toward the end of ages have started, and that this revival was unlike other evangelical revivals. It is the presence of the Spirit that explains the possibilities of miracles, healing, and power. These pneumatic resources of the gospel were available in the contemporary life of believers and were not mere creedal assent.

Quite notable is the fact that charismatic power reshaped the lives of individuals as tools for building a beloved, new community. In this community, intergenerational significance was highlighted as children (boys and girls) receive the experience and gifts. It noted the increased level of generous giving, and especially the experience of love within the community "such abounding love! Such compassion seemed to almost kill me with its sweetness." The Azusa Street revival was notable for its counterestablishment origins and its countercultural potential. Its ecumenicity and racial mixing was a defining characteristic that defied acceptable social norms; this dimension would be replicated in far distant lands when the wind of the Holy Spirit would blow through weekend retreats forcing white missionaries and indigenous

Christians to be soaked together. The newsletter could not resist taking a swipe at Roman Catholics and mainline Protestant churches, recounting with joy the saving grace that came to "Sister Wettosh, a German sister of Pasadena who was in the darkness of Romanism." Another young man so delivered started "telling the Catholics to get their own Bibles and to Protestants to get to God and not lean on preachers." Thus, in the midst of scholarly debates about who is a Pentecostal, these accounts are refreshing insider perspectives from the protagonists during its early stage. These characteristics reappear all over the world.

Scholars are conscious of the breadth of the movement but posit certain common denominators: Allan Anderson notes the primacy of experience of the Third Person of the Trinity and the practice of the charismatic gifts.[12] For Africa, the movement has been dubbed the "third response" to missionary message that privileged the place of the Third Person of the Trinity.[13] Harvey Cox approaches Pentecostal identity through the prism of history of religions: that they recover a primal spirituality comprising primal speech and utterances, primal piety in trances, dreams, and visions, and primal hope in the expectancy of miracles, supernatural interventions, and the *parousia*. This piggybacks on Simon Fraser's speculation in the *Golden Bough* on the origins of primitive religions that started with dreams and visions, before evolving into higher religions such as Christianity. The point is lifted up by David Martin who avers that the movement returns to repressed folk religiosity, and in L'Epinay's description of Latin American Pentecostalism as a continuation of folk Catholicism.[14] But the movement's image is that its spirituality counters the enlightened worldview of the modernity project. It did more: The Holy Spirit transformed the inner core of individuals, thereby assisting them to respond differently to life circumstances. David Maxwell argues that in Zimbabwe, Pentecostalism's success was most notable in the discipline of the body, of speech, and of sexuality, and it provided an alternative means to address the marginality suffered by the youth after the civil war and political independence.[15]

W. J. Hollenweger models the antistructural posture against modernity. But Grant Wacker nuances the image of early North American Pentecostals as people who combined the primitivist tendencies with a pragmatic trait to exploit the resources of modernity. As the movement grew, its charisma was routinized, and its bureaucratic organization enlarged in scale.[16] These assertions imply that Pentecostal historiography has a distinct character. For one, it "sets to work" the message of the mainline churches, and exploits the translated Bible to recover those elements that were ignored, lost, or muted in the process of institutionalization. Second, while a community may require a gospel bearer to access the initial faith, the baptism of the Spirit may occur without human agency as it did in young Asonye's life in 1934. The unpredictability encouraged indigenous agency and created the potential for multicenters. Third, this character became most visible within the global scope of this brand of Christianity. Scholarly emphasis on a global interpretation must respond to the complexity of data generated by local processes, indigenous roots, and higher rates of growth of the movement in Latin America, Africa, and Asia. Its different agency, coloration, periodization, and typology compel a different way of telling its story.

2. Genealogy and Character of Global Pentecostalism

In Pentecostal historiography, the North American voice dominates the story. The dominant voice claims that Pentecostalism is as American as apple pie, that it traces the genealogy to North America. From here it recounts how the movement started from humble roots in Los Angeles and flowered into a multimillion religious enterprise because it is a religion made to travel and that harbors a strong missionary impulse within its genes. It weaves a direct connection between Pentecostalism and the English language, though other language speakers participated in its early story. David Martin, Harold Bloom, and Harvey Cox point to the fact that "to attend a Pentecostal or evangelical church in Latin America or virtually anywhere else is to encounter an enhanced understanding of English and increased contact with Anglo-American world."[17]

Peter Berger puts it more bluntly that language is crucial in this cultural diffusion:

"The principal vehicle of Hellenism was koine, the rather vulgar Greek in which, not incidentally, the New Testament was written. Today, the English language, in its American rather than British form, is the koine of the emerging global culture. . . . People do not use language innocently. Every language carries with it a cultural freight of cognitive, normative, and emotional connotations. So does the American language, even apart from the beliefs and values propagated through American mass communication media."[18]

This profile has created a problem of externality (or extraversion) for protagonists outside North America. The first question in reimagining the genealogy of global Pentecostalism is to insist that the Azusa Street story is a local North American story and that the global dimension of Pentecostalism is not the geographical spread of a religious impulse and movement that started from North America and spread to other regions of the world. This sounds like a story about the travels and travails of the American apple pie. The image is that foreign culture bearers write their scripts on blank tablets.[19] On the religious level, worldwide Pentecostalism is imaged as the enchanted cultural version of globalization, or becomes the religious dimension of the cultural hegemony emanating from the North Atlantic and enveloping the globe.[20]

This view of globalism echoes Hilarie Belloc's "territorial complex" assertion that Europe is the faith. Or, as Paul Gifford has argued, "Whatever else it is, Christianity is a cultural product, honed in the West over centuries. The format of Africa's crusades and services, the music, the use of the Bible and even the selection of texts continually suggest the particular origins and betray particular roots."[21] Kwame Bediako and David Maxwell have adequately responded to Gifford.[22] The point here is that the Northern dominant voice is buttressed with a certain genre of the globalism discourse that distorts the image of African Christianity and Pentecostalism.

The globalization discourse raises two issues: The first is how globalization impacts local cultures and how local cultures respond. The appropriation of global forces within local contexts and communities has drawn attention to how local cultures gestate, absorb, internalize, domesticate, or transform external change agents. It rejects the binary view purveyed by the hegemony discourse in culture-contact theories. It could also be said that those who use modernity and globalization discourses to substantiate externality tend to use data from urban contexts, and by neglecting the realities of rural areas where most of the population live in the Two-Thirds World, they fail to explain the appeal of the Pentecostal spirituality.

Church historians therefore query the aptness of the concept of globalism in interpreting contemporary Christianity. Some substitute transnationalism, others prefer World Christianity or worldwide Pentecostalism.[23] Thus, the real question should be how worldwide Pentecostalism utilizes the resources of the cultural flows within the *oikumene*. This could be traced through the exchange of signs, symbols, and material things, through the patterns in the constraining embrace with other cultures, and in everyday life of the people of God. Peter Berger in the radio lecture cited earlier, puts a redemptive face on the matter, arguing that for people caught in the early stages of the modernization process, the new global culture is widely attractive because it gives a sense of open possibilities and aspiration for greater freedom—the sense of burden usually comes later! He recognizes the Janus-face of cultural globalization process as both a threat and a promise, as an intensified and accelerated form of the perduring challenges of modernization and its fruit, the great challenge of pluralism: the breakdown of taken-for-granted traditions, and the opening up of multiple options for beliefs, values, and lifestyles. This should be the salient dimension that is essential for modeling a deconstructive historiography.

The second issue is whether the story line in the dominant voice is accurate, and whether the unidirectional perspective constitutes the global genealogy of Pentecostalism. Did worldwide Pentecostalism emerge from North America and spread like the nineteenth-century missionary enterprise into all the world? Clarity demands that the question of genealogy should be separated from the profile or the character of Pentecostalism, and that both the genealogy and global character of the Pentecostal movement should be subjected to a closer examination.

3. Naming the Movement

The question raised by the above scenario is how to name the phenomenon. Scholars complain about the confusing categories used by David Barrett in his annual attempts to provide the statistics of the worldwide movement. The confusion stems from the fact that the North American categories do not replicate easily outside the region. He is annually compelled to invent new categories to deal with empirical observations in the non-Western world that could not fit into the mold of Western categories. In these far regions of the world, Pentecostals center the Bible as the origin of the movement. The question is often about the manifestations of the pneumatic dimensions of the gospel in various regions and cultures and how the people appropriate these dimensions. Perhaps they privilege the supernatural origins that enlightened concerns have blotted out of the literature in pursuit of the modernity discourse. This explains why Allan Anderson characterizes Pentecostalism as part of a larger nineteenth- and twentieth-century charismatic movement that embraced the Irvingites among others. Ian M. Randall in an earlier study of English Evangelicals indicated the negative attitude of the Keswick movement to early Pentecostalism.[24]

Undoubtedly, the Azusa Street revival is very important, but it is a North American event, and a certain movement that first called itself Pentecostal, and whose genealogy may be traced to a host of religious antecedents such as holiness movements. But other regions experienced the move of the Spirit independently; therefore, there is need to reconstruct the historiography of the movement worldwide, and to interrogate the extant literature. For instance, Dale Irvin admits that Azusa Street was a "local history with a global design" because missionaries were sent from Azusa Street. But he used the concept of "the logic of Pentecostal spirituality" to explain the global dimension. One is not sure about the content of the "logic," but it allegedly "resulted more often than not in the immediate localizing of these global designs in the new situations to which they were communicated. The result was the rapid adoption and adaptation of Pentecostal spirituality and practice far beyond Azusa Street often without any reference or deference to the Azusa Street experience. . . . One can trace some form of historical line of apostolic succession from virtually every Pentecostal and Charismatic movements today back to Azusa Street."[25]

This is a stupendous claim that assumes that all the protagonists in the non-American Pentecostal and Charismatic movements trace their genealogy to Azusa Street and merely adopted and adapted the spirituality without paying due deference to the origin. It echoes Karla Poewe's assertion that "what is global are traditions that reach across national boundaries, take local color, and move again."[26] The most benign response is that the story line ignores the clues from different regions that the same Holy Spirit started the process by manifesting itself to believers all over the whole inhabited earth without deference to any single geographical source. This was a repeat of the astonishment that perplexed Peter in Caesarea or the Swedes from North Dakota who went to South Africa at the turn of the century and were scandalized when the heathens spoke in tongues. In fairness, both Irvin and Poewe are attentive to the process of indigeneity. As Irvin argued in a different setting, "A new framework or mission studies is actively under construction today extending these insights in light of the growth of Christianity world-wide. In the emerging paradigm we find the agency not just of western missionaries but of the prophets, catechists, preachers, priests and other indigenous church leaders who were responsible for constructing the history of Christianity in various global regions figuring more prominently."[27] Contemporary scholarship recognizes the role of and connection with the United States, but distinguishes between pervasive and minimalist presence, funding and non- or limited funding, and being a catalyst/spark and creating/constructing a movement. The implication is to examine more clearly the dynamics of the American connection in each region because the pattern of relationship changed through time.

In many parts of the world there are three caveats that must be emphasized: Charismatic revivals started without such catalytic sparks. People received Holy Spirit baptism before inviting outsiders. Moreover, the size of Pentecostal missionary enterprise in the early period between the years 1900–1914 (when the First World War broke out) was relatively small. First, the failure of tongues to breach the language barriers was accentuated by the limited success of many solo enterprises that had insufficient funding. Second, the attempt to mobilize a group effort from 1909 failed in the United States. In Britain, it gave rise to the Pentecostal Missionary Union of Great Britain and Ireland. In 1926, they had only twenty-six missionaries: seventeen in China, six in India, two in Japan, and one in Africa. Allan Anderson has used their journals to reconstruct the sources of their failure. In spite of the missionary impulse within the movement, and the hyped reports in the newsletters, the story in the field was less edifying: missionaries lacked cross-cultural training and orientation; they were insensitive, impolite, patronizing, racist, and wrote tendentious, confrontational, inaccurate reports.[28]

In Africa, for instance, branches of classical Pentecostal churches are fewer in number than the indigenous ones that did not originate from the classical group. Among the latter, many early devotees of the new birth did not know about Azusa Street, and do not refer to themselves as "Pentecostal." In Congo Brazzaville, they refer to themselves as revival churches, in Congo Kinshasa as *bakristu*, in Ghana as charismatic churches, and in Nigeria as born-again Christians. The pattern of naming memorializes the experiences that constituted the origin of the phenomenon. For instance, in Uganda, though they have The National Fellowship of Born Again Churches of Uganda, the movement is popularly referred to as *Biwempe revival*. *Biwempe* is papyrus and the movement is named for the papyrus structures that once served as churches. It was known as a revival because it was perceived as a continuation of the *balokole* movement whose early protagonists emphasized the miraculous, especially healing miracles.

This makes periodization important for naming the movement because a number of the indigenous group developed contacts with the classical groups later. Each of the indigenous group designates itself by its ministerial emphasis, such as evangelicalism, deliverance, intercession, fellowship, Bible distribution, child evangelism, mission to other African countries, mission to the unreached communities within each nation, or by the theological emphasis, such as prosperity, holiness, witchcraft cleansing, spiritual warfare, prophecy, and so on. Many are so eclectic in their doctrinal emphases that the contentious matters in North America do not arise, and do not define the identity of the Pentecostal. Few trace their genealogy to North America. Are they distorting the Pentecostal genealogy or merely identifying where the rain of the charismatic gospel or showers of blessing met them?

4. The Historiography of Pentecostal Genealogy

African Pentecostalism should be reconstructed from four discourses: the historical, cultural, instrumentalist, and the religious. These are not discrete discourses. Thus, the scholar exploring the genealogy of Pentecostalism must be attentive to the historical dimensions, especially the preceding revivals (revitalization movements). Some had indigenous origins. Among those that had external contacts, the cultural or interior dimensions of the context are crucial in appreciating the pattern of convergences. As David Maxwell said in characterizing the religious change among the Shona when doubly confronted by internal contradictions and the pressures from externally induced process of rapid change: "The north-eastern Shona have seized upon Christian beliefs and practices, in response to locally-specific conditions, and in process have transformed their own pre-existing religious system."[29] This means that the religious dimension must not be ignored. The design of time frames should first reach back to the past of the community, and then forward to the encounter with the change agents. Attention must be paid to the process of change (its direction, pace, momentum, magnitude, and effects). The cultural dynamics and worldview (interior contexts) determine the vertical and horizontal patterns of expansion, and explain the emergent forms that appear in the convergences. Interpretation must start from the people's past because people respond to change agents based on where they are, how they live, and how they organize themselves, and respond to the numinous world and the external forces around them.

To tie the three issues into a bundle, as the gospel spreads into various regions of the world and encounters different peoples, mental and material cultures are shared, and people appropriate the message and new ideas and material cultures through the prism of their worldviews and cultures, they become creative in demonstrating the indigenizing capacity of the gospel to answer questions raised within the interiors of those cultures, and they weave emergent cultures that create new challenges in daily living. New forms of religious expressions emerge in the multilayered encounters. As time goes on, people move from accepting the new gospel and abandoning the gods of their forebears to a different level in which they seek a closer, personal relationship with Christ through an experience of the power of the Holy Spirit. The pathway is the indigenous religion. The element of continuity must be stressed before identifying the breaking points in this religious journey. Robin Horton's seminal paper "African Conversion," therefore, sought to enrich the social-structural analysis with the intellectualist discourse in probing why people would make the double jump in their worldviews.[30]

The process of conversion is beyond mere adaptation. As Paul argued in the early church period, a convert is neither a proselyte nor a God-fearer. The convert turns all that is important in the individual and communal contexts toward Christ, who makes all things new. The urge for a revitalized, trans-forming spirituality puts the born-again Christian at odds with the mainline churches. In Uganda, the charismatic (*balokole/tuketenderazza*) youths told the principal of their Anglican teachers' college (Mukoni) in the 1930s that they were "obedient rebels" contesting the modernist views of some of their teachers.[31] They set on wheels what their teachers had shown them in the Bible, and brought puritan ethical challenges to the old mission institution in which the evangelical zeal had routinized. The *balokole* youths insisted upon the gospel demands on the lives of the Spirit-filled believers. In other contexts, the new ethical challenges resembled the situation in Corinth where the question about the propriety for the Christian to eat meat that was acquired from idol temples could only arise from the encounter of the gospel with non-Jewish cultures. Paul's answer demonstrates a great sensitivity to a new culture and the need to privilege indigenous appropriation. Theories of culture teach us that culture contact generates a spectrum of responses best understood within the totality of the culture. In the encounters, emergent cultures arise that are new.

As the Indian scholar Mathias Mundadan observed, the history of Chris-tianity is the history of the encounter of the Jesus' gospel message with different peoples: "The impregnation of these contexts by the gospel, the assimilation of the cultures of the peoples by the gospel and that of the gospel by their cultures, and the consequent changes in the Christian movement and of the cultures of the people."[32] There are different stories within the Pentecostal story and the stories move along different time frames. But there are large areas of convergence that redefine the contours of each experience, and may even create homogenous dimensions. Christianity has a global impulse that Pentecostalism inherited and intensified.

To reemphasize the perspective on the genealogy of worldwide Pentecostalism, there are two issues underlying the historiography on genealogy: The first is what constitutes global Pentecostalism? The second is how the story should be told. I have argued that the extant literature is unidirectional, profiling the global in terms of Western spread to non-Western contexts, or the missionary extension of the North American Pentecostalism to the rest of the world, or, in essence, how the yeast from North America leavened the whole inhabited world. To the contrary is the image of encounters with the Holy Spirit in universes filled with many spirits, and the expressions of conversions that enabled the Holy Spirit to perform in better ways the roles that the indigenous spirits played in the individual and communal lives. People express the new relationships in various ways that reflect on their indigenous cosmologies. As they come into contact with others who share the same charismatic spirituality, they reconfigure certain aspects of what they teach, believe, and practice, and translate the charismatic affirmations and expressions into the language that people understand and in ways that serve the people's needs. They build international and intraregional linkages that enhance their evangelical capacities and image. There will be a tendency to avoid foreign control and yet a desire to be recognized as a ministerial partner.

A global perspective recognizes the integrity of the multiple contexts. It is beyond geography; it involves the enlargement of the religious space in the interior and at the surface levels. The global perspective consists of the various ways in which charismatic spirituality is appropriated, expressed, articulated, and lived in response to the challenges from indigenous cultures and ecosystems and other competing religious forms. There is no center and there is no periphery. Wilbert R. Shenk, therefore, urged that we should enlarge the story; that, "if we observe that history's river has overflowed its traditional banks and is cutting new channels, then the emphasis falls on discontinuity and we recognize that our perspective framework must be modified if we are to do justice to this dynamic reality." He pointed to three forces that compel the enlargement of the story: the shift from being a Eurocentric church to a polycentric one; the multiple sources of growth-biological, missionary, and indigenous dynamics; and the dynamic social, political, and economic environment that has contributed to this rapid change.[33]

5. American Connections and Multiple Sites in Global Pentecostalism

This brings to the fore the issues about time frame, nature, and dynamics of North American Pentecostal contact with the non-Western world. It must be recognized that the stories of Latin America, Asia, and Africa are like different streams that contribute to the river of life. For instance, the African contacts and networks with American Pentecostalism increased tremendously in the 1980s. There were occasional evangelistic thrusts from the late 1950s before the tempo increased in the 1960–1970 period. The televangelists escalated the contacts from the 1980s through their television programs, books, videos, cassettes, and ministerial organizations that are set up in different parts of the world to coordinate or facilitate outreach events. The impact on the character of worldwide Pentecostalism cannot be denied, but the outpouring of the Spirit was experienced long before these encounters. There were many revivals in yesteryears; and many indigenous people spoke in tongues without the presence of missionaries, much to the consternation of mainline churches. Indeed, many Classical Pentecostals were invited by local believers; and most Pentecostal missionary incursions to Africa in the period 1900 through the 1910s yielded little dividends or simply collapsed. A reconstruction of the genealogy of the movement must distinguish between the outpouring of the charismatic power, the arrival of Pentecostal groups from the outside, and the survival, development, and growth of both strands of the movement.

From the 1980s, the dynamics of Western relationships with non-Western Pentecostal groups intensified into a complex permutation with about a dozen patterns:

1. extending invitation from non-Western believers;
2. allowing indigenous leaders to controll a classical Pentecostal church;
3. funding indigenous groups externally;
4. offering networks of partners for outreaches;
5. creating an external operation that controlls leadership and funding;
6. financing an external operation that controlls leadership with locally sourced funds;
7. locating Western-based partners that sponsor non-Western leaders to attend seminars, train in Bible schools and annual workshops, and offer opportunities to preach;
8. engaging Western sponsors of diaconic services (socioeconomic projects);
9. broadcasting television and radio ministries (for instance, Trinity Broadcasting Network, 700 *Club*, Daystar, and others);
10. exporting material culture: books, videos, and cassettes;

11. creating international fellowships run by indigenous leaders (for instance, Full Gospel Business Men's Fellowship, Women's Aglow, Gideon Bible International); and
12. organizing outposts of Western-based ministries.

The periodization of charismatic movements in Africa highlights the significant charismatic outbreaks before and after the 1970s when an outpouring of the Spirit occurred literally from the mouth of babes. Here again the youthful puritan preachers known as the *aliliki* (Malawi) or guerrillas of Christ (Kenya) had nothing to do with the charismatic renewal movement that occurred in the West from the mid-1960s. We image the post-1970 charismatic movement as a catalyst of the decolonization of the church in Africa. Within a decade Benson Idahosa reshaped African Pentecostalism in five ways.[34] He brought the prosperity gospel, the episcopal polity, televangelism, megachurch with mega projects, and theological education that sponsored a large group of African students who spread the faith and deliverance theology throughout the continent. The watershed was the Fire Convention organized by Reinhard Bonkke in Harare, Zimbabwe, in 1984 under the banner "Africa Shall Be Saved."[35] Four thousand evangelists from forty-four African countries participated in a tent supplied by Kenneth Copeland at a cost of $1 million. Idahosa was the lone African among the keynote speakers.

But from the late 1990s there were six significant shifts:

1. a criticism of prosperity theology;
2. a return to holiness ethic;
3. the blossoming of intercession ministry;
4. an intensified evangelism;
5. engagement of the public space; and
6. a massive charismatization of the mainline churches.

An Africa-wide organization of intercessors developed, armed with new doctrines about spiritual warfare and land-cleansing projects.[36] Meanwhile, a strong missionary impulse and engagement of the public space emerged in the midst of untoward socioeconomic and political turmoil and the second liberation of Africa from military dictators. This period also witnessed the impact of African and Latin American Pentecostalism on North America as the Third Wave movement (led by Peter Wagner, Charles Kraft, and others) became prominent. The debate around spiritual warfare revealed how the face of global Pentecostalism was changing. The West was confronted with a new expression of the movement.[37] The spin-off to this debate was the allegation by Western scholars that the Korean David Yonggi Cho was indulging in shamanism![38]

The American connection in shaping the character of worldwide Pentecostalism from the 1980s onward can neither be denied nor ignored. But as

American Pentecostalism impacted the non-Western world, so did the spirituality from those regions flow into the North American religious environment. Clues point to multiple origins of Pentecostalism in various regions of the world. It is interesting that just before the Welsh revival in 1904, Korea experienced the beginnings of a revival during an interdenominational Bible study meeting conducted by R. A. Hardie in 1903 at the Methodist Church, Kwangwon Province, Wosan. This continued into January 1904. In 1905 a major revival started in Mukti, India, and flowed to Gujarat in 1906. The following year, Dr. Howard Agnew Johnston brought the stories about the Welsh and Mukti revivals to Korea and triggered another revival in Pyongyang. The Azusa Street revival flowered in the midst of these exciting events in 1906. The revivals in the Korean peninsula intersected with the spirit of the Welsh and Indian revivals. Their impact was felt on personal and social repentance; recovery of morality; church growth; an increase in the number of educational institutions; ecumenical cooperation; evangelism and missionary movement; an attack on social inequalities embedded in class-caste structure, gender, and slavery; and the flowering of nationalistic and patriotic movements in the face of Japanese rule. The distinctive power of the Welsh and Korean revivals was their use of vernacular. Revivalist Christianity became a marker for Korean identity.

People in Azusa Street heard about the revivals in Wales and India but neither precedent catalyzed the Azusa Street phenomenon. For instance, when Alfred G. Garr and his wife, Lillian, came to India from Azusa Street they exulted that "the revival had already broken out among the natives and some were speaking in tongues." The *Apostolic Faith* newspaper had declared the Garrs as the first pastors to leave Azusa Street for the "regions beyond." Later, they participated in the Calcutta revival of 1907–1910. In addition, 1910 was the same year when Wade Harris started a major charismatic thrust from the Grebo Islands off the coast of Liberia, through the Ivory Coast to the Gold Coast in West Africa. He itinerated, baptized, preached, taught new choruses in the vernacular, healed, and performed many miracles. He quickened the pace of Christianization and stamped it with a charismatic character.

Speaking in tongues appeared later at Mukti and was never regarded as an initial evidence or an identity marker. Minnie Abrams sided with those who opposed evidentiary tongues.[39] Some of these revivals may have been episodic, while others created new churches that blossomed into the future. The 1907 event has shaped the character of Protestantism in South Korea to the present day. The Azusa Street revival certainly had much significance and an impact beyond its brief lifetime. The Welsh phenomenon had an equally wide impact. Revivals broke out in distant places as people listened to the story of what happened in other places; thus, the events in Mukti were connected with the outbreak of Pentecostalism in Valparaiso, Chile. A keen eye to periodization helps us to reconstruct the genealogies and the changing faces of the movement. It shows the global convergences as well as the separate trajectories as each region confronts its specific problems or demons.[40]

For African Pentecostals, other directions and connections developed beyond the American connection: Rosalind Hackett has explored the inter-southern hemisphere connections, and Matthew Ojo probed the intra-African networks. Many Nigerian Pentecostal churches started branches in other African countries. An aspect of the contemporary era is the growth of immigrant churches in the Western world. A Nigerian evangelist has built the largest church in Kiev, while the Redeemed Christian Church of God, founded in 1952 by an illiterate preacher in Nigeria, recently paid more than $1 million to purchase 490 acres of Floyd, Texas (an ancient citadel of the Ku Klux Klan). Within its first decade (1982–1992), the Deeper Life Bible Church, founded by William Kumuyi in Lagos, opened branches in sixteen African countries. Gerrie ter Haar has examined the patterns of reverse missionary flows by African Christians in Europe, and Cephas Omenyo has pointed to the intensity of South Korean missionary enterprises setting up churches in Ghana.[41] African Pentecostalism has become a religious force that is sensitive to the socioeconomic and political terrains. Its adaptability in various regions has been one major source of growth even though it has been accused of being otherworldly.[42]

The complexity and fluidity of the movement is notorious. As David Martin intoned, "Movements play different roles at different times in different places, even while they retain continuity and family likeness."[43] Martin emphasizes the ambiguities born of the dynamism of the movement as it assumes different colors in various parts of the world:

1. even when it crosses borders, it goes native;
2. there are some cases of Anglo-Saxon origins, but many more where it is freestanding;
3. in some places it expresses folk religiosity but also ingests it;
4. the class content of its membership cannot be easily classified;
5. it may be varied but retains family likeness;
6. it fuses the modern mode with an ancient spirit or primal piety; and
7. it recovers the Word but also transcends it.

It is a movement characterized by variety, flexibility, and an expanding continuum of adaptive social inventions traceable in its ministerial formation, liturgy, economic practices, organizations, and infrastructure that range from storefronts in poor *favellas* to imposing structures in cities. A viable study of its genealogy and character begins by collating the rich cameos of local histories. In these resides its global identity.

In summary, this chapter revisits the historiography of Pentecostal identity by setting the movement within its pneumatological emphasis, and by using a global perspective. It alludes to the events in Wales, Latin America, and

Asia between the years 1903–1910 to illustrate the multiple sources of the movement. Azusa Street falls within a wave of ferments. It argues that Pentecostal historiography, therefore, differs from missionary historiography. Its register includes:

1. an attention to space-geographical, territorial landscapes, or outer contexts, and to worldview and cultural contexts or interior landscapes;
2. attention to time, an eye to periodization that historicizes and distinguishes the precedents or ferments of revivalism before and after the 1970 charismatic resurgence;
3. convergences, interpenetrations, and emergent outcomes;
4. the indigenous roots, translation, local agency, and patterns of appropriation;
5. the resources of externality: intensified missionary influence especially by televangelists from the 1980s that influenced Pentecostal culture and contested the independence of local actors;
6. the emergent forms of the movement, exploitation of the resources of externality in the new culture of Pentecostalism, and network patterns intensified by a process of reverse flow; and
7. the impact of the movement's theology and practice on the public space; its psychological impact on the individual in the urban and rural contexts, in the midst of changing socioeconomic realities, and in politics. Instrumentalist discourse must be balanced with the historical, cultural, and religious perspectives.

Local actors were crucial in the story of the early movement and are still reshaping the faces of the movement characterized by rapid growth. African Pentecostalism embodies the character of the changing faces of world Christianity. As Lamin Sanneh observed,

> The resurgence is not simply a matter of new names being added to the rolls, but of the accumulating pressure to accommodate new ways of life and thinking that are creating massive cultural shifts. ... An impressive picture now meets our eyes: the exploding numbers, the scope of the phenomenon, the crosscultural patterns of encounter, the variety and diversity of cultures affected, the structural and antistructural nature of the changes involved, the shifting *couleur locale* that manifests itself in unorthodox variations on the canon, the wide spectrum of theological views and ecclesiastical traditions represented, the ideas of authority and styles of leadership that have developed, the process of acute indigenization that fosters liturgical renewal, the duplication of forms in a rapidly changing world of experimentation and adaptation, and the production of new ... music, ... songs, and prayers.[44]

2

Bakuzufu

Contested Identities and the Quest for Power in African Christianity

1. The Third Response: Introducing the Historical Discourse

From the earliest contact with the gospel, Africans have tended to appropriate its charismatic dimensions, attracted to the extra power offered by the new religion, and stamped it with an African identity. This charismatic and revivalist ferment could best be described with the Luganda word *bakuzufu*. It means reawakened, or renewed, or even resurrected. It is a very apt description for the English word *revival*. In the interpretation of global Pentecostalism, the historical discourse argues the necessity for appreciating the contexts and periods from whence the movement flared up. It argues that the stories of various revitalization movements within such contexts provide the backdrop to the contemporary manifestations of Pentecostalism. These past events charismatized the religious landscapes, providing the agency, goal, popular perception, and naming of the movement. The failure of some historians to pay adequate attention to these precedents, historical roots, and multisites produced misinterpretations. In African Pentecostal historiography we must distinguish between the precedents in the colonial period, 1900–1960, and the charismatic flares in the independence era, from the 1970s forward.

In the nineteenth century, prophetic figures emerged in one place after another at the heels of the missionaries, engaging the indigenous worldview with charismatic elements of the Christian canon and symbols. Soon, the first generation of educated Africans caught the spirit of the prophets, and gave voice to a new brand of Christianity that sought to protect the innards of the indigenous spirituality as a pathway for appropriating the gospel. The movement, dubbed Ethiopianism, could be regarded as the first response by Africans. It challenged white representation of African values, cultures, and the practice of the Christian faith. It challenged white monopoly of the cultic and decision-making powers within the church, and the monopoly of the interpretation of the canon and the cultural symbols of worship. Ethiopianism countered the denigration of indigenous cultures with a nationalist antistructure, and a quest for the Africanization of the gospel. A religious interpretation of this movement sets the stage for understanding the patterns of Africans' quest for identity through religious power in the period under the colonial canopy and thereafter.

The aftereffects of the First World War unsettled African communities. The influenza epidemic that followed the war and the intensification of racist policies, alienation of land, and political disenfranchisement of Africans combined to aid the upsurge of spiritual movements that sought to succor Africans through prayer. Dubbed *Zionists* in southern Africa, *Abaroho* in eastern Africa, and *Aladura* in West Africa, they all privileged prayer, miraculous healing, indigenous symbolism and liturgy, and African agency in Christian matters. The African Initiated Churches (AICs) constitute the second form of response to the missionary message. But within the mainline churches, charismatic revival movements occurred during the interwar years that were variously termed as *bakuzufu*, *nguza*, and *balokole*. In the post–Second World War period, the revival movements accelerated the pace and shaped the direction of Christianization of the continent. The trail of ferment occurred in all types of churches, including the holiness and Classical Pentecostal churches that encountered Africa at the turn of the twentieth century. The argument here is that the charismatic revival movements within the mainline churches, the holiness missionary enterprises, and the cross-cultural Classical Pentecostal missions constitute the precedents to the third response of Africans to the missionary message. The response became sharper and flowered to greater heights from the 1970s forward. The goal of this chapter is to design the typology of revivalism in African Christianity that constituted the precedents to the contemporary Pentecostalism that holds the cutting edge in Africa's new Christianity.

In the twilight of colonialism, Max Warren, the secretary of the Church Missionary Society, wrote a book in which he revisited the revivalism of the 1930s that reshaped the face of Christianity in eastern Africa. The book is significant because it identified the charismatic character of African Christianity that had appeared amid the colonial restrictions as the single factor that aided the survival of Christianity in eastern Africa during the dark days of Mau Mau insurgence, triggered by an insensitive missionary cultural policy. Commenting on the conferences organized by the *balokole* advocates that attracted over 15,000 people from various tribes and tongues in the region, Warren exalted that

> here was the evidence that the Church in Africa was coming of age and that where men had been deeply committed to the Holy Spirit there were latent capacities for administrative and spiritual leadership which only needed the occasion to be deployed as Christian statesmanship. Only those who are aware of just how disastrous for the Church's unity elsewhere in Africa has been the inhibiting of leadership, how fruitful this has been of schism, can gauge the enormous significance for East Africa that there a spiritual movement giving full scope to African initiative has from the first been in and of the Church.[1]

Warren's posture is significant for this reflection because he was not talking about the emancipation efforts by either philanthropists or missionaries, precisely because the word *emancipation* conjures a reflexive, reactionary nuance. Rather, he pointed to the latent, interior, pristine spirituality that fueled African responses to the power of the gospel and left a trail of ferment throughout the story of African Christianity. African Christian initiative came from the depth of their being, became increasingly proactive in spite of efforts to throttle it, showed a deep commitment to the Holy Spirit, and absorbed the pneumatic tradition in the biblical story (that missionaries tended to mute), a trend that put a charismatic stamp on African Christianity.

Central to missionary presence were the questions of power and truth; often, it is the method of sharing truth that determines the relationship between the speaker and the hearer. Power shapes the environment of mission and the mode of sharing truth; a controlling power may be blinded to the other modes of perceiving truths in the environment. African encounters with the gospel betray the various dimensions of this interplay of power and mission: power of the gospel contested by the power of indigenous cult; power of the gospel bearers and colonial officers challenging the power of chiefs, the emergent, educated elite, or African interpreters; and the power of the masses as they tasted the fruits of charismatic power. This force will subvert institutional power or hardware of missionary enterprise. Finally, there was the clash of generational powers.

Warren observed that the revivalists betrayed a strong sense of joy, a burden to share this, and a bonding or fellowship that was both spiritual and a social reaction to the disintegration of their world. These are the roots of the contemporary growth of Christianity in Africa. The revivalists had no aversion to the institutional church but sought a space to express their joy, burden, and bonding freely. Warren emphasized that this matured growth occurred *within* the church, thus countering accounts of African responses that privilege the image of separation and sectarianism, as could be seen in R. L. Wilshade's portrayal of "simple secessionists" and "synthetist secessionists" among the churches of southern Nyasaland.[2] But, in fact, argued Warren, the Gikuyu who sustained Christianity in the face of the Mau Mau were the "saved ones," the spirit-filled, born-again Christians. Margery Perham gave a firsthand account of the brutality these people endured: "The priest on my right had been seized and slashed repeatedly—this by well-dressed young men talking in English— and asked at each cut to deny his faith and say that Christ was a European. Six others were killed nearby, and he was left for dead, one gash still visible on his head. Opposite sat another man, weak and limping from torture. Yet all looked calm, confident, even happy."[3]

From this perspective, Allan Anderson's study of *Moya*, the African con- cept of pneumatology, is an important background for the historical roots of African Pentecostalism, and one that we shall pick up in the next chapter.[4]

Ethiopianism and the prophet movements between the years 1860–1960 illustrate the trail of the ferment caused by Africans when they encountered the power of the gospel. Each provides a different vignette. It should be necessary to reimagine the movements beyond the characterization as schismatic sepa- ration. A number of explanations for the growth pattern are canvassed: At the cultural level, African responses to the gospel were determined by the fact that the gospel answered questions raised in the interiors of the worldviews. Afri- cans wanted the new religion to better perform the tasks of the old religion. Yet, Christianity served as an instrument or as a coping mechanism in the midst of rapidly changing socioeconomic and political changes. The historical discourse enables us to recover the purely religious dimension without nec- essarily subscribing to an obtuse version of the providential historiography and without denying divine interventions in the process.

2. *Bakuzufu*: A Typology of Revivals in African Christianity

Revivals are an endemic aspect of Christianity. At several points in time, a movement would flare up as certain elements in the gospel—either its char- ismatic/pneumatic resource or its ethical imperative—would be emphasized enough to compel a new expression of its spirituality and structure. There would be a great excitement and popular interest beyond what may have been witnessed in years. Efraim Andersson said about the *ngunza* movement, or revivalism, in the Congo that it was a different type of conversion from the normal reception of Christianity that was "quiet, almost passive, sometimes even routine-like confession to Christianity." In revivals, there could be "a violent expression of feelings with tears and cries, with shaking and convul- sion, with a falling to the ground and even unconsciousness."[5] Some have drawn attention to the element of individuality in such conversion experience without ignoring the communal impact. A revival is not the mere appearance of a new version of Christianity but one that elicits massive attention and acceptance; it brings a new life to an old religion.

A major characteristic of revival is to accelerate the pace of expansion, determine the new direction of growth, and reshape the religious landscape. Some revivals last long and have long-term consequences while others may be short-lived. Each brings new faces and styles of leadership to the fore and may aid or mar the quality of the biblical roots of the Christian expression; thus, not all revivals could be positive. Some have caused schism for the worse. At all times, revivals are the responses to the character of Christian living and message at certain times, in certain contexts, and may reflect the impact of external secular forces as people seek answers from the religious sphere. A revival may, therefore, reflect the turmoil and dislocation in a community. For instance, Janet Hodgson set the prophetic careers of Nxele and Ntsikana within the disquiet among the Xhosa in the nineteenth century:

> During the nineteenth century the Xhosa-Cape frontier was moved
> eastward step by step, following conquests by the British Imperial
> and Cape Colonial forces. By the 1880's after one hundred years
> of war, the Xhosa-speaking people from the Zuurweld in the Eastern
> Cape to Pondoland, had been incorporated under the British sover-
> eignty, suffering dispossession of their ancestral land, destruction
> of their polities, and displacement and domination by alien rulers.
> Every aspect of their daily lives, their customs, and their beliefs had
> come under sustained attack from missionaries. But while the Xhosa
> lost the struggle to retain their political and socio-economic inde-
> pendence, "the colonization of consciousness" itself was never
> complete, even among the Western educated black elite. The battle
> for sacred power between the intruding culture and the indigenous
> cultures continued unabated. Over the years, a number of Christian
> symbols and rituals were appropriated into the African worldview,
> providing a spiritually liberating potential with profound political
> implications.[6]

In Africa, revivals occurred at different times, sometimes right from the early insertion of the gospel into communities; people responded to missionary messages by deploying certain aspects of its doctrines to arouse communal interest in ways that the missionaries may not have wanted. Thus, the character of revivals, would include:

1. a response to a prevalent religious structure, message, and their implications;
2. a tendency to privilege a certain dimension of the message found most appropriate, especially the charismatic resources; and

3. an effort to reshape the interior of a prevalent religious tradition by redirecting the core message to deeply felt needs within the community and thereby provide an answer to socioeconomic, political needs and restore moral order by appealing to supernatural intervention and anchor.

A revival may act as a counterculture by weaving a new identity with religious fabric to enable the community's survival in the face of new challenges. It may also create a new leadership that is able to deploy religion in the explanation, prediction, and control of space-time events. Thus, in spite of operating in the religious zone, revivals tend to have political overtones and could be perceived as alternative power nodes, and thereby would elicit resentment from power holders.

In Africa, many revivals appeared amid African efforts to cope with the encroaching powers of colonial officers, white settlers, and missionaries. Later, the challenges of modernity and globalization would trigger widespread revivals in the quest for supernatural responses. Racialism that fueled the Ethiopian movement remained crucial in explaining the increased tempo of religious revivalism. While Ethiopianism appealed to the African elite, the new prophetic movement created mass conversion and broadened the enlarging Christian frontiers into rural areas where missionary churches did not exist. Some conjecture that colonialism mellowed during the inter-war years to create a space for the new religious movements. However, one should be cautious with the predominantly functionalist interpretations. A religious explanation would emphasize that God has constantly renewed His people through the outpouring of the Holy Spirit. This has occurred in many places at different times as an aspect of His love. For instance, it is said that Koreans enjoyed a massive revival just before the wars that traumatized generations; that the revival empowered their survival and recovery. It can also be claimed that a series of these charismatic revivals reshaped the face of African Christianity and catalyzed the massive growth that is a part of the gravitational shift of Christianity to the south.

African Christianity experienced localized revivals in the nineteenth century, but the frequency increased in the period 1910–1947 when some revivals with a wide provenance (beyond country of origin) occurred. For instance, the *Balokole* (Luganda for *Saved Ones*) was a movement that flowed from Rwanda through Uganda to Tanganyika and Sudan. The effects lasted through five decades. Similarly, the massive Pentecostal/charismatic revivals of the 1970s provide another example that has continued with great intensity through decades, and covered the entire continent including states built on either Muslim or communist ideology.

In the course of this broad time frame, five types of revival could be detected:

Type 1: A diviner or religious leader from the traditional context would shift base by appropriating some aspects of Christian symbols and message to create a new synthesis or emergent religious form that could respond to the felt needs of the community. In seventeenth-century Kongo, Kimpa Vita started as an *nganga*, traditional diviner, a member of the *Marinda* secret cult, who claimed to be possessed by a Christian patron saint, St. Anthony. People perceived her as an *ngunza* or Christian prophetess, but her claims became too messianic for the authorities to suffer and she was executed as a witch.

Nxele and Ntsikana achieved an identical status among the Xhosa in the nineteenth century in spite of their differences. Nxele wove a myth that included a God for the whites and another for the blacks and redefined the massive European migration into the southern hemisphere as a punishment for killing their God's son. He delineated their potential threat to his people and turned his half-digested Christianity into a resistant religion. Ntsikana tried to persuade people to ignore Nxele's militant notions but to drive in the line of the skid by deploying an evolutionary process that would utilize the Christianity to cure the moral challenges in the primal religion and weave an organized, united community so as to preserve the race in the face of the incursions of land-grabbing Europeans. Ntsikana's spirituality could be detected in the rich language of his hymns, many of which have been retained in Protestant circles. Religious revivals had immense political implications, especially when both guardians of the ancestral calabash responded to the threat of new white immigrants after 1812. In faraway southeastern Igboland, Dede Ekeke Lolo, a priest of the gods of the fathers retained the tradition at the turn of the nineteenth century among the riverine Akwete community. But his revival was more revelatory than political because he heard whispers of a new covenant, and soon after his prophetic utterances, Christian missionaries came to the community.

Type 2: A prophet would emerge from the ranks of the Christian tradition, emphasizing the ethical and pneumatic components of the canon to intensify the evangelization of the community or contiguous communities. Sometimes, the tendency was to pose like an Old Testament prophet sporting a luxurious beard, staff, flowing gown, and the mixed imagery of the cross. Some would go further by enculturating aspects of traditional religious symbols or ingredients of the culture; yet the diatribe against the indigenous worldview and acceptance of Christian solution would predominate. The followers of such enculturation include Wade Harris, whose ministry started in 1910; Garrick Braide, who operated between 1914–1918; Joseph Babalola, who left his job as a driver in 1928 in West Africa; and Simon Kimbangu, whose ministry lasted one year, 1921, in the Congo. Each was arrested by the colonial government and jailed. Harris remained under house arrest until his death; Braide died in prison in 1918; Kimbangu's death sentence was commuted to life imprisonment and exile at the intervention of two Baptist missionaries. He died at

Elizabethville in 1951. Babalola was released from prison when some Welsh Apostolic Church agents intervened on his behalf.

I will write more about these men later in this chapter.

Type 3: A wave of African indigenous churches arose all over Africa at different times before the First World War and especially during the influenza epidemic of 1918. Dubbed *Aladura* in West Africa, *Zionists* in southern Africa, and *Abaroho* in eastern Africa, some of these churches caused revivals, while others did not. The earliest or classical churches emerged from mainline churches by recovering the pneumatic resources of the translated Bible. Later, new forms appeared that had no linkage with missionary churches. They institutionalized quickly into churches, and equally deployed traditional symbols or ingredients of the culture—as mentioned in the category above though to a larger degree. Soon differences among various groups appeared, based on the dosage of traditional religion in the mix: some messianic leaders claimed to be one or the other of the Trinity; the revivalistic promoted the ideological significance of indigenous religion by privileging the resonance with Christian symbols; the vitalistic tapped occult powers; and the nativistic were virtually indigenous cults operating with Christian symbols and paraphernalia. Thus, many forms operated beyond the pale of Christianity. The sub-typology is as wide as the range and enduring contributions to African Christianity are immense. Some worship on Sundays while others are Sabbatharians. Equally, the character of the sabbatharian variety is complicated by the fact that some are political while others are safe religious havens for the brutalized Africans.

Type 4: Sometimes, a puritan and fundamentalist expression of Christianity would occur within the boundaries of mainline denominations challenging the regnant affirmations and seeking to enlarge the role of the Holy Spirit within the denominational members' faith and practices. The hostile responses of the "rulers of the synagogue" would force an exit and foundation of new congregations; others would insist on reforming the denominations from the inside. Thus, some operate as churches or ministries while others remain as movements or sodalities within the main body. The degree of challenge may include doctrine, liturgy, polity, and ethics or any permutations. Many attract enough mass support to become revival movements. In many ways, they resemble those outlined in Type 2, but they reject the traditional cultural ingredients that some in this category utilize. Examples include the Ibibio revival that occurred within the Qua Iboe Church in eastern Nigeria in 1927; the Kaimosi revival that occurred within the Friends Africa Mission/ Quakers in western Kenya in 1927; the Balokole revival that swept through the Anglican Church from 1930 as mentioned earlier; and the Ngouedi revival that occurred among the Swedish Orebro Mission in 1947 and resulted in the creation of the Evangelical Church of Congo (EEC).

Type 5: The contemporary face of Pentecostalism in Africa was catalyzed by charismatic movements led by young people from mainline churches from the late 1960s, in some parts of the continent, but more especially in the 1970s. As Richard van Dijk stated it: "During the early 1970's the populace of some of the townships of Malawi's largest city, Blantyre, witnessed the emergence of a new religious phenomenon. Young boys and girls, referring to themselves as *aliliki*, preachers, began to attract crowds by conducting large revival meetings. These young people, some of them still in their teens, traveled from one place to another, and in fire and brimstone sermons strongly denounced the sinfulness and evils of everyday urban life."[7]

The phenomenon became even more pronounced in the 1980s, in all denominations and most countries. André Corten and Ruth Marshall-Fratani have collated the interesting case studies of the insurgence in Ghana, the Republic of Benin, Burkina Faso, the Ivory Coast, and Congo Brazzaville. In each case, the insurgence challenged the predominance of either voodoo or Islam, or changed the face of Roman Catholicism. Later, the movements in different countries linked through the activities of the students' organization, FOCUS, and the migrations of students engaged in foreign language programs.

The reflection here differentiates between the prophetic movements that arose from within the indigenous religious leadership and those that emerged from individuals who had committed contacts with missionary churches, and will pay more attention to the latter ministries represented by Wade Harris and Garrick Braide. Their ministries illustrate the battle for sacred powers that became important at the turn of the twentieth century. It is argued that such prophetic movements and a host of other, smaller revivals that occurred in the half-century between 1902–1952 serve as precursors to the contemporary Pentecostal movement in Africa. These prophetic movements remove the strangeness of charismatism by inserting it into the broad spectrum of African initiative, appropriation of the missionary gospel, and the relationship with charismatic missionary bodies from the West.

Equally important is the ecology of coloniality. Education enabled many people to access newspapers and magazines that connected Africans with Asia and Europe. A number of cultic and esoteric religious organizations advertised their wares in magazines and catalogs, often distributed for gratis. It became the pastime of the literate few to search newspapers, catalogs, and magazines for advertisements, and place mail orders for amulets, charms, rings, and other cultic paraphernalia that ensure success in examinations, promotions in workplaces, and personal security in the competitive and enlarged market created by emergent modernity and urbanity. Masonic and Rosicrucian lodges dotted the urban capitals of various countries just as the elite patronized the magazine *Psychology*. As A. F. Walls observed, "Islam expanded more in the wake of improved transportation and commercial opportunities created by colonialism than many jihads would have accomplished."[8] Since most of the population still lived in the rural areas, traditional religion predominated in many countries. Thus, the revivalism of the period must be examined with a balanced perspective. The point is that the cumulative effect of these revivals intensified the process of Christianization, catalyzed vertical growth, and increasingly stamped a charismatic character on African Christianity.

3. Ethiopianism: The Roots of the Politics of Religious Antistructure

Many scholars may not easily connect Ethiopianism with Pentecostalism. The argument here is that Ethiopianism emerged from the quest for spiritual power that manifested from the interior of African religious genius in its many guises. It set a precedence of creative contestation of African religious identity that future entrepreneurs expressed in predominantly pneumatological strain. It recaptured the spirit of resistance that motivated the early African Americans who pioneered the evangelization of Sierra Leone, described in Lamin Sanneh's *Abolitionists Abroad: American Blacks and the Making of Modern West Africa*. Ethiopianism is perhaps the most misconstrued aspect of African response to Christianity. The reasons include the fact that it was the first organized form of response that occurred within a few decades of Christian insertion into African communities. It bore the brunt of the conflicts in the early culture-encounter as a massive wave of Western migration into non-Western worlds occurred. At that time, missionary structures had just been set up under the colonial canopy and consolidation process was still in progress, while many communities in the hinterlands had not tasted the fruits of the gospel. Racism was rife. The colonial agents hardly understood African cultures and self-assertion was perceived as worse than a plague. Moreover, the rise of Ethiopianism coincided with a major shift in the European image of the African. The imperial idea doubted African capacity(both innate and for self rule) when the scramble to partition the continent among competing colonial powers was in full bloom. The tutelage of the man-child as a part of the manifest destiny of the European to civilize the noble savage was not an invention by Rudyard Kipling. He merely put it into crude verse for adults while G. A. Henty nurtured it in children's minds through novels. Social Darwinism could not brook the savage's self-assertion built on the pedestal of a curious exegesis of a passage from Psalms 68:31. The interplay between the representation and experience of the gospel was at the root of the story. Tony Chafer has shown that other Europeans such as the French shared the same ideology as the English.[9] White people presumed that they held power for promotion of civilization, commerce, and for ruling over the inferior races, with power encounters ensuing at both the spiritual and material levels.

The Ethiopianism movement should be reimagined as an early expression of the interior of African spirituality. It operated within the church to promote

Christianity, but of a different kind: one that was sensitive to the African environment and the dignity of people. Its concern was the *modus* in which the faith was communicated. Ethiopianism was biblically rooted on an ancient prophetic promise. The exegeses of the passage inspired generations of Africans in diaspora in the Americas, which explains the connection between African Americans and the movement. In its American version, the passage's exegeses inspired the blacks to regain a sense of their humanity, capacity to be creative, the hope that they will build a civilization of their own.[10] Black diasporic culture wove a religious fabric with a strong ideological motif as a survival strategy and to cushion social suffering.

Thus, a number of strands could be detected. Some thought that the promise was that the blacks would regain their liberty and build governments for themselves; others envisaged it as a prospective return to the old civilization of the Maghreb where black civilization made enormous contributions. Still others proffered the need for black people to access Western cultural achievements and professional skills to regain self-respect. Some, such as Bishop Henry McNeal Turner, argued that God deliberately permitted the horrors of the Middle Passage and slavery so that blacks could acquire Christianity and use its resources to rebuild the desolate homestead in Africa. The totality of these ideas fueled the movement that canvassed a return to the African homeland. Of course, many opposed such a campaign and mobilization as a white subterfuge for getting rid of blacks on whose backs the economic fortunes of North America were built. Opponents perceived the American Colonization Society as a white blackmail. At the political level, the Africanist ideology dovetailed with abolitionism of various hues to produce the foundations of Sierra Leone and Liberia. At the religious level, the ideology served as a motivation for mission, to redeem the motherland through Christianity, as Alexander Crummell explained of his sojourn to Liberia, and to foster a number of black churches in Africa linked to the black churches in the United States and West Indies.

The returnees and the black ideologues in the diaspora were the first to foster Ethiopianism. They implanted it in the consciousness of the recaptives as these recovered from their short experiences of slavery. In so doing, they created a tradition of self-assertion and contested identities. The ideas imbued a nationalist feeling among the educated Africans who chafed under the weight of white missionary structures. This is most clearly the root of the West African brand of the movement. It became the empowering ideology among the educated black elite of the West African coast under the colonial canopy. The variety of the movement in southern Africa also had American contributions that were more intrusive because of the context: The evangelization of the motherland by African Americans led them into southern Africa where white settler populations not only had no competition from mosquitoes but also intended to inherit the land with an invented covenant theology. White settlers created a different type of virulent racism. Moreover, missionary presence had a longer history, had built an enclavement Christianity that denigrated African reality, and was, therefore, hostile to the pretensions of African Americans. Matters became complicated by the insurgence of the Watchtower movement that was subversive to political authority. This movement combined with outright rumormongering to build a strong anticolonial temperament. The popular appropriation of Watchtower theology bred the belief among some Africans that the African Americans would come as saviors to rescue them from whites and give them a new sense of worth. These rumors, in turn, bred fear that haunted the whites. But it should be understood that the Watchtower movement was not directly connected to Ethiopianism. Indeed, it reflects a broader phenomenon; for instance, in Kenya, a certain Onyango Dunde, a Luo from Alego, founded a militant cult named after the big snake, *mumbo*, that would appear from the depth of Lake Victoria to prosper the redemptive task. *Mumboism* proclaimed the demise of the whites, *wazungu*. An enthusiastic audience among the Gusii believed Dunde. Some district officers warned about a renaissance of secret societies as an anti-white bonding. Colonial governments dreaded the competition to rational administrative structures posed by religious power nodes as secret societies, cults, and oracles. Ethiopianism, on the other hand, manifested certain unifying characteristics among the Africans in the diaspora, in the western coast of the continent, and in the southern regions. By understanding how it was conceptualized among the different regions, a clearer perspective would emerge.

But first, let me give some background for the meaning of the term *Ethiopianism*. It emerged from a conflation of myth and history. The word *aithiops*, the Greek for "black face," was mistakenly used in the Septuagint Bible to translate the Hebrew *Kush*. It is not certain that the Egyptians understood themselves to be a part of *Kush*; more probable, they applied the term to their southern neighbors beyond the first cataract of the Nile and, therefore, to the entire region comprising Sudan and Ethiopia only. But the Maghreb is African, and the Ethiopianist ideology was built on the scientific and cultic achievements of Africans from the Maghreb to Abyssinia, the boundaries of the Septuagint's land of the Kushites or Ethiopia. When Wilmot Blyden visited Egypt in 1868, he was awed by the achievements of his ancestors who built the pyramids; the experience inspired him into a crusading spirit to mobilize Africans to regain their heritage. The biblical reference was meant as a prophecy for the whole of Africa, urging its people to regain agency from the memory of the Egyptian civilization, African roles in the biblical saga and in the foundations of the early church, and, later, the defeat of the Italian Europeans by Ethiopians in the battle of Adwa in 1896, showing that whites were not invincible. It was a prideful heritage to be reclaimed even if the connections between the Queen of Sheba and the Solomonic dynasty, or between the kings of Ethiopia and the Ark of Covenant could not be easily substantiated. Inspiring ideologies are often hewn from the granite of invented history.

Imbued by this sense of a noble heritage before missionary incursion, the band of educated Africans responded to *both* the gospel and the intimidating and controlling missionary structures in at least three ways: Some remained loyalist while affirming their Africanness. They hoped to tap white cultural resources for the "upliftment" of the black races and, therefore, wrote thick narratives to educate Europeans about the genius of African cultures. Others voiced their discontent in more strident tones without abandoning the church. Still others decided to exit and form their own churches. It must be understood that Africans choreographed the three positions of loyalty, voice, and exit in responses to changing expressions of the missionary moral economy or structures. In post-coloniality discourse, loyalty included assimilation, tutelage, or participation in the indirect rule structure and infrapolitical discourse when the ruled freely comment on the rulers within a safe and distant zone. Voice encompassed dissent/giving voice, heritagist recovery of lost voice, primary and secondary form of resistance, and dissidence that consolidates voice and builds community. Exit from existing institutions could be separatist/seces-sionist or creatively radical and revolutionary involving the use of violence. Thus, Ethiopianism was a movement that could not be simply equated with exit or secession. It sought to express an inculturated Christianity, different from that installed with the missionary hardware. This stressed the fact that coloniality was constructed ideology and could be contested and deconstructed. The religious import is significant for understanding the story of African Pentecostalism. From the onset of the African encounter with Christianity, var-ied efforts to appropriate it became increasingly enterprising.

4. Prophetic Movements: The Reanimation of the Religious Landscape, 1910–1950

From the turn of the century to the twilight of colonialism, a number of prophetic figures emerged all over the African continent. These were the agents who reanimated the religious landscape with *moya*, the Sotho word for *spirit*. As we continue the exploration of strands of precedents to modern Pentecostalism, it is essential to distinguish between the early prophetic movement from the leaders of the AICs. Two examples from West Africa illustrate the character of this genre of prophetic movement as a response to missionary cultic and institutional power. The prophetic movements laid the foundations of modern Pentecostalism in Africa. As Max Warren would argue, these are people who caught the joy of the gospel, expressed it in songs, made strenuous efforts to share it, and built fellowships that bonded and served as a social security network.

Certain characteristics beyond the beard and emblem, a cross, staff, or a bowl with holy water distinguished a prophet. A prophet was a charismatic figure, stringently opposed to indigenous gods and yet critical of missionary methods as a replacement of one culture for another without confronting primary allegiances and covenants. It was as if Africans created a periphery where they dialogued with the missionary message while preserving a core interior or epicenter where traditional allegiances predominated. The prophets recognized the powers of the indigenous worldview but confronted these with the power of Christ. This is why the Bible was central in their ministration. For instance, Wade Harris used the Bible in a healing therapy by placing it on a sufferer's head. In many ways, these prophets were sometimes precursors of Zionists/Aladura/Roho leaders in that they exhibited the same features, such as praying and healing, for African societies for whom health care delivery was a major problem.

Wade Harris was imbued with a message, unwilling to found a church but eager to save through word and miracles. He deployed new missiological strategies that intensified the pace of evangelism, and appealed to the masses through the use of choruses and his response to the challenges of the indigenous worldview. This is clearly illustrated in studies of his hymnody. Similarly, researchers have retrieved and translated 173 choruses by Garrick Braide, composed in his native Kalabari language.[11] A simple one that his followers used at the beginning of an outreach simply declared that "Jesus has come and Satan has run away." As it was repeated many times, the evangelists would pour holy water on shrines that would burst into flames to the consternation and conversion of votaries.

Some prophets were educated and others not; however, both groups attacked the symbols of traditional religion and nominal Christianity with the same hostility as missionaries, except the prophets demonstrated their engagement with signs and wonders. In addition, their attitude to the colonial government differed. Wade Harris was more proactively critical. The colonial governments, both British and French, hounded each of the prophets into prison out of fear for an uncontrolled charisma. Braide was imprisoned on false charges in 1915 and died three years later. Strangely, his movement grew after his death. Similarly, Harris was confined to Cape Palmas where many came to visit and enlist his support. Churches grew in his name. Perhaps these prophets' misfortunes could be explained by the insecurity of the times when colonial governments were jittery. In spite of many similarities, it should be academically and historically important to demonstrate the differences among the prophets.

William Wade Harris (ca. 1865–1929) was a Grebo in Liberia. He became a Christian while he was a student at a Methodist school in Cape Palmas, Liberia. On leaving school he worked as a seaman before becoming a teacher in an American Protestant Episcopal Mission school for ten years. During that period he became a social activist against Afro-American domination and was, in fact, serving a prison sentence for participating in a failed antigovernment demonstration when he received a divine call in 1910. He said that he experienced a vision of the Archangel Gabriel who identified him as a prophet to prepare the way for Christ, and instructed him to abandon his European ways. Following his release from prison he began preaching to his fellow Grebo. He imaged himself as an Old Testament prophet, a hybrid of Elijah and John the Baptist, whose mission was to call people to repentance. He adopted a distinctive dress and carried a Bible, cross, walking stick, a gourd rattle, and a bowl for baptism. In 1913, he trekked through the Ivory Coast to the Gold Coast catalyzing an effective evangelical revival based on prophecy and healing. Christian communities were established and survived where no missionary had ever ventured. Wade Harris was particularly successful in the Ivory Coast precisely because of the pattern of Christian presence in that region. The French colonized it in 1892 and the first mission arrived in 1895. The French subsequently closed English-speaking congregations of the American Episcopal Mission. Consequently, the area became predominantly Roman Catholic. The missions had little success in spite of the support from the colonial government. The local populations were united in their resentment against the French colonial regime. As the First World War approached, the French colonists feared any uprising, including that which might arise within a Christian context.

As a commentator observed, throughout West Africa there was "a mysterious ripeness for conversion."[12] The success of the prophetic movement was, thus, connected to the struggles to cope with the new economic production system, changes in currency, the salary system, and domestication of cash-nexus as a means of exchange. Some Ethiopianists, such as Casely Hayford, took the African prophet Harris's agency very seriously as an example of how Africans must evangelize Africa. Like the Ethiopians, Harris did not condemn polygamy and appears to have had several wives. On the other hand, he appreciated the white man's insistence on education and hygiene.

On his return from the Gold Coast he was arrested at Kraffy, Ivory Coast, in 1914 because of homeland security during a time of war. Some say that it was because he protested against some shipmasters who insisted on employing African laborers to offload goods on a Sunday. He threw holy water on the ship and it caught fire! He was brutally treated and extradited in 1915 to Liberia, where he continued his ministry under house arrest until his death in 1929. His assistants, John Swatson and Helen Valentine, continued the actual ministry after his house arrest. Though he never intended to establish churches, Harrist churches did emerge in a context where there were no established communities. In these situations, Harris appointed twelve apostles to lead each community and pursue his vision. Though the Methodist and Roman Catholic churches were beneficiaries of Harris's work, a Harrist church survived in the Ivory Coast and the Church of the Twelve Apostles was established in the Gold Coast. Subsequently, many prophets emerged who originated from within the Harrist tradition as it spread inland to places where Harris himself never ventured. Although, even today they claim Harris's authority for their practices, they have evolved their own distinctive forms through the "minor prophets" who followed Harris.[13] His message did not deviate from that of the missionaries, yet he "represented a new and populist level of African Christian initiative, quite removed from missionary control"[14] and "an authentic Christian universality, yet one in which diversity–and Africanity in particular—was to be honored."[15]

Just as the unsettling First World War started, Garrick Sokari Daketima Braide (ca. 1885–1918) came on the scene in a different part of West Africa. He was born at Bakana in the north of the Niger Delta, in southeastern Nigeria. His mother was a Kalabari and his father an Igbo, possibly a slave. In early life he was a fisherman and a tradesman. He was baptized in 1910. As a member of the prayer band of St. Andrews Church, Bakana, in the New Calabar district of West Africa in 1912, he began to experience dreams and visions, healing powers and prophetic utterances. People flocked to his home and the church, and his pastor, Rev. M. A. Kemmer, was quite excited at the increase in membership. Popular opinion pronounced him as the "Second Elijah." Not only was he particularly creative with new choruses, he dug a well in front of his house, and healed many with water, and many people believed that Braide had power to protect people from evil spirits.

Soon a conspiracy brewed against Braide because the political authorities were tense about security and banned large gatherings of people. During the First World War, some chiefs were suborned to allege that he was a health risk because sick people gathered at Bakana. The real sources of their grouse were that he destroyed charms and shrines, opposed the lucrative gin trade, and confronted their sexual immorality. Most intriguing was the meeting between Braide and Holy Johnson who was now the assistant bishop of the diocese. Johnson refused to recognize the prophetic authority of Braide. Ironically, the leading Ethiopianist forced Prophet Garrick Braide out of the church. Yet Braide's fame soared.[16] So effective was his mission that a commentator observed that never was there "any instance where Garrick Braide consented to pray for any sick person in which prayers failed to be efficacious."[17] He died in prison in 1918. Oral tradition preserves this period with the memory of burning of idols and rapid process of Christianization.[18] But it was also the period when cost-intensive education became the prominent form of Christian presence. Thus, the initial growth of the Garrick Braide movement could not be sustained because of a weak funding and organizational or institutional base. The Braide movement could not compete. By 1939, a decline set in as poor funding stunted the growth of their schools and government inspectors refused to approve them for financial subvention. During this period, communities wanted schools and would accept a church only if there was a school along with it. By the 1940s some Ethiopianist leaders of the African Native Church movement recognized the ideological import of the Braide movement. J. G. Campbell from Lagos tried to take over the church and this action created a split within the church. Later, S. A. Coker was invited from Lagos to serve as the leader of the Christ Army-Garrick Braide Connexion. Coker brought together various strands that had originated in the power struggles within Braide's movement. This organization still continues to this day, linking the prophetic movement with the antecedent Ethiopianism.

Robin Horton argues that Braide's movement is a natural development of traditional Kalabari religion and a response to political, cultural, and social changes in the Niger Delta. E. A. Ayandele has suggested that the condemnation of the movement is an example of the collusion between the colonial government and the church. They recognize the fact of power encounter in two dimensions, countering missionary structures, promoting an ecumenicity that contested denominational boundaries, and challenging missionary interpretation of the Bible. As the Ethiopians used to intone, we are no longer slaves to accept every interpretation. The new spirituality and missiological strategy created a mass movement. Braide betrays both the continuities and discontinuities between the Ethiopian movement and the new charismatic spirituality that would shape the emergent African Christianity.[19]

In conclusion, the prophetic and revival movements were catalysts of change in communities and they altered the image of African response. Rather than produce black clones of white missionaries, they developed a distinctive and enthusiastic form of African Christianity. The ideological statement was more potent than its numerical strength. The mission churches wanted to control the "purity" of the converts by privileging intellectual grasp of the faith, commitment, and discipline. The prophetic and revival movements in the African continent were a necessary and vital indigenous response to the incursion of white colonization and missionary enterprise, and subverted the missionary patronage of the Enlightenment.

3

Moya

African Charismatic Initiatives and Classical Pentecostal Missionaries

1. Charismatic Flares in the Missionary Churches, 1920–1960

i. *Naked Faith People: The Faith Tabernacle*

The argument that African Pentecostalism has African roots does not ignore the roles of a variety of missionary influences. The implication is that many of the early classical Pentecostal groups came into Africa on the invitation of the indigenous Christians. In some cases, the same Christians disengaged from their white visitors because they dissented with certain liberal tendencies among the Europeans. For instance, in West Africa, some indigenous Christians from various places had contacted the Faith Tabernacle in Philadelphia because each group read their literature *Sword of the Spirit*. Ambrose Clark was responsible for the mission strategy of the Philadelphia headquarters and encouraged these disparate individuals to liaise and form worship groups. He built a copious correspondence mission that advised the new churches in minute detail and armed them with guiding rules on doctrine, polity, liturgy, and ethics compiled in a document called the *Blue Book*. The faith message was most appropriate during the ravage of influenza. In 1925, a schism occurred in Philadelphia when Ambrose Clark was accused of moral lapse. He left the Faith Tabernacle and formed his own church the First Christian Century Gospel. The Africans reflected the split: Many remained loyal to Clark; a few held faith with the Faith Tabernacle. The real problem was that neither of the divided Philadelphia groups could send missionaries precisely because they refused to take the vaccinations required for foreign travels; they did mission only through the post office. The Africans, especially in western Nigeria and the Gold Coast, turned to the Bradford Apostolic Church. The naked faith people in southeastern Nigeria continued with Philadelphia.

After a reconnaissance trip in 1931 to the Gold Coast and Nigeria by a delegation comprising Daniel Powell Williams, his brother William Jones Williams, and Andrew Turnbull, the church sent Pastor George Perfect and Idris Vaughan in 1932 to Nigeria. When George Perfect left Nigeria in 1935, he stopped in Ghana to enjoy the hospitality of Apostle Kwaku Anim Mensah (later Peter Anim, 1890–1984). This explains the plaque in the Apostolic Church of Ghana about its foundation date. However, many trace its roots to the joint ministry of Anim and James McKeown, who was posted to the Gold Coast in 1937. Later on, a split occurred because the Africans held firmly against the use of medicine while the white missionaries were driven by malaria to compromise on its use. The Africans in Nigeria and the Gold Coast carved out the Christ Apostolic Church (CAC) while the whites moved into new areas and continued to spread the British Apostolic brand. McKeown took over the Gold Coast ministry until he broke with it in 1953 over the doctrine of prophecy as an instrument of decision making, and his newfangled enthusiasm for the Latter Rain movement, a new wave of Pentecostalism that started in the United States of America. He then established the Church of the Pentecost that is currently the largest Pentecostal church in Ghana.

ii. The Assemblies of God in West Africa

Faith Tabernacle and Apostolic Church contacts flowed into early Pentecostalism by the late 1930s because, first, they linked the indigenous movements to external Pentecostal sources; second, their evolution fused into the contemporary Pentecostal movement in West Africa. In Nigeria, this evolution led to inviting the Assemblies of God (AOG) into southeastern Nigeria when five young men belonging to the True Faith Tabernacle spoke in tongues. They were expelled for speaking in tongues, founded Church of Jesus Christ in 1934, and invited the Assemblies of God, who in response quickly sent Rev. W. L. Shirer and his wife to take over the Church of Jesus Christ in 1939. The Assemblies of God started a rural ministry in Sierra Leone in 1914 and in Burkina Faso in 1920, and entered northern Ghana in 1931 and the northern sector of Dahomey (now the Republic of Benin) in 1947. W. Lloyd Shirer and his wife were crucial in the AOG ministry that linked Sierra Leone, Burkina Faso, Benin, Ghana, and Nigeria. The longevity of Apostle Anim aided the growth of Christ Apostolic Church in Ghana just as the Babalola revival enabled the CAC to spread in Nigeria. In 1928 a payload driver, Joseph Babalola, had a divine vision that he should preach and heal. He abandoned his job in the public works department in Nigeria and became a revivalist preacher, setting the western regions on their ears. It was the indigenous Babalola movement that caused a mass evangelization.

iii. Early Charismatism in Western Kenya

There was a second type of charismatic revitalization of the missionary churches that flared up in many parts of Africa between 1925 and 1960. These occurred within various types of churches including holiness groups, Quakers, evangelical Protestants, and Anglicans. A number of Pentecostal/holiness missionaries were established in various parts of Africa, especially western Kenya, Liberia, and South Africa between the years 1906–1912.[1] None of these made much impact or grew until the outbreak of charismatic revivals. However, it may be said that some of them were open to the move of the Spirit. In 1927, for instance, the Qua Iboe Mission (QIM) among the Ibibio people of southeastern Nigeria enjoyed an outbreak of spiritual outpouring during a weekend retreat of church workers. Samuel Bill started the QIM in the nineteenth century in Wales. His parents were adepts of the first Welsh revival. His ministry, therefore, continued a strong, public, tent evangelism and church planting. The Ibibio Revival caused much growth. By 1928, the mission felt that it was losing control and virtually instigated the district officer to intervene and suppress the spiritual overflow among the indigenous believers.

A more detailed example from eastern Africa will buttress this pattern. A revival occurred among the Quakers in Kaimosi in western Kenya in the same year, 1928, sporting public confessions, fasting, vigils, and spiritual emotionalism. The western province of Kenya was called North Karirondo in the nineteenth century when the British government staked its presence. It was an important link between the Kenyan coast and the new protectorate of Uganda. Missionaries surged into the area, aided by the completion of the railroad between the coast and Kisumu in 1901, and delimited their areas of operation. By 1920 at least six groups had consolidated: Mill Hill Mission (MHM), Church Missionary Society (CMS), South African Compounds and Interior Mission (SACIM), Church of God Mission (CGM), Apostolic Faith Mission of Iowa (AFM), and the Friends Africa Mission (FAM, Quakers). But during the interwar years, the Africans seethed with resentment and came under pressure from taxation, forced labor, and administrative restructuring that compelled communities to supply the labor for white plantations. Many white former soldiers were rewarded with large acreages of farmland. African discomfort could be gauged in the formation of North Karirondo Taxpayers' Association among the CMS in 1924 and in the North Karirondo Central Association organized among the Quakers in 1932. Yet missions thrived as the Africans wanted education.

Within this assortment of missions, two were outstanding in their charismatic religiosity: the AFM that allied with Pentecostal Assemblies of Canada
(PAOC) and the FAM (Quakers). The FAM had been deeply imbued by the
wave of nineteenth-century evangelical revival and the Pentecostalism of the
new century. However, they avoided ecstatic dimensions of charismatic spirituality. The FAM established in Kaimosi in 1902 was led by Willis Hotchkiss,
Edgar T. Hole, and Arthur Chilson. The choice of location was determined by
availability of land, good climate, and luxuriant forest for the sawmills. The
FAM engaged in industrial, medical, educational, and evangelistic ministries.
Progress was slow, so they turned increasingly to indigenous personnel for
assistance and thereby bred a cadre of capable evangelists who imbibed the
puritan version of Quaker spirituality. Moreover, the Bible had been translated
into the vernacular, *Oluluyia*, in 1925. The FAM occasionally organized leadership training retreats for workers and this became the context for the 1927
revival.

The story of the FAM begins with Arthur Chilson and his wife, Edna, who
came to Malava, another FAM station, in 1918. The people appreciated Chilson
as a very practical man who initiated projects to build roads and bridges. He
was also an electrifying preacher. In 1926, the couple moved to Kaimosi station
to deputize for Ford, the resident FAM pastor who was on furlough in
America. The Chilsons usually prayed with the Otto Keller family, who had
taken over the Pentecostal Nyag'ori mission station of the AFM from Clyde
Miller. Chilson involved some indigenous people in praying and preparing
for the 1927 annual conference; four other missionaries and some African
teachers from adjacent centers converged on Kaimosi. Chilson shared from
Acts 2:1–4 and Romans 10:9–13 and, as he prayed, the Holy Spirit fell on the
audience. Some cried, shook, fell down, and spoke in tongues while others
confessed their sins publicly. Participants spread the new spirituality with great
effect throughout the surrounding regions.

In January 1928, Ford returned to find a new dispensation as the young
people insisted upon tongues, public confession, prophecy, exorcism, and
night vigils with loud wailing prayers as mandatory components of the liturgy.
They were nicknamed *abandu wa rohi/abarohi* (people of the spirit) or simply
as *abakambuli* (people who publicly confessed their sins). When the elders
could not restrain them, they were forced out of the church in 1932 and formed
The African Church of the Holy Spirit that has blossomed and successfully
challenged the AFM in western Kenyan villages. In due course, however, they
developed new ritual and liturgical practices. With their vigorous evangelism,
they attracted the repressive attention of the colonial government. However,
the colonial governement registered it as an independent body in 1957.[2] It has
since splintered into four groups and with each shift veers more into an AIC
type of church.

iv. Early Charismatism in the Congo

Coincidentally, it was the same period, the 1930s, that witnessed the explosion of the *Balokole*. There are two noticeable dimensions to this explosion: First, little of it occurred within the Catholic Church until the *Jamaa* charismatic movement among the Catholics of the Congo.[3] Second, a number of the movements that started under the white missionaries were appropriated by African youths and reinvented into enduring new patterns. This dimension became even more glaring in Raymond Buana Kibongi's career and contribution to the *ngunza* movement in Brazzaville.

The Congo region was suffused with prophetic or *ngunza* movements. After the prophet Simon Kimbangu was deported to Elizabethville in 1921, where he died in 1952, other prophets claimed to be imbued by his spirit in very vibrant political rebellion against the colonial authorities. For instance, Andre Matswa formed the Association of Congolese in Paris and returned as a religious messiah before his arrest and deportation. But the revival that endured through the years in Congo Brazzaville was led by Raymond Buana Kibongi, beginning in 1947. It started among the Swedish Mission Covenant Church during a leadership retreat. The Swedish mission had two major centers at Kimpese in the Belgian Congo and the pastoral seminary and evangelical school at Ngouedi, situated 300 kilometers west of Brazzaville and just south of Loutete. In 1946, the Swedes engaged in soul searching because they felt their missionary work was progressing while the horizontal impact on the moral lives of their people was weak in the two Congolese states. As usual, the missionaries prayed for a revival.

Then, on January 19, 1947, during the celebration of the Bible Society day, something broke loose among the students of the school. Efraim Anderson, who witnessed the event, reports that John Magnusson, the secretary of the mission, preached on John 3:16. After the sermon, there was an invitation for prayers and Kibongi started to pray. Kibongi was a student and was the most affected when the spirit fell on the group. According to Carl Sundberg, "He prayed for the missionaries and for the seminary at Ngouedi, which is 'rotting in sin.' During the prayer, he became more and more excited and started shaking, as in ecstasy crying from his heart, '*Jesus, make me your servant, Jesus, Jesus, calm me down, calm me down*,' whereupon he sank on the bench exhausted."[4]

The course of the revival took different forms: people confessed their "*kintantu*," envy or hatred, and poor relationships across racial lines, and they changed dramatically. Others realized their Christian dullness and the low level of church attendance and poor prayer lives in the school and improved. Still, for others, a certain fire came on them. It was known as "the ecstasy of the cross." It gripped people as if they were touched by the suffering of Christ.

Some felt pains in their hands as if pierced by nails; others, such as Kibongi, would stretch out stiff on the ground. The movement spread as other *ngunza* adepts thronged to the site. Students spread the movement all over the Belgian Congo, and as it spread into the hinterlands east of Brazzaville, villages became reconciled under the power of God. As Kibongi would say, "Just as hard iron can only melt in fire, so the black man's stone heart can only be melted in the all consuming fire of the ecstasy."[5]

Kibongi grew to leadership heights and turned the church into the Evangelical Church of the Congo. He succeeded because his vision was centered on the unity of whites and blacks, an ecumenical vision for all churches in Brazzaville, and because the Swedish were already open to pietistic tradition. He was such a peacemaker and proponent of reconciliation in a violent society that he took the initiative in 1970 that led to the formation of the *Conseil Oecumenic des Eglises Chretiennes au Congo*, and became its first leader. His longevity until 1998 ensured that he provided many years of leadership and theological articulation. Unlike many others, Kibongi spoke in impeccable French and was rooted in the Scriptures, even though his church sports some ingredients such as holy writing, occurring when the spirit moves people's hands to write messages. He was a musical person, ecumenical, nationalist, and practiced Christianity with power. His influence remained so strong that contemporary Pentecostal churches in Brazzaville refer to themselves as *revival churches*.

2. Typology of Classical Pentecostalism in Africa, 1901–1960

i. Case Study: Clyde Tolliver Miller

As was mentioned earlier, the trail of ferment in African Christianity in this period includes the emergence of Pentecostal spirituality from external sources in the period between the years 1901 and 1960. This excludes a Keswick-type of evangelicalism that flourished among university students in Britain and was spread to many parts of Africa by university men and women who served as missionaries, doctors, schoolteachers or colonial government officers. First, there were some missionaries who expected that speaking in tongues might short-circuit language training. They were sorely disappointed. The resourceful missionaries changed tack; the frustrated ones returned home. Second, some missionaries were poorly funded solo entrepreneurs like Clyde Toliver Miller. Miller was associated with a city Pentecostal mission in Des Moines, Iowa, run by evangelist Robert Waldron and his wife, Vivian. They had come from Topeka, Kansas, where they received Holy Spirit baptism in 1897. A Mrs. Sturges served as the assistant and Clyde Miller later married her daughter. Without preparation or adequate funds the newlywed Miller left for Kisumu in Kenya in 1907 to work with the Nilotic Independent Mission. Later, Miller discovered that there was a huge tract of land available among the Nyag'ori

people. But because it was a crown land, he needed the backing of an organization to acquire it. Some members of the church in Des Moines quickly
formed an "Apostolic Faith Mission, Nyang'ori," and a business laymember,
John Buckley, provided the money for the acquisition. Trouble started in 1911
when Vivian Waldron and the Buckleys sailed out to join the Millers in the
belief that Clyde Miller was their missionary partner and representative. But
Miller had registered the 109 acres of land in only his name. In the course of a
struggle for the leadership, John Buckley died. Buckley's widow and Vivian
Waldron returned to the United States, along with Miller's wife and son. Mrs.
Miller refused to come back to Africa, while Miller soldiered on resourcefully
through twenty years in the Nyang'ori mission field, and tried to integrate
himself into the culture of the people by marrying a Kenyan convert.

Three facts ruined his mission: the prospective Kenyan in-laws (trusted
members of his church) dreaded the implications of an interracial marriage on
the kinship system, yielded to the taunts of their neighbors, and refused to
allow the marriage. This broke his heart. Second, the First World War disrupted his enterprise. And third, he changed doctrines during a furlough and
came back teaching Oneness Apostolic doctrine that caused a schism in the
church. He subsequently left Africa in despair.[6]

ii. Charismatism among Missionaries

Missionaries were the greatest purveyors of Pentecostal spirituality and dis-
tributors of Pentecostal tracts and magazines. Some served non-Pentecostal
churches; others were *sponsored missionaries* from Pentecostal groups such as
Seymour's Azusa Street ministry in California, or the Swedish group from
Minnesota, who in 1904 sent Mary Johnson and Ida Andersson to Durban,
South Africa. The image of Azusa Street as the new Jerusalem from which
missionaries moved into fifty countries including those of Africa within a few
years has been the staple diet of North American historiography. Recent literature has reexamined the numbers, biographies, support system, duration,
character, and achievements of these missionaries. Initially, Azusa Street
worked with many holiness groups who were willing to cooperate. Many independent missionaries from small holiness house cells who served with little
organizational backing may be mistaken as Azusa Street missionaries. In this
early period, there was little coordination and the spiritual hype in the house
magazine must be understood properly. Some of the missionaries may have
had official blessings without financial support. For instance, in 1906 Lucy
Farrow, who accompanied Seymour from Houston to California, went to
Johnsonville, Liberia, with some black Pentecostal missionaries such as G.W
and Daisy Batman, whose three children quickly died from tropical fever.

Farrow's service period lasted through seven months. The group was self-
supporting and had no financial backing from Azusa Street. Though she

claims that she was able to preach in the Kru language, the more successful mission was led by Edward McCauley, an African American pastor from Long Beach, California, who went to Monrovia in 1908, the same year as Henry M. Turney.[7] Seven years later, the Azusa Street mission sent William F. P. Burton and James Salter to open the Congo Evangelistic Mission, and Angel and Etta Post to Egypt. The case of J. G. Lake and Thomas Hezmalhalch, connected with John Alexander Dowie's Zion City, Illinois, will be dealt fully under the development of Pentecostalism in South Africa. Ironically, Lake complained in 1909 that some of the enthusiastic missionaries arrived without money including the required government's fee of $100, yet he himself arrived without enough funds to pay the same fee for his party of five in 1908. At that time, a stranger tapped him on the shoulder and gave him the money! But it appears that he was concerned to stem the influx of missionaries because there were enough Afrikaans and African converts to carry out the mission. As his letter to the house magazine *Upper Room* in June 1909 declared, "We have men here far superior to any that can come from America. Among the baptized people here are men who can speak English, Dutch, Zulu and Basuto." Indeed, he commended the Africans: "Some of the most used men in Africa are these young converts. God is using the timber right here on the field to make missionaries."[8]

The strongest agents of Azusa Street were *missionaries* who had been in the field. These were the targets of the early Azusa missionaries. Many received the baptism of the Holy Spirit and Azusa Street imprimatur when they came home on furlough. For instance, Samuel and Ardell Mead, who had been Methodist missionaries in Angola for twenty-one years, received the baptism during their furlough and returned to Benguela, Angola. In the same year, Julia Hutchins, an African American, left for Liberia with her husband and niece Leila McKinley.

iii. African American Pentecostal Mission

A major issue concerns the role of African American Pentecostals in the evangelization of Africa, a story that has not before been told. Many African Americans in this period went to either Liberia or South Africa; the former because it was founded by African Americans in 1822; and the latter because the African Methodist Episcopal (AME) Church had opened the field; and finally because it was felt they could better endure the climate of Africa. The African American contribution functioned in three phases:

(1) The early contacts by African Americans who were inspired by evangelical spirituality and the Higher Life Movement in the eighteenth century.

(2) The nationalist ideology of redeeming Africa through religion which was strong from the nineteenth through mid-twentieth century, served as the clarion call of the Ethiopian movement, catalyzed the flowering of black mis-

sionary enterprises as a sequel to emancipation and back-to-Africa movement, and became a core aspect of African Pentecostalism in the twentieth century. Various advocates articulated the strands of the stirring ideology. The argument is that Pentecostalism spread through southern Africa along the grooves of the Ethiopian churches. David Maxwell argues that many of the AMEC churches affiliated with Apostolic Faith Mission in a clever scam for funding; that they soon left to develop Africanized versions of Pentecostalism. Nonetheless, they contributed to the vertical expansion of Pentecostalism.[9]

(3) The missionary achievements of black Holiness and Pentecostal groups at the turn of the twentieth century.
This will be illustrated with two examples including the missionary enterprise of the largest black Pentecostal church in America, the Church of God in Christ, in Liberia during the period 1920–1950.

The key concern is motivation and rhetoric. Motivation in black missionary enterprise is quite complex. Sanneh paints a picture of an antistructural endeavor buoyed on American republican ideals; but he also adds the impact of evangelical spirituality. A typology is essential because different types of black enterprises occurred and each generated its own nuance. First, there were some who stayed home but organized, raised funds and supported missionary activities because they perceived mission less from the exilic posture but from the imperative of the Great Commission. Second, some believed in programs to uplift the black people. They sponsored Africans who studied in the United States but returned home to serve in their various countries and churches. These educated Africans created the political turmoil that produced political independence in their various countries.

Third, some African Americans emigrated to Africa in different time frames and, therefore, for different reasons; but they took their charismatic Christianity with them and hoped to practice it freely and create a new dispensation for Africa. Some of these emigrants believed in the "Blackman's Burden," a sacred duty to make Africa the garden of Eden again and to enable the black person to prove a sense of worth and ability. Others envisioned the leadership of Africans in Christianity. Walter L. Williams has used the sociological theory of metamotivation to explain this emigrant posture arguing that while the emigrants after emancipation wanted land and opportunity, they also acted out of a great sense of racial duty. As Alfred Reidgel (AMEC) put the matter, "Often I think of leaving the field and returning to my friends and relatives where life would afford more base and comfort, but in the midst of these meditations, the voice of the man of sorrows comes down the ages: stand to your post. Hold the fort for I am coming."[10]

In the reverse theory of providential design, Bishop Turner argued that God brought them to North America so that they will be equipped as agents to bring the gospel home and so that the status of the black person in the United States will change as a function of the success of the enterprise in Africa.

Fourth, some simply went on mission just like other white people of their age; that is by their own volition and inspiration and even through personal funding. Fifth, some were recruited by white organizations because the climate in those regions made it difficult for whites. There were many reasons for the recruitment of black people. For instance, working with Episcopalian data, Harold T. Lewis is convinced that Anglicans in the nineteenth century recruited blacks as missionaries with a certain method of solving the slavery issue, namely, to rid the country of surplus freed slaves and that the predominantly white Anglicans feared a possible insurrection by blacks and nursed other racist motives. After all, he argued, the Anglicans had been the least concerned with the abolitionist cause. They played no significant roles in abolitionist societies. Yet, they appointed sixteen out of the twenty-five African Americans ordained between 1795 and the end of the Civil War as missionaries to Africa. The same church brought West Indians to supply the needs in local American parishes.[11] The enterprise called African Mission School Society that set out to locate and train pious, intelligent Africans for cross-cultural mission failed partially because the early graduates preferred to work at home and to assist the cause of their enslaved kin. Indeed, opponents of the American Colonization Society (founded in 1816) argued that the organization was being hijacked for different agenda by the racially motivated and that those who could not argue against the enslavement of blacks in the United States may not show honest intention in their concern for benighted Africans in the homeland.

Similarly, Morrissinne Mutshi and Stephen Bartlett computed that the Presbyterians sent fifty-nine African Americans to Liberia between 1833–1895 though the number dropped to twenty-two between the years 1948–1992. Racial motives are also adduced. But there were other reasons for whites to scout institutions such as Oberlin College, Lincoln and Fisk Universities, Hampton and Tuskegee Institutes, Gammon Theological Seminary in Atlanta, Stillman College in Alabama, and the Stewart Missionary Foundation for able African Americans to be recruited for mission to Africa. Mosquitoes constrained white presence as malaria decimated white missionary personnel in West Africa. Various missionary agencies arrived at the same conclusion that black personnel must be the agency of sustainable crosscultural mission. The Wesleyan Methodists in the Gold Coast saw the longevity and success of Birch Freeman as connected with his racial profile. Andreas Riis advised the Basel Mission to recruit from the West Indies with equal success. Antwi and Jenkins have reconstructed the efforts of the Basel mission to recruit black missionaries in this period.[12] Anglicans did the same. Moreover, dearth of volunteers especially in the early years of British enterprises constitutes another problem. The legal nature of advowson or method of holding benefices in the English church meant that many priests could not give up their places for service abroad. The British missionary bodies relied on European volunteers many of whom met with early deaths.

When black churches stood on their feet, especially from 1815 to 1900, they sent missionaries to different parts of Africa as a symbol of their independence. Three black churches, the AMEC, AMEZ, and the Baptist National Convention sponsored seventy-six missionaries in Africa and educated thirty African students in between 1877–1900. Seventh, "recaptives" or Creoles (children of settlers) in Sierra-Leone later went on mission to other parts of West Africa such as Nigeria, Gold Coast, Gambia, Liberia and Cameroon. Eighth, the evangelical ardor among Holiness and Pentecostal groups emerged from the interior of their spirituality but the direction followed the black consciousness of the times.

African American Pentecostal missionary enterprise during the World Wars could be illustrated first with the story of Alexander and Margrete Howard who landed in Cape palmas in 1920. Theirs is a fascinating story with a strong human-interest angle. In 1914 Alexander was employed as a porter at the Palmer House Hotel in Chicago. In the course of his duties, he heard a voice asking him to go to Africa. It seemed impossible, but the urge persisted. He finally yielded, withdrew from the work, collected his little savings, and started the search for a sponsor for his trip. It was a forlorn hope because black churches could not afford to send missionaries, and white churches told him explicitly that God could not have called him.

Things changed four years later when he ran into Mother Florence A. Thomes in Philadelphia. The woman directed him to Cambridgem Massachusettsm to Rev. George Phillips, founder of Faith Holiness Church of the Apostolic Faith (55 Moore Street). Phillips's life story started from his home in the Bahamas. His father founded a group called "Christian Mission." But George did not follow in his father's footsteps; he wanted to make money and as a teenager escaped to work in Guyana. At nineteen, he left for the United States. A near-death experience struck the fear of God in him, especially as he came in contact with the Nazarene Church in Cambridge where Mary Vinton and the husband had started a charismatic ministry following the experience of the "fire" at Azusa Street. Phillips was baptized in the Spirit and joined in the ministry. He was ordained in September 1916 in a colorful ceremony. His ministry prospered. According to his biographer, "The normal capacity of the meeting house was overrun at every meeting, which inspired members to seek larger quarters." When Alexander met Rev. George Phillips in 1919, some synergy occurred. Phillips mobilized two other Pentecostal churches, founded by West Indian immigrants, to facilitate Alexander's dream.

The first was The Christian Mission Holiness Church started by Rev. Alfred E. Cragwell, who migrated from Barbados, British West Indies to Massachusetts. There he moved from a room on Harvard Street, bought the property at 789 Main Street, and chartered his church in Cambridge in 1917. It blossomed as "a fire house and soul saving station for the people of God" until he died in 1951. The second church was another West Indian church, the

Apostolic Pentecostal Church (aka Abundant Life Church) located in 45–47 Howard Street, Cambridge, Massachusetts, pastored by Rev. Conrad Dottin. The three churches formed the United Pentecostal Council of the Assemblies of God (UPCAG) with no connection to AOG Springfield. They sponsored Alexander and his wife so they could travel to Cape Palmas. Notably, the biographers pointed to a key aspect of Pentecostal missionary engagement:

After having received the baptism of the Holy Ghost according to Acts 2:4, and having many other wonderful spiritual experiences, the Lord showed Mr Alexander Howard that his field of labor was to be in Liberia, West Africa.[13]

In the earlier phases of African American missionary enterprises, motivation was theologized from the perspectives of *theodicy and human liberation.* Among Pentecostals, the emphasis shifted to premillenial *eschatology.* This did not make them less sensitive to racial and social justice issues. For instance, the white pietist group, United Brethren started a mission in Shebro Island in Sierra Leone after the Amistad case when 53 African slaves mutinied off the coast of Cuba in 1839. Through the Good Hope Mission the United Brethren (UB) participated in the repatriation of the hapless Africans and set up a mission for them. The enterprise collapsed for a number of reasons. The United Brethren secured the services of an African American couple who could survive the harsh climate to jump-start the enterprise. Mary and Joseph Gomer set out in 1871 motivated by a pietist spirituality. J. S Mill's contemporary account, *Mission Work in Sierra Leone* describes the motive as carrying "votive offerings to the sepulcher of a dead Christ . . . (carrying the) knowledge of that Christ to the sepulchers of those dead in trespasses and sin." Then he waxed more eschatological, "upon your head, at no distant future will loving hands be laid as our returning Lord stands glorified on Mount Olivet."[14] Joseph Gomer had a rough dealing from the white leadership because he soon discovered an ebony kinship with the indigenous folk, won their confidence, became a confidant of the warlord and chief and served as a judge to the people. His racial consciousness grew in the mission field.[15]

However, Alexander and Margrete showed their ideological commitment quite early when they refused to work on the coast and moved inland to the Fan ethnic communities, Bonike, in the southeast corner of Liberia, and Biabo, on the boundaries with the French Ivory Coast. The mission would later spread into the Ivory Coast.

In twenty-four years of service, the Alexanders built mission compounds, village schools, and a boarding school named after George A. Phillips. They labored for years in spite of malaria outbreaks and other hardships, sustained by God through local chiefs and communities. In November 1943, the *Apostolic Messenger* mourned and honored the memories of Alexander Howard and his wife. Their work continued with Sister Rosa Lee Wright, who sailed for Africa in 1937, and Sister Maryne Hathaway of Chicago, who sailed for Africa in 1940. Among many failed enterprises in these early years, the legacy of this intrepid couple, Alexander and Margrete Howard survived because we hear that in November 1982, a team (Herman Greene and Sister Marva Collins) went to appraise and shore up the legacy of the black Pentecostal missionaries.[16]

In the same period, the Church of God in Christ (COGIC) organized The Home and Foreign Mission Board in 1925 and sent their first missionaries to Trinidad, Costa Rica, and Turks Island in 1927. Two years later, it recruited Elizabeth White to the island of Cape Palmas. She had served for three years under a Miss January, a self-sponsored, female faith missionary in Liberia. Returning under a denominational sponsorship, White opened the COGIC mission at Bonika. In 1932, Mrs. Willis C. Ragland of Columbus, Georgia, joined White. During her furlough, Ragland recruited Beatrice Lott to Tubake while White moved to Wisseka. The Second World War disrupted missionary enterprises, but after the war, COGIC recruited Miss Martha Barber of Chicago who, with the help of an indigene, Valentine Brown, enabled the church to move into Monrovia in 1948. Five missionaries were deployed to the field between the years 1945–1956. The predominance of female personnel is a notable feature. It could be conjectured that the appointment of Charles Pleas in 1945 as the COGIC bishop of Liberia, and his visit with the president of the country, consolidated the work.[17] When William J. Taylor visited Monrovia and Cape Palmas in July 1956 as the secretary of COGIC's missionary agency, he found a receptive Liberian President William V. S. Tubman, a healthy missionary presence filled with new opportunities and land grants, and a competitive mission field sporting seven other African American agencies: Gibi Apostolic Church, United Pentecostal Mission, Carver Foreign Mission, Afro-American Missionary Crusade, Youth Mission of Life, United Church of America, and the Liberian branch of International Evangelistic Women's Workers Incorporated.[18]

iv. Ecumenical and Denominational Pentecostal Missions

In the story of Pentecostal missionary enterprise, there was an effort to coordinate Pentecostal groups to act in united missionary enterprises between the years 1909–1910, and Africa was one of the targeted mission fields. Indeed, in 1909, an effort was made to found the Pentecostal Missionary Union. It failed in the United States but motivated a missionary enterprise in Britain. The following year, the Bethel Pentecostal Assembly of Newark, New Jersey, organized the Pentecostal Mission in South and Central Africa and sent missionaries to Liberia, Swaziland, Mozambique, and South Africa. Later that year, it sent George Bowie, a Scot who received the baptism of the Holy Spirit in America, to South Africa. He founded the Pretoria Pentecostal Mission. He was later joined by a Welshman, Eleazar Jenkins, and an Englishman, Archibald Haig Cooper, who took over the leadership in 1913. In 1921, it was renamed Full Gospel Church and in 1951, it merged with the Church of God (Cleveland, Tennessee) to form the Full Gospel Church of God.

Among the denominational brands of Pentecostalism established in various parts of Africa, the most evangelistic was the Assemblies of God that started with rural evangelism from the outset. The AOG was established in Sierra Leone in 1914, and from there moved into French territories such as Burkina Faso in 1920. Pastors H. Wright, W. Taylor, and their wives, Miss M. Peoples and Miss J. Fansworth initiated a successful rural mission among the poor Mossi of the central plateau where they participated in the agricultural development of the semi-savannah ecosystem. The pastor as a rural chief and agent of change shaped the success of the missionary enterprise. This, argues Pierre-Joseph Laurent, explains the Mossi culture in its polity and the predominance of Mossi indigenes in the pastoral hierarchy. When the church moved into the urban areas, it retained a coherence in which the elite in the town provided the ideas and projects that the local pastors carried out.[19] Later, the AOG moved into the Cote D'Ivoire, Republic of Benin (formerly Dahomey), and South Africa. Other Pentecostal groups were the Pentecostal Assemblies of Canada, Church of God in Christ, Pentecostal Assemblies of the World, and International Pentecostal Holiness Church. The Foursquare Gospel Church came later in the late 1950s. One explanation for the emergence of the Foursquare Gospel ministry in Nigeria is that Rev. H. J. Curtis and his wife were invited by an indigenous believer in 1954. For most of the Foursquare Gospel's ministry, it has relied on indigenous manpower.[20]

3. Early Pentecostalism in Southern Africa, 1908–1958

i. Introduction

A major aspect of the rise of Pentecostalism in southern and central Africa in this early period was the importance of South Africa in the charismatic evangelization of the rest of the region. It served as a nodal point from which black and white missionaries sallied forth into the region. In some cases, white missionaries participated in evangelizing Zimbabwe, Malawi, Zambia, Mozambique, and other countries in the region. For the most part, migrant laborers and traders (mutchona) served as the core agency. African agency remained strong either as individual ministries from South Africa, as in the case of Nicholas Benghu, for those Africans who served on behalf of white-founded missions, or others who were suspicious of foreign missionaries, especially white missionaries, and founded their own ministries, as Ezekiel Guti did in Zimbabwe. The dynamics in the azungu-atchona, white-black relationship, became important for the future of some ministries and the story of early Pentecostalism. Adrian Hastings always exhibited a historical sense of placing past events in their contemporary context. Writing on the expansion of

Christian presence in colonial Africa, Hastings noted how improved communication, technology, education, the quest for employment, and the openness of colonial frontiers aided African agency in evangelizing Africa—the dream of Ethiopianism: "By the 1930s countless ordinary Africans took books, trains, and bicycles very much for granted as part of their own lives. In those days, they could have homes in northern Nyasaland and work on the Rand, or in Tangayinka and work in Uganda or Kenya. They spoke more languages than most missionaries. The very uniformity of the colonial order, the lack of manned frontiers, passports, or a clear sense of citizenship, all helped the emergence of an almost continentwide new society."[21]

Labor migration would become crucial in the spread of Pentecostalism, especially because most laborers stayed for only brief periods in one place. Therefore, there was a high mobility rate that opened more people's eyes to new ways and religions. An Igbo proverb says that a person who travels is wiser than a sedentary person. Thus, while the role and presence of classical Pentecostal groups were more prominent in this region than for the rest of the continent, as found in the AICs, spread more at the heels of labor migrants and traders. Indeed, the overall influence of many classical Pentecostals remained weak before the upsurge of the 1970s. Only about 2 percent of Christians in Malawi could be counted as Pentecostals by 1960 but the number rose to 20 percent by 2000. Let me illustrate these statements with the story of early Pentecostalism in South Africa, Zimbabwe, and Malawi.

ii. Seven Characteristics of the South African Story

The story of Pentecostalism in South Africa is often dominated by the pioneering enterprise of John Graham Lake (1870–1935) and the Apostolic Faith Mission. He is imaged as the father of the movement, having spent the years 1908–1913 in South Africa; the man who linked Africa with the classical roots of the movement in the careers of Charles Parham, John Alexander Dowie (1847–1907), and William Seymour (1870–1922). Vinson Synan intoned that African Pentecostalism owed its origin to John Lake and arose out of the Wesleyan holiness tradition. But revisions are rife in the literature stressing various characteristics of Pentecostal presence in South Africa. First, the biographical profile of Lake has become more nuanced. The most interesting reconstruction is by Kemp P. Burpeau who provides an outsider's balanced, critical appraisal. He notes that Lake's image covers the entire spectrum from saint to sinner; that out of about fifteen biographies, seven portraits by fellow charismatic leaders such as Robert Liardon, Kenneth Copeland, D. du Plessis, and William Burton paint him in the bright colors of a saintly, self-sacrificing evangelist. Some missiologists have been critical of his connection with the roots of the apartheid system in South Africa. His boisterous character, showmanship, exaggerations, controlling tendency, epic quarrels, flamboyant personality, and other warts have been reflected in these portraits with lurid colors.

Second, Lake came to a charismatized environment because there were three spiritual revivals in the nineteenth century within the Dutch Reformed Church (DRC) (in 1860, 1874, and 1884) that softened the grounds. More important, the Dutch Reformed minister, Andrew Murray (1828–1917), had established the charismatic tradition distinguished by emphasizing holiness lifestyle, spirit baptism, and divine healing. Murray was a frequent speaker in the Keswick conferences and had been healed at the Betsan Divine Healing Mission in London. His books on divine healing and spirit baptism—*Jesus the Physician of the Sick* (1884) and *The Full Blessing of Pentecost* (1907)—were in the public domain. Admittedly, he suffered much opposition from the DRC. However, his church still thrives in contemporary South Africa.

One of Lake's disciples was Pieter L. Le Roux (1864–1943), a DRC minister who was posted to evangelize Africans in Wakkerstroom (Transvaal). Le Roux's friendship with Johannes Buchler (1864–1944) produced two results: First, Buchler had founded the Zion churches, a name derived from an old Moravian hymnbook and not from Zion City, Illinois. But he later contacted Dowie's Zion City after reading its house magazine *Leaves of Healing* and was authorized to be the representative of the Christian Catholic Apostolic Church (CCACZ) in South Africa. Matters turned awry when he visited Dowie's utopian community. Buchler was so disgusted with Dowie's pretensions and the sycophancy of his followers that he disengaged from serving as the missionary agent of CCACZ. In 1904 Dowie sent Daniel Bryant to continue the work abandoned by Johannes Buchler. Pieter Le Roux teamed up with Bryant to catalyze a spiritual revival in the Zion chapels.

The spiritual revival in Wakkerstroom recruited a large number of Africans in the years 1904–1905. Wakkerstroom was the African version of Azusa Street that occurred around the same time as the Welsh revival. Following the rumbles of collapse in Zion City, Bryant returned home in 1907. Indeed, Lake's party, including Thomas Hezmalhalch (1848–1934), merely took over the Zion chapels when Le Roux teamed up with Lake's team in 1908.

Third, the importance of the AFM is recognized as long as it is realized that the Apostolic Faith Mission started in a Zionist congregation in Johannesburg in 1908 under the leadership of Hezmalhalch; the whites perceived Lake and his group as Zionists. After a leadership tussle in 1910, Hezmalhalch yielded the post to Lake, who was able to combine the core elements of Parham's spiritual baptism and tongues, Dowie's theology and practice of triple immersion and divine healing, and Seymour's synthesis of these elements with an egalitarian structure, lively liturgy, and ecumenism that embraced all races and classes of people. There was no doubt about Lake's energetic leadership and healing ministry. He was able to break the opposition of the Afrikaaner whites to the interracial worship services and attracted the

Africans. His childhood background in Wesleyan Methodism, professional career in business, and charismatic gift of healing enhanced his capacity to launch a ministry that endured. It is said that he was a talented preacher, hardworking and generous to a fault, but oftentimes at the expense of his family.

Fourth, it is argued that the AFM grew by leaps and bounds because it addressed the needs of the Boers after their devastating war with the English. But Lake attracted Africans because he resonated with the indigenous world-view and responded to African conditions through faith healing, exorcism, spirit baptism, prophecy, speaking in tongues, spiritual revival, vibrant liturgy in worship, prayer and evangelism, and sanctified life. He was able to recruit the services of many African missionaries, a fact that became crucial for the spread of Pentecostalism. All the classical Pentecostal missions depended on the contributions of Africans in their ministries. As Pentecostalism spread into urban and rural areas under African evangelists, many engaged in witchcraft cleansing as a major evangelical strategy. This was exactly the pattern that Pierre-Joseph Laurent has shown with the case studies from the Mossi capital of Ouagadougu. He argued that the businessmen in the urban context still felt the power of and used the idiom of their indigenous religions and cultures in discussing their conversion. He cited the oral interview with a businessman, P. W. Zoungrana, one the pioneers of the Wend-Yam, a peasant organization working for the social and economic development of Oubritenga province: "During the period when I had problems starting the Wend-Yam federation, I spoke to God. People consulted and paid witch-doctors to kill me. They sacrificed everything to their fetishes: dogs, goats, beef, everything except humans. When these things happened, I asked everyone to try to protect himself. Me, I have my God."[22] Mission to culture compelled the privileged focus of evangelism and the adequate responses to local exigencies.

The spread of either the AFM or AOG in southern Africa demanded similar responses. Of notable mention are the careers of Elias Letwaba and Mhalangu, who recruited innumerable other black leaders into the AFM. The Nicholas Benghu (1909–1986) factor in the development of Pentecostalism in southern Africa is a key theme. Unlike the AFM, the AOG in South Africa is an umbrella association of many groups run by white, black, and colored leaders. Benghu became connected to the AOG in the 1930s, and rose to prominence in the next decade through successful revival outreaches in Port Elizabeth and East London. By 1950 he founded the Back-to-God Campaign that served as an instrument for expansion into southern and central Africa. His ministry was distinguished by its capacity to address a combination of issues including personal renewal, and racial and social justice themes. He imagined the continent of Africa as a sleeping giant that must awaken to its greatness; he proffered Christianity as an instrument for achieving this from the "Cape to Cairo." His pan-Africanism was grounded in the ideology of Ethiopianism and the nationalism of the era: the negritude movement that emerged among African and Caribbean students in Paris in the 1930s. The responses to the Fascist Italian occupation of Ethiopia among Africans in the diaspora had risen to a feverish pitch in 1935 and, by the late 1940s, Kwame Nkrumah of Ghana mobilized the anti-colonial young radicals, leading to the Manchester meeting of 1945 and the quest for Ethiopian political independence in the 1950s.

Benghu's achievement was to provide the religious dimension of pan-African nationalism, grounded in the interior of the gospel message. He inspired future Pentecostal leaders such as Ezekiel Guti of Zimbabwe and Mensah Otabil of Ghana. His theological quest for African identity through religious power underpins the ideology of the Intercessors for Africa. Benghu urged Africans to build up the individual personality through hard work, hygiene, and discipline. He, therefore, constructed tight-knit communities in which members drew moral boundaries against popular culture such as drinking alcohol, gambling, dancing, and the use of traditional medicine. Members grew within the movement through discipleship or mentorship, and continually engaged in church activities and energetic evangelism. Nicknamed the black Billy Graham, commentators were impressed by Benghu's seriousness, commitment, confident demeanor, and the tensile strength of his simple faith. He became popular with African Americans and garnered support from many Western countries. From the mid-1950s, a number of evangelical American preachers toured eastern and southern Africa: William Braham (1952), Oral Roberts (1956), Frederick Bosworth, Lorne Fox, and Billy Graham. The impact of these evangelistic missions on early African charismatic movements has been mentioned elsewhere. Benghu immediately adopted these evangelists' style of holding revival campaigns in big tents. Thus, Pentecostalism in southern and central Africa grew long after the J. G. Lake period and on through black agency. Indeed, Nicholas Benghu and Ezekiel Guti are significant players in the period from 1950 to the end of the millennium.

Fifth, race soon became a major factor that led to the church schisms as the Africans started their ministries by 1917 using the Zion and Apostolic nomenclatures. Lake's role in the foundations of the apartheid system becomes crucial. Some image him as Machiavellian; others as a hypocrite who pretended to like blacks but used them as a fodder to nurture the church while soon after abandoning them. Some aver that he fathered segregation; defenders admit that he was a paternalist. Even if he was not a racist, he permitted the culture and social convention to separate the church. Before he arrived in South Africa, Lake was fascinated with the Boers, their alleged suffering, and their covenantal theology. The disdain of the DRC for him inspired an increasing desire in him to contact and minister to the Boers. His friendship with Botha,the president and architect of apartheid system in South Africa, his role in the fashioning of the Land Act of 1913, and his oft-quoted advice about deploying the example of the American segregated land allocation policy and establishment of reservations, using the example of white reaction to the First Nation Indians, set the pattern of white control of the church and collusion with apartheid power structures. In 1917, the executive council of the AFM enshrined their racial prejudice in a constitution:

> We do not teach or encourage social equality between whites and natives. We recognize that God is no respecter of persons, but that in every nation he that feareth Him and worketh righteousness is acceptable to Him. We therefore preach the gospel equally to all peoples, making no distinctions. We wish it to be generally known that our white, coloured and native peoples have their separate places of worship, where the sacraments are administered to them.[23]

From that date forward, the whites segregated and controlled the black sector of the AFM.

Sixth, besides the roles of Africans in the foundation and spread of Pentecostalism and the impact of racism, scholars have drawn attention to the presence and contributions of other missionary groups. For instance, Archibald A. Cooper, who converted Rodney "Gipsy" Smith (1860–1947) and assisted the foundation of the ministry in Cape Town in 1905, joined the AFM with Le Roux, and later split to freewheel as an evangelist. The AOG was a veritable competitor in the southern Africa scene. The roles of Charles William Chawner, a Canadian who planted churches in Natal and Transvaal, Henry and Anna Turney, Hannah James, and many others who worked in the region during the same period, compel a balanced perspective. Lake's contemporaries were just as creative and active. It would appear that some have imagined Lake's role in the story of African Pentecostalism from the impact of his ministry at the point when he returned to the United States.

Seventh, the multiple sources of African Pentecostalism are further buttressed by Gerald Pillay's story of the development of Pentecostalism among the Indians of Natal and Durban. The significant aspects are that among the Indian population, there is no confusion between Pentecostals and AICs. Out of 12.5 percent of the Indian population in South Africa who declared themselves Christians in the 1980 census, 7.5 percent were Pentecostals, especially belonging to the Full Gospel Pentecostal, AOG, and AFM. As Pillay argued, "Between 1925 and 1980 Pentecostals acquired more Indian members than all the other denominations put together." At that time Roman Catholics comprised 2.6 percent of those counted, and all Protestants numbered 2.4 percent. (compare those numbers to Full Gospel at 2.8 percent).[24] The rapid growth of the Full Gospel among South African Indians could be traced to the evangelistic ardor of a Bristol businessman, John Alexander Rowlands, who worked closely with South African Indians in an age of segregation. It was also the period when many Indians moved from rural areas into the cities for jobs on the railroad and in mills. The population bulged around Durban, Pietermaritzburg, the Natal coast, and its environs.

The increasing urbanization and its impact on family structures, argued Pillay, coincided with the rise of Pentecostalism in this region in the 1920s and the 1930s. Rowlands made enormous efforts to acculturate; he lived with an Indian family and later shared a room with F. Victor, one of the many Indian co-workers who ensured the success of Bethseda, the largest Full Gospel Church congregation. Rowlands was ordained in 1931 and started a revival-style ministry in the 1940s and 1950s that adopted a constitution and the Back-to-the-Bible campaign. Lengthy revival meetings and colorful sermons were followed by baptizing members by the hundreds. Within a decade, the church grew rapidly and established training institutions and several branches.

The development of the AFM and AOG among Indians took similar patterns. The AFM was organized in the 1930s when an American couple, Charles and Ida Flewelling, founded a small Indian AFM fellowship at Stranger. They nourished it to spread branches, which were often led by Indian lay leaders. Two AOG groups were founded between the late 1940s and 1950s. A Nowergian, F. L. Hansen, established one at Bethshan and distinguished its ministry with social outreach programs such as a safe home for orphans and destitute colored children. It remained under the control of the family and only eventually ordained an Indian in 1978. The other group, Peniel International Assembly, was established by an Indian evangelist, Stephen Govender, and moved into segregated zones when the Group Areas Act compelled Indians to leave the city centers. This made Merebank the center of the assembly, from where it has served and grown, however modestly. Pillay makes the significant observation that "among Indians there was little resistance to white missionary leadership as there had been elsewhere in South Africa among many Africans."[25] Explanations for this include the low level of education and familiarity with the Christian literature among Indians, a culture of obedience to gurus, a coping mechanism amid the exigencies of racism, and a tendency to shy away from expressing public criticism of apartheid because of the threat of repatriation. Still, there is no denying that these ministries expanded from the contributions of Indians preaching to their own folks. They built survival communities of suffering because of the double jeopardy of class and religion posed by their Hindu neighbors. In the mid-1970s, the Hindu launched their own Back-to-the-Ramayana campaign!

iii. Pentecostalism in Malawi

Pentecostalism in Malawi benefited from a number of streams: The evangelical revival of the nineteenth century inspired Anglican and Presbyterian missionary ventures, the holiness movement that created interdenominational fellowships such as the Scripture Union, Christian Students' organizations, and other evangelistic agencies. But the charismatic movements that endured owed much to the missionary zeal in the Apostolic Faith Mission and Assemblies of God in South Africa. As Klaus Fiedler concludes, "The two oldest Pentecostal churches both came to Malawi through the initiative of Malawians who had gone to work abroad, a phenomenon common to many churches in Malawi. Missionaries followed only after the churches had been established as what the then government called "native controlled missions."[26] In the case of the AFM, there were four important routes into Malawi within two crucial years, 1933–1934. Robert Chiguwo converted into the AFM while working in South African mines. He returned to Malawi in 1933 to open a station in a poor, rural community near Zomba, an area that had a large Muslim population. In faraway Mzimba, another *mutchona* repeated a similar pattern before some white missionaries came to visit. Still another indigene, Moses Banda, first established an AFM congregation in Cape Town where the Nyanja dialect was spoken and later brought it home to Malawi. The first white AFM missionary to settle in Blantyre, Malawi, was Eduard Wendland, a German belonging to one of the earliest Pentecostal churches in Europe, the Velbert Mission. He was a carpenter reputed to have built about eight churches. But Wendland positioned himself as the national chairman, an itinerant missionary who left the task of running the churches to Jim Phiri and Moses Banda. This posture caused much conflict of authority with indigenes. Jim Phiri was recruited by a *mutchona* who had been in Zimbabwe, called Rhodesia at that time. He built the strongest AFM presence in the Lower Shire region. It is conjectured that this area sported the most vibrant cult of affliction or spirit possession. As Pentecostalism paid attention to healing and deliverance ministry, the community found it to be a religious form more adaptable to their cultural situation, which allowed for greater participation and level of commitment. The evidence shows that early AFM presence was in poor rural communities rather than urban areas.

The missionary incursion by the AOG was made predominantly from an indigenous agency that served white-founded Pentecostal churches. In 1930 we find an odd Swiss Assemblies of God missionary living in the remote Igale Pass, halfway between Tukuyu and Rungwe. But the main story of the AOG in Malawi is about the pioneering evangelism by a number of returning migrant workers who founded "native controlled" churches in the Misuku Hills (Mubulu) in 1934. In the same year, Lyton Kalambule, who was first converted to the Full Gospel Church in Durban, returned to southern Malawi. It does appear that he changed stripes to the AOG, under the influence of Frederik Burke, an American who changed to the AOG in South Africa and moved to Malawi. We shall return to Kalambule's colorful career later.

Eliot Nkunika established the AOG parish in the Dedza area (Gilbert Village) where a seminary later developed. These details demonstrate African missionary initiative. In fact, five Classical Pentecostal Churches were established in Malawi between 1930–1958 under indigenous agency: Assemblies of God (1930), Pentecostal Holiness Church (1932), Apostolic Faith Mission (1933), Apostolic Church of Pentecost (1947), and Independent Assemblies of God (1958)—when Magnus Udd, the longest-serving AOG missionary, seceded from the church over its willingness to baptize polygamists. The Pentecostal missions continued to grow through schism and evangelistic fervor but generally operated in poor, rural communities with agents who did not possess much education. The focus was on the spiritual component of mission. These factors explain the slow vertical growth pattern and provide the backdrop to the surge in the post-1970 period, a pattern that could be illustrated from just about every country in the continent.

iv. Early Pentecostalism in Zimbabwe

The charismatization of Zimbabwe came initially from the AFM and AOG in South Africa. In 1915, an AFM evangelist, Zacharia Manamela, initiated the enterprise in Gwanda Reserve in Southern Rhodesia/Zimbabwe. He built up a vibrant congregation before two white Boer missionaries joined the enterprise. For the entire period, only a few whites participated in this mission field. A list of black missionaries carried the burden with a number of migrant workers This explains why many of them roamed the reserves looking like AIC prophets, sporting shaved heads, long beards, white robes; held mountaintop meetings and night vigils; and practiced exorcism, witch finding, and ecstatic possession. Their unorthodoxy alarmed the colonial officers who tried to hinder them. Some, like Joel Juma, a Nyasa migrant who was nicknamed *Alleyula*, set the Umtali region on its ears. The most obtrusive of these missionaries was Enoch "Deutoronomy" Gwanzura who, decked with his European-style pith helmet, would carry his salvation message into various communities, overturn beer pots, break up traditional ceremonies, and confront chiefs. The colonial government constituted a hindrance to charismatic Christianity.

By 1931 the official assessment put the AFM strength at three thousand members. Concentrating on a spiritualized agenda, it challenged official policy by preaching divine healing in the midst of the influenza; it built no schools for the civilizing mission; it ignored the delimitation of boundaries designed to keep peace among competing missionaries; its method jarred prominently; and it had the habit of rebaptizing other churches' members. Many of the evangelists were laypeople who had little education and did not fit the typical image of pastors. Politically, officials worried about the havoc that could be caused by the itinerant evangelists who would confront chiefs, attack local rituals, and provide young migrants and especially young women with legitimate reasons to challenge patriarchal authority. In the late 1930s, the AFM sent some white missionaries, who attempted to trim the long beards of the evangelists, curtail the activities of the lay preachers, and set up a more orderly missionary regime. But the AFM must have been pleased with the rapid growth achieved between 1915–1938 that included far-flung parts of Southern Rhodesia as well as the townships of Harare and Highfield.

David Maxwell's study of the evangelization of the Hwesa communities of the Katerere dynasty, Zimbabwe, underscores a number of facts: early Pentecostalism was not an urban phenomenon; and migrant laborers constituted the main agency for the AFM when they entered into this dynasty in 1946. Five years later the community showed more interest in the Elim Pentecostal group that came in 1951. African Pentecostal missionary enterprise was characterized by a vigorous missionary zeal that reshaped the indigenous religion and culture. As Maxwell argued, groups comprising women, youth, and labor migrants, in alliance with Elim Pentecostal missionaries from Ulster, destroyed charms and magic in a totalizing effect on the rural community. They erected boundaries with ethical values around personal morality (adultery), consumption habit (alcohol), crime (murder), and attitude to traditional religion and culture by attacking both the central ancestral *mhodoro* cults and the peripheral *ngozi* and *mashave* rituals. As mentioned before, some of the Shona missionaries, such as Johana Marange and Moses Masamvu, developed their own Christian versions of these cults, such as the Vapostori.[27]

Resentment against white control must have been at the root of the disengagement from AFM by a small group of artisans. They started as a choir and prayer band that gradually developed into a ministry. The prominent members were Joseph Choto, Raphael Kupara, Abel Sande, and Ezekiel Guti, a carpenter working for Fisons Fertilizer Company. Under the guidance of Gwanzura, the young group continued the intense prayer activities that spread into the rural villages. Quite early, Guti started an evangelistic band and offered private ministrations. By 1959 his small group felt confident enough to split from the AFM over authority and power issues and just at the time when Nicholas Benghu from the Assemblies of South Africa conducted an outreach in Harare with the cooperation of the PAOC. Guti and his friend assisted Benghu and became his "agents" in Southern Rhodesia. But Guti managed to use the resources from both the PAOC and Benghu to bolster his group until 1967, when a frustrated Benghu expelled Guti, who quickly rechristened his organization as the Assemblies of God African (AOGA) with himself as chairman, Choto as secretary, and Sande as vice chairman. This marks the birth of the organization that became the Zimbabwe Assemblies of God Africa (ZAOGA). It is the largest Pentecostal organization in contemporary Zimbabwe.

Finally, in both eastern and southern Africa, there was a lull in the operation of Classical Pentecostal missionaries during the period 1935–1955. Africa was rediscovered as a mission field in the late 1950s. While the early effort was dominated by the spread of the AFM, the AOG in its varieties dominated the second period from the 1950s. For instance, the Canadian Assemblies of God in Uganda entered the borders with Kenya in 1935 but its spread could be dated to 1962 when it entered the eastern region, and by the year 2000 it could claim almost 3 percent of the country's population. Meanwhile, the Full Gospel Church arrived in 1959, Conservative Baptists in 1961, and the Southern Baptists and the Elim Missionary Assemblies in 1962.[28]

In summary, the story has attempted to place the roles of Classical Pentecostals in the evangelization of Africa within its black perspective. Classical Pentecostals appeared early in the African religious landscape and operated with a muscular indigenous agency to charismatize Africa. Comparatively speaking, the achievement remained modest. The crucial point is that none of the classical forms of Pentecostalism became important in the religious landscape until they benefited from the spiritual renewal of the 1970s. Many missionaries did not stay long in the field or develop any missionary work that outlasted them. As the force of the "faith movement" weakened, so did the activities of intrepid solo entrepreneurs. Although the world wars disrupted many enterprises, the denominational genre succeeded more than the others and, in many places, solo entrepreneurs sought the patronage of denominational Pentecostal organizations. From the outset, the white Pentecostals accepted racial segregation; some doubted the possibility of Africans to speak in tongues. This explains the ambiguous image of Pentecostals in southern Africa as possible agents of the American Religious Right. However, these groups cumulatively added to the charismatic temper of the environment, provided the nuance in the story of Pentecostal origins in Africa, and certainly counter the impression that "new crusaders" recently forayed into Africa bearing the insignia of fundamentalism.

Pentecostalism emerged from the indigenous response of Africans to the missionary message; the missionary input from evangelical ministries such as Scripture Union, Campus Crusade, and such; from the increasing missionary forays of Pentecostals from the holiness tradition and Pentecostal denominations from various countries who utilized the labors of African agents; and from interdenominational parachurches, bolstered by the educational institutions of many American Bible colleges and many evangelical evangelistic outreaches.

4

Mademoni

African-Instituted Churches in Pentecostal Rhetoric

1. The Estranged Bedfellows: The Context of the Problem

There is a major debate in African church historiography about
whether to include the African Instituted Churches (AICs) in the
growing Pentecostal movement. Obviously, doing so will cause the
statistics of the movement to bulge. The question is whether the
insiders accept that they are Pentecostals. Is their inclusion the hand-
iwork of academics who may be outsiders? Moreover, how do we
explain the diatribe in Pentecostal rhetoric and practices that variously
demonizes the AICs as "white garment churches" or *mademoni*,
people covenanted to familiar spirits? For instance, those who come
for deliverance in a Pentecostal church are asked to fill out a form
indicating their life history, family and business contacts, and religious journey. If the candidates indicate an earlier participation
in a white garment church, the first process of the deliverance ministry would be to deliver the person from the foul spirits and covenantal rituals in those churches. Yet it is acknowledged that many
new Pentecostal churches had AIC roots. Is there a significant measure of continuity to dub all of them as Pentecostal? The sheer variety
of the movement beggars the imagination and this explains the
Babel of diversity.[1]

As an emergent religious form, the Pentecostal movement tends
to rub every other religious form the wrong way, as common parlance would put the matter. For instance, it alleges that the mainline
churches are suffering from "power failure" and indulges in powerless Christianity, dispensing Sunday to Sunday pills. The mainline

churches retort that the new fad engages in sheep stealing and propagates a crossless Christianity. Prosperity preachers, especially, are accused of merchandising the gospel, being veritable false prophets and wolves in sheep's clothing. Opponents treat the new Pentecostal movement the same way that Wole Sonyika's *Brother Jero* treats the priests of the AICs. Some scholars are more critical of the Pentecostal movement and show a higher level of appreciation for the religious creativity and achievements of the *Aladura* churches. For instance, Mercy Oduyoye portrays the new Pentecostal movements as a strain on the ecumenical endeavors of yesteryears; Paul Gifford images them as a threat to the pluralistic environment required for national development; while Adrian Hastings characterizes the movement as retrogression from the creativity achieved on the culture-gospel interface by the AICs. As Mercy Oduyoye intoned, "Today we have Christian missions in Africa who pour spite on African culture in its totality because of the negative aspects and yet subject their women members to exclusions and marginalizations [sic] said to be demanded by the Bible.... They are establishing Bible Colleges and Universities and will soon flood Africa with a theology ... making Africans hate their Africanness."[2]

The rituals, symbols, and the use of instruments such as candles by the Roman Catholic Church and the AICs have attracted the most severe diatribes from the Pentecostals. Digging deep into the ancient puritan rhetoric and anti-Catholic vituperations on rituals, symbols, and instruments, Pentecostals allege that it is easier for a camel to go through the eye of a needle than for a Roman Catholic to be born again. Ironically, recent "improbable conversations," seeking the death of stereotypes, betray the Roman Catholic roots of Pentecostalism.[3] Besides, the charismatic movement has flowered luxuriantly within contemporary Roman Catholicism in Africa.

The focus here is on the relationship between the two significant movements in African church history given the demonization of the AICs in Pentecostal rhetoric as unadulterated cults. For simplicity, we shall refer to the AICs as the *Aladura*, a Yoruba word meaning "praying people," though they are known mostly as *Zionists* in South Africa, *Abaroho* in East Africa, and *sunsum sore* (spirit worshipers) in Ghana.[4] "Zion/Apostolic," in southern Africa, refers to those churches that perceive themselves as being guided by the Spirit, *umoya*. This shortcut does not ignore H. W. Turner's typology; much to the contrary, the issue of typology is the heartbeat of this chapter because its neglect has been the bane of the dialogue. We shall apply a modified version of Turner's typology to underscore the lines of divide.[5]

Some scholars have imaged the Pentecostals and AICs as bedfellows. As Karla Poewe would say, these movements "have common roots and many links; they experience their religion similarly."[6] So the goal of this chapter is a historiographical survey of the discourses deployed by scholars to adjudicate the soured relationship and the estrangement of the odd couple or counsel them to live in peace and be counted in the same category as the map of world Christianity changes. As argued in a previous chapter, the AICs were the *second* response to the missionary message in Africa. But unlike the *first* challenge posed by Ethiopians, who were promoted cultural nationalism in a religious stroke, the AICs confronted the muted pneumatic elements in missionary theology and practice. As the *third* challenge, the Pentecostals have equally laid emphasis on the pneumatic dimension; that is, both the Pentecostals and AICs are operating in the same spiritual frequency. The vibrant spirituality in both groups produced creative liturgy, polity, ethics, and evangelistic concern for soul care and material well-being of members. Both groups are innovative and have developed doctrinal emphases that differ from the inherited traditions of the missionaries who responded with jaundiced perceptions of the world of power in indigenous African communities. At the cultural interface, both drink from the same wellspring of African primal worldview. Perhaps this is the rub: different approaches in appropriating the text.

Two positions have, therefore, emerged in African church historiography on the estrangement of the bedfellows: those who lay emphasis on the shared worldview tend to emphasize the elements of continuity, and those who deploy the Pentecostal covenant theology emphasize the elements of discontinuity. The first group portrays the AICs as the roots of modern Pentecostalism in Africa, or indeed, an earlier form of it. The implication is to posture the roots of Pentecostalism in Africa within the religious genius of the indigenous people. Within this camp, however, some arrive at the same conclusion through the prism of comparative religions, emphasizing the eidetic or common elements in some religions. They argue that there is a common current that runs under every form of religion, that this could be the bedrock on which to mount one-world ideology, that already global processes are webbing all cultures and religions. A vision of a religious terrain with the colors of the rainbow runs as an undercurrent in this mushy, reductionist approach. The predominance of Western sociologists, coming from cultural contexts that emphasize inclusivism and promote religious pluralism, has informed the study of both the AICs and Pentecostalism. They ride roughshod over distinctions that matter to the practitioners. Outsider perspectives have trumped the insider perspectives. Thus three fields have determined the discourses: phenomenological, sociological, and those who emphasize the shared historical roots.

Those who emphasize discontinuity or the estrangement explore the deployment of covenantal theology in the Pentecostal arsenal. This argues that both in primal religion and in Pentecostal theology, human beings and communities relate to spiritual powers through covenants. Covenanting rituals predominate in religious acts, symbols, and oral liturgies. With libations, sacrificial objects, powerful incantations, and other acts, individuals and communities covenant themselves to the spirits in the sky, land, water, and ancestral world. Christians do the same in consolidating their relationships to saints, angels, Jesus, the Holy Spirit, and God. Covenants are legal, binding, and confer privileges with responsibilities; they dominate worldviews, ritual activities, and religious ardor; and they determine the destinies of human beings and communities. This view images the Christian life as a power-encounter and a spiritual battle, requiring a certain attitude for the spirits at the gates of communities, and asserts the need to be wary, to test the spirits, for not all spirits are of God. This perception tends to emphasize the elements of discontinuity and may produce the demonization of other religions. This is the bed, the contested space. I now elaborate on these historiographical contours by examining the life of the bedfellows or the arguments for continuity, and then analyze the estrangement or the rhetoric of discontinuity. Certain conclusions will emerge on the implications for African church historiography in the throes of an exciting process of revisioning, reconceptualizing, and recommissioning. The trend is a response to three facts: First, the shift of Christianity's center of gravity to the Southern Hemisphere has turned Africa into a veritable laboratory in Christian development, eliciting new forms of interpretation. Second, this theme plays into the larger resurgence of religion in Third World development. Elements such as ethnicity and religion that were supposed to be too primitive to withstand the insurgence of modernization have refused to die and are, in fact, holding the center stage in social analysis. Sociologists speak about the "re-religionization of the world" that has come about because of the breakdown of modernity, a process that has become most obvious since the 1970s. Third, the *finger of God* is a conceptual scheme that explains how inexplicably God acts in certain ways at certain times. There appears to be an outpouring of the Holy Spirit in large measures in these times and, in its wake, a re-evangelization process is occurring in Africa, which queries old positions.

2. The Bedfellows: Links and Parallels

Stepping outside the compounds of those who see all religious forms as the different roads to Rome or the colors of the rainbow, one engages about four group of advocates linking the AICs and the Pentecostals based on the pneumatic emphasis. The first group of advocates consists of H. W. Turner, Walter Hollenweger, Rosalind Hackett, Allan Anderson, and Kwabena Asamoah-Gyadu, who uses C. G. Baeta as a referent point. A second group includes Poewe and G. Oosthuizen and those who focus on the genealogy of new religious movements or the linked roots in the historical discourse of origins. A third group, comprising Andrew Walls and Kwame Bediako, points to the kindred atmosphere or shared worldview of the AICs and Pentecostals. A fourth group, led by J. B. Tinney and Inus Daneel, points us to the social context, ideology, and the reintegrative response to social predicament. These are representative nodes in the historiography and have been selected to balance the data from southern and western Africa. In addition, some commentators gyrate between postures and may not wager their academic reputations on any single position. It takes much hubris to try to pigeonhole them.[7]

The *Aladura*, Zionists, and *Roho* emerged as a reaction to various aspects to colonialism: the monopoly of power in the church; the strangeness of the polity, ethics, and doctrine; the dullness of liturgy and modes of expressing the spirituality; and as a quest for a place of belonging in the midst of political oppression and marginalization. African Instituted Churches(hereafter refered to as AICs) benefited from the achievements of Ethiopianism but went beyond it to tap the pneumatic emphasis in the Bible story. It was this emphasis on the spirit that dominated scholarly discourse on the movement. The World Council of Churches (WCC), for instance, initiated a number of conferences in the 1950s to probe whether AIC movement was a Christian form or a return to the promotion of pagan spirits. As decolonization loomed large on the horizon, disquiet over the durability of the missionary enterprise intensified. This question of authenticity lay at the back of research by Bengt Sundkler in the 1940s,Victor Hayward in 1957, and C. G. Baeta and Harold Turner in the 1960s. In church history, the manifestation of the Holy Spirit has consistently bobbed to the surface like a cork that cannot be suppressed. So, the sympathetic scholars sidestepped the nuanced concerns of the rulers of the synagogue and imaged the AICs as "Independent African Pentecostal Churches."[8] H. W. Turner's article "Nigerian Pentecostalism" in *Orita* dwelled fully on the *Aladura*. As the early or Classical *Aladura* emerged from mission churches, there was much curiosity and even respect for them as a form of African creativity, response to the gospel, and contribution to the universal church. They were imaged as separatist churches that had the same affinity with the mission-founded churches. But some people may have noticed that they were different from the African churches among the Yoruba studied by J. B. Webster in 1964. The problem would arise when new indigenous forms proliferated that did not have any missionary roots. Thus, the image of the AICs as the African version of Pentecostalism became significant and set the tone for younger scholars such as Rosalind Hackett, Allan Anderson, and Kwabena Asamoah-Gyadu. The perception is that the pneumatic common denominator makes both the AICs and Pentecostalism birds of the same feather who should flock together. As Anderson variously put the matter:

- Because of the similarities and the historical and theological connection between these churches and African Pentecostal Churches of Western origin, I propose to refer to them as African Pentecostal churches.[9]
- The historical and theological affinity between the present-day Zionists and Pentecostals justifies my using the term *African Pentecostal*

rather broadly. In fairness to both groups, however, the differences that emerged in later years result in a distinctively "Zionist" or "Pentecostal-type" and "Pentecostal" churches. But these distinctions were not at all clear in the early 1900s.[10]

- Although there are clear affinities and common historical and theological origins shared by African and Western Pentecostals, the passing of time and the proliferation of AICs may have accentuated the difference.
- In doctrine there are no significant differences between Zionists and Apostolic churches, on the one hand, and Pentecostals churches, on the other hand, but in ritual, the differences are marked.
- There is an emphasis on healing, although the methods of obtaining it differ. Whereas Pentecostals generally practice laying on of hands and prayer for the sick, these will usually be accompanied in Zionist and Apostolic churches by the use of symbolic objects such as blessed water, ropes, staffs, papers, ash, and so on.
- The attitude to traditional religious practices is generally ambivalent, particularly when it comes to ancestors; and some of these churches allow polygyny.[11]
- The use of the term *Pentecostal-type* to describe those AICs that make up the bulk of African Pentecostals in South Africa is an attempt to avoid generalizing or overlooking the obvious differences that exist, acknowledged by the church members themselves. Referring to these churches as "Pentecostal" does not in any way overlook their distinct liturgies, healing practices, and particularly their different approaches to African traditional religion, and their unique contributions to Christianity in a broader African context.[12]

Thus, Anderson struggled to argue for the lack of distinction, but at the same time was puzzled by:

1. the obvious differences in practices;
2. the impact of time and schisms on the character of the *Aladura* movement; and
3. the insiders's self-image or what the members themselves think and say. In a surprising passage he observed that "Harvey Cox is at least partly correct to refer to the Apostolic/Zionist, Lumpa, and Kimbanguist churches as 'the African expression of the world-wide Pentecostal movement,' but these churches do not usually define themselves in this way."[13]

Little did Cox know that the Kimbanguists would soon be embroiled in a strong disagreement with both the WCC and the Organization of African Instituted Churches over the claim of its leader's divinity. At the heart of

Anderson's position is a phenomenological bias that eschews the exclusion of other religious forms. But analytical clarity may demand that we separate both movements and appreciate them better through a healthy comparison. Moreover, Anderson's method ignores the typology within the movement and insiders' self-perceptions. The distance between some of the types could be farther than a journey from Jerusalem to Tyre and Sidon! Furthermore, his method questions whether all the flares of revivals should be treated the same. In West Africa, for instance, there were a number of spiritual revivals before the strictly *Aladura*-type emerged. Should the revivals led by Wade Harris (1910), Garrick Braide (1914), and the Spirit revival in Ibibioland (1927) be treated as *Aladura*? Obviously, revival leaders had no agenda for starting separate congregations and were driven beyond the pale by the hostility of mission churches.

This hostility resulting in new churches is similar to the fortunes of the *Balokole* revivals that swept from Rwanda in the 1930s through Uganda, Kenya, and most of eastern and central Africa, yelling *tukutendereza Yezu,* "We praise you, Jesus!" It may, therefore, be possible for the sake of clarity to distinguish between the Classical AIC-types that flared up in the colonial period and the spiritualist AICs that appeared later. In the genesis of Classical *Aladura* movement in Nigeria there was much connection between those chruches that mutated into Pentecostalism and those that remained *Aladura*. Both rejected some of the resources of traditional religion, but by differing degrees. A classical *Aladura* group such as the Christ Apostolic Church (CAC) has a pedigree running from Faith tabernacle through Welsh Apostolic Church to the modern Pentecostal congregations. It used a close reading of the Bible to express caution toward certain esoteric dimensions in the Church of the Lord Aladura. The CAC refused to associate with Joseph Oshitelu because of his secret names for God and other doctrinal and ritual idiosyncrasies. However, much was shared in common. Tangled roots ensured that William Kumuyi's Deeper Life Bible Church, which is certainly one of the largest Pentecostal enterprises in Africa, traces its roots through the Apostolic Church to Babalola's revival, except that the CAC separated from the Apostolic Church. Can we still claim that Deeper Life has *Aladura* roots?

In Ghana, Wade Harris inspired Apostles Sampson Oppong, John Swatson, and Peter Anim, who charismatized various Protestant churches, as well as John Nackabah and Grace Tani, the founders of some *sunsum sore* (spirit worship) churches such as the Church of the Twelve Apostles.[14] In Nigeria, a number of the youths who later used the Scripture Union as the vehicle for entering charismatic organizations had earlier contacts with *Aladura* churches.[15] The crossing of boundaries may point to the same historical origins, but the differences are manifest. This explains the gyrations in Anderson's positions.

In Zimbabwe, Inus Daneel notes that the prevalence of such terms as *Apostolic* among the indigenous churches "in itself indicates that most of them are strongly pentecostally-inclined, or at least give prominence to the work of the Holy Spirit."[16] Southern Africa presents a peculiar case in which racism forced the exit of some African members from the Apostolic Faith Mission (AFM), and as it splintered, many developed new religious spiritualities. As the AFM spread through indigenous Shona missionaries of the Masowe and Maranke movements into Zimbabwe and Malawi, it encountered different religious problems that compelled an emphasis on witchcraft eradication. The exigencies of the religious environment led it to deploy new religious symbols and liturgy more attuned to the indigenous spiritual environment.

Indeed, David Maxwell made the most robust case for continuity based on shared historical roots. He argued that the Hwesa people of Katerere dynasty in northeastern Shonaland "seized upon Christian beliefs and practices, in response to locally specific conditions, and in the process transformed their own pre-existing religious systems."[17]

As the AFM splintered into various religious groups such as Vapostori, Mughodi, Torpiya, Zviratidzo, Samanga, Rujeko, and Borngaes, under the leadership of migrant workers, traders, and refugees, they all emphasized the same goals of renewal movements in traditional religion, namely, fertility, abundant harvest, successful hunting, material wealth and prosperity, protection against evil, sorcery, or witchcraft. Maxwell argued that the origins of the distinctive rituals and taboos of Zionist churches emerged through a process of osmosis with early AFM branches, and that these taboos were first preached by John Alexander Dowie in Chicago and taught in South Africa by J. G. Lake and Thomas Hezmalhalch. Zionist identity markers such as prohibitions on alcohol, pork, and smoking; rituals such as baptism by triune immersion; ethics and practices such as pacifism; the style of preachers' certificates; the use of white robes, colored sashes, and staff did not emerge from kraal splitting but was inherited from Zion City, Illinois. Maxwell concludes: "The AFM would doubtless have looked more like Zionism if Lake and Hezmalhalch had remained in South Africa." But Maxwell admits that divergences emerged after 1915, and the AFM took a different path.[18]

Even more astonishing is the fact that some of the founders of contemporary Pentecostal megachurches came from *Aladura* backgrounds: The Redeemed Christian Church of God was founded by a member of Cherubim and Seraphim. The complete realignment of the church occurred only in the 1980s under new leadership. The founder of Winners Chapel or Living Faith Church remained a pastor of the Cherubim and Seraphim until the 1980s. In his last post, just before he left for Kwara Polytechnic to study architecture, the chief of the village presented him a lantern as a significant symbol of the light that he brought to the community. This church leader changed to Pentecostalism through a vision he saw after his graduation. His brother is still a prominent pastor of that *Aladura* church. Even more poignant, as the spirit revival that occurred around the globe in the 1970s hit Nigeria, many *Aladura* groups abandoned the use of candles and other instruments and became fully Pentecostal. The split in the Christ Ascension Church (Aladura) produced Mike Okonkwo's large True Redeemed Evangelical Mission, Lagos. Victor Onuigbo's Victory Christian Mission in Enugu (southeastern Nigeria) is now a leading Pentecostal body participating in the Council of Bishops. These are examples of a trend that increased in frequency.[19] The verdict is that the same *providential* outflow of the Spirit operated in the early AICs and later flowed into modern Pentecostal movements, mediated directly through African religious genius, and linking some of the by-products. The caveat, however, is that there was a religious shift from one to the other, indicating that they were not the same. The remaining question is about the reasons for the change and the direction.

One dimension of the link and parallel stresses the African genealogy of African Pentecostalism to a certain spirituality and intense quest for religious power that yielded various permutations and constantly changed the shape of the religious landscape. Poewe makes this case strongly for southern Africa:

> It seems to me that Sundkler is wrong when he insists that the impetus for the "black charismatic wave" came from whites like Le Roux, Cooper and Dowie among others. Rather, the impetus came from the black. The contribution of white missionaries was of a different nature. Having lived among blacks, and being deeply influenced by the reality of black religiosity, some white missionaries moved away from tradition to a much more experiential form of Christianity. When they reached this point—the point of Zion and Pentecost—they had the doctrine for which the African was ready and waiting and of which he was aware long before colonialism.[20]

The direct links and parallels between Azusa Street, African Pentecostalism, and Zion that the South Africa data contain is peculiar to the region. They were not easily replicated in the eastern and western regions of Africa. As argued before, some American Pentecostal groups sent missionaries to Africa, but these did not generate the origins of charismatic flares in the continent. Poewe argues that the AFM-Zion linkage makes the case for the love affair of the bedfellows but runs a certain risk by "assigning an undue importance to foreign influence on local religion." "It was the contact of African religious culture (consisting as it did of tongues, Spirit, healing, and joyful worship) with the Pentecostal gestalt that sparked the new experiments of Black and White independent churches."[21] Crucial to her perspective is the debate raging within Pentecostal studies about race ideology in the interpretation of the history of the movement. The blurring of the line between Pentecostals and AICs could use the race factor to link the black protagonists among AICs and Pentecostals. Hollenweger, Tinney, and Leonard Lovett are a few of those who have forged the link between the two groups by urging the blackness of

Pentecostal origins.[22] Poewe and her husband, Irving Hexham, have pitched in their academic effort for the recovery of black contribution to early Pentecostalism.

Closely related to this emphasis on racial ideology is the resurgence of a cultural-historical model in the study of revivalism in Africa. The doyen of African church history, Andrew Walls, has made the point most cogently. He argues that the shift of Christianity's center to the South, especially to Africa, is not a matter of numbers but requires that the method of studying African Christianity must be reconceptualized to highlight the strands of continuity in African religious history, Christian and pre-Christian, with no sharp break in African understanding of relationships with the transcendent world. As Andrew Walls argued, "The continuity in African religion, pre-Christian and Christian, is due in large measure to continuing worldviews, the application of the material of the Christian tradition to the already existing African maps of the universe."[23] Christianity in Africa has absorbed the old goals of primal religion while reordering the worldview and introducing new symbols and sources. From this perspective, Walls comments on the "sharp conflict between the old type Independent churches, the spirituals, and the new type, the Pentecostal and charismatic radicals":

> Perhaps the core of the conflict, the element which makes relationships so tense, is the issue whether subordinate spiritual beings, who represent the continuity of the religious consciousness demonstrated in the divinity element in the older cosmologies, may be recognized as the obedient agents of God, or must be anathematized as evil entities opposed to Him. What both groups take for granted is the existence of this element. In this radical evangelicals are as much the children of Africa as the older Independents, the prophet-healing churches. *They use the same maps of the universe—even if they color them differently.*[24]

Walls brings to the fore the pursuit of strands of continuity in African church history and theology, linking these to their primal roots, kindred atmosphere, shared worldview, cosmology, and internal architecture of the movements. He argues that in the contested religious space, both AICs and Pentecostals are engaged in the same task and share much in common; that both movements are engaged in mission to culture, and are religious responses to the challenges from the indigenous worldviews. We shall focus on this theme more adequately in a later chapter.

Like Walls, Hollenweger had arrived at the same conclusion by a combination of structural and functionalist analysis. In a seminal article, he argued that the religious register of *Aladura* Christianity include the following: racism (European superiority complex) versus intercultural and interracial understanding of Christianity; literacy versus orality; abstract concepts versus narrativity; the anonymity of bureaucratic organizations versus family and personal relationship; medical technology versus a holistic understanding of health and sickness; and Western psychoanalytic cliques versus a group and family therapy that centers on human touch, prayer, and a daily informal education in dreams and visions.[25]

These characteristics are deliberately chosen to emphasize the "Pentecostal" or pneumatic elements in AIC spirituality. They also provide the bases for innumerable articles on the functions of AIC spirituality in the African environment. Some, such as Daneel, have examined the "liberative value of a ministry which appears to confront the existential needs and fears of people in a ritually understandable and, therefore, psychologically and religiously satisfying manner."[26] Oosthuizen argued that, rather than being apolitical and otherworldly, the AICs have been sensitive and active in social and environmental issues.[27] Daneel further emphasized the tree-planting Eucharist of the AICs: the pursuit of social justice cause from a spiritual perspective. All these sound like the same explanations proffered for the rapid proliferation of Pentecostalism in modern Africa. It should be added that Daneel stresses the difference between Pentecostalism and the AICs even though they share the same perception of the victorious life in Christ.[28]

The scholars' verdict is that there is no reason why the bedfellows should not live happily and that with the implosion of charismatic groups within mainline churches, the stage should be set for a massive process reevangelizing Africa. The grounds for the optimism are that AICs are the earliest version of African Pentecostalism; the historical roots of modern Pentecostalism in *Aladura* spirituality; the direct links between Azusa Street and Zionism through the Apostolic Faith Mission in southern and central Africa; the black liturgical initiative that AICs contributed to charismatic religiosity; and the shared worldview, kindred atmosphere, interior architecture and texture, and the functions of a new spirituality in both religious and political landscapes of Africa.

3. The Estrangement: The Demonization of the AICs

The first clue that all that glitters is not gold is indicated by deploying a typology in the study of the religious forms in Africa. Many of the scholars avoid the use of typology, and do not even discuss its viability. Yet, as H. W. Turner shows, it is possible to represent the relationship on a chart based on a typology that he designed in the early 1970s. Turner designed a multivariate typology and, therefore, it is possible to extract and update the theologically predicated dimension. It must be spelled out at the outset that while a typology brings order out of chaos, as Stephanie Douglas argued, it must be used cautiously because of its limitations.[29] This particular typology reflects the

Sola Scriptura		Scriptura et Traditiones	
Pentacostals	Protestants	Roman Catholics	Aladura
Evangelicas	Ethopians		
	Charismatic Movements		
Christians			Zionists

Non-Christians

	Nativistic
Russelites	Messianic
	Vitalistic
	Revivalistic

changing face of Christianity in Africa and is theologically based to test African Christianity against biblical and historic Christianity. To use an ancient predicate, Christian forms may be typologized between those that stand on "*Sola Scriptura*" and those that affirm "*Scriptura et Traditiones*": The ancients understood "traditiones" to include rituals and instruments, as well as other traditions whose use has been inherited through ecclesiastical history. The clarion call in the Reformation was the denial of these traditions and a veritable stand on the Scriptures alone. Perhaps, the bare form of Calvin's church in the old part of Geneva illustrates one dimension of the puritan assertion. With mainline Protestants in the center of this form, Evangelicals stand to the left, and Pentecostals farther to the left. Ethiopianism, at least in West Africa, in the nineteenth century, did not differ much from mainline Protestantism except on the issues of allocation of power and the admissibility of certain cultural forms in Christian life and worship. To the right stood the Catholics, and to the farther right would be the *Aladura*, based on their use of rituals and instruments—alum, green water, candles, colors of vestments, staff, and such. Here lies the irony: Based on pneumatic emphasis, the *Aladura* and the Pentecostal would be situated near each other. If the chart were to be folded, this would become obvious. But, if it were presented on a flat surface, one could sing Nat King Cole's song about the lover being so near and yet so far away!

The plot thickens because of the amoebic nature of the *Aladura*. Oosthuizen draws a distinction between independent and indigenous churches. The resulting consolidation of the terminology, the African Instituted Churches, emerged only in the late 1980s in Nairobi when it became necessary to officially register the umbrella organization, The Organization of African Instituted Churches. Oosthuizen avoided the official nomenclature so as to show that the earlier forms (that we have termed classical AICs) that broke away from mission churches retained much of the theology of their heritage. In the proliferation or mutations, new indigenous forms appeared that lost the tradition. For instance, as the Cherubim and Seraphim split into fifty-one branches, some must have lost touch with the original vision and character of the founders. At some point in time forty-nine came back together into an uneasy family reunion in which many could not recognize their cousins. Indeed, some did not accept the centrality of the Scriptures and the affirmation that Jesus Christ is Lord.

Two factors mattered: The lack of literacy among the leadership may be an aspect of the problem, as well as the pressure to demonstrate the possession of spiritual power. It is said that similar pressure forces the televangelist to fake healing miracles. And in fact, some of the AICs resort to occult means to meet popular demands. In Pentecostal rhetoric, a boundary of acceptability is drawn after the Apostolic and Zionists. The rest of the AICs, such as the messianic, vitalistic, nativistic, and revivalistic types, should not make any pretensions to be Christian. One cannot have Halloween without pumpkins or Christianity without Christ. This affirmation is built on the interface of theology and church history. A definition of the church as *ekklesia* must perforce mean that church history is the reconstruction of the experience of what God has done in Christ through the power of the Holy Spirit in individuals and among communities.

Harold Turner made this point many years ago but it seems to be ignored in the headlong romanticization of the AICs by Western sociologists. In his seminal paper "Pagan Features in African Independent Churches," Turner first separated the healing homes (nativistic), the eccentric prophets who claim to be one or the other of the Trinity, whom Turner calls charlatans (messianic), the occultist, spiritualist groups who quest for power (vitalistic), and the revivalistic forms such as Reformed Ogboni Fraternity, Godianism, and Afrikania. Second, he drew attention to the Christian elements in the Zionist forms. And third, he pointed to the residual cultic elements with the hope that the founders will deal with these. As I've indicated, some have.[30]

The contested areas within these churches, therefore, are:

1. modes of receiving and transmitting spiritual power—dreams, visions, laying on of hands, anointing with oil, prophetic speaking, and intuition or the still, small voice;
2. crisis control—discernment, diagnosis, cleansing, deliverance, and healing;
3. rituals of rejuvenation, recovenanting and reenchanting the world ancestral cults, festivals (especially agricultural); and
4. empowerment rituals—for life force, tangible material things such as goods and wealth, and intangibles such as status and power.

There are wide areas of agreement in many of these. Lack of space constrains a detailed discussion of these weighty matters. However, an example may suffice.

Since healing is central to the practice and allure of the AICs, R. C. Mitchell examined the healing practices of various *Aladura* genres, the Zionist, nativistic, and evangelical *Aladura*, by which he referred to the Apostolic types. He showed that the Apostolics were very biblical in their healing practice; that the Zionists paid the Bible some attention, though some critical, questionable elements could be detected; that the nativistic genre veered off the biblical maze. The occult nature of the vitalistic *Aladura* goes beyond the use of holy names and the *Sixth and Seventh Book of Moses*—a cabalistic collection of spells and incantations. The *Aladura* produced a booklet entitled *Spiritual Uses of Aroma Candles*, published by "Besade Aromatic Industries, Ondo, Ondo State, Nigeria," and purportedly "compiled by spiritual experts from Israel, India and Nigeria for all people of the world for use in prayers and supplications." It describes the guidelines on how to use a number of ritual candles. For instance, the Elephant Candle is said to be "good for Bishops, Archdeacons, Apostles, Ecumenical Leaders to maintain their positions." The appropriate ritual is as follows:

> (i) Get a small piece of paper about the size of exercise book (sic) and write all that you like in it. Place it on the ground in front of you.
> (ii) Light the candle and place it on the paper and let it burn on until the paper becomes waxed or burnt off.
> (iii) Read Psalm 48, 68, 63.
> (iv) Try to give alms during the time you operate it.

Adherents offer varieties of aromatic candles for all manners of life ambitions.

A good illustration of the messianic group's affirmations comes from G. I. S. Amadi, the ambassador who literally "lies abroad" for the Brotherhood of the Star and Cross (BSC). He said that "elements of its peculiar ideology include the belief in the deity of its founder/leader, Olumba Olumba Obu, held to be Christ in His Parousia . . . (the mother's place is) perhaps higher than that accorded to the Virgin Mary in the Catholic faith, being thought of as the mother of God. . . . He never reads the Bible and yet is able to quote, teach from and expound every section of it authoritatively."

Amadi said all these things openly at the Edinburgh-Yale Seminar at the Center for African Studies, University of Edinburgh, in the summer of 1992. When he finished, the late professor Adrian Hastings objected that his paper could be published in the same volume as Amadi's! Helen Ukpabio's book *The Seat of Satan Exposed* is an exposé of the same messianic form. It was published in the same year, 1992, in Calabar where the "Obu Obu Olumba" ("OOO as the BSC is called) built its headquarters.[31] Ukpabio was formerly an insider in the organization. But here is the note of caution: Some African groups think functionally and not ontologically when they refer to their leader in messianic terms. It could mean that they perceive him as a pre-Christ figure, like John the Baptist, or as a successor to Christ, and either imitating Christ's work or serving as Christ's replacement. That the impact of the colonial context may have led the followers of Shembe or Kimbangu to claim divine authority for their leader who will lead them to break the yoke of foreign domination is under-standable. This is Irving Hexham's point that is echoed by Adrian Hastings.[32] The modern versions of some messianic churches are making enormous ef-forts to change the message because it jars prominently against biblical au-thority. But others insist upon the divinity of the leader.

For instance, both the Brotherhood and the Kimbanguists in the Congo are clear about the divinity or messianic character of their founder. The WCC and the Organization of African Instituted Churches are currently locked in a surrealistic dilemma in their dialogues with the Kimbanguists over their doctrine. So far, the WCC has refused to accord membership to a number of new applicants from the AIC camp. Other messianic forms in Nigeria include the Jesus of Ikot-Ekpene, and the Jesus of Onyingbo, who built a large com-mune, *Aiyetoro*. Both Jesus figures are dead. The belief in the divinity of the leader is not a mere matter of hyperbole, as some Western Aladura-lovers would like to pretend.

A genre of *Aladura* that has received inadequate attention is the growing band of Sabbatharians. Both Israelitist and Judaistic forms have grown into all the categories found among Sunday worshipers. The doctrine on angels among the Sabbatharians needs theological critique as *Kairah* dominates on Monday, *Holy Michael* on Tuesday, *Uriel* on Wednesday, *Raphael* on Thursday, *Holy Gabriel* on Friday, and *Fisitah* on Saturday. Some of Sabbatharians reject Jesus.

The Pentecostal point of contention, therefore, is not whether the Holy Spirit can perform many things, but that there are other spirits in the universe that are not wholesome from the Christian perspective. All miracles are not from Christ or the Holy Spirit of God. Much to the contrary, the book of Revelation refers to a symbol of flies as representing the spirit of false miracles. The Bible cautions that all spirits should be tested. Pentecostal rhetoric alleges that many of the *Aladura* forms do not sufficiently test and some deliberately tap into the unwholesome spiritual sources. When these adherents hear and talk to ancestors and replicate some rituals in primal religion, they open the gates or break the hedge for the enemy. These examples show that attention to typology and thick description is essential for understanding the diatribe in Pentecostal rhetoric and for doing church history.

Sympathetic studies exist. For instance, Daneel explained the use of the symbols of exorcism, such as water, red cloth, money, new plate, fowl, and such, by Bishop Nyasha. Interestingly, these are the symbols used in marine spirit cults in the primal religions among many ethnic groups in West Africa. Numerous studies have proliferated from two sources, either from the in-creased interest on spirituality or from gender-related ardor for female god-desses. Anthropological studies show that the *Mami Wata* (or mermaid) cult, the *Ogbanje* or *Abiku* cult (of twin children), as well as prosperity cults related to marine spirits all utilize the same symbols that Bishop Nyasha deploys. An interdisciplinary approach may aid African historiography on this matter. The retort would be that the inner meaning may have been reinterpreted. But are the biblical roots clear in the New Testament? Translation is inescapable, but how could this be done faithfully? A certain level of continuity in religious symbolism may be at the expense of the discontinuity in the message affirming that Christ alone saves by the power of God. While it is true that many AICs reject some ingredients of indigenous religion, the point of contention is that they retain many other ingredients. As I said earlier, the quality of the mix becomes the matter of contention.

This brings us nearer to the core of Pentecostal virulent rhetoric that is theological. It arises from their reading of the African map of the universe with covenantal theological lenses. The operative map of the universe is one in which individuals and communities weave covenants with the gods in the sky, land, water, and ancestral worlds. These are legal and binding; the obligations can be inherited, deliberately entered into, unknowingly covenanted into, and transmitted into the genes of progenies. It is as if the iniquities of the fathers could be transmitted into the children to the tenth generation of those who fail to renounce the covenant and the requisite obligations. In this worldview, the things that are seen are made of things that are not seen. Circumstances of life are determined at the spiritual realm. It does not negate personal responsibility, but rather enjoins a more alert and honest life. Pentecostals take the African map of the universe very seriously. The spirits are real just as Christ is real. Three levels of spiritual conflicts ensue as Pentecostals' concern: low-level demonic attacks, occult level warfare, and territorial spiritual warfare. The world *kosmos* is really the world order or system over which Satan has cast a pall or control after the Fall. Much of human cultural production is imbued with *kosmetikoi*, the embellishment or allurement with which Satan weans the world from the designs of God. A process of re-creation and redemption has started in Christ. The keys to the Kingdom have been given to the people of God to do battle against the demonic forces that hold people in bondage.

The articulation of this type of spirituality has been the staple diet of Third Wave Pentecostals and Deliverance ministries. The attendant scholarly battle has been constantly fought in the pages of *Pneuma* and bears little repetition here. The covenant discourse produces a certain jaundiced perception of primal culture as the theater of a battle of covenants. A successful conversion to Christianity will require that a Christian exchange primal covenants with a new one with Jesus Christ, and this involves deliverance and an alert attitude against the wiles of the enemy, the *kosmetikos* and pollution by primal covenanting and covenant renewal. Symbols and rituals used at the primal context must be rejected without any effort to reinterpret them in such a manner as to perpetuate their validity. For instance, it will be considered dangerous to kill a fowl and smear the blood on someone as a sign of the blood of Jesus.

In Pentecostal rhetoric, dalliance with such rituals potentially exposes the votary to attack from familiar spirits parading as angels of grace. The new dispensation in Christ provides an avenue for escaping from the rituals of bondage or entanglements. The language of power is a different intriguing aspect to this issue that Walter Wink (1984–1992) has pursued in a trilogy (naming, engaging and unmasking the powers). In spite of a most sympathetic view, H. W. Turner was insistent on the dangers of dalliance with familiar spirits in AICs spirituality. The problem of "false pneumatology," as a scholar of the old brigade called it, has remained a central feature in the demonization of the AICs.[33] The question, says Anderson, "is whether African Pentecostal churches conceive of the Holy Spirit's power in a Biblical sense, thus transforming traditional power concepts, or whether continuity is maintained by giving traditional power concepts a 'Christian' guise."[34]

Thus, a theological typology of Christian forms is bound to betray the reasons for the estrangement. The proliferation of the AICs may have reared mutations away from the affirmation of the centrality of the Bible and the confession that Jesus Christ is Lord. An understanding of the Pentecostal covenant idea breaks open the seemingly shared worldview. It may be argued that Pentecostal understanding and use of the Bible as normative makes it easy for Pentecostals to give those who take a different posture the back seat. Also, Pentecostals have built an intriguing and elaborate system of demonology. Opponents accuse them of seeing demons everywhere. Indeed, so do the AICs, and that is why the Pentecostal virulent rhetoric hits home.

Many of the scholars under consideration failed to be strict about typology, just as Turner admonished. To these children of postmodernity, such sensitivity appears like "tunnel-vision," lacking inclusiveness. The paradigm shift in the theory of knowledge, consequent of the breakdown of the Enlightenment worldview, turns religious inclusiveness into a fad. It will be interesting to explore how the vogue of liberal theology has affected doing church history. For the Pentecostals, a theo-christological affirmation is the core of lived faith and a means of understanding the new face of Christianity in Africa. Christianity has come of age and must come to terms with the complex issue of Christology or faces of Jesus. Pentecostal critique is not just about historical origin and some ingredients of theology, but about ritual practices because of the relationship between religious experience and religious expression. Rijk van Dijk put the matter succinctly, saying that Pentecostals

> effectively took a third way from which their present-day popularity may be explained. They critiqued the missionary churches for denying what was so obviously a part of everyday African life: occult forces. These were and still are in Pentecostal ideology understood as manifestations of satanic power. It was also on this account that these Pentecostal churches have remained dismissive of the healing churches' syncretic practices. As the traditional practices for healing, protection or exorcism may in themselves be contaminated by

demonic influences, it followed that these churches could not be trusted either. Instead, the Pentecostal churches began stressing ecstatic deliverance sessions in which prayer healing and possession by the Holy Spirit is sought. Herbs, candles, water, fire, or other substances that are commonly used in both traditional healing practices and in healing churches tend not to be found among these Pentecostal churches, nor in the practices of the street preachers.[35]

We could perhaps see a process (to borrow from Birgit Meyer's title) that was continually untangling as religious innovators moved from African independency to Pentecostal-charismatic religiosity.[36] To write romantically about the AICs without spelling out the type is neither good for the subjects of one's study nor for good scholarship. It is such lack of clarity that instigated philosophers of history to berate social historians for sloppy terminologies.

4. Implications for African Church Historiography

This discussion has wide-ranging implications for doing church history in the African environment, by raising the debate on the relationship of sociology/ anthropology to church history, especially the inability of the former to deal with religious experience. The predominance of social scientists in the study of the *Aladura* has influenced the discourses. Beyond the structures and functions of various forms of religious expression, we must recover the fact that faith is lived. Church history must interface with theology because of the nature of the church and the peculiarity of that branch of history. Church history thrives on unabashed confession of the reality of Jesus Christ of Nazareth. Otherwise it is not the memory of the people of God. This does not deny the requirement to be irenic and ecumenical, and to apply all the scientific tools of inquiry. Church history is a critical, interpretative, but nonetheless confessional enterprise. A romanticized approach that ignores a typology of religious forms fails to assist the people of God as they reflect on their past as an empowerment for the future.

In conclusion, the bedfellows have recovered the pneumatic emphasis that sustained the survival of early African Christianity during the dark days of onslaught in the Maghrib. There is a measure of recognition for African initiative, creativity, and genius in Christianity. Both the AICs and Pentecostals are challenged by the fact that African Christianity is an extension of African indigenous religions. Indeed, under the colonial canopy, many guardians of indigenous deities heard whispers of new covenants and persuaded their progenies to listen. David Maxwell puts it differently arguing that "the religious map of central and southern Africa has long been colored by great regional religious identities. Before Christianity established itself, territorial cults of

Mbona in Malawi and *Mwari* in Zimbabwe received streams of pilgrims from polities hundreds of miles away."[37] This environment facilitated the appropriation of the charismatic dimensions of the gospel.

Two key issues about the relationship between the AICs and Pentecostals are crucial. First, insider perspectives distinguish both strands. Lurking in Pentecostal rhetoric is a challenge to the ecumenical spirit. It betrays Pentecostalism as a movement that lacks a strong theology of interfaith and interreligious dialogue. Amos Yong has explored the possibilities for Pentecostal participation in global theology. He urges that theology should affirm the significance of providence in the existence of religions because God is over all and working for all. Second, Pentecostalism ought to understand that salvation is much richer and fuller than we might have ever imagined; that it encompasses others in ways we had not previously supposed. Grace is not confined and therefore we should witness with love and dialogue, not diatribe and inflammatory attitudes, and by simply depending on God to judge.[38]

PART II

The Modern Pentecostal Movement, 1970s–1990s

5

Aliliki

Charismatic Resurgence of the 1970s: A Regional Comparison

1. Introduction

Rijk van Dijk writes: "During the early 1970s the populace of some of the townships of Malawi's largest city, Blantyre, witnessed the emergence of a new religious phenomenon. Young boys and girls, referring to themselves as *aliliki* (preachers), began to attract crowds by conducting large revival meetings." At the background was the intense evangelization of Zimbabwe and Malawi by indigenous agents of the Apostolic Faith Mission (AFM) and Assemblies of God African (AOGA) in the first five decades of the 1900s. Van Dijk described the evangelistic style of the *aliliki*:

> They fulminate against adultery, promiscuity, violence and theft. Furthermore, the satanic habit of frequenting bars, hotels and discos are condemned, clear demands for a rejuvenated strict morality are put forward in an atmosphere of religious excitement and emotionalism. While the audience is urged to sing, dance and clap, sinners are commanded to kneel in front of the young people, who insist that evil objects such as knives, tobacco, stolen goods and magical amulets be handed in.[1]

Those baptized in the spirit after the altar calls in Zimbabwe and Malawi became *kubadwa mwatsopano*, born again. They were also known as born again or Bible carriers in Nigeria. But in Kenya they boasted that they were guerrillas for Christ. These puritan young preachers from secondary schools and universities catalyzed the modern Pentecostal movement, thus giving it a different stamp from previous genres. From a certain perspective, the phenomenon complemented other forces that catalyzed the decolonization of the African church in the period 1970–1975 and stamped the character of the future.[2] It successfully challenged the hostile responses of the missionary-founded churches and broke through the controlling hurdles.

A key contention in this book is that by keeping an eye to periodization, it becomes clear that there was a major difference between the charismatic flares in the early period and the phenomenon of the post-1970 period. Most parts of Africa witnessed the sudden surge of young puritan preachers in the 1970s, who signified a new cycle of revivalism that swept through the continent in the post-independence period, bringing with them a religious tradition whose face has changed drastically in every decade and whose full import is still in the making. This will be illustrated with two brief sketches of the rise of charismatic movements in western and eastern Africa (Nigeria, Kenya, Uganda, and Tanzania) between the years 1966–1986. It is argued that this form of pneumatic response to the gospel bore deep resonance to the earlier phases as a "setting to work" of missionary preaching, a recovery of the old evangelical spirit that had catalyzed mission, a seepage to the surface of the type of charismatic Christianity that appealed to Africans, and the new missionary opportunities unleashed by the process of decolonization. The case studies demonstrate that an indigenous missionary impulse has been central in African Christianity and that the quest for African identity in religious power has taken different routes.

2. The Birth of the Born Again: Youthful Charismatic Power in West Africa in the 1970s

In the Nigerian context, the born-again movement included both Pentecostal and charismatic movements. It has acquired various hues and become complex but its origin was a wave of charismatic movements among the youth of various denominations that occurred in different parts of the country, challenging the parent groups who allegedly suffered from "power failure." The charismatic goals were both to reevangelize the mainline churches as well as to win new souls for the Kingdom. Evangelism and passion for the Kingdom remained central to whatever followed.[3]

In order to show lines of continuity with older flares of revivals, these lines must be put in perspective. Nigeria witnessed a number of charismatic stirrings between the years 1914–1975: First were the scattered flares of 1914–1939, which were not part of the *Aladura* movement, but which ended with the emergence of the Christ Apostolic Church; second were the specifically *Aladura* movements; and third, the 1970 phenomenon. It is possible to weave connections among the three and to show the differences. The third phenomenon did not benefit from the proverbial resources of externality. Its significance was to challenge the indigenization model by the mission churches with a charismatic religiosity and intense proclamation of the gospel. There were five components to this phenomenon in Nigeria:

1. the Hour of Deliverance ministry that operated in Lagos before the Nigeria-Biafra civil war broke out;
2. the charismatic explosion that occurred within the Scripture Union in eastern Nigeria between the years 1967–1975;
3. the emergence of the Hour of Our Freedom ministry in the midst of the civil war in 1969 and its bloom in eastern Nigeria;
4. the growth of the Christian Union movement in Nigerian universities; and
5. the Benson Idahosa ministry that linked the new Christianity with American televangelists.

Other developments consolidated the trend: In 1971 many university graduates from southern regions of Nigeria served in northern Muslim regions under the compulsory National Youth Service Corps program and founded the "Corpers as Preachers" project. Meanwhile, some Roman Catholic students joined the charismatic fellowships. These trends catalyzed the movement before divisions emerged and some of the young men established their own independent charismatic churches. Perhaps we can use the Scripture Union as the marker to reconstruct the spiritual temper of the times and to demonstrate how the various groups cooperated under the fire of the Holy Spirit. It should be added that a similar trend operated in Ghana but there the movement started from prayer and Bible study groups among Protestant churches. For instance, the first national conference of such groups within the Presbyterian Church of Ghana met in 1965.[4]

The Scripture Union, or SU, as it is called, was introduced into Nigerian Protestant secondary schools from Britain in the 1950s. It was an interdenominational group that focused on Bible study, prayers, and hospital ministry, and served as the character formation component of mission education. It was an innocuous body until the Nigeria-Biafra civil war broke out in 1967. When schools closed as a result of the war, the new travelling secretary, Bill Roberts, who had just arrived from Britain, decided to hold Bible classes for the students around SU House in Umuahia. The house cell soon developed into a prayer camp, engaging in deep conversion, deliverance, village evangelism, and relief work. Its reputation spread like wildfire as young people formed prayer and evangelistic bands in their villages. By 1969, the character of the SU had changed tremendously as people gave their lives to Christ in large numbers, and healing occurred during many hospital visits. To illustrate the temper, Roberts tells the story about some young men in a village outside Umuahia who refused to participate in a communal oath-taking, a form of witchcraft-cleansing ritual. Threats against these men from parents, elders, traditional priests, and even some church members failed. Instead, they retreated into a church to pray against the deity and neutralize its hold on the community. On the day that the village set to take the oath, a violent quarrel broke out among the elders, scuttling the ceremony. The young men, by their open resistance exposed the compromising ethics of the members of the mainline churches. They crested on their victory to engulf the village in a new charismatic spirituality.

A key aspect in the revival is the participation of university students. Matthew Ojo's account in *The End-time Army: Charismatic Movements in Modern Nigeria* concentrates on the pioneering activities of university students in southwestern Nigeria, where he locates the source of the stream. Ojo ignores the data from southeastern Nigeria.[5] My effort here is hardly to repeat that part of the story, but to argue for multiple sources that later flowed together. A number of southeastern university students participated in the charismatic activities during the civil war and took the movement to their universities at the end of the civil war. Richard Burgess argues that a spiritual revival occurred in southeastern Nigeria starting from the civil war period, 1967–1970.

The religious landscape during the Nigeria-Biafra civil war is an important backdrop. Burgess argues that decolonization and the disorder caused by the civil war contributed in the origins of the movement. The socioeconomic and psychological profiles of the times included a cultural renaissance of the ancient cultures, especially the social control models of the communities, because scarcity of money and social suffering enlarged the space for native doctors and compelled one to resort to the things that worked in the past. Traditional social groups and occult groups flourished because dire times needed quick solutions. Among Christian groups, the *Aladura*, who had not been very successful in southeastern regions of the country because of the competing strength of mission churches, now proliferated as the prayer houses were established in the hinterland at the heels of fleeing refugees. The mission churches had much competition because their organized structures could not be maintained. Priests and nuns ran for safety after losing their congregations in the urban areas. British support for the Nigerian government disillusioned and angered many who thought that "Christian" England would easily recognize that eastern Nigerians constituted the bulwark of Christianity in the country. Patriotic propaganda harped on this perfidy, leaving the insinuation that Western-style Christianity was not a reliable path. Many turned to the syncretistic prayer houses to deal with the inner and physical needs of the war condition. So, ironically, Christianity's middle ground gave way when prayer houses and young radicalized Scripture Union boys and girls seized the cutting edge.

Just before the Scripture Union Secretary Bill Roberts left Biafra, he came into contact with three lads who had been members of a prominent *Aladura* band, Cherubim and Seraphim. They later joined a more powerful prayer house located at Ufuma. They had risen to high offices variously as "visioner," "cross bearer," and "clairaudient" (one who could hear from the unseen world). They were groomed in the *Book of Mars, Sixth and Seventh Books of Moses, Springfield Books*, and other mystical, esoteric literature. Roberts ministered to the lads; they converted, renounced their dealings in candles and occult, and preached Christ to other votaries of prayer houses. Of course, the prophetess at Ufuma chased them out of town for ruining her business. Penniless, Stephen Okafor, Raphael Okafor, and Arthur Orizu formed The Hour of Freedom Evangelistic Association(hereafter, The Hour of Freedom). The name significantly emphasized the passion for soul as the dominant concept of mission in this period.

The Nigeria-Biafra civil war ended in 1970. Based in Onitsha (a commercial nodal town, located on the bank of the Niger River), the Hour of Freedom members itinerated all over the eastern region with a vibrant evangelical fervor. They built a support network of prayer groups, as many young people from schools flocked to the outreach programs. Many were members of the SU. Within the decade, a revival hit Igboland. The Hour of Freedom became famous as healings and mass conversions occurred in one town after another. Prayer bands formed in various towns such as Enugu (the administrative capital), Owerri, Aba, and more. Many of the young people, ranging in age from seventeen to twenty, boldly evangelized rural villages. Those who had joined their parents in *Aladura* churches caused splits within these churches as they challenged the use of certain symbols and rituals in the liturgy. For instance, the Christ Ascension Church splintered and the leader of the young rebels, Mike Okonkwo, formed a Pentecostal church, the True Redeemed Evangelical Mission. He later became the president of the Pentecostal Fellowship of Nigeria. Vibrant SU branches spread in the secondary schools while the university students formed Christian Union branches as formidable interdenominational evangelistic groups.

Just at this time, Benson Idahosa, who was converted in the early 1960s by an Assemblies of God leader in Benin City, built up a vibrant ministry with the aid of his AOG pastor and a Welsh missionary, Pa G. Elton. Elton who came to Nigeria in 1954 as a missionary of the Apostolic Church but separated from it when he joined the Latter Rain movement. Elton lived as an apostle who discerned the new Christian temper of the nation and chose to rear these young firebrands. He put Idahosa in touch with Gordon and Freda Lindsay, who sponsored him to attend Christ for the Nations Bible Institute in Dallas. However, Idahosa left before completing the course because, as Ruth Garlock, his biographer said, the young man had "fire in his bones" for soul winning. Idahosa later founded the Church of God Mission. By the 1980s, his theology was developing some of the themes from T. L. Osborn as Idahosa waxed strong with prosperity motifs that sounded like music in the ears of those who had just come out from the civil war. His huge Miracle Centre, television ministry,

All Nations for Christ Bible School, and the effective musical group called "Redemption Voices" grew rapidly.

The leaders of Hour of Deliverance (Mike Oye, Muyiwa Olamijulo, and J. M. J. Emesin) from Lagos, Pa G. Elton of the Apostolic Church, Emma Harris, a Baptist missionary, and a few other older charismatic leaders provided advice and encouragement as a youth-led religious revival enveloped Nigeria. By the mid-1970s, the center of charismatic influence passed to the students of the universities of Ibadan and Ife when members of the CU started to speak in tongues during their Tuesday prayer meetings and later organized national conventions to arouse other universities. The CU broke away in 1962 from the Student Christian Movement (SCM), after accusing the SCM of being spiritually and ethically tepid. As this was happening, Pa Elton, who lived at Ilesha, turned his attention to fostering charismatic spirituality in the universities and curing the disunity among the young people. Rivalry had become rife as a harbinger of future Pentecostalism.

These young people graduated just when Nigeria's federal government made the National Youth Service Corps compulsory for university graduates. As they dispersed through the nation, they formed charismatic groups; those who traveled abroad for foreign language courses in neighboring French-speaking countries took their spirituality with them. Those who attended the Fellowship of Christian Union Students (FOCUS) took the message to Kenya. In northern Nigeria, they set out to establish themselves in Muslim strongholds by forming branches in Ahmadu Bello University, Zaria, and Kaduna Polytechnic. They also took over the travelling secretary jobs in such organizations as Fellowship of Christian Students, New Life for All, and the Nigerian Fellowship of Evangelical Students. A central body, Christian Youth Corpers, was constituted in 1973 to mobilize the dizzying number of evangelical enterprises. Some of the southern youths who had not gone through universities, but drank in their charismatic spirituality in secondary schools, surged through Muslim northern Nigeria founding ministries just about the time when many northerners were returning to the north after the civil war. About ten ministries blossomed in Jos, Kaduna, Kano, and Zaria between 1973–1976. Northern indigenes have since converted to Pentecostalism and become leaders. But later I shall argue that the reinvigorated evangelism by Pentecostal youths in Islamic northern Nigeria has strained the concept of dialogue and interreligious relationship in the nation and may partially explain the heightened level of religious violence.

Raphael Okafor meticulously kept a diary of the activities of the Hour of Freedom movement and this section relies mainly on these entries. One entry is intriguing:

28th March 1971: Enu Onitsha campaign continues. Emmanuel
Church authorities refused their church compound again. We moved

to the Anglican Girls School, Inland town, Onitsha and began around 5.00pm. People still attended despite the disruptions. Michaelson gave his testimony. Brother Stephen preached while Brother Arthur interpreted. Emmanuel Ekpunobi who said the opening prayers also prayed for the converts and later gave them additional instructions. . . . TO GOD BE THE GLORY.[6]

Diary entries are often cryptic, so certain aspects need comment: the impact on mission churches and their responses; the gender factor; the impact on the entire religious landscape, including occult groups; the relationship of literacy, Bible, and revival; and the further radicalization of the SU as it worked in agreement with the Hour of Freedom. There are other ironies: Mission schools that were created as means of evangelization fulfilled the goal to the then-ironic chagrin of the proprietors who were dismayed by the religious exuberance of the youths. Schoolchildren, on the fringes of mission power structures, created a challenge that was more radical than anything the missionaries could have anticipated. The youth, both in secondary and tertiary institutions, created a new culture of Pentecostalism in which the leadership was more highly educated than in the earlier pneumatic challenges by the *Aladura* or the prophetic movement. But despite this higher level of education, the fluid dynamism in a spirit-driven movement deconstructed the Western model of the mission churches.

At first, the responses from the mainline churches varied in their degree of opposition to the youths. The Roman Catholic Church was initially hostile, and Archbishop Francis Arinze of Onitsha defrocked two priests who supported charismatic spirituality in the hurry to rebuild after the Nigeria–Biafra civil war. The church faced a double-edged challenge, the first from the youths, and the second from the impact of the prayer houses, which intensified during the war. Archbishop Arinze responded by appointing Fr. Geoffrey Ikeobi to start a charismatic service in Onitsha that used Catholic liturgy, and included healing and exorcism. Later on, Fr. Emmanuel Edeh returned from the United States to begin a healing center at Elele, near Port Harcourt.

In addition, in 1974, the Dominicans at Ibadan sponsored the visit to Nigeria of a charismatic team from the United States led by Fr. Francis F. MacNutt. MacNutt and his team claim much success. Though Archbishop Arinze allowed the team to operate in his domain, and it was even rumored that his mother was healed by Fr. McNutt, the diocesan priests treated the team with much suspicion because of their ministerial formation; but the laypeople lapped up the opportunity and the import of the challenge was not lost on the "rulers of the synagogue" who had to ensure that their flock would not drift away.[7] These are some aspects of the origin of the Catholic charismatic movement. Turning to the Protestants, the Anglicans were friendly to the people, while the Presbyterians were downright hostile. The Minute Book of the

Session at St. Andrew's Presbyterian Church, Enugu, contains the accounts of a strongly patriarchal attitude toward the young people, and their order to the SU to stop using the church facilities because of charismatic manifestation and noise. In Ohafia Parish located in Cross River Igboland (southeastern Nigeria), the young people were forced out of the church membership and formed the Church of the Evangel. This ministry grew rapidly and competed favorably with the mother church. This cryptic account highlights how the youth subverted the doctrine, liturgy, and patriarchal ideology of the mission churches, and how females embraced charismatic fellowship as a safe zone that also enlarged the level of their participation. The young people evangelized Africa with a home-grown spirituality that was beyond mere adaptation and was notable for its vigor.

The impact of this evangelism was to challenge the mission churches to either allow the young people more roles in the churches, and permit charismatic activities, or risk the exodus of young people and women to Pentecostal fellowships. An encapsulation strategy triumphed. Initially these young evangelists stayed in their churches and met to share fellowship, but later, some founded churches specializing in evangelism, deliverance, or intercession, while a few remained as ecumenical fellowships. Most secondary schools and all universities have charismatic fellowships comprising young people in various denominations.[8] Initially, these fellowships served as the ministerial formation sites. The missiological model was reminiscent of the combination of the nineteenth-century Keswick model and the faith missions. The young people walked along the railway line from one town to another preaching, sleeping in open classrooms, living without money, and depending on the hospitality of strangers, and trusting that God would miraculously meet their needs. The millennialist beliefs added urgency to their evangelism and inspired one and all to be agents of God's work in these end-times. The potentially democratizing and nonelitist ideology spurred the pace of these evangelists' activities.

3. Guerillas for Christ: Youthful Charismatism in Eastern Africa in the 1970s

The massive *balokole*, a movement of "saved ones," set the stage for the charismatization of eastern Africa in later years. It started in the Rwanda Mission that was led by evangelicals from the CU of Cambridge University, most of whom had contact with the Keswick movement. Dr. Joe Church's connection with some Ganda Christians, such as Blasio Kigoli and William Nagenda, produced a revival that had two foci: attack on lukewarm, inclusive, Anglican churches that compromised with indigenous cultures; and the theological modernism among some Anglican missionaries such as J. C. Jones, the warden of the Mukono (Uganda) theological college. It was a revitalization movement indicating that traditional ways of being church are no longer appropriate, and no longer consistent with the gospel message. The Mukono students called themselves "obedient rebels." They held revival and evangelistic conferences that emphasized separation from spiritually harmful cultures, confession of personal sin, and baptism of the Holy Spirit. It was moralistic and conservative. Some encouraged people not only to cut down plants used in brewing local beer, but to cut down coffee cash crops because the *abomwoyo* (people of the spirit) should have no investment in earthly things. Exclusive, enthusiastic, and belligerent in confronting indigenous cultures, the movement privileged preaching and witchcraft cleansing as its missionary method, and spread rapidly into Kenya, Sudan, and Tanzania. With a signature tune from the Luganda hymn *Tukutenderezza Yezu,* "we praise you Jesus," they challenged the foundations of various missionary churches, disrupted the regimen of the theological colleges, and established a vibrant, ecumenical, missionary movement.[9]

In Kenya, the *balokole* youths were prominent in the western and central regions in the mid-1930s; spread into Kabete and Pumwani in 1937–1938; and Nyanza, Chigori Presbytery, and North Kiamba in the late 1940s. By the 1950s, they spawned the Kenya Students Christian Fellowship (KSCF) and bred CU types who later became legalistic. Some students belonging to the Scripture Union sought an alternative to the legalism and found an answer during a camp meeting in 1959 when they experienced a new spirit baptism. Some formed the Trinity Fellowship, others started the Ambassadors. The youths enthusiastically crisscrossed the secondary schools all over Kenya to unite and radicalize the CU organizations. They held camp meetings and prayer retreats in various regions, and these turned into revival centers by the next decade. Thus, when Billy Graham evangelized in 1960 in Nairobi and Kisumu, the tradition of public preaching and outreach invigorated the young secondary-school students who came from many types of mainline churches. Some teachers opposed their activities with futile restrictions. Holiday periods were consumed by charismatic camp meetings. Miracles of healing and even cases of raising the dead followed these meetings. One of their leaders, Watson Omolukoli, is now a professor and chaplain in Kenyatta University, Nairobi. When he was leaving for postgraduate training in 1973, he gave the leadership of the Guerrillas for Christ to Henry Mulandi, who expanded the activities of the movement.

Some of the students formed "neo-Pentecostal" ministries after their school days. For instance, Margaret Wangari one of the active members of the revival in this period, returned from a prayer camp held at Njoro High School, west of Nakuru, in 1974, to find that her grandmother was dying. She placed a blanket that was anointed during the camp meeting on her grandmother, and she was immediately healed. The Banana Hill community broke loose as sick people gathered near her for healing. She later studied in Benson Idahosa's Christ for All Nations Seminary in Benin, Nigeria, and founded the Church of the Lord, a predominantly rural evangelistic church in the Kiamba district of central Kenya.

When the American evangelist Oral Roberts visited Kenya in 1968, one of the former KSCF founders, now itinerating from Kenya to Uganda and Tanzania as a missionary under the aegis of the Regions Beyond Ministry, named his son who was born that year after Oral Roberts. Such outreaches by Western evangelists benefited from the indigenous charismatic movements and equally encouraged or inspired the young people.[10]

The point is that the charismatic movement in eastern Africa was built on the achievements of the *balokole* movement, just as indigenous Shona missionaries spread it in central Africa. The story in Uganda underscores the youthful character as well as the harsh terrain of the 1970s, when Idi Amin ruled with a determination to wipe out Christianity. In 1977 Idi Amin murdered the Anglican bishop Jana Luwum (who in his youth was a leader in the *balokole* movement). Simeon Kayiwa, a twenty-year-old philosophy student at Makerere University, Kampala, said that this was the critical year when he heard the Lord not only telling him to wake up other Christians, warn people against witchcraft, and call them to rededication, but promised him miracles as a proof. Kayiwa set out to build a corps of born-again evangelists who would achieve the vision. Because the church was illegal, he took refuge in a small papyrus sanctuary on Namirembe Hill. The church became the rendezvous point for many young people who later founded churches emphasizing a New Testament style of miracles. Kayiwa has written an account of these miracles in the midst of social suffering entitled *Working Miracles*. His ministry received foreign media attention from the British Broadcasting Company and the London newspaper *Daily Mail*. It is claimed that Kayiwa is the father of almost 90 percent of the thirty-five thousand Pentecostal churches in Uganda; that he has raised up to eighteen people from the dead; and that he unites the vast movement that now claims the allegiance of one-fifth of Uganda's twenty-six million residents.[11]

Josiah Mlahagwa's account of the story in Tanzania further underscores the impact of miracles in church growth.[12] He started his story of the rise of Pentecostalism in Tanzania from the contemporary period and moved backward. He began his account with an example of a leadership conference of the Evangelical Lutheran Church that met at the foot of the Uluguru Mountains in Mongoro in January 1997. By that date it had become impossible to resist the exploding growth of both the Pentecostals and their cousins, the charismatic movements, within the mainline churches. The quantitative and qualitative growth of Christianity in Tanzania was palpable and due mainly to the charismatization of the religious landscape. Churches were bursting at the seams. The Lutheran church leaders resolved that the charismatic movement was the spinal cord of the church and should be actively promoted. Mlahagwa shifted his glance back to the 1940s when the *balokole* movement emerged in Tanzania not only through the evangelistic forays of Kenyan students, but even more so from the arrival of one particular Ugandan member, Festo Kingevere, who later became an Anglican bishop. He was employed by the African Inland Secondary School at Dodoma and soon became a household name as a powerful evangelist in central Tanzania. Soon a revival fire started whose flames reached into every church: the Anglicans in Lake Tanganyika and Bukoba, the Africa Inland Church in Mwanza, and the Lutherans in the Kilimanjaro region. In this early period, laypeople and priests were involved; some priests, such as Kingevere and Yohana Omari, who converted from Islam in Kasulu, became ardent revivalist and later bishops in the Anglican Church.

By the late 1960s, the mainline churches became alarmed because of their loss of control and desertion by members, and were torn by doctrinal concerns over glossolalia and the tendency to rebaptize their members by immersion (*maji mengu*), and subsequently sought to douse the fire of the charismatic movement. When Moses Kulola, the fiery preacher who pioneered charismatism in the African Inland Church in Mwanza, teamed with Emmanuel Lazaro to establish the Assemblies of God Tanzania, mainline churches' worst fears were realized. Catholics and Protestants stopped their rivalry to combat the new challengers by drawing up a concordat that forbade pulpit exchange between Pentecostals and mainline churches, and threatened to excommunicate deserters. This policy to throttle the new movement operated through the years 1970–1990. But certain developments challenged the policy. First was the inexplicable ministry of John Edmund that appeared within the Anglican Church. He saw a vision where God commanded him to preach from door to door with a powerful ministry of healing. An interdenominational group formed around his House to House Anglican Prayer Ministry. Its popular name was HUMANN from the Swahili: *Huduma ya Uinjilisti na Maombi Nyumba kwa Nyumba*. Edmund's puritan and ascetic lifestyle and extensive ministry shortened his life. But his followers continued the Big Harvest Crusades.

Second, the split between Kulola and Lazaro led to the formation of a new Evangelical Assemblies of God of Tanzania, thus bringing more competitors into the religious marketplace.

But it was the third development, namely, the rise of crusades, that became a clincher. A group of charismatic laypeople and pastors organized a big crusade at the Mnazi Mmoja grounds in 1986. This cooperation among pastors contested the hostility of yesteryears and created a new interdenominational spirit. It was repackaged as the Big November crusade that was held annually at the central Jangwani grounds. Branches of this crusade were formed in the twenty regions of mainland Tanzania. Soon, the local organizing committee was consolidated as New Life Crusade Ministry. Each crusade lasted for two weeks and invited international speakers; it initiated evangelization into Muslim Zanzibar; and it drew up a twelve-point doctrinal statement. While avoiding the contentious issues about glossolalia and immersion, the first three articles affirmed the Bible as the inspired word of God, the Trinity, and Jesus as savior. Articles four to eight of the doctrinal statement insisted on the born-again experience, infilling by the Holy Spirit, and miracles and the holiness of life. Articles nine to twelve focused on eschatology: rapture, last judgment, millennial reign, and a new heaven and earth. Other parachurch groups, such as the Africa Evangelistic Enterprise and the Tanzanian Fellowship of Evangelical Students, complemented the intensifying charismatic presence that transformed the religious landscape, and thwarted the opposition of the old church leaders within two decades.

The astonishing aspect of this charismatic growth is that the stories from Kenya, Uganda, and Tanzania resemble the story of young charismatic students in eastern Nigeria as recounted earlier. The key issue is their conception and practice of mission. They were on fire for the Lord, and expected to experience miracles in everyday life, such as the supplying of one's everyday needs, healing, raising the dead, and especially their witnessing one making a moral change in lifestyle. They nurtured a theology of individual salvation built on strong puritan ethics. Every Christian had an obligation to evangelize because of an imminent rapture. With a strong evangelistic zeal, the Kenyan students evangelized other eastern African countries and forayed into Muslim communities in the coastal seaboard of the Indian Ocean, while the Ugandans took the message into Kenya and Tanzania. In a similar vein, the Nigerian students evangelized the Muslims in northern Nigeria and forayed into other West African countries. In all the countries, the youthful movement tended to show the same developmental phases: They started as an interdenominational Bible study and prayer group among students such as the Scripture Union, Student Christian Movement, New Life for All, and so forth. Members soon formed fellowships, perhaps as charismatic house cells; then some metamorphosed into ministries with specialized or personalized goals, and formed around strong personality types, with a nucleus and a broader patronage. They would not meet on Sunday morning so that members could attend their own churches. Finally, the group would develop into a church and create the necessary structures. As the secondary-school students matured, some founded independent ministries, while others remained as the evangelical wings of mainline churches. In all the countries, some of the radical youth would later rise to the episcopacy in their churches. Later, the Fellowship of Christian Union Students (FOCUS) brought together the students from the eastern and western regions of the continent. These constituted the founders of contemporary indigenous Pentecostal churches in Africa and set the intense missionary tone of the post-1970 period.

4. *Aliliki* in Central Africa

The impression that the young preachers came out of the wormwoods ignores the backdrop consisting of charismatic flows in Malawi. Moreover, the phenomenon must be interpreted from a broader perspective. We can argue and demonstrate that the charismatic renewal of the 1970s occurred all over the continent and with an identical pattern. Some may add that it was a worldwide phenomenon, but it must be stressed that the events in Africa had little to do with what happened in the United States from the 1960s onward. In Malawi, the revival was rooted among interdenominational parachurch groups such as the SU, Students' Christian Organization, and New Life for All, which was a drive mounted by evangelical missionary groups such as the Sudan Interior Mission and Sudan United Mission in the late 1950s. These were not necessarily Pentecostal movements, but became increasingly radicalized in that direction in the 1970s. Pentecostal ministries became important in Malawi from the 1980s onward. Prior to that period, Pentecostal influence was spread by the Apostolic Faith Mission, the Assemblies of God, Pentecostal Holiness Association, and Full Gospel Church of God. As mentioned earlier, the impetus came from two directions: South Africa and Zimbabwe, and the agency was preeminently African. The point is that none of these organizations experienced rapid growth. In 1960, Pentecostals constituted only about 1.2 percent of the population of Malawi. The evidence points to a rapid growth of Christianity since the 1970s with the charismatic dimension holding the cutting edge. Klaus Fiedler profiles the new trend as consisting of a great diversification of the religious field, a gradual move away from the more established denominations, a move toward churches that allow for greater participation of all, and churches that provide for a greater level of commitment and identification. But dating the explosion of Pentecostalism in Malawi to the 1980s has been connected with the worsening of African pathology. As David Maxwell argues, "Africa's born again explosion also coincides with, and was stimulated by, the beginning of its socio-economic malaise; crippling external debt; state contraction; dramatic population rise and food scarcity. The retreat of the state from welfare provision forced by structural adjustment programmes both prompted a flood of secular NGOs and provided opportunities for new types of mission work and church involvement, much of it originating from North America."[13] This is the staple explanation from the instrumentalist perspective, and it has its merits. Maxwell had earlier argued that these movements embody a systematic attempt by young men, women, and youth to restructure social relations in the face of the intransigence of male elders; and that they represent the continuing search of the wider community for healing and liberation.[14] Other scholars combine the generational factor with deprivation, postcoloniality, dependency, and externality discourses. Missing is the religious explanation that the young people were questing for a deeper Christian life or that this may be an African Reformation in the making. This study is attentive to the sociocultural interpretation because people seek health, power, and wealth through deeper commitment and relationship to Christ, concerns that also feature prominently in African indigenous religion.

Indeed, the background of the charismatic explosion in Malawi was connected with reinvigorating activities of Nicholas Benghu's Back to God Campaign that expanded from his base in East London to South Africa into Zimbabwe and Malawi in the years 1960–1977. One of Benghu's early disciples, Ezekiel Guti, grew a sprawling movement of his own in Zimbabwe. As Maxwell describes it,

> By 1977 AOGA had over 40,000 members in Rhodesia, 185 branches (with thirty-four in Salisbury), fifteen church buildings, and six in progress. With the title Forward in Faith Mission International (FIFMI) it had also grown considerably elsewhere. There were over 50 branches in Mozambique, thirty-two in Malawi, five in Botswana and four in Zambia.[15]

The Malawi agent was J. P. Chitakata, a labor migrant who worked in Rhodesia. He had joined the Apostolic Faith Mission (AFM) and was a member of a prayer group that organized Nicholas Benghu's mission to Rhodesia. Later, this group left the AFM in 1959 under the leadership of Ezekiel Guti and teamed up with Nicholas Benghu before establishing a group of their own. In 1961 Chitakata returned to Nsanje, Malawi, to build a church as an agent of Guti's Assemblies of God Africa (AOGA). Within three years, Chitakata deserted Guti's AOGA and merged with older Pentecostals Lyton Kalambule (d. 1990) and Magnus Udd (who left Malawi in 1997). Kalambule was a former labor migrant, serving as a cook in Durban. He joined an American missionary who had deserted the Full Gospel Church and both converted to the AOG. When Kalambule returned to Malawi in 1950, his energetic ministry soon made him a linchpin of the AOG advance in Malawi. But he had a testy time with white leadership. To clip his evangelistic wings, the AOG leadership once confined Kalambule to his village of Ntcheu. It is alleged that he rejected the compromise to baptize polygamists, but he did not resign until a white missionary accused him of being a liar (*wabodza*). He had a fellow traveler, Udd, a maverick American who left the AOG over the same issue of refusing to baptize polygamists. The three rechristened their organization the Independent Assemblies of God (IAG). In 1967, Udd reconnected with Nicholas Benghu and the AOG in East London, South Africa. By 1969, Guti was expressing great fears that Benghu would use Udd to recover the AOG churches in Malawi and Rhodesia. Just then, Chitakata founded his own African Assemblies of God, withdrew from the IAG, and rejoined Guti's AOGA from a stronger bargaining position. The fissile character of early Pentecostalism caused growth as other enterprising Malawians, such as D. Chiteka and F. S. Phiri, joined the AOGA work in the late 1970s.

From the 1980s, a host of independent ministries appeared in Blantyre, with the list topping fifty at the end of the millennium. Many are small but all are vibrant. Here is a list of the larger ones.

Name	Year Founded	Founder
Blantyre Christian Center	1980	Barbara Tippet
Agape	1982	Pastor Mgala
Faith of God	1984	Pastor Matoga
Living Waters	1985	Pastor Ndovi
Glad Tidings	1986	Group initiated
All for Jesus	1993	Pastor Zalimba
Flames of Victory	1993	Pastor Katchire
Calvary Family Church	1994	Pastor Mbewe
Vineyard	1994	Pastor Gama

Charismatic movements within mainline churches proliferated, many causing schisms and dissension. The AOG grew tremendously as a leading Pentecostal church, especially after it was adopted in 1982 by the Crossroad Cathedral in Oklahoma for spiritual and material support. Membership escalated by 40 percent while infrastructure and schools improved.

Though commentators have focused on Pentecostalism as an urban phenomenon, many in the movement operated in rural areas and among poor neighborhoods in the towns. Harri Englund studied one such poor township, Chisanpo, in Lilongwe, the state capital. Two conclusions emerged: The collapse of the Malawian economy created a dependency and a moral discourse of failure that Pentecostal discourse contested and sought to reverse. But the conditions compelled the "quest for missionaries" to provide assistance and care for poor congregations. A missionary is not necessarily a white foreigner; it can be a local rich man and benefactor. To study the new face of Pentecostalism solely from the modernity and globalism discourses could neglect the transnational blockages in the country and the hierarchies within the movement. A comparative perspective may show that the character of the movement differed from one African country to another, and its membership embraced a wide range of economic and social classes. It would also show that the African communal ethos was not abandoned. The link to one's village of origin is not cut by the individualistic ethos of the town. Rather, "the village of origin continues to play an important role in the lives of most Pentecostal Christians in Chisanpo township, in both material and spiritual respects."[16] Englund's perspective is that the focus on relationships in everyday life in the study of Pentecostalism "allows for an appreciation of multiple translocal currents in the practice of particular persons."[17] In fact, some churches are relocating from the rural to the urban areas while others are expanding from the towns to the rural areas, or foraying into rural communities on land deliverance missions.

6

The Big Man of the Big God

Pentecostalism, Media, and Popular
Culture in the 1980s

1. Introduction: Pentecostalism and Emergent Cultures
   of the 1980s

There are a number of issues in this reflection: African Pentecostal
use of media and response to popular culture should be examined as
an aspect of its evangelical strategy and as a dimension of its engagement with both indigenous culture and contemporary or emergent culture. We, therefore, broach the theme of cultural discourse
in the interpretation of Pentecostalism: How does Pentecostalism
engage the indigenous and contemporary cultures of Africa? Does this
process provide clues to the success and prospects of the movement?
Media use became most prominent in the period from the 1980s
onward and, therefore, reflects the Pentecostal response to contemporary or emergent culture. Since Pentecostals image themselves as
being engaged in the re-evangelization of modern Africa, how has the
intensive use of media enhanced, reshaped, and even endangered
Pentecostal missionary strategy? One could ask if it was employed "to
raise a new society of persons unconditionally committed to the
Lordship of Christ in every aspect of life while exchanging the values
of the surrounding society as well as the world at large for the standards of God's kingdom; a new breed without greed, and a radical
opposition to corruption; an alternative society and counterculture
to the kingdom of Babylon; a new social, economic and political reality which reveals the true nature of God's reign and the likeness of
Christ through its renunciation of the world's definitions and tactics."[1]

In contrast, the character of Pentecostal missionary strategy in the 1970s was the direct, puritan, oral, and revivalist model. Although enormous changes occurred in the character of the movement in every decade, the 1980s proved a heady period because of the vast changes including vast socioeconomic and political collapse, the enlarged networking with external, Western forms of Pentecostalism, and the liberalization of media space following the "second liberation" of Africa from dictators. The combination of religious and cultural changes, especially, increased contact with external change agents, and catalyzed the intense use of media as an instrument of evangelization. Given the fact that media technology has an innate culture and that popular culture is driven by a different spirit, how do these serve as resources and challenges in Christian evangelism and representation? We reflect on how the Pentecostal movement has reshaped the religious landscape using media technology and popular culture and has, in turn, been shaped by both popular culture and the media technology.

We shall be attentive to the concerns from the critics of the movement. It is germane to profile the contours of the Pentecostal movement in the 1980s since by this time, many of the youthful protagonists in the charismatic movement who were students in both secondary schools and universities in the 1970s had graduated, gone into the main world, founded their own ministries, and even networked with international Pentecostal movements. A second generation joined them in the heady 1980s under new circumstances and with a different ethos.

Unlike leaders of the youthful charismatic movements of the 1970s, many of the leaders were now highly educated and professional people. For example, in July 2005, The Mountain of Fire Miracles Ministries celebrated its tenth anniversary in Lagos. The leader, Dr. Daniel Olukoya, became a born-again Christian when he was a secondary-school student in the late 1970s. He graduated with first-class honors in microbiology at the University of Lagos and completed a doctorate in microbiology at the University of Reading in the United Kingdom. In July 1989, he claimed that God called him to start a house fellowship that has blossomed within a decade into a megachurch with three hundred branches all over the world. His brochure claims that "the ministry is a full gospel ministry devoted to the revival of apostolic signs, Holy Ghost fireworks and the unlimited demonstration of the power of God to deliver to the uttermost. Absolute holiness, within and without, serves as the greatest spiritual insecticide and a pre-requisite for heaven."[2]

Olukoya represents the trend at the end of the 1980s in many ways, including the emergence of highly educated young ministers who quickly established megachurches. Toward the end of the decade, criticisms against the excesses of prosperity preachers emerged, and holiness ethics flowered again. Emphasis shifted to church growth, and the megachurches, aided by media technology and led by a powerful "big man of the big God," consolidated into an enviable pattern.

2. Pentecostalism, Media, and Popular Culture: The Terrain

A central feature of the African religious landscape of the 1980s was the contestation between prosperity that came with an elaborate media representation, including electronic communication designed to reshape religious consciousness and holiness theologies. The valorization of the mode of communicating the gospel created a new culture, values, and meaning system. This new way of communicating had an enormous impact on doctrine, polity, liturgy, and ethics in the Pentecostal movement. Driven by ideological concerns, scholarly analysis in the 1990s leapfrogged a wide range of background issues about media technology to hail the triumph of modernity and externality signified by the homogenizing cultural flows of global cultural influences.[3] Scholars extolled how the electronic synthesizer trumped all other musical instruments, and televangelism dominated the practice of mission. The argument here is that cultural analysis should include:

1. a typology of media forms;
2. historical analysis that places media in their cultural contexts;[4]
3. the history of the medium or technology involved, and the institutions that support it;
4. the immediate and intermediate points of the production process;
5. the point of consumption of particular media/cultural products;
6. the impact of the media on believers and on the movement; and
7. the historically changing relationship between social institutions and media technology.[5]

It should be realized that electronic media technology became available to both the American Pentecostals and their African networks around the same time and elicited much enthusiasm as a new instrument for forging transnational relationships, greater mass reach, direct encounter, potential promotional attraction, and world evangelism. They saw a medium that could reinforce the message and vision. Therefore, we must attend to the two contexts (the external source and the African local context) with a thick description that embeds the technology within these cultural contexts. In the United States, the Evangelicals and Pentecostals accessed print, radio, and television at different points in time. The success of media technology in reshaping the character of Pentecostalism was fueled by its combined power and its novelty. In 1950 only 5 percent of Americans owned a television, although the percentage escalated in the next decade. Indeed, Evangelicals fought hard to broadcast on the radio up through the 1940s, and were gradually shut out of broadcasting on television during the 1970s when technological, religious, and cultural changes, and relaxed state regulations that required "sustaining time," or free air time, for religious organizations were changed to allow for "paid time" that enabled the emergence of elaborate television access.

Using a decadal analysis, Billy Graham, Rex Humbard, and Oral Roberts experimented with television from the late 1950s, and Pat Robertson's *700 Club* joined the airwaves in the 1960s. Graham's appeared to be the most successful. But Robertson's *700 Club* was the first of the Christian talk shows of the electronic church era, and the first to lease satellite time to distribute his product to cable television systems. The 1970s opened a window featuring Jerry Falwell and Jim and Tammy Bakker's *Praise the Lord Club* (PTL). The PTL that functioned from 1974–1987 was important for the Nigerian Pentecostal movement. The PTL's initial talk show format tried different commercial techniques, operated a national satellite service to cable systems, raised funds within the format, and built a state-of-the-art studio. Bakker expanded into Nigeria through the ministry of Benson Idahosa. Meanwhile, others joined in the ranks of television broadcasters in the 1980s and thereafter. And today the Trinity Broadcasting Network broadcasts in many nations. The point is that novelty, experimentation in cultural production, and expansion into the outside world occurred in the 1980s in both cultural contexts, which reinforced the novelty and attraction of the purveyed theologies.

Television penetrated lightly into most of Africa in the decade of 1960–1970, and more deeply only in the 1980s. Before then, orality and print were the chief media for evangelization. While missionaries concentrated on oral communication, education, and charitable institutions, Evangelicals exploited magazines, tracts, and radio because of their mass exposure, simultaneous coverage, and penetrative power. Most West Africans listened to the Christian broadcast from the Eternal Love Will Win Africa (ELWWA) Radio, Monrovia, founded in 1954 by three young Evangelicals from Wheaton, Illinois: William Watkins, Abe Thiessen, and Merle Steely. The success of this tropicalizing of the radio ministry was due to the wartime advances in high frequency transmission, availability of surplus military equipment, and the domestic resurgence of robust evangelicalism.[6] This history of ELWA radio still needs to be written as the backdrop to the excitement of 1980s televangelism. Indeed, the Muslims were still debating in the 1960s whether the Koran should be broadcast by radio. The concern was that radio technology might resignify the holy words into a particular, desecrated material form because broadcast pulses move through cables or waves that pass through the air and are reassembled into sound. In the last two decades, the novelty of increased media presence in Africa has not worn off. The market is largely unregulated partially because the constitutions of various African nations usually enshrine freedom of religion as a price for decolonization. None actually separates religion from the state's concerns. Much to the contrary, media resources in Africa have become sites of the politics of religious difference and conflicts.

There are certain dimensions of the increased deployment of media that should be spelled out: First, every transcendental idea must be mediated. So religion is intrinsically woven into various forms of media representations. Communication is essential for building community. It is at the heart of the church's existence. The church is under mandate to communicate the gospel, reveal itself to the world, and dialogue and guide through a creative use of symbols and media. Thus, each new form of media provides the church with new language. Second, the Pentecostals were not the early adaptors of modern media technology but, in fact, were latecomers. Third, religious broadcasting is shaped by the technology and the industrial values and culture that sustain it. Electronic media has its own version of reality, reshapes the contact environment, and concocts a culture for the consumption of images that support life structures understood as patterns of choices and ways of living. Some may argue that the media system and field (context) harbors democratic deficits: It may fail to constitute a democratic public sphere because of the centralization of symbolic and political power; the ownership by the wealthy creates unequal representation, homogenized value, declining sense of community, fragmentation of the public sphere, and elitism because of the secrecy of decision-making processes.

Corporate agendas may enforce gender, racial, and religious biases. In some cases, state censorships and journalists' values shape the product. Therefore, we should expect that media could be both a resource and challenge to the gospel message and mission of the church, whether taking the form of evangelism, discipling, Christian nurture, or inculcation of family values. Religious users could attempt to shape media to their needs, but media too could reshape the religions, and even trivialize the content and create a religious counterculture.

Fourth, there is often a thin line between religious and secular techniques in the use of media communication. Improved technologies define the style.

Fifth, the religious media that hit Africa in this period was produced from a certain religious and cultural context, namely by neoevangelical, fundamentalist revivals that occurred in recent years in America and were tied to the conservative mainstream who shared common symbols, values, and moral culture with African Pentecostals.

This profile raises several questions about how local actors appropriate these new media and fit them into new cultural contexts. Other questions should ask how African churches have used the new media technology, and how the technology, characterized by a culture of packaging, merchandising, competiing in a cost-intensive market, and legitimizing popular culture, reshape the message of Christianity—its authenticity, its capacity to speak prophetically to power, and as a source of salient moral values. Sometimes the message is cut to a size and format that fits the tube, applause is canned, and certain ethics of electronic media—such as personality cult, individualism, commercialization, and marketing of spiritual services—are injected into an African cultural context where communalism is privileged, and ritual agents neither advertise nor emphasize fees. In traditional religion, a ritual agent becomes famous based on efficacy. In fact, it is believed that the gods would "slap" a greedy agent to death.

Under the colonial canopy, an egotistic virtuoso missionary would cause conflict within the corps. How has Pentecostalism used today's media in the task of doing intercultural theology and evangelization? Another contentious matter is the impact of electronic culture on the personality of the pastor—clothes, demeanor, popularity, and consumption. As R. E. Hiebert and others argued, "The mass media bestows prestige and enhances authority of individuals and groups by legitimizing their status. Recognition by the press or radio or magazines or news reels testifies that one has arrived, that one is important enough to have been singled out from the large anonymous masses, that one's behavior and opinions are significant enough to require public notice."[7]

3. Discourses on Pentecostalism and Media in Africa

Certain discourses have dominated the study of religion and media in Africa: The globalism/modernity discourse traces the linkages to transnational and homogenizing cultural flows, and networking at the global level. This buttresses the image that Pentecostalism in Africa is an extension of the American electronic church and a vanguard of the political agenda of the American moral majority. Close by is the market theory built around the rational choice concept that profiles the religious space as being similar to a marketplace, and examines the commercialization of religion as a commodity, because messages are packaged as products in a competitive marketplace. This theory argues that marketing strategies enable religious businessmen to dupe gullible consumers by selling their books, videos, and audiotapes, and all manners of wares, using the sales techniques honed in the secular marketplace. It adds that the glitz mixes religion with entertainment. The preacher and television star become inseparable as the big man of the big God. Media pander to materialism and financial gain, and focus on the individual's desires and quest for prosperity.

The rebuttals to this theory state that a predominant globalization discourse misses the cultural nuances of a region;[8] that entertainment appears crucial for the survival of religion in the marketplace of culture; that it is an inculturating pathway for touching youthful audiences who are already enmeshed, wired in the electronic culture and bored with the equally packaged institutional religion. Religion and popular culture must be enmeshed to attract the youths, just as mainline churches experiment with new liturgies and music. However, this has not sufficed, as Quentin J. Schultze argues in *Tele-vangelism and American Culture: The Business of Popular Religion*. Schultze argues that religion and popular culture have a reciprocal influence on each other in creating a Christianity wherein it is difficult to distinguish popular entertainment from religion. But Jeremy Carrette and Richard King, authors of *Selling Spirituality: The Silent Take-over of Religion*, provide the flip side of the coin by arguing that the secular corporate interests have taken over spirituality to subvert individuals and seduce them into consumerism; that advertisements utilize their cultural cachet and brand products by associating them with personal fulfillment, inner peace, happiness, and success in relationships. Management efficiency is packaged as religious paths to enlightenment. Michael Warren concurs: "*Merit* is a cigarette, as is *True*. *Life* is a cereal for breakfast. *Joy* and *Happiness* are fragrances for the body. Unlike the human values they are drawn from, these names are all of products available for a price."[9]

These authors conclude that the market has taken over the responsibility of religion, and neoliberalism attempts to revalue all values and define the goal of life itself. The convert and consumer are one. If religion is commercially minded, commerce may be deemed to be religiously minded! The entire communication industry produces, reproduces, creates, and fosters a commodity culture. All communication production is under the economic control of the production and orchestration of consumption, whether used by Pentecostals or others. Should Christian missionary strategy contest and avoid electronic media as a satanic realm? Pentecostal diatribe about the satanic potentials of electronic media falls short of avoiding its glaring possibilities.

Other analyses image the primary goal of media as an enabling, valorized strategy for making disciples, and proffer advice on how to counter its dangerous dimensions. The Web site of the *Living Projects Media Network*, Nigeria, intones that that it is "using timely technology to preach the timeless truths to a dying world."[10] The magazine *Charisma* carries many articles on how a ministry could use media resources to launch, grow, makeover, face-lift, maximize presence, become a household name, build brand strategy, evangelize, and find and reach "the most powerful audience on earth": women! The Affiliated Media Group (founded in 1989) promises to serve as a media consultant that will assist ministries to access more channels and also join in the fight against the government interference and regulations that hinder Christian programs.[11]

Marla Frederick of Harvard Divinity School raises questions about one of the challenges Christian programmers face: how televangelists respond to the spiritual needs of people and help them grow and absorb Christian spirituality in everyday life. Television programs serve as a counseling discourse; a means for individual transformation; as motivational, self-help, teaching resources that change lifestyles; and a source of achieving progress and social uplift. But Frederick asks: Do televangelists encourage people to engage society or do they merely encourage listeners to contribute to their own individual social and spiritual advancement? For an answer, she avers that conversionist theology (with emphasis on sanctification) tends to be apolitical, focuses on the emotional and spiritual needs of individual believers, and suppresses focus on social ills; that although televangelism entertains and constructs an integrationist multiculturalism, it may psychologically create self-empowerment by pointing inward because the new individualistic faith is a matter between the individual and God and does not foster community.[12] Does this lead to an apolitical posture? Kwame Bediako argues in a nuanced conclusion that the significance of Christ's paradigmatic ethics for the public space is that "however essential it may be that transformation should find expression in sociopolitical institutions and structures, it needs also to find incarnation in personal lives."[13]

Another challenge for programmers is maximizing the impact of worship edited into a thirty-minute, individually centered clip, while not compromising the authenticity of the gospel and its message. Packaging the message does a number of things: It could distort the gospel, promote the creature instead of the creator, and encrust a certain interiorized ideology. This, argues Frederick, has an enormous ideological import for the black church, which has served as the forum for civil rights agitation. In Africa, privatized spiritual ethics could emasculate the political relevance of Christianity in an environment that needs a strong prophetic voice. But there is still another dimension: Is the allotted television time too short to achieve much? How effective is the television medium as a mission tool? Berit Brethauer responds about the inherent limitations of media evangelism and the ineffectiveness of evangelism via media by arguing that effective recruitment follows the warm lines of personal contact and trusted networks of family and friends. Therefore, "televangelism is hardly an effective way to provoke change in religious identity. Nor do religious media often bring about a radical personal transformation from a born-again experience."[14]

Kwabena Asamoah-Gyadu brings together the two dimensions about media as resource and challenge. He argues that the increased media use has reshaped the structure and ethos of the new Christianity in Africa: It has shaped a youth-oriented culture and encrusted modernizing tastes in ethics and liturgy while dispensing of the old missionary taboos that were used to inculcate frugality and asceticism. Media exposure has changed attitudes to created order and given the leadership and their organizations high public profile, sometimes to their detriment. The media's mood shapes the doctrinal emphases and fosters an international image. Indeed, the prosperity theology is moored to the upbeat mood and glitz of television for nurture, expression, representation, and propagation. But, "This new type of Christianity, as a result of its media presence, continues to have a much more diffused impact on African Christianity in particular and popular culture in general. The presence of the new Pentecostal/charismatic movements has literally transformed the religious culture of Christianity in Africa, leading to what may be referred to as a pentecostalization or charismatization of African Christianity."[15]

4. Pentecostal Representation in Advertisement and Print Media

i. The Message, Messenger, and the Medium

Scholars have focused on various genres of the media. We should examine and show the impact of each of them on African Pentecostalism, and balance authoritative voices that have monopolized the theorizations on African Pentecostalism by recovering the voices of African authors. Critics image advertisements as vehicles of commerce. But Martyn Percy rebuts that advertising is not necessarily selling: It does not convert but persuades people to take a second look; it is a legitimate option given the pluralistic nature of the modern world characterized by freedom of choice and competition. He revisits advertisement theory in posters, handbills, billboards, domestic goods, clothes, and television spots, and argues that advertisements can inspire, evoke affection, and impart useful public information and, therefore, are beneficial to religious groups in a pluralist age. Asonzeh Ukah focuses on the use of posters among Pentecostals in Africa. He concurs that posters are accessible and adaptable because the technology builds around a plot (problematic), actor, mood, message, and a resolution offered with certitude and authority. Thus, "Pentecostal entrepreneurs use poster to contest and create visibility, shape and influence people's attitudes to religious producers, break down resistance to social acceptance of the new religiosity, shape expectation, and create *needs, desires* as well as spiritual threats."[16]

Handbills, for instance, are essential for evangelism because they alert people about programs. In urban areas they supplement other modes of passing information. In rural areas, culture change has affected models of information dissemination: Whereas the village announcer ("town crier") once passed information with a gong, popular culture now uses handbills, leaflets, and posters to announce meetings, funerals, or celebrations of rites of passage. Pentecostalism has adopted, adapted, and disseminated the new vogue.

On a closer look, popular culture has influenced Pentecostal use of print media in its aesthetics. This reflects a paradigm shift because, as William Dyrness argues in his book *Visual Faith*, Protestant traditions have problems with visual arts.[17] Early Pentecostals deployed the puritan attack on certain forms of art by drawing on the diatribe in the aniconic/iconoclastic passages in the Scriptures. They preferred the use of images from nature—flowing rivers, budding plants and flowers, meadows, or scenes from the Holy Land and from the Bible. Early Pentecostal posters and handbills from the 1970s to mid-1980s were relatively austere, and emphasized the words of the message in a black and white background. The newsletters during this time consisted of biblical teachings. But by the late 1980s, Pentecostal representation borrowed heavily from popular culture. For instance, it was the political class who initiated the advertising style using glossy, iconic, color photographs of the electoral candidates. Government leaders installed huge billboards from which they smiled down at the public with the assurance that the country, state, or city worked best under their leadership, and photographs of completed public projects would adorn the billboards as veritable proof. Pentecostal leaders soon abandoned the old aesthetic scruples and promoted their anointing as successful "big men of a big God."

There is a linkage between the iconic image of the leader, the message, and the lure to mimesis. The dress and lifestyle of the big man of God become essential ingredients of the composite culture. Asonzeh Ukah aptly observes:

> The aesthetics of the poster, therefore, reflects the underlying doctrines of the new religion with its thematic emphasis on an expansive God whose wealth is located in the market place of commercial practice; its design is partly governed by local practice of exhibiting one's best as a way of seeking notice, of symbolically communicating one's worth to a public that recognizes and desires wealth and grandiose. Part of the proselytizing potential of the poster thus is located in its design to appeal to an audience that understands the logic of its image, a public willing and desirous of sharing in the wealth of God displayed in the life of the pastor whose image proudly gazes out from the poster. The power of the gaze to focus, channel and organize attention is generally recognized therein.[18]

Thus, beneath the need to disseminate information and evangelize may lurk the intricate relationships between evangelization and commercialization and a significant modification of the image of the pastor/shepherd. Where Paul called himself a bondservant, the new pastor engages in a personality cult, and flaunts his person, wealth, and status. Does the medium reshape the messenger, trivialize the message, and distort the image carved by the simplicity of Jesus? Indeed, the attack on prosperity theology from a certain sector of the same movement used a spiritual index to warn against the "spirit of things," a materialism that could entrap, capture, and lock up the preacher in bondage in spite of Paul's warning: Love not the world. Bakker's confession after his jail sentence becomes apropos of the need to be attentive to boundaries and motives. House magazines, T-shirts, and calendars are used to build the beloved community, to bond, and to raise funds for the ministry's growing list of projects.

Generally, in the media industry, style is important for enhancing the message and the messenger: The glossy photographs of the leader, his wife or family, and members who celebrated happy events serve as mission statements asserting the believer's capacity to refuse defeat from the harsh, disabling environment, and to pose as an overcomer. The house magazine set inspirational goals. With desktop publishing facilities becoming more readily available, the number of Christian magazines in Africa has rapidly increased, and many ministries own printing and publication facilities. As a result, a body of Christian journalists has been constituted. Pentecostals accessed the print media more easily as the vehicle for propaganda. Matthew Ojo listed over forty-two magazines produced by charismatic groups within western Nigeria in the decade 1970–1980.[19] The numbers escalated thereafter.

ii. Reinventing the Big Man from Indigenous Society

In addition to the various media mentioned above, there is more to consider: the ambiguous concept of "big man" in traditional African societies. Among the Igbo of southeastern Nigeria, it represented an achieved person who had, by the support of his *"ikenga,"* performed all the traditional rituals and taken all the titles, fulfilling the dream of old age lived with dignity, *nka na nzere*. But this title was loaded with moral implications demanding that the person's tongue be as sharp as that of the tiger; that is, he was to always tell the truth according to his conscience, ignoring whether his family's sheep must be gored. This is an ingredient of indigenous wisdom and expression. If one lost a case, the person would pay a goat or sheep that will be slaughtered and the meat shared among the elders. An honest person will tell the truth even if his family had to slaughter a sheep for the elders He was to be a person endowed with wealth and moral integrity who would carry his carved stool to sit among the elders and judge the community. The community was keenly aware that not all wealthy people were morally upright. The enlargement of the political space from the village into the new national theater, and into the emergent culture of urbanity created a zone where the big man would be able to achieve wealth and status without the ethical demands in traditional society.

This ambiguity is similarly found in the works of Ben Jones on Teso village, Uganda, and by Rijk van Dijk's study of youthful Charismatics in Malawi. Jones paints the big man as a person who assiduously climbs through the status ladder by being elected to hold civic offices.

Van Dijk argues that the word *kukhwima* meant a "ripened" or "empowered" person, a person of immense status and power; being a *kukhwima* for the elderly meant having a secure power (*mphamwu*) and stronghold in the home village. But it was suspected that the *kukhwima* secured a powerful position by using witchcraft and sorcery and by patronizing ancestral cults and covenants. Early Pentecostal youths of the 1970s fulminated against these negative ways of obtaining power by insisting that authority rests on divine inspiration and not on an influential position in society. By the 1980s, the fascination with media technology and the hypnotic allure of prosperity gospel quietly reshaped the Pentecostal attitude toward status, elitism, and the big man syndrome. The pastor, especially the "powerful man of God," took over the local image and idiom of the big man, no longer to be suspected but seen in its traditional sense. This image was not based on patronage of the traditional cults, rather it was God who has "rubbed oil on the head of His servant," which signifies anointing for leadership. A chorus proclaims that "God has rubbed oil on me, that is why I am gleaming with anointing." As God was praised, so was His visible viceroy on earth. The image and idiom of the pastor as a superhero was derived and translated from the indigenous language and perception of the hero as someone who was chosen and anointed by the gods.[20] The pastor replaced the witch doctor.

Equally, the use of books written by indigenous pastors has increased enormously. In the decade of 1970–1980, many used imported books until these became expensive with the collapse of economies and poor exchange rates. Some Christian publishing businesses acquired the copyrights to re-publish foreign books locally, but by the end of that decade indigenous authors became prolific. It became the mark of a successful pastor to publish books. Whether these are ghostwritten or are derivative must be determined by scholars. My initial conclusion is that these books demonstrate a significant capacity to address everyday problems of the cultural context. This are of the media is where local appropriation has been most visible as self-help resources and commentary on political matters. Many ministries have set up publishing houses precisely because the production of books, house magazines, posters, and handbills could sustain a desktop publishing enterprise and enhance the image of the ministry.

5. Television and Videos in Pentecostal Missionary Strategy

There are certain characteristics unique to the African Pentecostal way of uti-lizing media as a means of doing evangelization: First, certain aspects of to-day's media that constitute a challenge to the churches in the West do not exist in Africa: for instance, Internet addiction disorder based on cybersex, cyber-gambling, and cyberinformation such as chat rooms.[21] The level of Internet penetration in the African continent is still very low because of the high cost of bandwith, computers, and Internet infrastructure. In the current migration from analog to digital systems, there is a wide berth in the digital divide be-tween developed and developing nations. These facilities are too expensive on the continent to permit extensive and easy indulgence. Above all, the unreli-able power supply stunts growth and provides the milieus for discussing the impact of television. Harri Englund made a similar point for Malawi in 2001:

> In Malawi, for example Pentecostalism hardly provides a truly global space for people's lives. The country's poor links to the electronic

means of mass mediation contrasts with the diverse uses of the electronic media among Pentecostal congregations in countries like Ghana and Nigeria. In Malawi, the only nationwide radio station has long been under tight government control; Malawi Television was launched only in 1999 and even then for viewers living within an 80 km radius from the commercial city of Blantyre; the ownership of even a simple transistor radio indicates relative affluence among the urban and rural poor alike. Video and audiotapes, magazines and pamphlets are accessible through some Pentecostal congregations, but they become scarce resources in the overall poverty of the Malawian mass media. As such, in transnationalism, blockages are as important to understand as flows and the transnational networks which Pentecostalism appears to support are not always enabling and empowering.[22]

But there is a linkage between television culture and the prosperity gospel that promoted the concept of the big man and the big God whose will is to prosper His people materially, physically, and spiritually because the blood of Christ's atonement and many promises in the Scriptures assure these.

As mentioned at the beginning of this chapter, when Benson Idahosa linked with Bakker's PTL and other proponents of the faith/claim theology, the character of Pentecostalism changed dramatically in nine ways:

1. the rise of the megachurch with its thousands of members and branches;
2. the success of the rich big man of God;
3. the creation of mega projects, such as the elaborate church center, Bible school, businesses, and elaborate stadia outreaches;
4. the increased access to electronic media, such as radio, television, video-, and audiocassettes;
5. the increased access to print media, such as glamorous house magazines, handbills, posters, billboards, and books;
6. the availability of clothes such as T-shirts, caps, fashion;
7. the means to hear and perform new forms of music;
8. the radical shift in ecclesiology from congregationalist polity to episcopacy with centralized, bureaucratized administration; and
9. the emphasis on fivefold ministry, where prophets and apostles controlled evangelists, teachers, and deacons (lower cadres of church workers); the wife of "the man of God" organized sodalities for women; and pastors acquire degrees especially doctorates either *honoris causa* or by outright purchase. In fact, Idahosa became a reverend, doctor, professor, and archbishop! And in Zimbabwe, Ezekiel Guti virtually developed a cult around his person.

The shift in ecclesiology, the importance of titles, and the size of projects were connected with profile and visibility of a ministry. The high visibility, iconic image tangoed with intense spirituality to draw public, national, and international attention. These were essential for getting the political ears of the government to listen to pastors who control a large constituency of voters. Enlarged scale and increased advertisement yield more devotees and income though these projects are cost intensive. Marleen de Witte studied the Altar Media built by the Ghanaian pastor Mensah Otabil, and showed the infectious character of Pentecostal style of mass mediation.[23]

The religious trend reflects the shifts in popular culture in the social, political, and economic spheres. Both the secular and religious entrepreneurs use the same communications strategies and interact closely. In his article, Asamoah-Gyadu reproduced the photograph of a billboard advertisement in Accra on behalf of Kingsway International Church, sponsored by Borges, a company that markets olive oil, because the members of the church use the oil in their liturgy.[24] Some businesspeople see the potential in the critical mass of the new movement and target the symbols and core message in their sales strategies. For instance, anointing became a major and attractive feature from the late 1980s to the early 1990s. Its increased use tallied with the rise of the prophetic movement within Pentecostal theology and ecclesiology. Anointing deepened the appropriation of the Pauline teaching on the *charisma* and *charismata* connecting these to the fivefold ministry. Similarly, Nigerian breweries exploited the moral boundaries such as the prohibition of alcoholic beverage as an identity marker of a born-again Christian. Though the company produces alcoholic drinks, they chose to underwrite the huge, annual outreach event by the Redeemed Christian Church of God that attracts over three million participants on condition that their product, Maltina, will monopolize the sales of nonalcoholic drinks. In Ghana, some corporations compete in sponsoring the programs by Altar Media. For instance, the proprietor of Kingdom Transport Services says that his success came from the pastor's teachings. This reinforces the message that business success/prosperity comes from generous giving to ministries.

But African Pentecostals have not dealt adequately with funding the cost-intensive project of evangelization: There are no widespread secular product sponsorships, no fan clubs, and no elaborate structures for mailing and contacting "consumers." They engage in direct sales of religious wares and depend on the contributions of members. In the United States, many ministries differentiate the media ministry from the church. In Africa, the two are interlocked and the members' tithes, offerings, and earnings from business ventures constitute the major sources for prosecuting cost-intensive projects. The level of intensive use of African televangelism should be reexamined. I suspect that there must be few people in Africa who have left their churches to depend upon "tele-churches," as might be the case in Western countries. But powerful men of God receive gifts from nonmembers of the ministry who may have benefited from televangelism. For instance, the house magazine that is produced by Chris Oyakhilome's ministry Christ Embassy claims that people come from all over the nation to attend the healing sessions dubbed as Healing School, and offer their resources in gratitude.

We should examine cultural production at the point of consumption. For instance, do colorful handbills, posters, and billboards sporting photos of iconic, rich pastors and scriptural promises convert, allure, or persuade the unbelievers? They may attract attention and create a religious culture that offers solutions to everyday life challenges, hopes, and fears; and they may invite and allure, but it is another thing to get the fish to bite. They could construct how reality should be imagined and create an atmosphere suggesting that religion is important for the nation. Birgit Meyer raises another challenge to be confronted at the point of consumption:

> By going public Pentecostalism recasts Christianity as distraction, both in the sense of deliberately adopting an entertainment format and dispersing the message without bounds. In doing so the Pentecostal message is dismembered into mediated religious forms and elements displayed everywhere in public urban space.... Religious authority over practices of mediation is, to some extent, undermined.[25]

As in all interpretations of the movement, sociologists contradict themselves. De Witte sees it differently:

> In this new public sphere religion intertwines with both national politics and commerce and entertainment. Charismatic Pentecostalism is part and parcel of the business and entertainment culture of the commercial media, just as entertainment, business, and marketing are integral to charismatic churches. Its impact, then, lies not only in its institutional forms and rapidly growing number of followers, but also in more fluid forms of consumer culture and entertainment business. Through the media, it has widely diffused influence on general popular tastes and styles, that may not be religious per se, but are clearly shaped by charismatic-Pentecostal discourse and practice.[26]

This is a more perceptive interpretation.

When speaking of religion in media, a number of facts have to be examined: First, the proliferation of religious television programs may turn off many people. In England people refer disdainfully to "God channels." In many African countries such channels do not exist. In many others, efforts have been made to restrict "miracle outreaches" from television programs. This could arise from state policy, opposition from competing religious forms, or from secularists.

Second, there are few statistical studies of television and digital media usage in Africa to determine the percentage of ministries that use the television medium. My suspicion is that there are fewer than imagined because television stations and channels are few in each country, though recent privatization broadened the scope. In many African countries the state and regional governments own most of the television stations. To illustrate with Kenya: According to Steadman Media researchers, Kenya Broadcasting Corporation (KBC) covers 40 percent of Kenya's land mass and concentrates on urban areas. In 2000, 1.8 million households owned a television and adult viewership was 29 percent nationally. Kenya Broadcasting Corporation radio has a longer reach. However, a competing Christian television station, Family Media Television, had approximately 27 percent viewership and 47 percent radio listenership in 2000. Because the cost of broadcasting is high, few ministries can afford more than brief exposures of badly taped videos.

In an earlier period, state broadcasting provided religious items free as a public service. Indeed, state broadcasters are willing to break the broadcasting code that allocates only 10 percent of airtime for religious broadcasts. But now, 40 percent of the revenue of the Nigerian Television Authority comes from Pentecostals, so there is no reason to provide free services when there are people willing to pay. No Pentecostal group owns a television station because no religious group is permitted by law to own a television station. Few own their own recording studios. Admittedly, The Redeemed Christian Church of God embarked on extensive development of Dove World Media comprising Dove Television, a satellite channel run from Dallas; Dove Link, a wireless Internet provider; Dove Billboards, a celebrity-driven magazine with a Christian flavor; Dove Music; Dove Movies; a Christian music television network; and two shortwave channels. The media assault is akin to penetrating hostile regions by air before sending ground troops. In 2003, Christ Embassy pioneered the first twenty-four-hour Christian network based in Africa to be broadcast to the rest of the world. It broadcasts from twenty-two different channels in the United States, Canada, Australia, India, Europe, the Middle East, and six African countries.

Third, Harri Englund rightly concluded that in Malawi many of the ministries are not operating as large, rich outfits; rather, they are just struggling to survive in an intensely competitive arena.[27] Costs, rather than antimodernity ethics, deter the African Instituted Churches from extensively using television. Some Pentecostal megachurches, such as David Oyedepo's Living Faith, do not spend resources on television but on university and other business projects.

Fourth, one needs to focus attention on the impact of the contents of television programs consisting of healings, miracles, people slain in the spirit, short motivational homilies, and the promotion of literature and goods. Generally, television attracts and has impacted evangelism in rural areas. Its power is poignantly indicated by the phenomenon of television ritual, as many dev-

TABLE 6.1. Christ Embassy International Television Schedule

Country	Time	Number and Name of Station
United States	Morning/Evening	7—TBN, Fox 35 (Mississippi), Word Network, Church Channel, WATC (Atlanta), WJYS, KTLN (California)
Canada	Evening	2—Miracle Channel, CTS Canada
Europe	Morning/Evening	1—Sky 679 (Love World TV)
Abu Dhabi	Morning	1—LoveWorld Christian Network
Australia	Evening	1—LoveWorld Christian Network
South Africa	Morning/Evening	2—TBN South Africa, Love World Christian Network
Kenya	Daily Evening	1—Citizen TV, Kenya
Uganda	Evening	1—Uganda TV
Ghana	Evening	3—TV Africa, Cable Gold, Metro TV Ghana
India	Evening	1—Miraclenet (India)
Togo	Evening	3—TVZion, RTDS, TV2
Zimbabwe	Evening	1—ZIM TV

Composed from information in *Healing School Report* (Ikeja, Lagos: Christ Embassy, February 2006), 16.

otees either stretch their hands toward or put their hands on television sets so as to receive blessings or healings during the broadcast. Here, the use of olive oil, and recitation of positive mantras become important.[28]

The question still remains: When the image is carefully packaged to convey a defined message, create an impression, and elicit imitation, does this affect the nature of the gospel? Many testify that the teaching in favorite programs helps to deepen their Christian lives. This cannot be ignored because of the lurking dangers in the relationship between gospel, popular culture, and televangelism. Berit Brethauer acknowledges that participation in televangelism with a global outreach catalyzed the growth of Robert Schuller's ministry. The only problem then was ensuring that a local community was sustained while engaging the global scene.

Pentecostals have been more successful in utilizing drama productions on video. Home videos in English and its various vernaculars have become important tools of evangelization and have provided Pentecostals with lucrative vehicles for projecting ideas and images.[29] The power of this vernacularization in mediating the gospel has been a staple of church historiography. It fits the message into popular culture and uses entertainment as a mode of insertion. An example is the connection between the Pentecostal videos and the lucrative and imploding local movie industry in Nigeria nicknamed *Nollywood*. This industry's presence and quality have been discussed by *The New York Times*, and its films are now widely distributed in the Western world. Pentecostals have invested heavily into this industry by producing films that critique the ethics of contemporary society, by dramatizing how and why the audience should seek Christ as the solution to many life problems. Critics point to the lurid emphasis on the demonic in the portrayal of spiritual warfare and deliverance themes. Others argue that films produced in Ghana are more subtle in their plots. But there is no denial about the popular interest in these films and their didactic, moralistic character. Jordan Smith explains the popularity of the videos with an instrumentalist theory: the connection between inequality in economic distribution and appeal to the supernatural. But Akoko Mbe's account of Pentecostalism in the wake of economic crises in Cameroon provides a nuanced analysis. The availability of home videos rentals and video clubs in many townships enhances access. Bus companies show such movies on long trips, and advertise them as competing attractions.

Pentecostal growth is partially explained by the vigor of its evangelism so that it ignores the costs. For instance, since cellular phones have penetrated Africa deeply in the last three years, some Pentecostal churches have expanded the range of their digital electronic evangelism by sending inspiring text messages to bless subscribers who may not be members of their churches. For instance, a ministry sent me such a message, originating at 05:25:25 AM saying [sic]: "May d glory of heaven, d vry face of Gods countenance, shine upon u, causing a cascade of favors, an ocean of peace & a fountain of joy. Hv a dy of grace!"

6. Radio, Cassettes, and Music in Pentecostal Mission

i. Radio and Charismatic Cassettes

Africans have manifested greater cultural agency with audio- and videocassettes and music. Audio materials, whether sermon tapes or music, are easily dubbed or pirated, and widely used in trailer parks, homes, offices, taxis, and buses. The retreat of the state from control over media and the accessibility of cheap media technologies gave rise to a new image economy.[30] Three important changes on the social terrain occurred in the 1980s: an emergence of highly educated, young adults who established their ministries. Many had enlarged contacts with Western, especially American, televangelists who introduced them to media use in religious communication and invaded the African air space. These two factors have been aided by a third, namely the liberalization of the media space. Apparently, the democratization process dubbed as "the second liberation of Africa" included the liberalization of the state's stranglehold on the media sector, the dismantling of state monopolies, and the commercialization of airtime and ownership. The media landscape opened to a cacophony of sounds. One index of the relaxation of the state's rule over the airwaves is the number of radio stations in West Africa, which increased from 40 in 1993 to 426 in 2001, including sixty community radio stations in South Africa, 117 private FM stations in Uganda by 2002, more than one hundred stations in Mali, and two hundred new local rural FM solar stations in Niger.

Someone quipped that Africans had more radio stations than portable water.[31] In addition to spoken-word programs, radio promoted music and dance.

Muslims have abandoned old taboos to imitate Christians. Charles Hirschkind has examined the use of cassettes in public piety in Egypt where Muslims have developed a genre known as Cassette-Dahwa built around sermon tapes to be used in fulfilling the duty to actively encourage fellow Muslims in their pursuance of greater piety, and to evangelize.[32] All over the continent, radio is the fastest means of disseminating information. From the interwar years it has served as a prized possession in many homes, a veritable symbol of modernity. Many agro-industrial development projects include the distribution of radio to rural farmers, and the proliferation of Non-Governmental Organizations (NGOs) in the 1990s further broadened the use of radio in the hinterlands. Missionary-founded churches tend to depend on government patronage to access the radio network, but while small Pentecostal groups aggressively buy time to air pretaped programs, the bigger ones set up their private radio stations. Perhaps radio ministry in Ghana is more vibrant because of the proliferation of over twenty radio stations and their special product, the call-and-response method excites public interest and devotes much air time to religious content materials.[33] In South Africa, broadcasting is still controlled by the state, and there is an ongoing struggle to change from the apartheid tradition and from new forces of secularism to an inclusive mediation of diverse religious faiths.[34]

ii. Music and Dance

There are a number of approaches in studying radio and video media. Here, they will be considered through their impact on music and dance. The concerns here are, first, to shift perspectives because the tendency has been to study Pentecostalism through space, describing its spatial and vertical expansion and its numbers. Moreover, media studies tend to focus on the glare of television and the multicolor billboards showing the big man of God staring down on the traffic, promising liberation and prosperity. The goal here is to change the focus by studying the sounds of the born again through music and dance of the Pentecostals. Second, Pentecostalism is reshaping the religious landscape by creating a new religious culture whose force is mirrored in its respose to popular culture. This is best illustrated with charismatic liturgy that is one of the biggest attractions to the movement. Dubbed "praise-co," Pentecostal music and dance traditions have attempted to supplant the music and dance of discotheques. A number of high-profile secular or "juju" musicians (who create new rhythms from indigenous musical culture) have become gospel singers, evangelists, and pastors. Politicians and the celebrants of rites of passage borrow freely from gospel music and dance. The goal is to trace how the new musical tradition or gospel music originated and developed; how the

Pentecostals who were initially wary of popular cultures negotiated between sacred and popular music and dance.

Ezra Chitendo aptly defines gospel music as

> an artistic product emerging from cultural workers who are influenced by the Christian cumulative tradition. These artists utilize various musical styles and instruments to communicate Christian themes. These include the *mbira* beat from a traditional Shona musical instrument, *sungura* or *museve* (like an arrow, it pierces the heart) from Zimbabwean popular music, rap and hip hop from African American culture, reggae from the African-Caribbean culture, Congolese *soukous* and other types.[35]

Popularity has its price and Pentecostal churches are now competing among themselves in adopting new musical and dance choreographies. The empire of popular culture has struck back and reshaped the character of the movement. The papal exhortation *Ecclesia in Africa* (1995) had noted the use of media as a resource in evangelization but cautioned that media "constitute a new culture that has its own language and above all its own specific values and counter-values"[36] and could pose a challenge to Christian users.

The significance of the problem can be illustrated in an example from the Republic of Congo where the Pentecostal/charismatic devotees are called *bakristu* in the Lingala language. One noticeable characteristic of believers who live in this musical culture is how they are struggling to draw a line between sacred Christian music (*mabino ya Nzambe*) and the polluting secular music (*mabino mabe*) that fills the air in the urban areas and percolates into the remote villages via radio and other electronic technology. Yet the line is receding. The *bakristu* declare that the Holy Spirit (*Molimo Mosantu*) inspires a certain type of appropriate music, while the evil spirit (*molimo mabe*) inspires different types of music and dance that seduce and ruin morals. Preachers eloquently entertain and exhort their audiences by choreographing diatribes against the influence of popular culture on believers. But change in the style of gospel music is unstoppable because of creativity, rivalry, the pressure of popular culture, and shifts in technology as digital recording and video took over from vinyl records. Meanwhile, distributing these recordings became easier because of piracy and hawking them in trailer parks and on buses. Music and dance constitute an important dimension in the prolific mass mediation of religion among the Pentecostals. The use of mass media has given the movement a higher public visibility, profile, and influence than their statistical share of the contemporary religious market would warrant.[37]

7

Elijah's Mantle

Pentecostal Re-Evangelization
of Africa in the 1990s

I. Introduction: The Trauma of Growth

This chapter continues the interpretation of Pentecostalism by closely
following the changing face and emphases in various decades. I argue that the explosive growth of African Pentecostalism intensified in
the 1990s through a vigorous evangelization program and thereby
created a very complex religious environment. Another dimension of
this argument is to revisit the aftereffect of the movement's growth.
The literature exults about the unstoppable growth of the movement
in Africa, but what about the aftermath of growth? Growth can be
traumatic. One example of this growth is its impact on ministerial
formation as the movement sought to mobilize the personnel to
match its passion for evangelization. Many young people—educated,
professional men and women—sought to wear the surplice as the
numbers of converts overawed the infrastructure. Meanwhile, rivalry
yielded new visions, theologies, and styles of leadership. Elijah's
mantle became a dominant imagery; the altars of the Old Testament
legitimized the formation of new churches and ministries under
new leaderships that had not tasted formal theological training. The
models of ministerial formation in Africa became scrambled. Since
the ancient prophets bestowed their mantles upon their disciples or
sons of the prophet, the African leaders reimagined themselves as
prophets and apostles. This is best captured in Basil Ibe's book *The
Ultimate Generation: The Emergence of the Prophetic Company*. As
prophets, they groomed the future leaders through apprenticeship,

unaccredited Bible schools, short-term crash courses offered by well-meaning global partners, awards of doctorates, outright sale of certificates by wolves in sheepfolds, and a host of other strategies. Soon, young people started preaching without even undergoing apprenticeship. They deployed the power of mimicry, as young men and women who watched enough videos and listened to enough cassettes started to imitate what they saw and heard, and preached to large public audiences until these preachers were discovered and absorbed by larger ministries as apprentices. One could hear the distraught prophets declaiming that all equipment have manuals and people should endeavor to study under somebody and learn how to read the manuals before operating the equipment.

The emphasis on the leadership of the Holy Spirit created conditions in which people could declare that the Spirit called and gave them visions. No one could query the authenticity. Ironically, as the fellowships routinized into churches, and the youthful radicals aged, bureaucracy and institutionalization challenged the new youthful disdain for authority. Leaders encouraged members to refer to the leader either as "father/mother in the Lord" or as "daddy/mummy"— warm images of intimacy drawn from the family setting used to encrust patriarchal and gerontocratic authority patterns. In the 1990s new forms of ministries sprung up all over the continent. In this chapter we shall focus on how the Pentecostals responded to the problem of ministerial formation and prosecuted robust evangelical visions that had Africa as its main target.[1] Starting with the charismatic movements of the 1970s, many young people boldly moved across national boundaries with the gospel. Notable is the pan-African nationalist ideology that fueled this process. Reuben Ezemadu, the leader of the Christian Mission Foundation, recalls in the "Ife Declaration" among Nigerian university students in 1977 that "the Lord was preparing his children for missions to other parts of Africa. It was clear to us that Nigerian Christians will send the light of the gospel to many dark places in Africa and to change the stigma of Africa as a dark continent to stem the tide of opposition and resentment to white missionaries in Africa." Emeka Nwankpa, one of the leaders in what he and others labeled as a Christian Evangelical Social Movement, later became a leader in the Intercessors for Africa, and networked throughout the continent focusing on redeeming the land, as he entitled his book.[2] The avowed goal of Intercessors for Africa was delivering African nations from spiritual forces that have stunted economic growth and scourged the fate of the black race. Concomitant with intercession was a call to transform local churches into apostolic and prophetic praying assemblies, and to evangelize other African countries and unreached peoples within each nation. Africa became the privileged site for evangelization and the racial motif was linked to the eschatological theme of what God was doing in the end-times. The tone of evangelization was prophetic and didactic. The vision was to intentionally mobilize an army for what God was about to do in Africa. In this chapter, I shall use the mission to Muslims and Francophone Africa as an example. I shall also point to the political implications of the rise of intercessory ministry.Indeed, the role of intercession as a form of political praxis was not lost on the political leaders who often sought the services of charismatic intercessors.

Many churches, especially Pentecostal, have founded private universities as a means of changing the moral temper of nations through faith-based education. Amid these frenetic shifts in the core elements of mission, issues of poverty, failed political leadership, civil wars, and HIV/AIDS stared communities in the face. The political and religious implications of the cost-intensive investment in new universities and their capacity to achieve the avowed goals have not been adequately explored. We shall, therefore, pay attention to their mission statements that are blazoned in Web sites.

The arguments here are, first, that from the long view of the development of African Christianity, we can see how the rise of Pentecostalism intensified the passion for mission and enlarged the scale of missionary enterprise. Pentecostals were the inheritors of the core ideology in the Ethiopian movement. We also see how the conception and practice of mission changed as people redefined the needs of their contexts. New visions compelled changes of strategy. Second, many of the Classical Pentecostal churches, such as the Assemblies of God and International Foursquare, who came at the invitation of the indigenous folks but had not made much impact on the religious scene, benefited tremendously from the charismatic resurgence of the post-1970 period. Third, Pentecostals benefited from their increased media access. However, the prosperity gospel and some of the theological tendencies were robustly challenged from the mid-1990s onward. Fourth, the parachurch organizations—such as Full Gospel Business Men's Fellowship International, Women's Aglow, and The Gideons Bible International—simply exploded into many parts of the continent within the last two decades.

Pentecostal emphasis on evangelism compelled shifts in ecclesiology, and raised the issue of money and charisma and the problem of mobilizing the whole people of God through a salient gender ideology. It should be re-emphasized that the concept and practice of mission in African Pentecostalism emerged just as much as responses to the indigenous worldviews and cultures, the contemporary experiences of communities in the face of the collapse of their economies, and their appropriation of biblical resources as they did for the surging intensity of secularism.[3] The question is whether the contemporary African Pentecostal movement recognizes the mandate to engage the whole of culture. Does it practice a holistic mission?

2. Emergent Forms of Ministerial Formation

i. Pentecostalism and Missiology

The character of Pentecostalism informs its activities: With the understanding that the mainline churches have practiced powerless Christianity, which has left the spirits that govern the gates of communities unconquered, there is a process of reevangelization of the entire continent. Missionary fatigue has produced compromises of the gospel, allowing people to have their feet in both primal religion and biblical Christianity. The answer is to utilize charismatic or power evangelism, as well as modern resources such as media and management techniques, in promoting a personal faith commitment to Jesus Christ and Holy Spirit baptism. Typical is the lucid and bold mission statement of the Redeemed Christian Church of God (RCCG): "It is our goal to make heaven (sic). It is our goal to take as many people as possible with us. In order to accomplish our goals, holiness will be our lifestyle. In order to take as many people with us as possible, we will plant churches within five minutes' walking distance in every city and town of developing countries; and within five minutes' driving distance in every city and town of developed countries. We will pursue these objectives until every nation in the world is reached for Jesus Christ our Lord."[4] Commentators have also observed that the missionary motif is reinforced by the liturgical creativity that brings the impact of the gospel into the daily lives of the people as a transformative experience. Pentecostals have recovered the centrality of mission as the only reason for the existence of the church.

Pentecostal critics acknowledge the emphases on witness and proclamation, liturgy, and prayer and contemplation, but they question Pentecostal commitment to sociocultural transformation through social justice, peace, integrity of creation, dialogue with other faiths and ideologies, inculturation, and reconciliation. Critics point to the Pentecostals' lack of engagement in the public space and against structures that dehumanize. Thus, in examining the conception and practice of mission by African Pentecostals and their zeal to re-evangelize Africa, we must be attentive to what the critics are saying, for in such listening lies the possibilities for healing the trauma of growth.

ii. The Problem and Context

Ministerial formation is a key component of mission. The quality of Christianity in Africa would depend on how churches train their leadership. The Pentecostal dilemma should be set within a larger picture that shows that ministerial formation continues to be a problem for all the churches in Africa, because the rapid growth calls to question the viability of inherited patterns and walled institutions. The process of producing a minister used to begin with a careful selection of candidates for the ministry, followed by a number of years training or forming them for the ministry. Now, the numbers of believers, types of Pentecostalism, forms of Christian worship, high level of competition, conflicting theologies, rivalry and jealous demarcation of turf among groups of believers complicate the problem. Many churches have been compelled to experiment with inadequate strategies. Deschooling in theological education predominates. Confident of a spiritual experience and a divine call, many people start their own ministries without formal training. Divine call testimonies replace accreditation. Thus, large numbers of church leaders with good qualifications in professional areas such as medicine, architecture, academics, and finance desert their professions for full-time ministry.

In this scrambled pattern of ministerial formation, many pastors train their own leaders. Some ministries begin by establishing an in-house Bible college within their churches, where the pastor teaches all the subjects, while operating without the need for an external accreditation. Others build more elaborate seminaries, though they could be of low quality. There are, however, many seminaries with reasonable infrastructure and an adequate number of instructors. Few are accredited though, because some state governments restrain the granting of degrees by insisting that approved seminaries must be affiliated with state-owned universities. The financial cost of such affiliation is usually high. Many seminaries bypass the state regulations by awarding degrees from foreign universities, or students obtain degrees by taking correspondence courses from American or South Asian institutions. Some of these foreign institutions offer fake degrees. Singapore is a popular spot that hosts fake operators. In addition, there are groups of Americans who travel through the Third World granting degrees and ordaining bishops as a way of building a worldwide network. Many African countries, such as Nigeria, prohibit the awarding of offshore degrees. In Nigeria, some seminaries formed an association, the Nigerian Theological Education Council, and attempted to establish an accreditation body in 1999. These seminaries also operate under the Accrediting Council for Theological Education in Africa that is run by the Association of Evangelicals in Africa, with headquarters in Nairobi. The effort failed. In Aprils 2002 another group formed the Association of Christian Theologians in Lagos with the goal of establishing an accreditation body. They asserted that the state has no right to accredit purely religious institutions. The debate is ongoing about the credibility of the association and the powers that it arrogates to itself. But associational parties recognize the challenge of quality control in seminary educations, the need for an accrediting body and the ambivalence in state intervention in religious institutions within the purviews of a constitution that prescribes a separation of church and state.

3. The Rise of Christian Universities

A new phenomenon has emerged as the growth of private higher education in Africa has been spurred by the intervention of churches. Admittedly, some of the private universities are secular. As Bev Thavers says, "In East Africa, evidence points to the emergence of secular-based private higher institutions with profit motive that are managed by a new group of 'education entrepreneurs' deploying market principles in education. . . . The application of market ideology to higher education is related to a global ideology that defines education as a private good for economic growth."[5] She argues that a majority of the private universities in Kenya are secular. It is the opposite case in many African countries; the number of church-operated universities is much larger than that of secular institutions. Churches came to be the primary sponsors of universities in most African countries when the states' hubris evaporated with the collapse of their economies and their subsequent lack of ability to deal with huge population growth. For instance, with a population of more than 130 million, the Nigerian government can no longer afford the provision of adequate tertiary education, and can no longer afford to monopolize education. It would appear that the International Monetary Fund and World Bank have urged African governments to adopt an ideology of liberalization, privatization, and commercialization in their broad economic policies and practices. This has affected education policies and funding very dramatically. Education must be perceived as a good investment; it should pay its way just as any other enterprise should, and should be available for those who can pay. This view has necessitated the privatization of education. Churches that had been pushed away from primary and secondary levels of education during the heydays of national independence have reentered the education field to invest at the tertiary level.

The collapse of morality in state institutions has coincided with the Christian responsibility to regain a voice in a fundamental area of national life. There is so much desire for education in Africa that the number of tertiary institutions cannot adequately meet the need. For instance, in 1999, Central University College started in Accra, Ghana, with an enrollment of 428 students; increased to 952 students by 2000; and to more than 2,000 students in the 2003–2004 academic session. The bachelor's degree in business administration that includes a computer-training component is the most attractive sector. Some perceive this demand for computer training as being driven by the global market economy. But it emerges from the theology of Mensah Otabil,the leader of the church that founded the institution. He emphasizes what he calls practical Christianity that argues that the core moral values of Christianity are the pursuit of independence, human dignity, and excellence. People do not need to be poor because they are Christians, but should develop all their God-given resources and should strive to succeed in life. A vital relationship with Christ must result in an abundant and improved quality of life. Though the business sector of the school brings in much of its income, there is no attempt to articulate the goals of the institution in a market entrepreneurial manner.

Much to the contrary, Bishop David Oyedepo describes the vision of Covenant University (located in Ota, Ogun State, Nigeria) with the concept of Total Man: "This concept centers on developing the man who will develop his world. It is designed to produce students who are intelligently conscious of their environment and who know how to maximize their potentials in life. The programs of the University are first directed at the person before addressing his profession." He insists that the curricula would ensure "sound cultural and moral ethic, managerial and sensitive skills and self-development training designed to achieve integrated, holistic life-centered perspective."[6] The institution is built on a committed vision to raise a new generation of leaders with discipline and focus. Oyedepo's task is known as the Nehemiah Complex, rebuilding the education structure of the nation that has collapsed. He wants to reform the national tertiary educational ideology with a tailor-made concept that caters to the physical, spiritual, and psychological needs of mankind, a focused educational ideology designed to make extraordinary graduates out of the students. The institution graduated its first set of eight hundred students on July 28, 2006. The leader called them the first eagles, and tagged the event as the "release of eagles, "sent into the labor market and into the national institutions to provide solutions to its many problems from Christian moral values. This ideology weaves nationalism and religion into a tapestry just as Ethiopianism had done in an earlier period. The Pentecostals combine religious, moral, and political reasons in articulating the import of the Christian universities. Thus, the context of contemporary Christian education is characterized by an expanding demand for education, the dwindling resources of a contracting state, and a redemptive moral discourse and market discourse. With figures echoing Central University's growth, Covenant University opened its doors in 2003 with 1,360 students: 693 females and 667 males. The challenge remains how to provide an adequate faculty and funding to match the pace of growth. Central University, for instance, has invested enormous resources to send many of its faculty overseas to complete various programs in higher education. The sponsorship of its faculty in higher-degree programs is one of the centerpieces of its development planning.

The market for faith-based tertiary education is enormous because many church leaders do not have formal theological education and are hungry for it. For instance, a master's degree program designed for ecclesiastical leaders at the West African Theological Seminary, Lagos, was oversubscribed by bishops from Nigeria, Liberia, Sierra Leone, and Kenya. Daystar University's mission statement provides another reason for this development:

At Daystar, five African students can be educated for the cost of sending one student overseas. By educating committed leaders in an African context to address the needs and issues of the continent, Daystar is an important solution to Africa's "brain drain," reversing the loss of its talented young people. Daystar University provides some of the finest Christian education available in East Africa so its graduates are prepared to boldly lead communities, businesses and churches well into the 21st century.[7]

The Web site brags that many alumni are serving the nation in parliament, the education sector, relief agencies, and the entire society "with leadership rooted in Christian values." This statement combines two different arguments: First, it is cheaper and more useful to train leaders at home, since they could undertake such studies while still being employed in serving the church. Second, it harps on a typical theme that the problem of the continent is the lack of a leadership with a strong ethical orientation and adequate knowledge about the context of mission. It is, therefore, critical for these institutions to distinguish between entrepreneurial goals and Christian goals, especially because the cost of attending higher education institutions is high.

As universities grow, many of the mission statements posted on their Web sites may be challenged. For instance, Benson Idahosa University, Benin, has a vision to "raise an army of professionals and academics who would go in Christ's name to the ends of the world with the fire of the Holy Ghost to impart truth by precept and example." This leaves the impression that the university would remain engaged in training pastors. But recently, it decided to branch out into law, medicine, applied science, and management science. Obviously, narrow curricula could be self-defeating. But the concern is that many Christian institutions may find it difficult to maintain their Christian commitments when they turn into large universities.[8]

The negative dimension to this growth is that the culture of paper qualification is ingrained. Because a degree grants status, a pastor's doctorate degree becomes an essential sign of the quality of a church. In Nigeria, the National University Commission has approved about twenty church-related universities and many secular and Muslim ones in the last decade. Among the Christian universities, five are Roman Catholic Church–related, three are Anglican; there is one each for the Methodists, Baptists, Seventh Day Adventists, and the Evangelical Church of West Africa; and the rest are Pentecostal. Ghana has about eleven government-accredited degree-awarding institutions, most of which are church related. The trend of creating more church-related universities can be documented for the entire continent and is still spreading because many churches revamp old teachers' colleges and Bible colleges. The trend creates the problem of adequate funding, human resources, and academic integrity. The pattern of ministerial formation has been scrambled,

creating a trauma for African Christianity. Who could control all these institutions and ensure an accredited performance, a liberating curriculum, and an
adequate infrastructure? In 2000, the vice chancellors of five private universities met in Dar es Salaam to establish the Tanzania Association of Private
Universities to bring some order into the new system. Competition is rife among
the churches and hinders useful co-operation because the act of founding a
higher institution is the mark of a successful church in the African environment. A hopeful aspect for students is that after two surveys and accreditation
exercises in all Nigerian universities in 2005 and 2006, the national Universities' Commission declared that Covenant University ranked first among
twenty-four private universities and enjoyed as many accredited courses/pro-
grams as the best among the old-generation of federal government–funded
universities.

Finally, the classical Pentecostal churches used Bible school education to
form their ministries from an early stage. Many of these schools are not accredited by the host countries and this way of forming ministries has been copied
by the many branches of the Assemblies of God (AOG) and other indigenous
Pentecostal groups. Since the Pentecostals avoided World Council of Churches
and Vatican-related projects, they refused to be involved in continental projects
such as the Conference of African Theological institutions with their regional
branches. In time, some of the Bible schools were elevated to tertiary institutions. For instance, the American Assemblies of God has co-operated with sixteen African nations to run the East Africa School of Theology, Nairobi, and the
West Africa Advanced School of Theology (WAAST) in Togo. The Pentecostal
Assemblies of Canada operates the Pan Africa Christian College, Nairobi. All of
these basically offer bachelor's and master's degrees. Only The Apostolic Faith
Mission Theological Seminary in South Africa goes beyond this level. As
Kingsley Larbi argued, Pentecostal churches in Africa are just waking up to the
need for high-quality and accredited theological education.[9]

4. Mission as Re-Evangelization of Africa in the 1990s

In the 1990s, three crucial dimensions emerged in Pentecostal missionary
enterprise: an emphasis on re-evangelizing Africa based on revelations of
God's counsel on the continent, an intensified mission to Muslims and unreached people, and a strategy of manpower training through engagement in
the mission fields. The intensified pace of evangelization reimagined the
church as the presence, witness, representative, and foretaste of the kingdom
of God in communities. In its being, doing, and saying, the church affirms,
proclaims, teaches, and assists communities to experience and receive the gift
and resources of the Kingdom. This is the essence of *missio Dei*.[10] The church
has no other reason for existence than to continue the mission that Christ

started. From this perspective, the missionary engagement requires baptizing the cultures, nations, and peoples; unmasking the powers that dehumanize and deface people; and initiating a holistic engagement that is dialogical by identifying the signals of transcendence in cultures, affirming these, and bringing spiritual discernment to enable that people live truly human lives. This is a major shift in the style of doing mission. It is not about charity but a different style of presence. There were four types of presence:

1. the youthful charismatic insurgence into restricted Muslim areas;
2. the rise of the Intercessors for Africa;
3. the formation of evangelistic ministries that focused on neighboring regions; and
4. and the ministries that founded branches in other African countries.[11]

i. Mission to Muslim Enclaves

From the 1970s, the youthful, charismatic university students recovered a spirit of evangelization. Campaigns into Muslim enclaves and into unreached parts of the nations of Africa became a passion. Later, many ministries consolidated their visions to evangelize other African nations. This trend that has grown through the last three decades could be illustrated with about forty ministries based in Ghana, Kenya, and Nigeria. In Nigeria, the Calvary Ministries, known as CAPRO, was started by young southern Nigeria graduates who were posted by the National Youth Service Corps (NYSC) to serve in northern Nigeria during the mid-1970s. Both groups were connected with the Nigerian Fellowship of Evangelical Students. The initial goal was to minister to Muslims, a daunting task that collapsed. But they reorganized to include outreach to unevangelized ethnic groups in the north. Soon, the Missionary Crusades Ministry joined in the arduous task of reaching some of the sixteen identified unreached peoples in northern Nigeria. The mission to the Koma mountain people won national attention.

By the 1980s, CAPRO broadened its vision by sending missionaries to Gambia and the Muslim states of Senegal. In Gambia it cooperated with the British Worldwide Evangelization Crusade (WEC) missionaries. The WEC turned over the mission field to CAPRO. At about the same time, the Christian Missionary Foundation (CMF) was established in Ibadan (southwestern Nigeria). It, too, started evangelizing parts of the rural southwest and central Nigeria. Its strategy used agricultural projects and health-care delivery as entrée into communities. Soon, it sent missionaries to Cote d'Ivoire, Gambia, the Republic of Benin, and Liberia. In each place, it would assist the indigenes to form a local branch. For instance, in the Republic of Benin, Paul Zinsou started as a representative of CFM and later built a local group with about fifty-seven missionaries. Similarly, the CFM started the *Ministere de l'Evangelisation des Enfants pour l'Afrique Francophone en Cote d'Ivoire* and invited the partnership of a local church, *Eglise Evangelique de Reveil*. Other missionary groups, such as the Grace Evangelistic Mission, Harvesters Mission, and Children's Evangelism and Mission, sprouted. All these groups sent missionaries both internally and internationally within the West African coast.

By the late 1980s a number of Pentecostal ministries in Ghana started vigorous missionary activities along the Atlantic coast. The Ghana Evangelical Missionary Association, Christian Outreach Foundation (1987; church planting), African Christian Mission (1984; education), and Torchbearers (1987; medical work in Mali) are only a few. The picture is that African Pentecostals are crisscrossing the entire continent in vigorous evangelism: The African Christian Mission from Nigeria co-operated with Action Partners, formerly Sudan Interior Mission in sending missionaries to other African countries, the Deeper Life Bible Church created a ministry that forayed into other West African countries and catered to Burundi refugees in Dar es Salaam. The Church of the Pentecost in Ghana, and Redeemed Christian Church of God Mission in Nigeria have joined in various missionary enterprises. Malawi missionaries are laboring in northern Ghana just as Congolese Catholic fathers are working in Nigeria. I shall illustrate this further in the discussion about the television programs funded by The Redeemed Christian Church of God, The Deeper Life Bible Church, and the Christ Ambassadors in South Africa, Kenya, and many other African countries. The Christianity of refugee camps is another huge research topic because of the spate of civil wars in the last two decades in different parts of the continent. Many Liberian and Ivorian missionaries joined in the work among refugees. There has been a tendency toward the explosion of charismatic Christianity in many refugee camps.

ii. The Pentecostal Passion for Evangelism

A significant dimension of Pentecostal evangelism is the proliferation of missionary strategies among Pentecostals. This factor has been its source of strength. Evangelism is so significant in the lives of some groups that they hold a two-part worship service on Sundays. The first part ends with a teaching on evangelism and evangelistic materials are distributed through group leaders; then, believers go out to evangelize certain designated parts of the city. After three hours, they all return and report on the mission before the second part of the worship service follows. The whole day is virtually spent in the church. Traveling door-to-door; attending cottage meetings, crusades, and weekend retreats; doing ministry in motor parks, on buses, trains, street corners, and at healing camps are only a few innovative aggressive models. Everyone acknowledges the ubiquitous presence and heightened visibility of charismatic

Christianity and its message, which has elicited the competitive ardor among Muslims and other religious groups.

The outstanding strategy is the crusade. This is the weapon that has been forged to reach the hinterland rural areas and to mobilize teeming urban populations. During the Easter and Christmas periods, many believers living in urban areas mobilize funds to bring a powerful evangelist to their villages or clans. Huge billboards and leaflets decorated with a glossy photograph of the evangelist announce the event, urging everyone to return to the village. This is designed to counteract the materialism and commercialization of the yuletide and contest the indigenous rituals that are celebrated as recovenanting rituals during the epical point of the agricultural cycle, the New Yam Harvest festival. During the village crusade, the village leader or chief will be invited into the public square to hand over the land to the Christian God, who is the rightful owner, and to deliver the land from pollution caused by idol worship. The promise is that the ritual would liberate the indigenes from the bondage of covenants made with the spirits of the land, and would enable them to prosper in their jobs and businesses, to build ultramodern houses in the villages, to contribute to development projects, and to return every year with their own cars. The ability to return to the village with a personal car instead of depending on the chaotic public transportation system is a major goal for everyone, a veritable sign of success and a pride for the community. A car is a symbol rather than a mere means of transportation. Pentecostals have become the vanguard for reclaiming their heritage in the lands of their birth. Both in the rural and urban areas, every Pentecostal ministry and fellowship devotes a period in the year for a high-profile crusade that serves as a recruitment strategy. Intermittently, foreign ministries join the local sponsors. Reinhard Bonkee's ministry, Christ for All Nations (CFAN), has targeted Africa through crusades that draw millions. We are witnessing the enlargement of the crusades begun by the Evangelicals in the 1950s–1960s.

Another major feature of Pentecostal mission is the mission to unreached areas that have been bypassed by modernity. There are pockets of such small ethnic communities in each African nation. The isolation is often caused by the ecological factors, such as some of the people living in harsh mountainous regions. Others are mobile pastoral communities, or communities with very strong traditional cultures that resist the penetration of exogenous cultural forms, including world religions. Some Pentecostal ministries have mobilized resources to target such communities. In addition, the African missionary enterprise benefited from the campaign called "A.D. 2000 and Beyond" that encouraged many African missionary groups to pick up the gauntlet and expand evangelism. As the Ethiopianism movement of the 1890s intoned, Africans must evangelize Africa. Pentecostals set the goal of reenchanting the African religious landscape with a sense of certainty, religious experience, and lay commitment.[12]

5. Shifting Polities: Holistic Mission and Polity

i. Holistic Mission

In conclusion, we return to certain themes that were raised at the beginning of the chapter: Are Pentecostals practicing holistic mission that is sensitive to ecological ethics, social justice, and asymmetrical power relations? Are they sensitive to the fact that the freedom of the gospel is the liberating of people from "lordless powers," that the struggle against principalities and powers (archai kai exousiai) is not just spiritual but involves engagement and transformation of all institutions of society? What are the effects of the muscular evangelism on the polity? Some critics argue that Pentecostal spirituality is individualistic, private, mystical, ecstatic, and confined to the temple walls; that the movement not only encourages a biblical church at the service of God's kingdom whose purviews are narrowly defined, but also refuses to embrace the openness of the Spirit as God's agency in rescuing a grieving world. Others perceive the potential for empathy and mission to the poor, the marginalized, and those who suffer; that the resources for theologizing such an orientation are available within the Pentecostal spirituality; that salient social ethics could be designed and practiced. But as a wisecracker observed, Pentecostals prefer the prayer of Jabez, who asked God to rescue him from poverty, and ignore the prayer of Jesus that pointed to the obligation to respond to the needs of the wider society. Stephen Bevans's analysis of the content of contemporary missiology pointed to a growing sensitivity to issues of structural injustice and environmental protection. This raises a concern about the level of social sensitivity in the Pentecostal urge to evangelize Africa. Roswith Gerloff has argued that black churches in England are especially involved in social services and building the community because they are compelled by the poverty and racial discrimination against people of color.[13] A holistic conception of mission demands attention to both the spiritual and physical needs of the people of God and the salvation of the whole of creation that groans for redemption.

Others counter that the movement is young and has functioned in Africa for only two decades, therefore, it is still in its teething stage, consolidating in a terrain that has been dominated by the mission-founded churches and African Instituted Churches (AICs) for a long time; that the movement is deeply engaged in social services; that the Pentecostal community encapsulated in the terminology of "brethren" serves as a social security network that brings solace to a community of suffering. Megachurches provide employment for thousands in their industrial projects such as bakeries, laundry services, transportation, banking, electronics, construction, and many more. The NGO-ization of churches that grew with the collapse of the state economies and catalyzed the new trend in Western intervention in African countries implicated some Pentecostals churches. Pentecostals in countries such as Congo, Zambia,

Zimbabwe, and others incorporated agencies that participated in the governments' development projects and poverty alleviation interventions. For instance, True Redeemed Evangelical Mission in Lagos founded an NGO, the African Mission Committee, to "support the RCCG in reaching its vision for Africa in fulfillment of its end time mission of saving souls, particularly the oppressed and underprivileged; to eradicate poverty by providing self-enrichment courses and community development programs; to educate on and reduce the spread of the HIV/AIDs epidemic in many African countries."[14] The mission offers the less privileged a free educational and vocational training in artisan vocations such as soap making, barbering, hairdressing, and hair weaving. Their Redeemed Aids Program Action Committee (RAPAC) was specifically focused on the issue of HIV/AIDS. In recent times, the conditions in Africa have forced attention to health issues. Many charismatic groups have engaged HIV/AIDS prevention and care programs. The Africa House of Prayer held a conference on "healing Africa's diseases," which focused on using indigenous herbs such as *Phyllanthus Niruri/Amarus* to respond to the health needs of the continent.

The question still throbs whether they imagine the entire society or use the social services and their evangelism as means of growing their numbers. The evidence differs from one country to another because this is a movement that plays different roles at different times in different places. In some countries the movement has matured sufficiently to move beyond personal piety and personal concerns to engage social justice issues at the national level. An example comes from Uganda, where the government deliberately turned to Pentecostal churches to intervene in the rebellion and civil war prosecuted by the Lord's Resistance Army. The civil war has an ethnic and regional dimension as the Acholi people rebel against marginalization by a central government that has been dominated by a different ethnic group. For them it is a nationalist war of liberation garbed in religious symbols. It has been reported that the Pentecostal intervention brokered the peace overtures that produced a cease-fire and direct negotiation because President Museveni's government realized that a military solution was not possible. Matthew Ojo has demonstrated through the pages of the Christian Students' Social Movement of Nigeria publication, *The Way Out of Our Predicament: A Clarion Call on the Church* (December 1983), and other sources that the charismatic movement has sustained a critical attack on the state's social policies using the printed and electronic media.[15]

ii. Shifting Polities

The rapid growth of Pentecostalism catalyzed major shifts in polity and ecclesiology. It has often been argued that the Holy Spirit nurtures egalitarianism; that speaking in tongues is endowed with a democratizing principle; that the muscular evangelical thrust comes about through a valorization of the charismata, and has generated lay, participatory, charismatic fellowships in which the daily lives of members become the multiple sites for mission. Pentecostal preference for a charismatic-driven ecclesiology contests the hierarchical structures of the mission-founded churches that image the church as an organic reality where every member is taken up in the "whole of Christ." Pentecostals perceive a social and interpersonal body where every member is related to others and the Lord. Rather than seeing it as the universal church, Pentecostals image the church of Christ that has local assemblies and whose eschatology is futurist rather than fully realized. The egalitarian base of the movement feeds the voluntarist principle, mass appeal, and mass participation. It produces a muscular internal critique in the midst of an adoring loyalty to the leader. Many pastors cajole and threaten the members about the evil habit of gossiping about the pastor. They warn about judging another man's servant and doing harm to God's anointed. They are keenly aware of the powers of restrictive social control in holy gossips by the members. Mass appeal, and concerns for numbers and tithes produce rivalry and competition.

But the mass movement has its ecclesiological problems, namely, an unstable base. Many ministries adopt numerous encapsulation strategies to keep the members from straying to other churches. Some scholars have argued that Pentecostalism cannot generate democracy or serve as a "school" where people learn democratic ways precisely because leaders become controlling and dictatorial. Growth compels megachurches to develop corporate, modernized characteristics such as rational calculability (biggest is best); predictability of visible benefits, consumerism, systemization, and ritual and order; efficiency and bureaucratization, standardization of procedure, and concern for status, role, and differentiation of functions using committees and cell groups; and control of the spirituality of the people through enhancement with media and marketing strategies, lavish facilities, and communication technology. Critics have harped on the dangers of institutionalization and quantity-driven culture that silence the Holy Spirit. Happily, there are few Pentecostal megachurches in Africa located in urban areas that could compete with the decor of Roman Catholic cathedrals. Studies tend to focus on urban megachurches.

Growth has changed the leadership ethos. In the 1970s, the youthful charismatic movement deployed the concept of the priesthood of all believers as a strategy to pry open the ecclesiastical space, challenge the elders, and contest the monopoly and control mounted by the old mission churches. Within the next two decades, 1980–2000, a major shift in ecclesiology started at the top layer of the movement. The older generation of Pentecostal leadership institutionalized and sought new imageries for legitimizing their positions. At first, they exploited the iconic images of prophets and apostles with the task of mobilizing an end-time army. They mined the indigenous polities for images of leadership and family institutions for warm images, just as the

AICs had done. They turned to African American sources for new styles, and adopted the pursuit of doctorates, vestments, electronic preaching gadgets, and enlarged roles for the wives of pastors.

By the 2000s, Pentecostal practice shifted further to full-blown episcopacy. About five competing houses of bishops emerged in Nigeria alone. Rationalization runs into a number of grooves: biblicist (following the footsteps of icons in the Bible), restorationist (recovering the model of the early church), logistical (social control and order amid rapid growth), and pragmatic. A political motivation has been canvassed: When the government invites clerics for consultation, the bishops from the mission-founded churches quickly grab the leadership roles and show up in colorful garbs while the Pentecostals are treated as mere members of new religious movements. The pragmatic excuse is supported by the decision of formerly congregationalist Methodists to ordain bishops in the recovery of the polity of the early Christianity in Africa. Recently a debate has ensued among the African Presbyterians about episcopacy! Some of the peculiar requirements from the houses of bishops include possessing a doctorate degree (virtually always honorary), having branches in many towns and villages, building an impressive cathedral and bishop's court, and ordaining a number of pastors. This shift or great reversal in ecclesiology from an egalitarian to an episcopal structure has taken place within three decades under the banner that even God himself is not a democrat. But it not only challenges the full implications of the ancient doctrine of priesthood of all believers, but appears to be happening at the top while the base leadership remains intensely egalitarian and prominently lay. It is an open question whether the striving for the bishopric has increased the pace of evangelization or may centralize authority sufficiently to encourage a holistic mission. Undoubtedly, it fosters authoritarian personality types—a characteristic that runs through a number of African churches irrespective of denominational stripe. Personal loyalty to a pastor runs deep in many churches.

iii. Membership Structure

From a certain perspective, the shift in Pentecostal polity reflects the changes in the membership structure. Generally, membership is predominantly youthful and female. This is especially so in the rural villages. But there have been major changes in urban areas as professionals and adults have embraced the Pentecostal movement. Some parachurch groups, such as the Full Gospel Businessmen's Fellowship International and Gideons Bible International, have targeted professionals and have successfully contested the growth of humanistic sodalities such as Rotary Club and Lion's Club in Africa. The town dwellers, in turn, sponsor the outreaches in their village homelands. Some have argued that the collapse of the economies encouraged many professionals to seek solace in a spirituality that proffered the prospects of recovery. Beyond the pleasant sounds of prosperity gospel, Pentecostal ethics empowered survival through the inculcation of self-control, discipline, initiative, aspiration, mutual self-help, economic thrift practices, spiritual healing, ethics of trustworthiness, cleanliness, psychological cleansing from insidious corruption, and wholeness through the expulsion of unruly spirits. Pentecostals erected strong boundaries by recovering the dualistic imagery of light and darkness. Peter Althouse argued that the character of Pentecostal spirituality holds the clue in analyzing Pentecostal ethics; that Pentecostal spirituality operates like a rhetorical device, a cipher indicating the insertion of a confirmatory, differing, or contradictory opinion in a conversation. It is like an appeal to be heard, a counter-appeal to authoritative voices. It rejects the claims of failure and hopelessness; it replaces ideology, cant, and theory by inserting a conviction that there is an exit that lies beyond oneself and through a structure of consciousness.[16] As one chorus puts the matter, "Whose report shall we believe? We believe in the report of the Lord!" It proceeds to affirm the Lord's desire to counter the evidence and effects of economic collapse.

Pentecostal optimism has been a strong weapon in changing the social structure of Christian membership. Some of the early class analysis of the membership no longer holds up because the movement includes membership at all levels of society. The mobilization of youths and women has been crucial. In the universities, many academics patronize the charismatic ministries and are playing important roles in the parachurches. This geological shift in the character of membership in the 1980s catalyzed the rationalization of polity because the problem of discipline, authenticity, and the exploits of fake adventurers threatened the reputation of the movement. The issue of grace and malpractice is a significant aspect of the critical profile of contemporary Pentecostalism. This explains the formation of national associations to provide a measure of control within the movement. Many cases have shown that such associations have only moral clout and lack enforcement instruments. But in each country, Pentecostal churches have formed one or two umbrella associations to serve as pressure groups and to instill discipline among the members.

6. Charisma and Money

The discussion on Pentecostal missionary practice raises a major question related to money: How do Pentecostals finance the vigorous evangelistic enterprise? There are two cogent reasons for raising these questions. First, the maturity of the movement in Africa is demonstrated by the self-funding capacity of many of the Pentecostal churches. Some of the incautious literature canvased Western sources of funding and dependency models even as many African churches struggled to promote independence by paying honorarium to visiting pastors, asserting their independence while forging links that could aid the funding of projects and exchanging of pulpits. Second, charisma and scandalous malpractice are close neighbors. It could be that intrinsically, the charismatic mood creates a degree of exuberance that could overflow the boundaries of the moral control system. Accountability arises from the youthfulness of the movement, while a lack of precedence, structure, and ethos, and the revered presence of the founder are found in a culture with a strong deference ethos. The polity of mainline churches provides both a social control mechanism and a means of damage control when a scandal occurs. Pentecostal polity is characterized by a democratizing influence of charisma, the regular diet of diatribe against the worldly ethics of other churches, and the privileging of holiness consequent on the emphasis on the Holy Spirit. These combine to ensure that any scandal among the brethren will enthrall the public, elicit screaming and exaggerated headlines, attract the hostile attention of opponents, and may lead some young believers to backslide out of disillusionment.

Scandals such as betrayal, hypocrisy, abrogation of religious authority, and affront against the goals of the ministry could be quite devastating and have led to schism and the total collapse of many ministries. It is often very difficult to sweep a scandal under the rug since some moderates would use some Pauline verses to restore the erring brethren, while ardent ones would counteract with other Pauline verses to insist that the brethren should not eat with the offender. Three issues have caused the highest number of scandals in churches, namely, money, sexual misdemeanors, and fake anointing. An example of all three issues is the case of the flamboyant Kenyan televangelist Archbishop Gilbert Deya, noted for his "miracle baby" ministry in the United Kingdom and Kenya, in which he promised infertile women they could bear children after his groups prayed for the women. In 2004, it was alleged that the high-profile, high-living pastor was engaged in a child trafficking syndicate, when it was reported that babies stolen from Kenya were taken to Great Britain in order to make the previously infertile British women think they'd given birth to a healthy baby. One of London's newspapers, the *Evening Standard*, on Friday, November 12, 2004 reported that the judge in the case described Deya as a man driven by ruthless financial greed to hurt many women desiring babies.

There are two dimensions to the problem of money and malpractice: Evangelization is a cost-intensive enterprise in the modern period. To focus on the offering plate and the lifestyle of the few successful pastors distorts interpretation. But the average African Pentecostal invests a larger share of earned income in ministries and missionary projects than their compatriots in the West. Robert Garner argues that in South Africa, Pentecostals and Apostolic Christians give a higher percentage of their income than many in mainline churches and Zionists. Since Pentecostals foster the old evangelical voluntarism and are outside the ruling corridors, they lean less on state funding, foster a certain sense of survival, and pursue skill acquisition that will open the economy for God's blessings. One migrant congregation often prayed that God would open the gates of the hard city for them prosper within it. Few studies have compared the real wealth of mission-founded churches with the new wealth of Pentecostals. Andrew Walls observed that

> the view is sometimes expressed that the recent growth of Pentecostal forms of Christianity in many parts of Africa is a product of a new North American missionary presence backed by massive North American money. The studies do not support this view. North American Pentecostal mission in Africa had only a modest impact until the indigenous Pentecostal movement began. African Pente-costalism is very much aware of its world links, reads the North American literature and invites North American preachers, but it is financially self-supporting.[17]

Money matters are important in the ministry. Resource capability often determines what a church can achieve, and its identity, public profile, and growth potential. This is why many ministries cluster in urban areas. Strangely, many commentators describe the Pentecostals' rapid growth, use of media, crusades, and expansive infrastructure without paying attention to the costs. The incorrect outsider perspective or impression is that pastors grow churches just for the money. However, one should realize that money and human re-sources enhance the churches' capacity to witness. But money could also be-tray the moral underbelly of a Christian group, because accountability and honest service are connected to faithful stewardship. Pentecostals affirm that when the Holy Spirit calls and sends, He will supply the material needs to fulfill the mission. But churches do not sit down and wait for the manna; rather, they engage in a number of strategies to raise funds. Aggressive, in-novative fund-raising strategies jar prominently against the inherited tradi-tions of mission-founded denominations.

Funding strategies differ among various types of Pentecostals. Fellowships have a different membership base and raise funds differently. For instance, parachurches such as Women's Aglow, Full Gospel Business Men's Fellow-ship International (FGBFMI), and The Gideons Bible International raise monies differently. All three recruit members from mainline churches and insist that membership should be open only to those who are fully and actively engaged in church assemblies. They perceive themselves as "extensions" of the missionary activities of churches and, therefore, encourage members to pay tithes to local assemblies according to the Word. To cover the costs of their operations, FGBMFI and Women's Aglow "promote offering" by using scrip-tural verses to exhort members to give generously. They also encourage mem-bers to underwrite the cost of projects. Many company directors use grants from their companies to fund projects or pay for breakfast prayer meetings.

These groups contribute to the coffers of the international headquarters instead of getting any financial assistance themselves.

The Gideons Bible International in Africa, however, started by receiving free Bibles donated by various camps from the United States. Some African nations have now grown to the point that they could pay for their Bibles. The organization is divided into camps and zones and each zone sets a financial target for itself and may achieve it by levying its members. At weekly prayer meetings, each camp will collect offerings for purchasing Bibles. Members could also give thanksgiving offerings. It is mandatory for each camp to organize visits to the Protestant churches to raise money for Bibles, and to encourage believers to give money for Bibles in honor of those celebrating rites of passage such as baptism, confirmation, birthday, marriage, age- grade outings, promotions, and funerary rites. Glossy cards are used to congratulate and inform the honoree about the "placing of the Bible." Friends are encouraged to pay for Bibles to be distributed free during a celebration, festival, or a funeral instead of sending flowers.

Ministries that are engaged in mission to unreached peoples or to other culturally contiguous regions raise funds differently. These charismatic ministries fund themselves by asking the prospective missionaries to source their funds from a group of supporters/partners. Generally, the ministries depend on the faith of the missionary and pay low stipends and honoraria to missionaries to be supplemented by other mission partners. A "gospel bankers" group was formed in Jos (the plateau region of Nigeria) to assist missionaries to the unreached peoples.[18] Missionary outreaches engaged in reaching the previously unreached, witnessing among Muslims, or operating in other African countries through missionary associations that encourage professionals to offer short-term free services at cost. Doctors, nurses, teachers, and others went to a number of war-torn African countries as led and sustained by the Spirit. Some of the intracontinental missionaries are linked with the Third World Mission Association that was inaugurated in Portland, Oregon, in 1989; others with World Link University, an education project. A couple of Africans serve as executives of these associations, but these are not funding agencies.

One genre of Pentecostal scholarship has focused in a journalistic manner on the wealth and lifestyle of some leaders of the new-generation churches. It focuses on urban ministries, especially the mega types, ignores the rural-based ministries, and notes the wide differential among the ministries. The founders are referred to as "founder-owners," so as to suggest that they collect and control the finances and live comfortably, often flaunting their wealth in an obscene manner. Others have focused on the cost-intensive, innovative missionary strategies that emphasize the self-reliance motif and demonstrate that the ministries have structured polities that ensure a reasonable degree of accountability. Afe Adogame examined the funding strategy of the Redeemed

Christian Church of God (a predominantly urban megachurch in Nigeria) from this perspective to show that it funds huge projects and sends millions of dollars from Nigeria to pay for land purchases and television programs in the United States.[19] Until recently, Christ's Embassy Church with headquarters in PortHarcourt, Nigeria also remitted thousands of dollars per month to the United States to pay for television time.

The money situation is explained from the vision and focus of the new Christianity that is preeminently concerned with success, plenty, and victory, and believes that there is a connection between mood, charisma, materialist theology, and money. The conclusions are drawn from the fascination of the prosperity gospel comprising some questionable practices. The emphasis on wealth and money produced rituals such as employing the covenant hand-shake anointing the mantle or white handkerchief; conferring double anoint-ing; blessing instruments of destiny that signify work tools such as pens for teachers, scissors for dressmakers, pliers for electricians, and hammers for construction workers; and washing the feet of believers so that they could step into wealth, victory, and promotions. It is acknowledged that all Pentecostals are not prosperity preachers, and that many offer self-help seminars for wealth generation and skill acquisition and education.

The connection between money and charisma is a gray area precisely because it could encourage fakes. There is no attempt here to join the affray in defense or otherwise. Rather, the argument here is that the picture of depen-dency on Western sources for sustaining Pentecostal mission in Africa distorts the reality. However, there is a consensus that foreign assistance could be beneficial and should be sought. As some say: "God's work must be done by God's money. God's money comes from the God's people. And God's people are everywhere." International partners are appreciated because Pentecostal growth is cost intensive and the pace challenges the resource capacity of members.

Indeed, a closer look shows two aspects: First, many international evan-gelists based in the United States do not fund local ministries in foreign countries. A visit to Lagos by Benny Hinn in 2005 caused a furor and revealed much. Someone in Hinn's ministry made a careless statement that the min-istry spent about $4 million on the outreach, implying the local organizers were laughing and praising their God to the banks. The Pentecostal Fellowship of Nigeria waded into the scandal only to discover that Hinn's ministry said that it brought equipment worth $3 million that was shipped back to the United States after the outreach, and that it collected much of the offerings while leaving the hapless host with debts. The major organizer had, in fact, mortgaged some church property to fund the program.

However, some ministries receive financial assistance for projects from the Western world. There are evangelical ministries in the West that believe in sending funds to indigenous ministers rather than going into the mission fields by themselves, and because the local people are expected to do a better job. This is an evangelical effort to reshape missions for a new age. Others send short-term missionaries to serve as partners with the indigenous missionaries. Among Classical Pentecostals, there has been a tendency to support theological education projects while retreating from direct missionary engagement or funding the recurrent expenses of overseas churches. This support is sometimes connected with organizational structures. Many Classical Pentecostal denominations have autonomous congregations.

Second, African Pentecostals have for the most part subscribed to the three-self formula. Antidependency ethos is matched with innovative strategies for raising funds from internal sources. Soon, tithing acquired the status of a cardinal doctrine. Tithing ceases to be about money but about obedience to the Word, and people are encouraged to tithe from gross earnings, before the government takes taxes, and to tithe more than 10 percent of their earnings as a sign of commitment and covenanting with God. Pentecostals took over many of the fund-raising strategies of the mission churches, rejected some, substituted others, and devised more ingenious additions.

For instance, Pentecostals reject the notion of paying dues and raising money through bazaars. But they celebrate the church calendar that replaces the festivals in the agricultural cycle with harvest and thanksgiving celebrations, and they observe special days for mothers, fathers, children, and other arms of the church. Pentecostals celebrate the rites of passage and the agricultural cycle by encouraging members to make special offerings during the sacred periods. Each of these would be an occasion for raising money and targeting the funding of specific projects. On Pastor's Appreciation Sunday, members shower their pastor and family with gifts, and are encouraged to pledge to God, pay their vows, and to thank God with costly gifts and freewill offerings. Special prophecy may require an open invitation for members to be anointed for gaining wealth so that they can give back to God and thereby fund projects. Such special powerful prayers elicit grateful responses. Here, the costs for attending prayer-healing camps have attracted negative attention, although there is no study that confirms such concerns. Much to the contrary, it is said that people resort to spiritual healing because it is cheaper than Western medical facilities, and therefore, proliferation of faith healing may be an index of the collapse of health-care delivery in a nation.

Because many of its leaders are professionally trained, many Pentecostal organizations are able to invest in wealth-generating businesses that also provide jobs for members. Beyond self-help seminars, the educational ideology is skewed toward skill acquisition. Many organizations operate computer-training facilities, and, as a result, the computer and business technical courses offered in the evening and weekend programs yield the bulk of the funds for Pentecostal universities. Some ministries have used bank loans to finance crusades, university projects, and leadership conferences. Many such projects depend on donations from wealthy patrons and politicians, which raises awkward questions about church connection to money earned from fraudulent and illegal enterprises. A few scandals have linked such people to Pentecostal churches to the amusement of those in yellow journalism.

On the whole, Pentecostal critics have been most hostile against the seed of faith method of raising funds that is borrowed from North America. As mentioned earlier, this method could nurture corruption and a lack of accountability. Many churches generate funds through the sale of a variety of embossed materials and publications. These strategies for funding raise the problem of accountability and commodification of the gospel, and feed the rumor mills against Pentecostal pastors. It is the temper of spirituality that sustains the level of giving that occurs in Pentecostal churches. Ironically, mission-founded churches are now borrowing the Pentecostal strategies. African Presbyterians now tithe!

7. Money and Malpractice

There are a number of reasons for the attention on the new Christianity and its malpractice over money matters. As the new kids on the block who have quickly made good, the older ones watch them like hawks watching a young chick. The first attraction is the Pentecostals' unabashed teaching on money. By insisting that money is not the problem but rather the love of money that is the problem, it appears to have either opened a floodgate that could be misused, or affirmed similar values to the secular world. This opens the discussion on whether there are intrinsic Pentecostal values that encourage capitalist ethics and attitude toward money. Whether its embrace of modernity, popular culture, exuberance, youthful character, reflected in liturgical freedom and experimentation with musical styles attract individuals who are energized to pursue wealth and embrace capitalist ethics. Of course, the range of teachings includes the perception of money as an instrument for mission and cure for poverty, deprivation, vulnerability, and protection from the consequences of mismanaged political economy. Money may be connected to salvation precisely because wealth is a component of the divine economy. Pentecostal preachers assert that in spite of the doctrine of redemptive suffering, Jesus fed multitudes; that He stopped the law of nature to ensure that the multitudes did not faint on their way home. He performed a miracle with few fishes and loaves.

However, the flamboyant lives of the new generation of pastors jar prominently with the puritan ethics of the 1970s and the emphasis among establishment churches. Quite crucial is the variety of the state's regulatory capacity over church finances. The environment within churches is usually laissez-faire. Churches are exempted from taxation, their financial records are not examined. The state's constitutional guarantees protect them from state financial oversight, and churches are registered with the state as charities. In addition, umbrella associations among Pentecostal groups lack the legal mandate to interfere with the affairs of members. The air of independence, freedom, and existence beyond the regulatory capacity of any body feeds the street radio with gossip about the wealth of new-generation churches.

Asonzeh Ukah's research in Cameroon is instructive because the state monitors the finances of Pentecostal churches. It insists that "religious congregations shall keep an account of their revenue and expenditure and draw up an annual financial account for the past year and an inventory of their moveable and immoveable property."[20] Officials of such churches are obliged to present their records for inspection at the impromptu request of the minister in charge of territorial administration. Pentecostal leaders perceive a deliberate policy of harassment because Pentecostalism arrived late in Cameroon, has a strong Anglophone background, was founded there largely by Nigerians. The state uses security forces to control the proliferation of churches and ensure that the foreigners are not using the church as a subterfuge for commercial profiteering. In many African countries, the majority of Pentecostal and charismatic ministries are unregistered with the state. But research also highlighted the difficulty that a researcher can hardly gain access to the account ledgers of ministries, leaving much of our contentions imprecise. Suspicions of malpractice abound because, as Ukah postulates, there is a distinction between the "front region" and "back region" activities where the former describes official social encounters where persons carry out socially acceptable formal performances, and the latter describes maneuvers and subterfuges. The great interest shown by big ministries in establishing banks and insurance companies cuts both ways: They are entrepreneurial in growing their ministries and may be making a different statement about money and may promote the logic of the market.

More important, we need to know whether the experience of Korea is repeating itself in Africa. There, the entrepreneurial character of Christianity has unleashed a measure of social disillusion because it threatens the ethics of holiness and the moral boundaries that separate the religious and secular worlds. The Pentecostal fellowships in Africa are cognizant of the challenge and hold seminars on appropriate business ethics for born-again Christians. But many wonder whether the power of wealth generation and the environment of doing business in the continent will taint the saints. Many are concerned about the relationship between magic moments of healing and money. Are the healing miracles contrived and faked? The attempts to ban them from national television emanated from such concerns, though the Pentecostals invoke the persecution from Satan and his human agents. "Money and malpractice" is a lively feature of Pentecostal magazines and Web sites because of a habit of self-criticism.

8

Gendered Charisma

Charisma and Women in African Pentecostalism

1. Introduction

This chapter continues the discussion on Pentecostal missionary practice by focusing on another major question related to women: Do Pentecostals adequately conceptualize and utilize the resources of women? How do women theologize the feminine roles in the African Christianity and especially in the Pentecostal movement? What is the impact of Pentecostal missionary impulse on gender ideology? Does the Spirit-driven temper dissolve patriarchy? Instrumentalist analysis has argued in the literature that the Pentecostal atmosphere is friendly toward women, who make up the bulk of the membership. But what about the underlying gender ideology that determines access to ritual and administrative power? The first step is to clarify the distinctions about Pentecostal image of womanhood. Pentecostal discourse navigates various realms of the gender discourse: the domestic realm, ritual power, ecclesial participation or women's role in the public sphere, and the possibilities of gender partnership in the Pentecostal ministry.

Second, we should draw a distinction between African and the Western contexts, where women operated more freely during the early days of the movement but were reined into submission. All over the world, prominent and fiery female preachers and administrators assisted the spread of the movement.[1] It was one of the features of early Pentecostalism that angered the fundamentalists and fueled their virulent attacks. This forced the restriction of women's ritual power that was installed based on some Pauline verses of terror. Exclusion of women consolidated a patriarchal ideology.

Third, we place Pentecostal feminist theology within the larger framework of Christian feminist theology. This should profile the loyalist posture more clearly.

2. Charisma and Women: Founders, Sisters, First Ladies, and Jezebels

Patriarchy is the government of the fathers. It suffused the Hebrew religion and society, Victorian morality, and African indigenous religions and cultures. Mercy Oduyoye argues that patriarchy in African Christianity could be traced through language, culture, theology, and ecclesiastical practices, and that the church borrows its practices from the society. She nuanced the variations in Africa by distinguishing between theory and practice among patrilineal and matrilineal kinship societies.[2] The mission-founded churches were built on patriarchal gender ideology. The African Instituted Churches (AICs) may be presumed to have opened the space for women. But on a closer look, despite the fact that female prophetesses and founders exercised ritual and administrative powers, women were still restricted through the enforcement of Levitical prohibitions and gender ideology sourced from indigenous society. Not only have African female theologians approached the gender discourse with a plurality of voices, Pentecostal gender study have also benefited from the larger discourse.

There are four prominent categories of female discourses within African Pentecostalism: founders, sisters, first ladies, and jezebels. There are female founders who exercise more power than females in male-founded churches. Many of them who specialize in healing and deliverance ministries are taken seriously because these are the roles played by women in indigenous religions. I shall illustrate with a few cases. Since the 1970s, ministries and churches founded by women have multiplied all over Africa.

In Kenya, Margaret Wangare started having religious experiences such as dreams and visions when she was in high school in Banana Hill, Kiambu District, in 1974. She was a member of the student revival movement at the time. She operated as an itinerant revival evangelist before she founded her own church. Her ministry involved faith healing and the preaching of salvation and revivalism. Initially she operated in her parent's compound, but later she traveled all over the country from the 1980s until today. She is now the presiding bishop of the Church of the Lord. In 1980, Wangare underwent theological education in the All Nations Bible School in Benin City, Nigeria, under the tutelage of the late archbishop Benson Idahosa, founder of the Church of God Mission International. Other recent founders of charismatic churches and interdenominational ministries in Kenya are Margaret Wanjiru, of Jesus Is Alive Ministries (1993), and Teresia Wairimu, of Faith Evangelists Ministries (1989). These female leaders have managed to empower fellow women who have established churches elsewhere.

In Nigeria, Bolaji Olayinka has commented on the increase in female-founded Charismatic/Pentecostal churches, particularly in Yorubaland since the 1970s. Typical is Dorcas Olayinka, who founded the Agbala Daniel Church in 1979, after several religious experiences were interpreted as signs of her call to ministry. She is currently the archbishop of her church, which has opened several branches in Nigeria and New Jersey, and holds a master of divinity degree. Another female church founder is Stella Ajisebutu, minister of Water from the Rock Church (Faith Covenant Church), whose religious experiences and activities as leader of a prayer group started while she was a university student. In 1999 she established her church under God's command.[3] Analyzing the role of female leaders in the new generation churches, Olanyiki poignantly states that these women have become effective role models in promoting equality between men and women in church and society. They have given credence to the view that "failure to make use of women's potentials represents a serious under utilization of human resources and abilities for the development of human society."[4]

The female leaders are renowned just like those of an earlier generation for faith healing, pastoral care that is gender specific, motherly concern for their adherents, and capacity to inspire and support other women in the ministry. Many of these churches have established Bible schools for training pastors, and college enrollment comprises a sizable number of female trainees. Their promotion of theological education is a radical departure from leadership in the spiritual AICs, which are purely based on charisma, and end up being ceremonial. Until the 1980s only men would acquire theological training and hence become evangelists in AICs such as the Twelve Apostles, while women would be confined to the roles of healers and prophetesses. The AICs still limit the role of women by sourcing their gender ideology from traditional society. Charismatic and Pentecostal groups have provided a larger space, though some groups still debate women's sanctuary roles. Explanations for providing the enlarged space include the fact that many of the women are educated and operated in universities with their male counterparts. Some even acquired proficiency through Full Gospel Business Men's Fellowship International, which admits female membership, unlike its counterpart in the United States. Sodalities like Women's Aglow have also equipped many. Some women trained alongside their husbands and ministers. Indeed, it is quite fashionable for couples to found and minister together. As in the case of Benson Idahosa, his wife inherited the mantle of leadership at his death.

In Malawi, Bishop Mercy Yami is another example of a founder and leader of a charismatic ministry. Born in 1950, she had her spiritual formation in the

Keswick movement, which was introduced to Malawi through revival meetings, and was organized by the Evangelical Christian Association. She became "born again" in 1976 and was discipled in the Assemblies of God until 1978, when she started working part-time for "New Life for All," a fellowship established in Blantyre to nurture new converts in the faith.[5] In 1978, during an Easter Fellowship, she rededicated her life to God and was called to preach whenever she found people, whether they were on the streets, in prisons, or were blind and destitute. In accepting this call, she had to choose between evangelism and marriage, and consequently left her marriage. In 1994 she started Zodabwitsa (Miracles) ministry at Chilomoni in Blantyre, and later teamed up with a certain charismatic male simply known as Pastor Lumwira to establish Blessed Hope Church. Bishop Mercy Yami (meaning "Jesus in me") became the office director while Pastor Lumwira was the field director. Bishop Yami's work involved overseeing pastors' training, managing the finances, and grounding new converts in the Word. Soon a controversy started because Pastor Lumwira was not comfortable with female leadership. He claimed that female leadership was contrary to biblical teaching. They parted ways in 1995 and she founded "The Love of God Church." This leadership dispute is quite common among Pentecostal churches. Sometimes, opposition to female ritual leadership is voiced; at other times, a highly visible female organizational leadership is resented. Men tend to use the Bible to justify women's exclusion or relegation to the periphery. However, some Pentecostal churches, like Vine Branch Church and Christ Life Church in Nigeria, have numerous female priests.[6] Churches like Redeemed Christian Church of God, Winners Chapel International, and Lighthouse Church offer prominent roles for women as wives of pastors, evangelists, pastors, and even heads of departments.

The story of Margaret Wanjiru, founder of Jesus Is Alive Ministry in Nairobi, has been told by Philomena Mwaura of Kenyatta University, Nairobi. Wanjiru is a dynamic evangelist and pastor of a megachurch. She was born in 1961 into a polygamous family in Thika District, Kenya, and had a rough childhood. Her father was an alcoholic. The family moved into the Kangemi slums in Nairobi where Wanjiru's mother brewed illicit gin to sustain the family financially and to pay the children's fees in the local Anglican school. Wanjiru often tells her life story during her sermons, and says that she was initiated into witchcraft at a tender age through a strange man who came to their house when her sister fainted and was presumed dead. The mysterious man brought her sister back to life and became a regular visitor to their home. By Wanjiru's teenage years, both sisters had become wayward. At sixteen years of age, Margaret became pregnant. She describes the father as "a man I hardly knew. He ducked soon after and reappeared a year later. Before I could figure out what was eating me, I was pregnant again despite all the counseling and cautioning by my mother." While Wanjiru's mother cared for the two children, Margaret finished elementary school, worked as a cleaner, enrolled in a course in marketing, and rose through the job ranks by selling Marlboro cigarettes. As a beautiful model, she smoked and lived in the fast lane until she lost her job after throwing coffee on her boss. She got a new job with a Non-Governmental Organization (NGO) and decided to acquire wealth by all means. She joined satanic cults and attained a high degree known as Red Witchcraft. She competed with a young, Christian woman over the control of a business enterprise and wanted to eliminate the opposition through witchcraft. She failed. Instead,, a measure of emptiness in her soul combined with an inexplicable event to change her life.

Wanjiru attended a crusade by the Nigerian evangelist Emmanuel Eni at the Uhuru Park, Nairobi, in March 1990. Eni is famous all over Africa as a former Satanist who converted to Pentecostalism. His book detailing his sojourn has sold millions. His ministration at the crusade was so powerful that, despite Margaret's resisting the self-abasing altar call, she later paid the evangelist a modern-day version of Nicodemus's private visit, confessed her seamy past, was delivered, and started a new faith journey. She gave up all her possessions and joined an evangelistic group World Intercessory Ministry and itinerated widely as an evangelist, ministering in South Africa and other neighboring African countries. Finally, she started the Jesus Is Alive Ministry in Nairobi in September 1993. Later, Bishop Arthur Kitonga affirmed the calling by ordaining Wanjiru in 1997 and elevating her to the bishopric in 2002. Her vision included the revival of Africa by rebuilding the nation and cultivating a devotional life of humility. As soon as her ministry was growing, terrorists struck Kenya near her church in 1998. She joined in ministering to the victims and became a highly visible beacon of hope to many. She utilized the print media, radio, and television effectively. A beautiful woman who resembles Kathryn Kulmann's theatrical mannerism, she draws a crowd of about five thousand people into the Sunday morning service and holds twenty-two other services during the week. Her facilities are ultramodern and the liturgy is carefully packaged. Still her forte is the emphasizing spiritual warfare and deliverance ministry. Her magazine, *Faith Digest*, and television program, *Healing the Nation*, have touched many lives.

Helen Ukpabio in Lagos is also engaged in deliverance ministry. Her story goes back to the early 1980s when she finished her primary education and lived as a housekeeper in the home of a lecturer at the University of Calabar, southeastern Nigeria. The university is located close to the headquarters of the Brotherhood of Cross and Star, a messianic AIC founded by Olumba Obu Olumba (aka OOO). One day she strayed into the worship service. Before she knew it, the wardens grabbed her after the service and said that the leader wanted her. She was detained inside the sanctum because the leader said that Satan wanted to marry her, and she was to be groomed for this. At some point she was sent to a maternity hospital, where she would participate in collecting the blood of babies and initiating others into witchcraft. She was admitted as a nursing student without passing an examination. Later, she was delegated to attack a Pentecostal evangelist, Omoba Jesu, who held an outreach in Uyo. The encounter between the two is an intriguing story in her book, *The Seat of Satan Exposed* (1992). In the end, the preacher "arrested" her and delivered her. She became engaged to a lecturer and preacher and started a ministry. She itinerated to tell her story in Full Gospel conferences and finally opened a flourishing deliverance ministry in Lagos. Her colorful, huge posters adorn the city.

In Ghana, Christy Doe Tetteh, pastor and founder of Solid Rock Chapel, located in North Kaneshie, Accra, is a highly respected deliverance minister, who is nicknamed Fireball by her colleagues. Her journey is connected to the career of the Nigerian pastor Benson Idahosa. When Idahosa visited Accra in 1978, Tetteh was a receptionist in the Riviera Hotel, where the preacher lodged. She was a Roman Catholic who later answered the altar call at Idahosa's crusade. Idahosa invited her to Nigeria where she enrolled in his All Nations Bible School, from which she graduated in 1982, and became a secretary in the flourishing Church of God ministry. Tetteh says that from 1983 to 1989 God kept promising to use her mightily if she returned home. But the crash of the Ghanaian economy induced her disobedience until 1989. Since then, as claimed in her house magazine, *Solid Rock*, she has healed and delivered many, and their testimonies adorn the pages. Her style is the bold style of her mentor, who built his cathedral in a bush regarded as being possessed by demons, and who proclaimed that he was "sitting on the devil"! Tetteh dubs her prayer band Striking Force, and she attracts a couple of thousands of worshipers in her regular services.

These three women—Margaret Wanjiru, Helen Ukpabio, and Christy Doe Tetteh—have challenged the conservative segment of Pentecostalism that restricts the level of a woman's ritual status. There are many others like them in each nation, though scholarly attention has been lavished on male-governed churches.[7] The ministries of the women emphasize deliverance, which they interpret as part of the Divine plan for them and legitimized by an encounter with God either through a conversion experience or through a subsequent endowment with divine power that manifests itself in the ability to heal and deliver from demonic powers.

Generally, Pentecostal and charismatic movements recognize "sisters" and give women who are endowed with charismatic gifts the opportunities to minister those gifts at the ritual level without challenging the patriarchal base of the polity. This has enlarged the female role. Variations abound because some Pentecostal churches are so literalist in their reading of the Bible that they exclude women from the pulpit. However, commentators observe that women join the charismatic movements as vantage points for challenging the old, male-dominated order, patriarchal ancestor cults, and indigenous religions. The demonization of indigenous religions, traditional spirits, and possession cults is liberating and enables these women to contest the holy sites that are usually cordoned off against them and uninitiated youths. Women are particularly zealous in evangelism. For instance, a large percentage of those engaged in transnational mission within Africa are women, either as single women or as pastors' wives. In the mission fields they have an untrammeled space to exercise full responsibilities—just as it happened to missionaries' wives in the colonial era and other women during the faith movement in the West. Other specialized ministries within a church, such as the music ministry, prayer cells, and so forth enable women to manifest their gifts and give input in policy decisions. Some churches are more open to women's input than others: Some permit women to preach to the whole congregation, while others restrict their teaching to cell groups. The eclectic nature of Pentecostal theology in Africa creates the niches that could be exploited by some women who were perhaps stakeholders in the foundation of a ministry.

In Pentecostal churches, the pastor's wife, or first lady, serves as a nodal power point for mobilizing and deploying female evangelical power. V. M. Mackenzie provides a typology based on black churches in the United States, which is where the status of first ladies emerged. Some pose as the "queen leader" who takes charge and rules some segments of the church. The men give her much space because she is the adviser and partner of the founder. Today, it has become fashionable to give television time to the pastor's wife. These women image family values and a certain theology. But in this model, the queen's dress and front pew seat in the church make a statement of her importance in the life of the congregation.

Some other styles women adopt include that of "the mama," a woman who lovingly organize everyone. No one can refuse anything she requests. Some adopt "the wise woman" persona, the sage who advises everyone and has a word of comfort to dispense. "The sister/girlfriend" is usually very active and hands-on, engaged and involved in activities alongside everyone else. Critics argue that while "the first lady" can be helpful, she also perpetuates a myth that could distract a ministry. As the media packages the images of the pastor, the first lady also becomes more visible. Many acquire theological training and take over the ministry after their husbands. Female succession has caused splits within many churches.

The instrumentalist discourse has avoided the negative discourse about women as jezebels. "Preying pastors" who fall into sexual sins usually avoid taking personal responsibility by alleging that "Jezebel" attacked and seduced them in order to ruin their successful ministries. The explanation of causality by appeal to demonic attack is deployed to explain sexual immorality. Pastors pretend that the enemy counterattacks against any ministry that confronts and delivers people from the kingdom of hell. As pastors would intone, "Light the fire and a viper would appear!" The enemy attacks a ministry by sending a woman in the guise of an active believer, but whose mission is actually to seduce the leader, since capturing the shepherd or leader causes the sheep to scatter. The image is consolidated with references to the number of women involved in cases of spirit possession. There are many strands of the Jezebel discourse: One images Jezebel as a controlling, immoral woman, who uses beauty and harlotry as a weapon of a ministry's destruction. She is imaged as a powerful queen, a regal figure who nurtures and sends out her minions to ruin charismatic churches. Her father, Ethbaal of Sidonia, named her after Baal and she later seduced Ahab into idolatry. A second strand links Jezebel to the Mami water spirit in traditional religious cults. Pentecostal ministries, therefore, design rituals of identification akin to witchcraft detection strategies to ferret out such females before they do any damage. Rational and decorous rules are adopted during deliverance ministrations to ensure that more than one person attends to a female client; that females are properly attired, preferably wearing slacks when coming for deliverance; and that ministers provide cloths for covering women who may be slain in the spirit. Ministrations must be done only in assigned areas and under observation. Still, a negative gender discourse lurks within the Pentecostal theology that broadens the career of Ahab's wife into a spiritual force against the born-again community and betrays a lurking patriarchal ideology.

3. Plurality of Feminist Voices: Rejectionists, Liberationists, and Reconstructionists

More fundamentally, an African Pentecostal feminist theology has emerged that constitutes a specific strand within the resurgent voices of women in African theology. Generally, African women do not subscribe to the radical feminist theology espoused by some white women. They do not reject the church, yearn for a women's church, or call for an exit from male-dominated churches. The educated women espouse critical feminist reading that reexamines the basis of patriarchy. But most remain loyalists. The loyalist posture runs in different grooves: Some are "survivalists" who use the religious space as a survival kit through the socioeconomic and psychological pressures of life. Others are "elevationists" who wish to improve or uplift the quality of communal life through charismatic spirituality. This spirituality empowers women's capacity to confront society and to use the literacy and other skills that are nurtured within the church as tools in their daily lives and professions.

The liberationists are like southpaw boxers who fight within the system, attack the system without confronting it directly, but seek to transform it by using its internal logic. For instance, they require that both men and women take Paul seriously because he was preaching a radicalized form of submission in which everyone in the family submitted mutually to one another as unto the Lord. They would not debate the authenticity of the biblical passages as high criticism would, but would encourage Christians to accept the dictates and apply them to daily living. Like the other feminist models liberationists are against the male domination that hinders their practice of spiritual gifts in the church. They are also concerned that both males and females bear their God-given roles, which may differ in some aspects but are reciprocal. At stake is how to garner both personal freedom and the responsibilities of interdependent relationships. How much chance is there for partnership, given the historical and cultural realities? It is germane to explain these categories more.

The character of the problem is generally agreed upon; so is the villain's identity easily paraded in the market square. How to remove the fly from the cow's eye without blinding the cow, and how to do this through a concerted effort is the task at hand. In all forms of feminism, gender comprises a central focus; it is viewed as a problem because in virtually all social relations, institutions, and processes, many social inequities, strains, and contradictions abound. Gendered relations are not viewed as either natural or immutable, but rather as products of sociocultural and historical forces that are created and are constantly re-created by humans; therefore, these forces can be changed by human agency.

Strategies differ among feminists and across cultural boundaries. Of course, the first distinction would be between those who are secular and who pursue the feminist cause without any concern for the women's role in the church. They have to defend themselves against those who allege their activities point to a goal of lesbianism in the guise of the advocacy of women's freedom. The Christian feminists have the added problem of seeking an enhanced or uninhibited female participation in church matters. Among the latter, there are possibly four positions under which feminists could be labeled:

1. rejectionist;
2. loyalist;
3. reformist-liberationist; and
4. reconstructionist.

Like all labels, inaccuracy and overlap are routine. The differences among these four groups occur because some are doing theology manqué, while others are engaged in biblical scholarship, and there are different ways of engaging in the hermeneutical task. H. G. Wells divides the spectrum of feminist theologies into Trinitarian and non-Trinitarian, with the hope that the former holds the promise of a successful integration of feminist insight into the regular preaching and teaching of the churches.[8] The concern here is on explicit contextuality, to show the peculiarity of African articulation and yet place it within the larger context of what others are saying, both for the sake of interpreting Africa to the world and for linking the church in Africa to the global church. All Christians drink from the same well. However, there is nothing among Africans that fits as well in the category of rejectionist as one finds with some white feminists, such as Joanne Carlson Brown and Rebecca Parker.[9]

Some rejectionists, in their exile in the wilderness, find ethereal comfort in nature religion or mysticism based on women's consciousness. They are attracted to the role of the Earth deity in primal religions. The contributions of African women in eco-theology focus on utilizing the salient ingredients of a primal worldview as a channel for domesticating change agents. This is a far cry from propagating nature worship or romanticizing tradition. Isabel Phiri's study of the role of women in the *chisumphi* cult in Malawi brings out their difference from white fascination with native religions.[10]

Many African female theologians are reformist-liberationists; that is, their posture is to be in continuity with Christian tradition as much as possible, indeed, to search to the fullest possible extent for the liberating elements within the Christian tradition. They exhibit all nine characteristics of a Christian feminist, culled from literature, namely

1. sharp critique of patriarchy in church and society;
2. rejection of exclusively male metaphors for God language (though language concerns are muted because of innate structures);
3. opposition to the legitimization of male dominance through maleness of Jesus, the disciples, and Pauline theology;
4. concern for the emancipation of women and of all the marginalized;
5. explicit contextuality;
6. a large place for the category of experience;
7. hermeneutical suspicion of long-standing interpretations of Bible;
8. hermeneutical suspicion of long-standing interpretations of doctrine; and
9. intention to bring social analysis into contact with the Scriptures and tradition.

Elizabeth Johnson in her seminal work, *She Who Is*, calls the reformist-liberation model "a footbridge between the ledges of classical and feminist Christian wisdom. Throwing hermeneutical span from side to side may enable some to cross over to the paradigm of women's coequal humanity without leaving behind all the riches of the tradition that has been their intellectual and spiritual home."[11] This sets the stage for the reconstructionist group characterized by a suspicious reading of the Bible as a document produced by men for men, and preserved and used by men for their androcentric and sinful purposes. The biblical canon must be seen as a prototype, not as an archetype.[12] The latter is unchanging, fixed, and timeless while the former is open to the possibilities of transformation. The Bible cannot be trusted as divine revelation. R. B. Hays has, however, pointed out that the danger with the model is the dissolution of the canon; this undermines the authority of the New Testament so thoroughly that its liberating power would be also lost. The church finds her identity increasingly shaped by the ideals of liberal democracy and the apparent dictates of contemporary experience.[13]

Where do African women fit within these categories? African feminist theology tends to borrow the rhetoric of the reconstructionists without going all out. There are three predominant voices in African Christian feminism, two of which are variations of the reformist-liberationist model, and one of which is in the loyalist band. As I said earlier, there are no discernible bands of rejectionists. We can hear Dorothy Ramodibe saying, "No, there can be no cooperation between women and men as long as the oppressive and exploitative structures of the church remain intact. There can be no cooperation as long as men retain their dominant position in the church."[14] But by the end, Ramodibe's paper was not written from a radical feminist perspective, but from a reformist-liberationist position, and delivered in battle rhetoric. In Africa, the female theologians are very ardent believers who have committed most of their lives to serving their various churches in many capacities. They still believe in the church as a vehicle for mediating Christ's glory to the disheveled continent. Indeed, a legitimacy crisis is increasing attention on the church. All churches are growing in numbers, so the post-Christian option is not attractive to African women. In terms of strategy, it would disable the women from being heard by the churchly masses. Quite poignant, therefore, is the paper by Therese Souga who started with her statement of faith: "Jesus Christ means everything to me.... Christ is the true human, the one who makes it possible for all persons to reach fulfillment and overcome the historic alienation weighing them down."[15]

Souga perceives a deep bond, even complicity, between African women and Jesus Christ. Louise Tappa, representing those who mine the ancient texts for signals of feminine transcendence, picks up from Souga to examine the attitude of Jesus to Mary Magdalene. Using sources such as the Gospel of Thomas, Tappa builds an empowering case that is followed by contrasting the Levitical laws against women with the manner in which Jesus responded to the unnamed woman who came for help at the same time as Jairus (who was named). She is the woman who subtly touched the hem of His garment. In a similar vein, Teresa Okure, who is a biblical scholar, reexamines the Genesis creation story, which is central to the anti-feminine practices in the church. Okure acknowledges the method advocated by Elizabeth Schussler-Fiorenza in her seminal work *In Memory of Her* (1983). Using the same critical tool of analysis, Okure argued that the two Genesis accounts do not provide any basis for the denigration of women; rather, certain elements in the story have been both misinterpreted and ignored because of predominant patriarchal ideology. She calls for a spirit of discernment in the use of the Bible so as to differentiate between the divine and the human elements, between the timeless truths and the culturally conditioned.

Because rereading the Bible demands that one emphasizes the vocation of women as mothers, Okure portrays Mary as the epitome of women's vocation in the divine economy.[16] It should be pointed out that Okure seeks ways of reinterpreting the texts so as to remove the patriarchal slurs. The Bible is her starting point, a normative and theological resource used so that women's voices will be prophetic in the midst of desolation caused by male domination of decision-making processes. Okure's liturgical intent is to shape the biblical narrative into the feminist agenda. Hers is a hermeneutic of trust rather than of consent and affirmation. When one is a Roman Catholic, ecclesial tradition is one leg of the tripod in doing theology. Of great interest to Catholics is the return of Mariology into the center of theologizing among Third World women. Mariology signifies the ecumenical dimension in the sisterhood.[17] However, it does more by providing a link between feminist theology and the issue of poverty. Mary is portrayed as the patron of the poor.

Drawing from varied theological traditions, it has been difficult to develop a systematic theology. So we find that many African female theologians have tended to utilize Western resources on the roles of women in the Bible as a means of dealing with fear, violence, and the marginalization perpetrated by men in church and society.

Jesus looms large in their theology precisely because, in his attitude, they perceive the restoration of women to their full humanity in partnership with men as integral to the coming of God's egalitarian order.[18] Cheryl Bridges Johns says that Jesus reconciled women unto himself, and in order to do this marvelous action he dared to enter their world of alienation and pain and critiqued the numbness of his society.[19] Hisako Kinukawa has explored many of the familiar themes in her focus on women and Jesus in Mark, in her book by the same name. In her book, the hemorrhaging woman is perceived as the challenge to the cultural norms on pollution and ostracism, the Syrophoenician woman raises the issue of cultic purity, the poor widow becomes the occasion to reproach the scribes, and the woman who anointed the head of Jesus is the most fascinating because of her bold intrusion into a male gathering and the significance of her action. The irony that it was a woman who anointed the head of a man is not lost on feminist theology. It was a prophetic action. The double irony was that although a woman performed the act, it was a man who was anointed. Kinukawa also dealt with the cases of female disciples, as well as Jesus' reconstructive attitude to marriage, divorce, adultery, and prostitution. The four crucial questions to consider are:

1. Were the Twelve the only disciples?
2. Were the Twelve disciples priests?
3. Why did God exclude the male factor in the birth of Jesus?
4. Did Jesus accept patriarchy?[20]

In spite of the use of these references in African feminine theology, there is little ideological theorization in application of the texts. Indeed, I. J. Mosala has warned that from a Marxist paradigm, the recourse by women to a figure such as Esther is misplaced because she operated within the domination system that the more revolutionary Queen Vashti had challenged. This does not mean that criticism of the use of the Bible in Africa is lacking. Oduyoye berates the tendency to absolutize the Bible, and its uncritical reading, outdated exegesis, and interpretation that have entrenched and nurtured the marginalization of women.[21] She traces the roots to Victorian Christianity. Philip Turner made this point many years ago in his study of traditionalism in African churches. He quipped that Trollope would find himself more at home in many Anglican churches in Africa than he would in those of contemporary England.[22]

Oduyoye represents a peculiar voice among the reformist-liberationist band and deserves special attention. She has provided leadership in mobilizing the female theologians, having participated in the beginnings of the theological ferment in Africa and the Third World. She used her position as a deputy general secretary of the World Council of Churches most effectively to entrench the women's cause in that body. The wide range of her publications, spanning a few decades of vibrant academic endeavor, has left an imprint on the articulation of female empowerment in Africa. Her work *Daughters of Anowa: African Women and Patriarchy* is the only consistent narrative on African Christian feminism so far. It brings together much of her writings scattered in books and journals.

Three aspects of Oduyoye's writings are crucial: First, she recognizes that the exploding charismatic spirituality, within and outside the mainline churches, holds much prospect for turning the church in Africa to the reclamation of the glorious face of God. Second, Oduyoye refers to Efua Kuma, who is a Pentecostal and not a leader in the AIC, as Oduyoye claimed as representing an untapped resource in the study of new liturgical trends in Africa that utilizes indigenous idioms. Evidence of such reappropriation abounds among the women's groups and charismatic bodies.[23] Third, she draws attention to the lack of motivation among the women, as shown by the detrimental effect of their silence about and lack of reporting of violence and the high incidence of woman-on-woman violence in Africa.[24] Oduyoye spends the last part of her book showing the consequences of disunity, class distinctions, and lack of conscientization among women. She uses the example of the achievements of the Hebrew women in mobilizing Israel to the liberation during the exodus event.

On the whole, Oduyoye's theological method follows the agenda of Ecumenical Association of Third World Theologians (EATWOT). She uses culture, primal religion, language, biblical materials, experiences of women, and a concern for the predicament of Africa as sources for doing theological ethics. Her goal is to build a band of new African women, standing with confidence under God's empowering Spirit to respond to the challenges of poverty and pluralism in Africa. Beyond mental reconstruction, she advocates an organized quest for more economic and political space. Oduyoye's posture has notable features that show the relationship between the various approaches, feeding one another and yet leaving distinctive African nuances. This may confuse some readers about her attitude to the Bible and whether her theology is sufficiently Christocentric. Her rhetoric uses some of Fiorenza's antiandrocentric declamations, and she pays close attention to concrete historical context that makes experience the core hermeneutical principle and discounts the speech of God.

To dismantle the antiwoman habits that have shackled the church and diminished its ability to mobilize full resources to combat growing challenges, the roots of patriarchy in the society must be dealt with. This is what Walter Brueggemann calls moving back into the deepest memories of community to activate those very symbols that have always been the basis for contradicting the regnant consciousness.[25] As Nyambura J. Njoroge said, the church in Africa needs a consciousness-raising education or a program of enlightenment.

4. Pentecostalist Loyalist Feminist Theology

This brings us to the fourth posture, namely, the loyalist. The loyalist band emerges from among Roman Catholic sisters, Protestant Evangelicals, Aladura (AIC), and Pentecostals. The core difference among the loyalists and others is how each reads the Bible. In *Engaging the Powers*, Walter Wink intoned that Paul did not write the verses of terror in Ephesians 5:21–33; 1 Timothy 2:8–15; 5:3–16; or Titus 2:3–5, though they are ascribed to him. Someone in the early church wrote them.[26] The loyalist will not debate the authenticity of the passages but would encourage Christians to accept the dictates and apply them to daily living. Like the other groups, loyalists are against male domination, which hinders their practice of spiritual gifts in the church. They are also concerned that both males and females bear their God-given roles, which may differ in some aspects but are reciprocal. They explore how to garner personal freedom, the responsibilities of interdependent relationships, and partnership, given historical and cultural realities.

As Judith Mbugua's titled her book, our time has come, and evangelical women believe that a resolution is possible by urging men to obey the Bible. Their belief is that the Scriptures contain enough to make men less chauvinistic, more loving, and family responsible. The Bible is, for them, God's hope for women. For instance, the Ephesians passage demands that men love their wives as they love themselves, care for them as they care for their bodies. The Greek word *ektrepho* requires men to nourish, bring up, care for, and protect their wives; *thalpo* demands that they cherish, foster, and keep their wives warm in their bosoms. Paul asked men to leave their parents and be joined to their wives.

In Paul's defense, women disregard the hindering statements on their being silent and their restriction from preaching, as arising from the abuse of freedom in Christ by certain Corinthian female prophetesses. They note the sociocultural dimension: Since the sacred and the secular spheres of Jewish society were intertwined, the inferiority and subordination of women were consequently present in both religious and civil areas of Jewish life. The resonance between African and Victorian morality should not be allowed in the new dispensation precisely because the redemption restored women, after the fall, to rule the earth jointly with men. Besides, many African women find nothing wrong with covering their hair, which is an aspect of feminine fashion. Rather they note that Paul laid an enormous responsibility on the men that, if fulfilled, would enhance the partnership necessary for a vibrant mission. Beyond the freedom that is in Christ, where there is neither male nor female, Paul's theology provided for the organization of the entire family such that it may be a sweet-smelling odor for God. While reconstructionists regard Paul as a transitional figure with one foot in the old ways, and the other foot in the new dispensation ushered by Christ, the loyalist position says that while some of Paul's pronouncements may have dire consequences for the women's cause, the church should take a more holistic view rather than hiding under Paul's mufti to practice discrimination. Scriptures should be interpreted within their teleological framework for effecting God's salvation history. They lay emphasis on the power of the Word.

The loyalist theology is very vigorous among the Pentecostals, whose authority pattern declares that God is not a democrat. The pastor's power can be extensive. But the pneumatic emphasis in Pentecostals' theology provides a counterpoise. Can anyone prevent a female from exercising her spiritual gifts? Much to the contrary, argues Lois Wafula, the power of the woman's intercessory prayers is like electric power plants, carrying a powerful force that brings life and light into our homes. G. Mwiti, one of the contributors in Mbugua's book, buttresses this affirmation with a study of the Matthean passage that says Jesus is the light of the world, and concludes that God's power can work just as forcefully in women.[27] Do we perceive here the complementarity in the Spirit between men and women that could provide an exit from the shackles of patriarchy? Women, as light, contradict the dark imagery in primal myths and folktales, which resonate with the fact that women played larger roles in early Pentecostalism.[28] Margaret L. Bendroth has explored how the rise of fundamentalism brought the cult of domesticity and legalistic structures into Pentecostalism with its membership in the National Association of Evangelicals. Thus, the Assemblies of God, which ordains women, allows them to rise only to the rank of senior pastor, barring the doors into the district and general council meetings.[29]

In Africa, the trend appears to be in the opposite direction, with the rapid explosion of the wind of God there is an equal explosion in the number of ordained women. In many cases, the male leader needs his wife to be ordained as co-pastor so as to control the finances and authority within trusted bounds.

In other cases, it is a response to enlargement of scale and the burst of inno-vation in the religious space. It may take some while before the Weberian routinization of the charisma would emerge. However, the family ethics ad-vocated are akin to those of the Promise Keepers. In the midst of changing family patterns, the high rate of divorce, and social instability, scholars have argued that females find the certainties and securities of Pentecostal family ethics reassuring and attractive; there is coherence and capacity for coping in the darkness. The women call on the churches, Pentecostal or otherwise, to hear their cries and deal justly within the precinct of the temple. This will empower the church to foray into society to combat the inequities of polygyny, female circumcision, early betrothal, forced marriages, divorce rights, menstrual taboos, and widowhood customs. The loyalists are emphasizing the loving relationship model that suffused Puritan literature, yet they are also concerned with constructing a means for women to engage the church to respond to the forces in the society that scar women and children. As Oduyoye would say, the daughters of Anowa, standing at the fork in the road, must determine which direction to take.[30]

The loyalist model reinforces the old evangelical emphasis on the domestic responsibilities of the Christian woman by building on the implications of the size of female population (and citizenry), the fact that women perform two-thirds of the productive work, which sustains the family and is dominant in reproduction, and the fact that patriarchal ideology plays itself out in the ethics of power. This can be illustrated with Rebecca S. Dali's book *Women in the Ministry of Jesus*. Dali dwells on how the women's Bible study fellowships empower women as Christian homemakers and in their petty trades, and have helped the women to build their personal spirituality.[31] Dali ignores the fact that women have been excluded from political leadership, which has been identified as the key to Africa's failure, where the tendency is for the leader to assume the role of the father of the nation, use national resources as his private wealth, and brutally respond to opposition as if it were being sacrilegiously rebellious to divine authority. Thus, the leader clothes himself in symbols of sacred authority and chieftaincy regalia. The fly whisk, the leopard skin, the hat, the walking stick, and the motorcade and siren all symbolize the awe of patriarchal power that disdains accountability. Rather, the loyalists seek the partnership of men and women as the solution to the lack of accountability. They point to the fact that the social wounds of the society, such as HIV/AIDS, corruption, indiscipline, and violence, are sourced from the dysfunctional structure of the modern family. All these imply that men and women should work in partnership, standing in the glory of God and in shared humanity, to rebuild according to the demands of the gospel.

In such calls, they ignore the structural fact that there is a relationship between polities and gender practices among African churches. For instance, in the hierarchical politiesamong the Roman Catholics and the Anglicans in

Africa, the emphasis is on the church as an institution with inherited traditions. The authority lines are well defined and do not allow for much local
initiative. Male priestcraft has bewitched these churches. Gender practices
arise from ancient traditions and are resistant to the ordination of women.
Among the congregationalist and presbyterial polities, there have been enormous shifts; for instance, the Presbyterians ordain women as ruling elders
and, from the mid-1960s, started the ordination of female ministers, who have
full parity with male ministers. The question is whether spiritual power or
charisma leads to open gender polities.[32] Among the Pentecostals, the distinctive character in Africa includes the large corps of ordained women in churches, women leaders, and founders of churches and female-led fellowships
such as Women's Aglow.

Even among the mainline churches, there has been a resurgence of lay
power. Within this ambit, the power of women's organizations has become
considerable. Numerical and financial influence are important. These organizations wield enormous power in the affairs of the church in spite of the
powers of laymen. The priestly powers are increasingly confined to the monopoly of sacraments. Vast social changes as well as the increased level of
education have improved the roles of women in African churches. This suggests the first of three solutions to the dilemma, namely, that women should
intensify their advocacy for improved legal, economic, and political power in
the various nations. Already, the upsurge of working mothers, and the rise of
professional women's organizations and nongovernmental organizations devoted to women's causes have increased women's roles in civil society. Social
activism in the society flows into the church.

The second solution is suggested by the fact that women access power in
the church or religious space more easily through the exercise of their spirituality, as seen among the groups that emphasize the pneumatic aspects.
Initially, to talk about feminine spirituality appeared as one of those attempts
to categorize women, when in fact the characteristic is culturally conditioned.
Recent scholarship is connecting the feminist revolution with the desire to
reunite sexuality with the experience of the sacred.[33] This is a larger issue that
cannot be adequately dealt with here. Suffice it to say that women have always
been healers—from ancient temple priestesses to the medieval herbalists to
today's alternative practitioners, nurses, and midwives. The image of women
as visionaries and spirit mediums is encrusted in the African worldview. The
potency of feminine spirituality is equally acknowledged and used to explain
the numerical strength of women in churches. The challenge for women,
therefore, is to push forward an agenda indicating how their innate spirituality
could be used to revive the church. Are the victims asked to save themselves?
Yes and no. Quite often rights are not given; they are repossessed by those who
have been robbed. The poor and oppressed have an innate power that must be
aroused to counter the monopolized verdict of the oppressor.

The third solution flows from the capacity to reimagine the feminine imagery of the *pneuma*. Feminine spirituality is radicated in the Bible with images of God as a mother in Israel, the awesome power of God mediated in predominantly feminine imagery. God's salvation was first broached and activated by Elizabeth, Mary, Anna, and Mary Magdalene. In each case, the heart of spirituality is yieldedness. These women had the courage to say yes to the overshadowing power of the Holy Spirit and were able to see the invisible, had recourse to the sacred, and became coworkers with God. Their apparent weakness turned into a powerful, prophetic recovery of both church and community. As one Church of England study group suggested: "If women are now to bring into the ordained ministry their embodied realities, there will be a major shift in our symbolic structures—to metaphors and symbols drawn from the womb, from the breast, from birth and nourishment; from feelings and relationships; from the menstrual and other rhythms which are constant in their inconstancy."[34] Marie Griffith used the case of Women's Aglow to illustrate how praying women banding together can become an instrument of the struggle. The purpose of the fellowship, says the brochure, is to"provide and support, education, training, and ministry opportunities to help women worldwide discover their true identity in Jesus Christ through the power of the Holy Spirit." Aglow's literature emphasizes its mission of bringing women hope, healing, and reconciliation. It forms a network of caring women. During its meetings, every woman is invited to speak about her life and to receive prayers of healing from others. Each is empowered to engage in social and economic pursuits with Christian ethics and determination in order to be open to God's prospering grace. In *God's Daughters*, Griffith explores the rich metaphor in the power of submission. Surrender and submission to God become liberating features both in concept and in practice as family ethics. Writing about the righteous discontent in the women's movement in the Black Baptist church during 1880–1920, Evelyn Higginbotham concluded that "the feminist theologians had operated from a stance of radical obedience. And indeed it was this vantage of orthodoxy that compelled the brethren to listen. The theological nuances of these terms, the careers, and experiences of African-American women offer food for thought to African women."[35] An aspect that requires emphasis in the literature of African female theologians (charismatic or otherwise) is the exploration of the power of prayer as a tool for hope or rousing what Fiorenza calls the angry power of the Spirit.

As Cheryl B. Johns argues, if women's advocacy taps into the pneumatic resources in the Scriptures, they will discover that the Pentecost story contains the story of the conscientization of women; that the mission of the Pentecost involves both men and women as co-laborers and as joint heirs as members of God's new *ekklesia*. The Holy Spirit empowered many spirit-filled women to perform priestly, charismatic roles; to obey the call to and move to mission without ordination and institutional support and, in a revolutionary manner, to posture themselves in the line of God's eschatological design. The Holy Spirit is the power that will enable the Circle in Africa to achieve its goals. Therefore, the feminist scholarship should pay more attention to the new Christian culture fostered by Pentecostalism in Africa. It should be more attentive to the move of the Holy Spirit among the women of contemporary Africa. Gordon Fee, in his *Gospel and Spirit Issues in New Testament Hermeneutics*, attributes the prominence of women as a result of the deeply populist roots of the New Testament church.[36] It is, he says, the reviving of the elements of populism that is providing female preachers of our contemporary period with new ministry opportunities.

To conclude: I will not summarize the argument thus far but urge a program of Christian education designed to enlighten and sensitize the whole people of God about the victimization of women. Most people act out of ignorance, without realizing that the full potential of the community are underutilized. One should leave it to women to design a program that will utilize all potential. As Oduyoye has urged others and done herself, "Be a woman and Africa will be strong."[37] The Pentecostal movement in Africa has provided leadership in this area. It realizes that the mission of the church demands the full mobilization of all sectors and that to ignore any would diminish the full potential to work with Christ in reconciling a lost world unto the Father. Pentecostal gender practice has been pragmatic: By enlisting their wives, by recognizing charismatic gifts and the presence of successful female-led ministries, by literalist reading of the Bible that often cuts both ways, by modernizing their institutions and engaging in large-scale mission, pastors have opened the space for women.

PART III

Pentecostalism in the African Public Space

9

Sankofa

Pentecostalism in the African Map of the Universe

1. Introducing the Cultural Discourse

The explosion of Pentecostalism in Africa needs an explanation. Recent scholarship on African Pentecostalism tends to start from the contemporary and urban experiences to explore the impact of external cultural forces and show how Africans respond to the forces of externality and globalization. Pentecostalism is imaged as the religious vanguard. From here, assertions are made that ignore in-depth ethnographical research and that presume a higher degree of urban ethos than exists in Africa. This discourse does not recognize the force of cultural villigization of the modern public space; that most of the inhabitants of the towns carry medicine made in the villages to empower their successful foraying in the towns. As Stephen Ellis and Gerrie ter Haar observed, "Many Africans today who continue to hold beliefs derived from the traditional cosmologies apply these to everyday life even when they live in cities and work in the civil service or business sector. Religious worldviews do not necessarily diminish with formal education."[1] It matters where an analysis starts or is located because many studies of African Pentecostalism that are placed in the contemporary period and in the context of urbanity and urban culture miss the force of the movement's fit into the indigenous worldviews and the Pentecostal practices in the rural contexts. To the contrary, the African moral universe comprises three interpenetrating publics: the village public, the emergent urban public, and the Western public that is represented by multinational corporations and international institutions. The cultural discourse examines how Pentecostalism engages with each public.

The burden of this chapter is a cultural discourse that reconstructs the movement's response to the system of meanings embodied in the symbols and worldviews of indigenous African religions and cultures. It starts from a different location to explore the cultural discourse that argues that Pentecostalism has grown because of its cultural fit into indigenous worldviews and its response to the questions that are raised within the interior of the worldviews. It asserts that the indigenous worldview still dominates contemporary African experience and shapes the character of African Pentecostalism. Therefore, African Pentecostalism is the "setting to work" of the gospel in Africa, at once showing how Africans appropriated the gospel message, how they responded to the presence of the Kingdom in their midst, and how its power transformed their worldviews. Exercising a measure of agency, African Christians absorbed new resources generated internally and externally in reshaping their histories. The face of Christianity acquired a different character in the encounter because it was now expressed in the idiom of the African world. This means that the conversation partners in shaping Pentecostal ideology and praxis are the indigenous religions and cultures, the experiences of individuals and communities of contemporary cultures and competing religious forms in urban and rural contexts, biblical resources and a certain ecclesiastical tradition or the pneumatically driven Pentecostal image of the church. These are not discrete categories but shape the being, saying, and doing of the Pentecostal movement. They are useful sources for revisiting the debate on Pentecostal response to African cultural heritage.

It is argued that when Pentecostal discourse is rooted in both the African past—an area that has received an inadequate attention—as well as the experiences in contemporary cultural terrains, its full character will be illuminated. But the task here is to fill the lacuna in Pentecostal scholarship by focusing on the specific contextuality, the Africanness of the phenomenon and its place within African maps of the universe. It argues that the contemporary experience in Africa does not start from globalizing cultural forces, though the implosion of these forces compels much readjustment. Rather, the force of traditional cultures in determining behavior and policy in the modern public space compels an in-depth study of its salience and resilience. Pentecostal cultural policy demonstrates an acute awareness of this powerful reality for the majority of Africans, in a continent where most people live in the rural areas and where the urban dwellers cultivate their roots in their home villages. Urban migrants are often engaged in circular migration from the rural-to-urban and back again.

2. *Sankofa*: Discourses on Pentecostalism and the African Past

The force of the past for the present is illustrated in the cultural policies of African governments. Many African countries have dug deeply into traditional values for cultural symbols of unity. In the rainbow ideology of South Africa, the television features a stimulating jingle: *Simunye-e-e-e*, we are one! In Ghana, *Sankofa*, a Twi word, is one of the symbols used to promote unity based on the recovery of Ghanaian cultural heritage. Each of the symbols affirms a salient value that should be cultivated. *Sankofa* is the bird that turns its head to look backward in the direction from where it came and is used to remind a person to be conscious about where a journey started, otherwise the person may not know where he or she is going. This symbol urges people to go back or look back and reclaim their cultural heritage.

There are two contested images of African Pentecostal cultural policy. The first is that Pentecostals essay to destroy the past. In his *African Catholicism: A Voyage in Discovery*, Adrian Hastings complained that Pentecostal attacks against indigenous culture constitute a regression from the achievements by the African Instituted Churches on the gospel-culture interface.[2] Apparently the matter is subtle. Birgit Meyer suggests that the Pentecostal attitude may be inherited from the missionary traditions; that the Ewe converts translated or appropriated the missionary message about the devil. Pentecostals have followed en suite to embed the missionary rhetoric about Satan in a wide range of the ingredients of African indigenous cultures. But, she added that "by emphasizing continuously that being born again entails a complete break with the past, Pentecostals even celebrate the notion of rupture much more than nineteenth and early twentieth-century Protestant missionaries."[3]

Other scholars argue that Pentecostalism merely valorized changes that indigenous religious movements had initiated; all parties are engaged in worldview maintenance with competing narratives, which explains why cultural tradition often attacks this new religious form as an invasive virus. Still others emphasize how Pentecostalism engages the resources of African indigenous cultures in pursuit of its own agendas. They draw attention to large areas of resonance between Pentecostalism and African maps of the universe. David Maxwell,[4] using data from Zimbabwe, illustrates the resonance between Pentecostalism and the spirit possession cults and traditional witchcraft-cleansing mechanisms. He argues that they share a common appeal, seek empowerment to combat evil, and share the egalitarian idiom. Yet Maxwell points to a second dimension of the contested perspectives: he images Pentecostal cultural policy as subtle; that while affirming the reality of the powers of indigenous gods and cultures, Pentecostals essay to transform these cultures by contesting patriarchal ideology and the control exercised by the elders and "big men" of the village and clan. The attraction for charismatic women and youth, Maxwell argues, comes from the fact that "the new churches are also the heirs of older witchcraft eradication movements." The Pentecostals do not ignore but engage the primal contexts and renew the social system by critiquing and redefining possession: They brand all cults (central and peripheral) as satanic, exorcise all, and breed skepticism. But they do not end there. They provide an alternative— "white," clean possession by the Holy Spirit (*Mzimu Woyera*) that is safer and less expensive.

Through a transformational cultural response, Pentecostalism becomes a new form of possession replacing the old by deploying an identical mechanism. Among the Igbo of southeastern Nigeria, the *dibia afa* and *dibia ogwu* (diviner and herbalist) recognized that this new religious form was a stronger competitor than the old missionary cultural policy because it was as much concerned with spiritual power as was the indigenous religion. Birgit Meyer observed that

> the proponents of Pentecostalization stood much closer to traditional worship than they themselves were prepared to acknowledge. Exactly because they regarded local gods and spirits as really existing agents of Satan, they strove to exclude them with so much vigor, thereby placing themselves in a tradition of *"Africanization from below"* which was developed by the first Ewe converts and which had much in common with African cults propagating radical cleansing.[5]

This explains why Pentecostals would speak about deliverance rather than exorcism. They do not just expel the demonic force but refill the person with a healthier, clean spirit so that the person can become truly human and achieve the vaunted life goals of a community. It is a revaluation of culture to transform it into an instrument for building *ubuntu*. Thus, there are three models of relationship instead of one hostile posture in the conversation between Pentecostalism and indigenous culture: they both inculturate its resources, prophetically contest them, and are often counterattacked by the guardians of the sacred groves.

Rijk van Dijk's study of Chilomoni, a suburb of Blantyre, further illustrates the subtlety. Van Dijk recognizes the Pentecostal interest and attention to the reality within traditional religions and cultures. But he argues that the movement's attitude highlights the element of parody and skepticism: "While Pentecostalism in its deliverance ideology and praxis has never been skeptical about the powers that lie behind manifestations of social, political or even religious authority, the bearers of those powers tend to meet in Pentecostal praxis a lot of parody and ridicule: a form of indirect contestation."[6] From a certain perspective, Pentecostal studies benefit from the scholarship in the broader field of African church history. There, recent scholarship has emphasized the continuity of African primal religions in African Christianity; the exchange of symbols, images, and material things; the agency of decoders as well as encoders; the modes of appropriating the message of the gospel by the hearers; and the varieties of ways that African cultures have reshaped the music, dance, and liturgy of Christianity, and raised new theological questions and grassroots reflexive theologies in response to contemporary experiences.

3. *Homowo*: Pentecostals and the Tradition of Hooting at Hunger

This argument sets the stage to comment briefly on Birgit Meyer's thesis. A covenant is about relationship, a legally binding structure. My contention is that just as God built a relationship with human beings through the structure of the covenant, so did Africans build binding, legal relationships with the gods in the sky, land, water, and ancestral world. They used a variety of rituals and festivals to revitalize and uphold their own part in the covenants. We shall use the illustration of the *Homowo* festival of the Ga Dangbe people of Ghana, mentioned by Birgit Meyer, to demonstrate how a born-again family deserted its cultural past. A thick ethnographic description can better inform an understanding of Pentecostal cultural ideology. *Homowo* literally means "hooting at hunger." Before the climax of the agricultural/ancestral festival, heads of families would sprinkle the *kpekple* (ground maize) during libation in their homes, and many rituals would have been completed by the chiefs, led by the *Naa Wulomo*, the chief priest of the Ga people. The ritual journey begins by visiting all the shrines and deities of the land to perform rituals of revitalization and propitiation. Then the priest will "wash" all the stools with blood, "wash" the ritual machete (the symbol of planting and harvesting processes), and cut the earth with this as a sign of dedicating the land to the earth deity who gives fertility, thus initiating the planting season. After that, they visit the lagoon with sacrifices to marine deities, because the Ga people are predominantly fishermen. Finally, they cleanse the whole land. In some African cultures, the priests perform a ritual walk around the territorial boundaries of the ethnic group. After these walks, all the families who have twins will be joined by friends to perform a ritual called "washing the horns."

On the festival day, the chiefs and the chief priest process to the river to ensure a good fishing season. Individuals invite friends and families to gather to sprinkle the libation, eat the *kpekple* with fish stew, and binge with gin and other kinds of liquor. Libations at the various levels of the authority hierarchy are used to covenant children and those who are absent into binding relationships with the deities of the land. Ignorance is no bliss; all are implicated into these binding relationships unless a renunciation is made. A number of prohibitions, including the ban on drumming, are installed during the period. A casual observer may miss the ritual backdrop that informs the Pentecostal response. On May 31, 1998, the Lighthouse Chapel International got into trouble with the Ga priests because the church uses indigenous drums in its worship and dared to use the drum during the prohibited season. A group of traditionalists from the Korle Gonno area of Accra then bulldozed the perimeter fence of the church that is located in the old section of Accra. Indigenous religious orthodoxy aggressively asserted itself in a clash of covenants. In Ghana, this has happened often as when the Ashanti decreed that people should not farm on a certain Thursday in honor of *Asaase Yaa*, the mother earth. The Elmina people prohibited fishing in the Benya lagoon during the *bakatue* festival in honor of *Nana Benya*, the lagoon deity; the Nzema people of the Half Assini in western Ghana imposed a ban on drumming during the *Kundum* festival in which the people perform a sacred dance in honor of the earth deity.[7]

In all these cases, the African quest for identity and survival through religious power creates a power encounter. The covenant concept postures the relationships between Africans and their gods as binding covenants, which explains why the clash between indigenous groups and Pentecostals is most serious during rituals and festivals or reenergizing sacred moments. Religious fervor is at fever pitch on both sides of the divide. The application of this concept argues that the clash of covenants challenges the church's method for doing mission. Pentecostals argue that mission churches had compromised and that the failure to adopt the right counteraction explains why the spirits that guard the gates of communities have remained unconquered, thereby creating a dilemma for Christianity and calling for a refining of inculturation theology. Covenants can only be reversed by recognizing their existence, potent reality, character, and the use of appropriate rituals of disengagement. Pentecostal achievement has been in recognizing that the matter is not about noise levels or even about making music with drums, but about covenants that are legally binding and may not be simply wished away without due processes.

Pentecostals are not breaking completely from families that keep the old ways but are arguing for a new method of studying African indigenous religions and cultures, no longer as fossilized or exotic religion but as a living faith to be taken seriously. The ingredients of traditional religion contain both elements that proffer abundant life as well as those that threaten life. Laurenti Magesa posits the pursuit of an abundant life as the goal of African indigenous religions.[8] The Christianization process must be cognizant of the element of continuity in the religious lives of Africans instead of banding everything under the umbrage of syncretism. Undoubtedly a dirty epithet, the concept of syncretism began life in the search for an appropriate quality of the mix, the enduring problem of Christ and culture. Africa is currently boiling with much religious ferment and has, indeed, become a "great theological laboratory, dealing with issues—literally—of life and death, of deformation and reformation, of fossilization and revival."[9] Finally, some years ago, Robin Horton drew attention to the intellectualist approach in explaining religious change. He was trying to deal with both primary and secondary levels of conversion:

What makes the African to, first, abandon the gods of his fathers for the Christian God and, second, shift from mere attendance to indulgence in charismatic spirituality? He suggested looking into the changes in worldview, wherein, he argued, reside the elements of continuity and discontinuity.[10]

In summary, African Christian scholarship has informed the Pentecostal emphasis on the African primal worldview in its theology and determined its responses to the challenges of that worldview. African religions and cultures have contributed a specific flavor to African Pentecostalism as the movement seeks to share the gospel with power amid the pulsating problems of the ecosystem. The quest by Pentecostals to root their message into the African maps of the universe is buttressed in its efforts by African Christians of various hues—whether scholars, novelists, or political nationalists—to interpret the gospel from their meaning systems. Admittedly, some of these efforts arose from antagonism, and others from antistructural intentions to install a different and more kerygmatic Christianity.

4. Precarious Vision: Anatomy of an African Worldview

Some scholars have argued that each culture is a universe of signs comparable to language, a configuration of images, concepts, and interpretations. Through the process of enculturation, this grammar is acquired unconsciously by the individual members of the society. Underlying culture is the worldview as the hermeneutic that interprets the creative pattern of human action or, as M. Kraft puts it, "the cultural lens through which human experience is viewed." Charles H. Kraft concluded: "At the core of culture and, therefore, at the very heart of all human life, lies the structuring of the basic assumptions, values, and allegiances in terms of which people interpret and behave. These assumptions, values and allegiances we call worldview."[11] Worldview is a picture that points to the deep-level assumptions and values on the basis of which people generate surface-level behavior. It provides the motivation for behavior and gives meaning to the environment. Like the rest of culture, it is inherited unconsciously but deliberately transmitted. It could be encrusted in customs, myths, proverbs, folklore, music, and dances. For instance, in many African indigenous cosmogonies, the human world began from an anthill sitting in a marsh; the Supreme Being then sent a deity with bellows to dry the land. Differences in such myths of origin tend to reflect the ecology of the community or other ideological considerations. This indicates that worldviews are not static but could be reshaped by culture wars. Cultural change can often be detected as battering waves chipping away the crusts, initiating a process of separation, reconstruction, and reprioritization as a new way of viewing the world emerges.

Africans conceive time in a cyclical pattern. Life moves from birth to death and back to life by reincarnation. This movement of time is derived from the agricultural cycle among preindustrial peoples. As people's predominant economic activities move from planting to harvest and back to planting, as the sun and moon appear and disappear only to return in an endless cycle, life is conceived to follow a similar pattern. Reality is divided into two: the human world and the spirit world. But each is a replica of the other; thus if an achieved person or a chief dies, he will still live like one in the spirit world. This explains why some communities bury slaves alive. They are laid in the grave with outstretched arms to hold the body and to continue serving their master in the spirit world. Tied to this is an anthropology in which a creator deity delegated subalterns to mold human beings from clay while he himself breathed life-giving breath into them. The blood transmits the life into all the body. At death, the personality—soul or life—breath continues a new lifecycle in the spirit world, now as an ancestor who is still a member of his earthly family. This is the concept of the living dead. Death is not an end but the beginning of a new vista of living.

This organic perception is underscored by the conception of space. The African perceives three dimensions of space: the sky, the earth (consisting of land and water), and the ancestral or spirit world. It is an alive universe as each space is peopled with some of the four components of spiritual powers. The first, the Supreme Being, inhabits the universe as the creator, while the second, the major subaltern divinities, inhabit the sky. Manifesting as the sun, lightning, thunder, moon, and stars, the divinities serve as oracles, arbiters in human affairs and agents in ritual dynamics. The major force or divinity on the earth is the Earth deity, which is responsible for fertility and the nurture of life in humans, animals, and plants. Land looms large in this cosmology. In many myths of origin, it is said that during creation, the Supreme Being sent some deities to perch on anthills and dry the marshy earth; thus was the world formed. Some stayed back and inhabited rocks, trees, caves, streams, and rivers and thus imbued physical nature with divine power. Beyond nature spirits are patron spirits for certain professions such as farming, hunting, fishing, blacksmithing, trading, and other economic pursuits. Thus, all the realms of life are sacralized; there is no distinction between the sacred and the profane. The eco-theology in this religious landscape is very important but cannot be pursued here.

There are human spirits on the land because each human being has a guardian spirit who determines his or her fate in the passage through life. In some cultures, the individual would make a wooden figure of the personal demon and sacrifice to it daily for empowerment in the pursuits of life. In the gender construct, the marine spirits are imaged as daughters to the Earth deity. Marine spirits can be munificent and give riches to devotees. Barren women propitiate marine spirits for children; musicians consort with them for melodious songs; and artists seek them for inspiration. The connection between commerce and the arts with marine spirits runs as deep as the depths of seas.

But marine spirits could be wicked beings that cause those under their control to be morally unstable and wayward. Their flashy gifts do not last; marriages contrived by them do not succeed; and children born from the intervention of marine spirits are often plagued by inexplicable illness. These elements of instability force the afflicted to diviners who will assist to extricate the individual from covenants made by parents or by the person seeking the diviners' help with marine spirits.

Next to the deities and spirits, the third component consists of the ancestral spirits, which inhabit the underworld. Imbuing the whole of the world of the living are the fourth component, spiritual forces, which individuals can acquire through rituals for enhancing life force. They are nonpersonal beings such as they call *mana* in Oceania: mysterious, ubiquitous power that permeates all areas of life and can be used for good or in an antisocial manner to harm or diminish the capability of another person's life force, fortunes, and resources. Their negative uses could be operated through words, thoughts, attitudes, and behavior in sorcery or witchcraft practices. Witchcraft is the use of human psychic powers to do evil, unlike sorcery, which employs magical incantations, implements, objects, medicine, and other paraphernalia. With either method, curses could be put on individuals and families by the envious or wicked people. Evil forces are without bodily forms, so they embody people, animals, and physical objects, and manipulate these to harm people. The vision of existence is a precarious one as evil forces, which invest the human world as a siege, endeavor to ruin the capacity of individuals, families, and communities from living a prosperous life. Ruth Marshall-Fratani has shown that this scenario holds as equally good for the modern urban setting in Africa. As she said,

> With increasing economic hardship and zero-sum struggle for survival, great strain is put on the extended family as the basic domestic unit. Relatively successful family members often resent the pressure put on them by a variety of near and distant relatives.... Young people striving for upward mobility not only desire a relative freedom from such pressures, but also protection from resentment and jealousy in the form of witchcraft, most feared and dangerous in the hands of blood relatives.[12]

Affliction is a pivotal issue in the theology of the African primal world. It can be caused by a contravention of moral code. For instance, the Earth deity supervises the moral order on the land. Matters such as stealing, adultery, incest, and other forms of wrongdoing, as well as breakdowns in social relations, are abominations to her. One who fails to propitiate her is visited with afflictions that take different forms, such as illness or misfortune. The afflictions may manifest themselves individually or communally, and may includde political instability, economic disaster, an upsurge in the mortality rate, an increase in robbery, and other unwholesome social facts, which are regarded as disease, requiring divinatory diagnosis and spiritual cure. Disease could, therefore, be caused by religious, social, and natural causes. In order to re-establish the security of the moral order and reconcile broken social relationships, medicine becomes important. A diviner diagnoses the problem and provides curative and protective spiritual powers—either through herbs or by covenanting the individual or community to protective spirits. Festivals, dances, masquerades, and commensality are employed to reenergize ancestral and other covenants and heal the community from untoward conditions. Finally, it has been shown through a survey of the Igbo of southeastern Nigeria that 615 spirits occupy their religious ardor, though different culture theaters in Africa prioritize which deities are central for their needs. The challenges of the ecosystem are core determinants for prioritizing their choices.

This is a charismatic worldview. Going through life is like spiritual warfare, and religious ardor may appear very materialistic as people strive to preserve their material sustenance in the midst of the machinations of pervasive evil forces. Behind this worldview is a strong sense of the moral and spiritual moorings of life. It is an organic worldview in which the three dimensions of space are bound together, and the visible and the invisible worlds interweave. Nothing happens in the visible world that has not been predetermined in the invisible realm. The challenge for Christianity is how one should witness the gospel in a highly spiritualized environment where recognizing the powers has not been banished in a Cartesian flight to objectivity and enlightenment. The power question is ultimate and suffuses an African primal worldview, demanding an answer from the new Christian change agent, and pointing to the need for continuity in change. Earlier missionary effort to sidestep the African primal worldview with charitable institutions and Western worldview failed, leaving the field open for re-evangelization. The born-again people have picked up the gauntlet. The argument here is that Pentecostalism in Africa derived its coloring from the texture of the African soil and from the interior of its idiom, nurture, and growth; its fruits serve more adequately the challenges and problems of the African ecosystem than the earlier missionary fruits did.

5. Kindred Atmosphere and Resonance: Pentecostal Reconstruction of the Primal Worldview

The major contribution of the Pentecostal movement is how it addresses the continued reality of the forces expressed in African cultural forms. They deploy four strategies: adopt a posture of spiritual warfare, use the covenant imagery to describe the relationship between human beings and the gods, explore swaths of resonance between the Bible and African indigenous worldviews, and reinvent a theology that reclaims God's rule over the whole inhabited earth. It resembles the old strategy of "spoiling the Egyptians."

Contrary to the early missionary attitude that urged rejecting indigenous African culture, Pentecostals take the African map of the universe seriously, acknowledging that culture is both a redemptive gift as well as one capable of being highjacked. Pentecostals perceive a kindred atmosphere and resonance between the Bible and African indigenous religions. Pentecostals, therefore, explore the lines of congruence that go beyond destruction of the old to a new construction of reality.

African worldviews share an identical creation myth with the Genesis saga, that of an earth created from a watery terrain. Among the Igbo, Chukwu, the Supreme Being, sent a smith with bellows to dry the land. Anthills appeared. At the structural level, there appears to be a major difference between the indigenous and the biblical worldviews. The New Testament worldview is constructed on a linear perception of time. Time moves as a continuum from the past through the present to the future. In the worldviews of most African communities, time is perceived as cyclical. But on a closer look, both worldviews are in the Bible and they share a three-dimensional perception of space. The Bible declares that, at the name of Jesus, "every knee shall bow" whether it exists in the heavenlies, earth (land and water), or in the underworld (ancestral world).

Both traditional African culture and Pentecostalism affirm that "things which are seen are made of things which are not seen" (Hebrews 11:3b) and that events in the manifest world are first decided in the spirit world, therefore, in salvatory, conflict situations, "the weapons of our warfare are not carnal." The biblical worldview images the Christian life to be just as precarious as the traditional African imagines. The enemy is arranged in a military formation as principalities, powers, rulers of darkness, wickedness in high places, and demons. The Pentecostal goes through life keenly aware of the presence of evil forces just as the African does. Life is secured through a good relationship with the supernatural. The Bible, for instance, prescribes both obedience and active maintenance of the covenant with God; it, therefore, contains a diatribe against the competing covenants with other gods. These are imaged as snares and, therefore, the need for testing of spirits. The promise of land was a key component of the covenant. Similarly, when there is a drought or famine or social distress, Africans look to the land and to their relationship with the earth deity because the earth deity sustains the economic and moral order. The Pentecostals do likewise: They bring to the problem the importance of the land among the Israelites. Walter Brueggemann said that this land referred to actual earthly turf, and also symbolically expressed the wholeness of joy and well-being characterized by social coherence and personal ease in prosperity, security, and freedom. Land as promise, holy, and a symbol of our covenant relationship with God has tremendous resonance in the attitude to land in African primal societies.[13] The "brethren" plumb the resonance and move to the impact of pollution caused by the actions of rulers and the ruled. Shrines, festivals to Baal and Ashteroth, witchcraft, and corruption are all listed by the brethren as sources of the woes. In addition, they view the International Monetary Fund and World Bank as evangelists of the Beast who is equally behind the European Union and the divinity of the market economy that is "SAPping" African countries with debt repayment. (SAP is Structural Adjustment Program and comes with "conditionalities" that exacerbate poverty.)

Pentecostals appreciate the tensile strength of the spiritual ecology in Africa and the clash of covenants in their efforts to displace the illegitimate spirits at the "doors" of individuals and "gates" of communities with a legitimate spiritual authority. Salvation is posed as a conflict scenario. The Garrick Braide missionaries reflected this in a simple chorus that declared that "Jesus has come and Satan has run away!" From this power and authority structure, there are human beings who are given false powers by evil forces in order to exercise control over individuals, families, and communities. Satan even promised Jesus some of these powers if he complied with him. Thus, Pentecostals perceive dictatorial and corrupt rulers as being "possessed" subalterns of higher spiritual forces. The Pentecostals imagine that these spirits exercise psychic powers over the individuals through witchcraft and sorcery that constitute soul-to-soul attack. This theory is built on the biblical anthropology. All of life is subjected to the authority of Christ and, while not denying personal responsibility, it recognizes that individuals and circumstances could be driven by forces beyond their control.

Here, the Pentecostal explanation for witchcraft and sorcery by appeal to a biblical anthropology is fascinating. By arguing that God formed man and breathed Himself into the body and man became *nephesh*, a living soul, the fall is imaged as a house that collapsed, burying the spiritual resources. The soul (*psyche*), consisting of the intellect, willpower, and emotions constitutes the strongest part of man, and seeks to dominate both the spirit man (*pneuma*) and the body (*soma*). Salvation comes by the spirit of God, taking over the *pneuma* and exuding the power into the *psyche*, redeeming the constituent parts and recovering the *soma*, which is driven by lusts of the flesh, eyes, and pride of life. In this anthropology, witchcraft operates in the quest to tap the latent powers of the soul and use these to perform false miracles or hurt other people by a soul-to-soul attack. Sorcery worsens matters by using things that provide contact with the victim. It could be the hair, clothes, food, and so forth.

Both worldviews, traditional African and Pentecostal, are attentive to the power of words and names. God spoke things into being. Jesus spoke and people were healed and situations changed. Similarly, in indigenous religions, covenants are spoken into binding relationships, libations are followed with spoken prayers, and incantations and curses are pronounced. In oral cultures, the words of parents are so powerful that they could affect the fate of their children. In Jewish and Christain worldviews, the power of the word is duly acknowledged.

Born again Christians are, therefore, admonished to also speak the reversal to curses by using the name of Jesus, and the blood and the resources of the Holy Spirit. Thus, Christians have been given power to speak changes into being, making human beings co-creators with God. As Walter Wink said, *onoma*, name, is a metonymy, the part representing the whole. Renaming people and places was a part of signifying new relationship with the divine. In African cultures names have meaning and importance. The Nuer name their favorite cattle after their best friends as a mark of love. The name of Jesus designates his office, dignity, and power of God in him. The often-cited text that recounts the powers of Jesus and his position in the God-head is 1 John 5:8, as well as many others. This explains why Pentecostals use command and the power of word and name in the deliverance process and avoid the use of instruments, limiting these to olive oil, anointed handkerchiefs, the and laying on of hands.

Finally, the Pentecostals completely took over the Pauline use of the word *kosmos*, which can refer to the material universe and the inhabitants of the world, but which Paul fastens on the third usage referring to worldly affairs— the worldly goods, endowments, riches, pleasures, and allurements (*kosmetikos*) that seduce one from God. Thus, behind the classical idea of *kosmos* as an orderly arrangement is a mind behind the system, a world system established after the fall by a *kosmokrator*, a world ruler, the prince of this world, in rebellion. Friendship with him is enmity with God. It is a short step from here to perceive territorial spirits allocated to various spaces for ungodly activities. This idea was, after all, very prominent in Judaism and in the early church. There is a confluence of the spiritual and material worlds denying the myth of materialism. Wink has in his trilogy explored the language of power in the New Testament and concluded that

> every power tends to have a visible pole, an outer form-be it church, a nation, or an economy-and an invisible pole, an outer and inner spirit or driving force that animates, legitimates and regulates its physical manifestation in the world. Neither pole is the cause of the other. Both come into existence together and cease to exist together. When a particular Power becomes idolatrous, placing itself above God's purposes for the good of the whole, then that Power becomes demonic... Principalities and powers are the inner and outer aspects of any given manifestation of power. As the inner aspects, they are the spirituality of institutions and organizations of power.[14]

Analyzing further, Wink argues that the language of power pervades the whole New Testament and while it could be liquid, imprecise, interchangeable, and unsystematic, a clear pattern of usage emerges. Powers could be used to refer to heavenly, divine, spiritual, invisible forces as well as earthly, human, political, and structural manifestations as long as we realize that the world of the ancients was not a physical planet spinning in an empty space in a rotation around a nuclear reactor, the sun; it was a single continuum of heaven and earth, in which spiritual beings were as much at home as humans.[15] Paul used *dunamis* to focus on the spiritual dimension of power in its capacity to determine terrestrial existence for weal or for woe. Later, *dunamis* assumed more the designation for God's enemies who were engaged in a cosmic struggle to assert lordship over the earth.

Some have assumed that African Christians have manufactured demons and enlarged their provenance. But they abound in Jewish literature as defecting angels or as sired giants who were drowned in the flood, although their spirits lived on as demons, evil spirits, or "powers of Mastema." Their leaders were variously called Azazel, Mastema, Satan, and Beliar. Early Christians devised elaborate instructions on how to discern them. Jesus' ministry was very much a cosmic battle in which He rescued humanity from evil powers. Therefore, African Pentecostals have equated principalities, powers, and demons with the various categories of spirits in the worldview and as enemies of man and God. Pentecostals reinforce the causality pattern in primal worldview before providing a solution beyond the purviews of indigenous cosmology. They rework the Pauline structure with native ingredients:

A. Principalities
    i. Apollyon Revelation 9:11
    ii. Abaddon
    iii. Belial
    iv. The beast; symbol; the leopard
    v. Ariel

B. Powers
    i. Ashteroth (agricultural deities)
    ii. Baal (shrines on the earth; worship of earth deity)
    iii. Magog (e.g., Ogun; the Yoruba powers for medicine related to cutlasses, guns, iron)
    iv. Beelzebub (god of witchcraft, wizardry)
    v. Asmodee (goddess of sexual immorality)
    vi. Mammon (spirit that induces the allure of money)
    vii. Paimon (celestial demons empowering occultists)
    viii. Aritan (magic, satanic justice)

C. Rulers of Darkness
    i. Ogeaso (Bini), Ogbanje (Igbo)—spirits of children who come with a pact to return early into the spirit world
    ii. Jezebel, dark goddess of the loins, seductive spirit, harlotry
    iii. Moleck, promoter of nudist fashion and pornography

iv. Leviathan, a spirit that attracts people into unwholesome covenants
v. Jeptha, patron of thieves and robbers

By turning the Bible into a canon of tribal history and weaving it into the indigenous worldviews, Pentecostals directly address the problems of evil forces in numerous ways:

1. they mine the interior of the worldviews to establish that the same covenantal structure exists in both; therefore, the solution to the problem of affliction and defeat in life is to exchange the covenant with the wicked spirits for the covenant with Christ;
2. they produce large quantities of literature as discourses that expose these forces, and show individuals and communities how to overcome their dangerous and destructive influences;
3. they enable individuals and groups to constitute historical agents, empowered to do battle with these principalities and powers; and
4. they incite public testimonies about the works and victory over the wicked forces. Former agents of the spirits describe in gory details their years of bondage serving the false spirits; they combine these accounts with a wide range of self-help discourses exposing spiritual machinations at ground, occult, and territorial spirit levels. Testimonies in public worship become ceremonies of degradation and bridge burning.

Pentecostals do not reject the past wholesale but engage with it, refashioning the history and domesticating it. They use the Bible as a resource for explaining the past and critiquing the present. Pentecostal approach to the African map of the universe comes out most clearly in the response to the current legitimacy crises and economic collapse. For instance, the corruption in the state is attributed to the operation of the hunter or Nimrod spirit among Africans rulers, descendants of Ham. The collapse of the African economy is due to the shedding of blood through internecine fratricide and civil wars. These bring curses reminiscent of the Cain/Abel saga in which the land withheld her increase because the land was polluted with blood. Emigration follows ineluctably as the earth spews out her people. After the spiritualized diagnosis of the political economy's malaise follows the task of raising an army that will rescue the land. As will be further discussed in the next chapter, the approach fits into the tradition of iconic prophets whose duty was to "forth-tell" the meaning behind events. The real question may not be the spiritualizing of events, but whether such prognosis is based on adequate empirical data. Philip Jenkins has, therefore, brought together the arguments by John Mbiti and

Kwame Bediako that scholarship should pay attention to the centrality and uses of the Bible among Christians in various regions of the world.[16]

The language of God in Pentecostal liturgy buttresses this fact. Pentecostals explore the language that communities use in addressing their sustaining divinities, ancestors, and the Supreme Being and use this to describe God and Christ, showing that they are superior to all the powers available in the people's map of their universe. The reconstructed world is brought home to individual lives and circumstances by applying a "bumper sticker" hermeneutics or "experiential literalism." Cheryl B. Johns said that Pentecostal hermeneutics is praxis-oriented with experience and Scriptures being maintained in a dialectical relationship, with the Holy Spirit maintaining the ongoing relationship. The truth must be fulfilled in life experiences. Lived faith is the result of the knowledge of the Scriptures.[17] The emphases of lived faith are on the experiential, relational, and emotional aspects of the faith, as well as on oral faith the immediacy of the text, and a freedom to interpret and appropriate the multiple meanings of the biblical texts. By a pneumatic illumination, lived faith recognizes a spiritual kinship between the authors and readers and ongoing continuity with the New Testament church. Personal and corporate experiences weave into the hermeneutical task.

The amount of literature on this matter has burgeoned; suffice it to point to emphasizing the power of the Word in spiritual formation, resisting forces that could lead one to backslide, reversing curses, bringing deliverance, and commanding the things that the Lord's hands have made. The "brethren" arrive for Bible studies and Sunday worship with notebooks to take down the message or "revelations" so as to apply these during the week for victory. Everyone is urged to be an overcomer and "demon destroyer." This language is hermeneutics for conscientization, choreographed with a vigorous homiletic that mines the people's experiences, dramatizes these, props them with "real-life" testimonies, and brings the promises in the Bible to respond to the problems so that no one should leave bearing the burdens of yesterday. A pastor would tell the story of a woman who was carrying a heavy load. A car stopped and offered to assist the woman; she accepted the offer, got into the car, but continued to carry the load on her head instead of setting it down. The congregation would indicate that it was a foolish thing to do. Often a sermon would be interrupted with choruses to bring home a point. Pentecostal homiletic is language crafted in a transformative manner and choreographed as a ritual of validation and commitment. As L. Rambo argues,[18] the songs, dances, and the yells elicit audience participation and aid believers to perform religiously before rationalizing the process. Such rituals offer knowledge in a distinct form that enables the believer to understand, experience, and embody the new way of life.

6. Swallowing the Magicians' Serpents: A Conclusion

Generally, Western scholarship brands African Christianity as conservative and Biblicist even though some of the literature on the end-time prophecies from the Western world provides the armory for this application of the Bible to both contemporary events and the African primal map of the universe. Pentecostal leaders bring together materials from both internal and external sources in a manner that the unlettered can understand because behind the macroeconomics of the global market is the divine will. Pentecostals urge members to avoid judging by sight but by revelation as to which spirits are operating behind manifest events. Land deliverance is only one of the strategies employed. It is subtle and avoids overt iconoclasm: Believers can "walk" around shrines as hostile, polluted ground and command the spirits to leave. Sometimes, during emotional crusades, those with authority over the land and affairs of the community will be asked to confess the iniquities of the fathers that are being visited upon their progenies and to hand over the land to the authority of Jesus. This symbolic action will ensure prosperity for all the people. In these ways, the born-again brethren in Africa bring a spiritual solution to the great issues of the day, taking the context, the worldview, and the ecology seriously but doing so within the gospel mandate.

When Moses encountered the magicians in the house of Pharaoh, the narrative pointed to the undeniable fact that the magicians were able to produce serpents. They had and exercised powers. But the serpent produced by Moses swallowed the others to indicate that his rod of authority was more powerful. This informs the attitude of Pentecostals to African traditional cultures and religions. Unlike the enlightened missionary cultural policy, Pentecostals accept the power and reality in the symbols and rituals of communities and bring a "pneumatic knowing" to respond. Just as the primal societies wove covenants and encapsulating strategies to maintain cosmic order, Pentecostals essay to reshape the covenants, worldview, social control model, and individual life journeys and goals so that not only will individuals and communities have a better life, the community will also have a reshaped sense of order. These strategies could be illustrated with cultural ingredients from domestic and social domains, arts and aesthetics, religious life and public space, and especially with communication—the use of symbols, speech, and media to construct a new reality. The vibrancy and efficacy of the combined force of these strategies have given the new movement a high profile.

The movement can best be understood within the strand in African church historiography that has urged attention on the weave between religious ecology and the forms of Christian allegiance. It is a response to the deep-level challenges of the eco-theater, applying the pneumatic resources of biblical theology that missionary theology and practice had muted. Working within African maps of the universe, Pentecostals have shown how a creative use of biblical promises can transform the lives of many with tools of hope in the midst of the darkness that has hit Africa at noontide. They have exploited the elasticity in African worldview—and its capacity to make room—within its inherited body of traditions for new realities, which, though seemingly from outside, come in to fulfill aspirations within the tradition and, then, to offer quite significantly the basis of self-understanding within the tradition. Kwame Bediako says that this is what Paul did with Jewish traditions in the letter to the Hebrews.[19] Pentecostals have fleshed out their faith in the context of contending religious and social forces in Africa. The use of external cultural resources to create an emergent culture started with Western encounters with Africans. The genius of the movement lies in the degree of cultural creativity in appropriating, gestating, and reconstructing the extravenous with fresh imagination and energy. Culture and race were the contested set of signifiers in action in colonial Christianity, and African Christianity was stamped with values of anti-structure from the onset. Pentecostalism has produced a culture of continuity by mining primal worldview, reproducing an identifiable character, and regaining a pneumatic and charismatic religiosity that existed in traditional society. In conclusion, the achievement of Pentecostals lies in their innovative responses to the challenges embedded in the African map of the universe.

IO

Masters on Horses

The Roots of Pentecostal Public Ethics

1. Introducing the Instrumentalist Discourse

This study has been attentive to two concerns: the generational factor in the changing faces of African Pentecostalism, and the movement's response to both the indigenous and contemporary cultures of Africa. In the last chapter we concentrated on the indigenous culture. In this chapter we shall turn to the contemporary culture using the political theme as the illustration. Pentecostal political theology and practice reflect its responses to African political cultures. It used to be confidently affirmed that Pentecostalism is apolitical; that it ignores the issues of social justice and inequities in the political structures and focuses its message on the salvation of the individual soul. This characteristic, the argument continues, absorbs the individualism of Western Christianity and plays directly into the hands of right-wing religious conservatives whose political program is unhealthy for Africa. Another perspective is that African Pentecostalism is the religious face of modernity in which issues of political exclusion, frustrated economic aspirations, and overburdened kinship networks are confronted and renegotiated. It is said that Pentecostalism is a religion for the upwardly mobile, young, urban, educated generation who deploy it as an instrument to contest the constraints of ancient traditions. Both of these assertions constitute the heart of the instrumentalist discourse, a discourse that explores how religion serves as an instrument to achieve other goals that provides political, economic, and psychological adjustments to new realities by vested interests.

This discourse is prominently functionalist in its interpretation of the role of religion in the public space, and has been utilized by the social scientists who dominate the study of Pentecostalism. They explain the attraction of the movement to Africans as the allure to the cultural resources of externality. The discourse rejects Pentecostal use of providential language to attribute vertical expansion to the hand of God, as God's new move in contemporary times. Rather, social scientists perceive the invisible hand of the market forces, or the deprivation that compels people to seek a religious resort. The instrumentalist discourse brings to the fore the various, often oppositional, approaches to the study of religion: the normative, the historical–descriptive, and the theoretical. It has attracted the attention of post–colonial sensibilities, especially on the matter of indigenous agency and creativity. Obviously, the interdisciplinary approach to interpreting African Pentecostalism could gain much from the discourses on modernity and globalism as long the limitations are noted. The instrumentalist discourse tends to emphasize only the external contributions to African Pentecostalism, questioning the creativity of Africans in the Pentecostal explosion. Rebuttals abound.[1]

This chapter will achieve three goals. First, it will profile the globalization discourse as a version of the modernity discourse writ large, and point to its limitations. Second, it will illustrate the application of the instrumentalist discourse in the work of one of the avid commentators, Paul Gifford. Third, it will build the backdrop for a different understanding of Pentecostal practice by arguing that the practice is a response to the substratum of African political culture. In the following chapter, we shall then explore Pentecostal political practices.

2. Global Processes and Local Identities

The interest here, however, is the conjuncture of the rise of Pentecostalism with both the concept of globalization and the shift in the theory of knowledge held throughout the Enlightenment and modernity to that espoused in post-modernity. Is this fortuitous? The instrumentalist discourse favors the Pentecostal movement's avid exploitation of the resources of modernity. It views the movement as being so locked into the mindset of modernity that it is largely assumed that Pentecostalism worldwide serves as nothing more than the enchanted cultural version of globalism. Is African Pentecostalism an aspect of Western religious influence, "an extension of American electronic church"? How has African Pentecostalism responded to the external dimensions of the religious surge or utilised what Bayart calls "the resources of externality"? In other words, to what extent has the salience in the African religious landscape been a reproduction of the extravenous factor rather than African indigenous creativity?

An attempt to answer these questions begins by examining the theoretical exploration of the concepts of glocalization and its application to local religious contexts. *Glocalization* is understood as the process of domesticating the global in local contexts. How does globalization impact local cultures and how do local cultures respond? The appropriation of global forces within local contexts and communities—or the relationship of the macrocosm to the microcosm—has intrigued scholars, raising the question about how local cultures gestate, absorb, internalize, domesticate, or respond to external change agents. It might be useful to turn the question around to explore how African Pentecostalism utilizes the African worldview. Do African Pentecostals merely implant global cultural forms?

The argument here is that Pentecostalism is, in fact, colored by the texture of the African soil and derives idiom, nurture, and growth from its interior. It does not merely adapt, it gestates the resources of externality, transforming it to serve its needs. This explains why the fruits of the Pentecostal movement, therefore, more adequately answer the challenges (of power and evil) in the African ecosystem than the fruits of earlier missionary endeavors.

Since literature on the subject has burgeoned, suffice it to summarize that globalization is a relational concept to explain the increasing culture contact that has reduced distances in space and time and brought civilizations and communities into closer degrees of interaction. Not everybody is amused by the process, but many find it ineluctable. Everybody is affected by the integration and differentiation of global societies, which not only influences the theory of knowledge but has two other results: the emergence of a new culture and the intensification of culture and value clashes. As cultures are pressed together, the problem of identity looms large. Some argue that the new culture is not from any particular region but is an emergent culture, neither indigenous nor Western but a new culture. The key concern here is the application of the model in the study of religious systems, and Pentecostalism specifically. The issue has been addressed in the works of Roland Robertson, P. Beyer, Karla Poewe, Mike Featherstone, David Lyon, Rosalind Hackett, and Brigit Meyer and Ruth Marshall-Fratani. Much of the early discussion, to which Robertson drew attention, concerned the worldwide resurgence of religion contrary to the earlier predictions about the death of religion and ethnicity in the insurgence of modernity. Jeff Haynes analyzed the contrary trend in the Third World and especially Africa, while Peter Beyer demonstrated the failure of the prophecies of secularism by examining the insurgence of religious fundamentalism and ecological spirituality in many parts of the globe. It was Karla Poewe who reinterpreted Pentecostalism in South Africa as a form of global Christianity, contradicting those who imaged it as the religion of the disoriented, put it into the fundamentalist mold, or viewed it as part of the American right-wing insurgence into Africa. Rather, she argued, Pentecostalism reflected a spiritual flow from an ancient source coursing through the

Azusa Street impulse into the interior of the globe, including Africa.[2] Interest soon shifted to the conjuncture of modernity and postmodernity, probing the impact of media and technology as it empowers religious crusaders, the cultural discontinuities that must follow, and how it becomes an agent in spreading the psychology of modernity. In traditional society, ways of understanding the self, the other, and the past are very different. Does Pentecostalism attack the sustaining value of communalism in Africa by legitimating individualization and the nuclear family, or does it liberate members from the burden of the past?

Robertson first applied the concept of glocalization to deal with the global-local theme, borrowing from the Japanese *dochakuka*, a micromarketing technique for adapting a global outlook to local conditions. Long before then, *traditionalization* was the favored term, also using the Japanese pattern of industrialization along the grooves of traditional mores as an example. Factories operated as families, using the deference system and loyalties derived from traditional ethics. Glocalization is a concept designed to explore the interior dynamics and processes of culture contacts in contexts of asymmetrical power relations. It is not about globalized religion or increased homogeneity and sameness, but about how global, transnational cultural forms are set on wheels, domesticated, or refracted through the local cultural lenses. Viewed from several perspectives at once, it is the motor in the process between the encoder and the decoder, the interconnectedness of local distinctiveness and global generality, akin to the biblical understanding of the indigenous and pilgrim principles in Christianity. It emphasizes the initiative and creative responses and character of the local. Africa was not a tabula rasa on which foreign culture-bearers wrote their scripts with abandon. This concept makes it possible to demonstrate how global cultural forms are mediated in everyday lives of ordinary people in local places, expressed with the evocative phrase, "the epic of the ordinary." Finally, emphasis is placed on the sense of fluidity and flux in social analysis by restoring the initiative to the underdog and reducing the triumph of the presumed top dog. Globalism has usually been defined by the ideological bias of where one is located in the process. But local conditions and cultural patterns do still filter the flow of global ideas. As Marshall-Fratani puts it, "appropriation of the new occurs in an endless inventive process of cultural bricolage."

E. H. Carr intoned that all history is interpretation because facts are fragments. Using the rules of evidence as a restraint, the historian reconstructs events of the past from an articulated bias known as a conceptual scheme or discourse. The perception here is that Pentecostalism in Africa has indigenous roots, while also benefiting from external interventions and spiritual flows. When considering the appropriation of a religious phenomenon, it must be realized that religious networks do not operate within the same logic as banks and corporations. For one, most "hi-tech" networks are not deeply implicated in African settings; more cogently, votaries are self-conscious agents and do not simply adopt innovations unless they answer local questions and meet deeply felt needs.

Andrew Walls would further argue that Christianity was *always* global or universal in principle and simply became more so in practice from trends that appeared from the time of Vatican II to the present; that the real difference was a shift from *proselytism* to *conversion*, a process whereby communities turned the very core of their cultures to the glare of the gospel. The changes that may occur in such contexts would not be mere replications of the West, but would create a new experience for both the gospel and the new stakeholders. Christianity has, in recent times, voyaged into new terrains and expressed its message in new ways. When Paul Gifford intoned that "whatever it is, Christianity is a cultural product honed in the West over centuries," he was being ahistorical. As Walls countered, "At the beginning this story of Christianity appeared to be a Western religion. Appearances were deceptive; there was nearly a millennium and a half of active and expansive Christianity in Asia before the first Western missionary arrived there. There were also Christian communities in Africa that could claim a continuous history from sub–apostolic or early patristic times."[3]

Equally to the contrary, cultural flows are not unidirectional; rather, each cultural artifact acquires significance in each context. One of the complexities of Pentecostalism is that there are no fixed geographical, economic, or even symbolic centers for the movement. Heterogeneity and mutual dependence are core characteristics. Unlike the old missionary endeavor, the cultural flows and blockages are multidirectional, south-south, intracontinental, and north-south. This view, therefore, posits modernity as both a resource and challenge to people bringing the gospel mandate to bear on real issues of life and death in Africa. It explores the force of this form of religion in catalyzing both religious and social changes and thereby imperceptibly transforming the cultural landscape of which religion is a part. People remember Karl Marx's observation of the opiate effect of religion; they forget that he also said that religion was the heartbeat of a heartless society. As Harvey Cox would expand, "Religion is the royal road to the heart of a civilization, the clearest indicator of its hopes and terrors, the surest index of how *it* is changing."[4] Therefore, a close reading of Pentecostalism takes us to the heartbeat of the contemporary religious quest in Africa, which is simultaneously intense, pervasive, and multidirectional. African religious expression is a very alive universe in which all religious forms are exploding in numerical strength and have gained a voice in the public space.

The explosion of Pentecostalism has provoked an enormous upheaval in the African religious field and has acquired great visibility within a short period, both in urban and rural areas. The ordinary Pentecostal in Africa is less concerned with modernity and globalization and more focused on a renewed relationship with God, intimacy with the transcendental, empowerment by the Holy Spirit, and protection in the blood of Jesus as the person struggles to eke out a viable life in a hostile environment. It could be that they enjoy a certain "moral innocence of the global economy." As Harri Englund concludes in his study of Malawi, "Most Christians in Chisanpo are too poor and too unfamiliar with English to detach themselves from their immediate relationships in the township and country; ... the stuff of their Pentecostal lives is their personal relationships."[5] He warns fellow sociologists to "keep their abstractions in close dialogue with ethnography." This raises two important questions: How is Pentecostalism in Africa a force engaged in the religionization of cultures, at institutional and personal domains? And, in the process, has Pentecostalism itself been reshaped by cultures?

This chapter revisits the relationship of Pentecostalism to the contemporary African culture by posing the problem broadly. I shall summarize and view the application of this discourse on the political theology and practice of the Pentecostals through the lens of an articulate commentator, Paul Gifford, who has been a most engaging theorist. I shall also emphasize the need to locate Pentecostal theology and practice within the challenges of the African political culture suffused with religion. Quite often, scholars pay inadequate attention to the religious substratum of the modern African public space as a background to political discourses. Yet the modern African public space, in which secret societies perform as if they were open secrets, is so imbued with ingredients of resilient indigenous religions that it would be impossible for Pentecostalism to avoid the political implications. Instrumentalist discourse could be greatly enriched by examining cultural discourse. This would enhance the capacity to redefine the ambits of the political before determining the character of Pentecostal political engagement in the public space. Pentecostal political theology and practices are not heuristic.

3. Illustrating the Instrumentalist Discourse: Ghana's New Christianity

We shall use Paul Gifford's study of Ghana's Pentecostals as an illustration of this discourse.[6] Gifford, who teaches at the School of Oriental and African Studies, London, has a longstanding interest in the charismatic movements in Ghana: He wrote on them in 1993, 1994, 1998, and 2001. In 2004 he revisited the terrain with a detailed description of Pentecostalism in the Greater Accra context.[7] There is little doubt that he is very familiar with the territory, has a capacity for in-depth research, and embraces the burgeoning literature. Considering that most commentators read hardly any of the literature generated by the indigenous leaders, Gifford's scholarship is quite remarkable, and he is gifted with clarity of expression. The purview of his in-depth study is delimited to the Accra metropolis. Within this context, Gifford chose four megachurches and one prophet-type church as examples. The megachurches are those founded by Nicholas Duncan-Williams (1979), Mensah Otabil and Charles Agyin Asare (1980s), and Dag Heward-Mills (1991); while Elisha Salifu Amoako's church (1994) serves as an example of the prophet-type. These sample congregations were chosen to show the rich texture of the movement, and provide a window into other facets of the movement in the city. This is not a history of Pentecostalism in Ghana, but a sociological analysis of a small urban sample. Two critical observations must be made: the instrumentalist discourse privileges sociological interpretation rather than the historical and the sample is composed of urban megachurches and is hardly representative. Many scholars have drawn attention to rural features that disagree prominently with the urban phenomena. Gifford acknowledges the wide diversity in the sample and the marked changes of the churches over time "which make generalization even more difficult."[8]

He is equally clear that his two goals are to "establish what this Christianity is—what is its religious vision," and "to engage in the debate on sociopolitical role of this Christianity."[9] This political tail wags the religious dog. The time frame for this endeavor begins during the period when Jerry Rawlings ruled Ghana, first as a military dictator and later as a civilian president, and ends around 2002 when Rawlings failed to hand power over to his wife. Gifford's concern is to assess "the ways that (the) new Christianity might have helped, or currently helping, to bring Ghana into the world's modern political and globalizing economic system."[10] This, he claims, should be the ambition of any sensible Ghanaian and any viable Christian church. He paints a backdrop characterized by Ghana's pathology under Rawlings: personalized governance, economic failure, and patrimonial political culture.[11] Gifford's point is that the movement emerged during the closing years of dictatorship, the beginning of the democratization era, in the midst of economic collapse and legitimacy crisis.

Gifford acknowledges some positive dimensions of the new Christianity, emphasizing the rapid growth, youthful character, music, lively liturgy (consisting of praise, worship, sermon, offering), and sense of fellowship found in his sample churches. These congregations espouse a healthy gender ideology and advocate peace. Indeed, these churches catalyzed the charismatization of the mainline churches. But, he says, they inculcate the wrong ethics: the new Christianity de-emphasizes sin and hard work because "faith, giving, deliverance and the pastor's gifts are more important than hard work." Gifford examines the recurring emphases in the sermons, publications, and fund-raising strategies of the charismatic leaders, and concludes that:

1. they place spiritual over economic factors, and focus on the miraculous for success;

2. it is axiomatic that no country could hope to modernize until it has interiorized the importance of time and hard work and the new Christianity does not inculcate either of these; and

3. Ghana is webbed into global economic forces, yet the new Christianity obscures rationality by appeal to the demonic, ignores democratic values, and fails to mobilize social capital.

Generally, Ghana's charismatic Christians are portrayed as a collection of "divine pool players." This image contrasts sharply with other portraits by indigenous scholars like Emmanuel Anim and Kwabena Asamoah-Gyadu, who profiled the charismatic Christians as an army of reenergized business entrepreneurs using biblical words as business logos. Indeed, many commentators point to the work ethic among Pentecostals who name their businesses with Biblical affirmations as if they were protective charms of some sort.[12] Gifford rejects the argument that explains Pentecostal response to the contemporary environment by appealing to the force of continuity with traditional religion and culture, or attributes the success of the prosperity gospel in Ghana to the resonance between that gospel and indigenous spirituality. "I would argue that in Africa it is obvious that the faith gospel builds on traditional preoccupations. Africa's traditional religions were focused on material realities. Last century, Crowther wrote of the Yoruba religious search for 'peace, health, children and money.' This preoccupation has been noted several times since. But Africa's current Pentecostalism is increasingly articulated in terms of the faith gospel normally associated with a standardized Americn form."[13] The concern was to force the data into the mold of external influences, without reference to any contrary data. Also, the portrait of lazy charismatics waiting for manna to drop from the skies contrasts with the image of the consumerist, upwardly mobile groups who donate big sums to exploitative pastors. How do they access the fancy cars and material signs of success, described by Gifford? While some say that Pentecostalism has intensified the old Protestant ethic of hard work, Gifford insists that hard work is not in Pentecostal religious vision and may only occur as an unintended consequence.

Daniel J. Smith wryly concludes that "Pentecostalism is positioned in somewhat contradictory ways."[14] Andre Droogers concurs that commentators indulge in diverse and conflicting images of the movement: at once emphasizing the external and the indigenous; claiming to be global and showing the capacity to localize, to be sectarian and to drive for respectability; to be both authoritarian and democratic, world-rejecting and world-embracing; asserting both freedom and control; hard working and expecting miracles. These images could be based on the methodology, biases, and ideology of scholars as well as the inherent contradictions, diversity, and tensions within the movement. Geopolitical factors add pepper and salt to the broth. Droogers concludes that "people involved in globalization processes tend, like the above-mentioned church elder in Africa, to protect themselves by trying to remain who they are and what they are (identity as root), while simultaneously developing their own history, and making strategic use of all new opportunities that present themselves (identity as route)."[15] This is another way of stating Grant Wacker's notion of the interweave between the primivistic and pragmatic instincts within the movement.

Gifford's analytic method becomes more intriguing when he discusses the growth of deliverance and prophetic ministries that are, in fact, connected with political practice. The Pentecostal churches may believe that they are manifesting what the Bible calls the "word of knowledge" and are recovering the prophetic ministry from the Old Testament, but Gifford profiles them as lacking moral agency and deploying impartation, anointing, mantras, and testimonies to encourage members to do nothing because success must be miraculous. He contrasts these views by extolling the virtues of Mensah Otabil, a figure in African ministry who insists on self-development, mutes demonic activities in explaining human destiny and the fate of the nation, emphasizes human responsibility for failures, and advocates human agency in creating change both at the individual and national levels. Otabil advocates a cultural change for Ghana, and Gifford insists he was the only pastor who refused to be coopted by President Rawlings and dared to speak truth to power.

On the specific forms of Pentecostal political engagement, Gifford acknowledges that a modicum of "development activity is also found in some Pentecostal denominations," some established, and the charismatic leaders show incredibly diverse political attitudes. During the 2000 Ghanaian elections, some used the Bible to support different candidates. Some critiqued the political culture, while others explained its dynamics with spiritual eyes. The spiritualization of politics has various strands in Gifford's account: First, in the enchanted approach, the new Christianity makes demons responsible for the national problems. The demons are either ancestral spirits or territorial spirits. A second strand, the biblical approach, alleges that past leaders had indulged in apostasy and that liberation could only come from public repentance and by allowing the Holy Spirit to be in charge of the affairs of the nation. A third strand of spiritualization utilizes the faith gospel or the "power of the word" to insist that Christians must guard against negative pronouncements on the affairs of the nation. All of these discourses debate national issues in terms of morality, and Gifford expresses discomfort with all these strands because they diminish human responsibility: "Not only is it God who will bring about the deserved order, but nothing else is required of Ghanaians but the worship of the true God."[16] This affirmation, Gifford argues, will not be recognized "in modern political science departments or discussed in World Bank Reports."[17] Note the two sources on which he predicates the modernization of Ghana. He continues on the same page, "this understanding would not normally or naturally lead to pressure for an independent judiciary, accountable systems at the bank of Ghana, transparent tendering at the Divestiture Commission, or procedures rather than personal whims in approving rice production schemes."

By "spiritualizing" politics, the charismatic churches ignore the wider body politic. Gifford thus rejects as "slippage" the views by Birgit Meyer, Gerrie ter Haar, Stephen Ellis, and Ruth Marshall that conceptualizing evil could be politically salutary, and "that Africans use this demonic cosmology to make sense of the evils that befall them, and that many African Christians claim to be transforming the societies around them."[18] He also critiques David Martin's argument that Pentecostals who might be powerless in the public arena deploy the power of implicit or covert politics. Martin had argued that the internal organization of Pentecostal cell groups enable individuals to learn how to function democratically, elect their own officers, develop and exercise leadership skills, handle money and budgets, plan and execute projects, and critique the results. These functions groom citizenship, encourage democratic culture, incubate a civil society, and bear seeds of a critical populace, says Martin. Others add that Pentecostal morality has broad sociopolitical implications because it cures wastage from undisciplined, dissipated lifestyles; fosters a strong work ethic; and cures dysfunctional macho male behavior. Still others aver that spiritual intercession may be a form of political praxis when people seek to shape history through prayer and fasting. Gifford argues that much of this argument is wishful thinking. Because Pentecostal organizations are authoritarian, the faith gospel and emphasis on miracles foster passivity rather than a healthy work ethic. And since the churches themselves are not transparent in their accounting, they certainly cannot challenge unaccountable governments.

There are a number of ways that a reader could respond to the typically outsider hardware comprising of a Western enlightenment worldview, a World Bank yardstick, and a Weberian rational system of governance. African political analysts contest this dismal perception by rejecting both the Afro-pessimism and New Realism discourses and promoting a new discourse—labeled African Renaissance or Afro-optimism—that rejects the loss of hope in the destiny of Africa, and recommends a new strategy that mines African indigenous cultures, knowledge, and religious traditions for a viable political culture and system. African scholarship perceives the World Bank prescriptions as the source of the present scourge of poverty, since changes at the macroeconomic level do not easily change the suffering at the microeconomic level because of the slow trickle-down effect. One cannot ignore the external dimension to the fate of an African nation; structural adjustment programs were installed by Western countries that were unwilling to spend a certain percentage of their gross domestic product on poor countries but still wanted those countries to service their huge debts. Afro-optimism discourse recognizes that, in spite of failures by the African leaders, some measure of progress has been accomplished in many African nations, including the democratizing process in Ghana.[19] Given the impact of the democratizing process on the religious field in many non-Western nations, these strategies honed in the West are not necessarily panacea.

This leads to the examination of the purview of the political field and the complex character of the church's engagement in a pluralistic public space. There is no gainsaying that the church exists to serve the community; that the church, as a member of the civil society, could serve as a pressure group. The problem is the measure of balance between an activist church focused heavily on issues of social justice and a conversionist church focused on individual salvation. The greater concern is to live dialogically, lest politicians manipulate religion to their own agenda and religion become a dysfunctional force. A comparison with mainline churches who "have been characterized by an element of direct political involvement, which has led them to pronounce on issues of human rights and even to train election monitors,"[20] certainly ignores the history of collusion with forces of oppression by these denominations, exaggerates the churches' role in the post–colonial state, and underestimates the lack of the access to correct information for influencing change in this environment. Do Africa's leaders actually listen to the church's pronouncements?

The purview of the political field and the range of political activities are broad and complex. Commentators argue that being apolitical should not be construed as being antipolitical. It speaks to a symbolic framing that is covert; it is a certain level of political participation, perhaps within a civil society that could engage in fostering education, healthcare delivery, and participate in associational life within the infrapolitical zone. Covert activities could be effectively antistructural; homiletics could be imbued with images, symbols, language, idiom, and protocol that induce opposition to the power holders. Intercessory prayer could be a form of political praxis attacking the immorality of rulers, insisting upon individual ethics as the basis of political morality, focusing on the family as the basis of political practice, and defining the shape of a new environment. This is unlike an antipolitical posture that indulges in an enclave mentality. Indeed, voting does not necessarily enable the people to make their leaders accountable just as political structures do not necessarily mean the consolidation of salient political values.

Similarly, there are various levels of overt political participation, either engaging in governance, electoral processes, or in opposition movements. For instance, many researchers are hardly aware of the wide range of religious movements on the continent. There are groups such as Intercessors for Africa, whose main focus is redeeming the public space for Christ and who organized the SALT Project to inculcate a higher sense of accountability among top civil servants in West Africa. The imagery is borrowed from the Bible's requirement that Christians should be the "salt" of the community. In the early 1970s, the

Nigerian Christian Graduate fellowship published a magazine called *ALARM: Prophetic Publication for the Church and Nation,* indicating that the young Pentecostals were not other-worldly but had a clear political vision.[21]

There are various views about the character of Pentecostal political practice. For instance, some argue that Chiluba's declaration of Zambia as a Christian nation did not enlist the input from mission-founded churches, that he opened the road to Pentecostal naivety in politics, that he could not restrain corruption and may have actually participated in it, and that he became increasingly dictatorial. Others argue that he fell off the Pentecostal wagon and consulted a spiritualist church in Nigeria. The bottom line is the issue of whether one assigns a spiritual explanation or a secularist, empirical causation to the political condition of a nation. This is the method in the modernity discourse. From an ecclesiological perspective, some prefer an activist church or a countercultural confessing church that insists upon rational governance and compels the government to improve society. As Gifford put it "Nobody denies that Ghana would change if all citizens became paragons of love, truth, justice," but change could also come from insisting upon transparent and efficient instruments of governance.[22] Others want the church to be both conversionist and prophetic.

In spite of Gifford's achievements a methodological problem lurks under his works, as Karla Poewe and Irving Hexham noted in their critique of Gifford's work on South African Pentecostalism.[23] For instance, Gifford's skewed portraits of two pastors, Dag Heward-Mills and Abu Bako, in the attempt to underscore his position. I shared a copy of the book with one of them and he observed that the researcher must have visited on the day that they were completing a forty-day fast; that the liturgy described was far from being the regular liturgy; that if the author had talked to him or any of the leaders, these issues would have been clarified. Pastor Abu Bako added that when he was a lecturer in the university, social scientists applied better research methods. The crucial point is that these men are educated and respected Bible teachers whose sermons focus on the Scriptures. Abu Bako, the leader of Logos Rhema Church, was formerly a lecturer at Ahmadu Bello University, Zaria. Like Derek Prince, he roots his teachings on spiritual warfare in rigorous biblical scholarship. Dag Mills, a medical doctor, makes every effort to ground his ministry on the word; his liturgical arsenal includes the use of skits as a teaching technique to deal with moral issues. Every year, he produces three ninety-day Bible Guides that teach those things that Gifford found lacking in the sermons on the days that he visited.[24] Gifford's image of the new Christianity in Africa is that the leaders lack a valid theology, proclaim a gospel that is hardly classifiable as evangelical, and contribute to the poverty of the nation by failing to inculcate values that could liberate Ghana.

Yet Gifford's critical profiling deserves much attention because it may assist African leaders in reexamining the quality of their witness. Of particular importance is the quality of biblical exegesis by some leaders, and the biblical pedigrees of many of the church's practices. It is not enough to merely insist that the critic must be a Pentecostal. However, this work raises the question of insider and outsider perspectives because Gifford disagrees so strongly with indigenous scholars; it appears that the critic does not feel the same spiritual power that the people feel, and from which they make their decisions and derive what they say. It is like a thick description of dancers without hearing their music. Worse still, he devotes great uncritical attention to cataloguing the discomfort of secularists, Muslims, journalists, and synods of mainline churches about the so-called false prophets. It is dangerous to write the history of a young movement from only the perspective of its enemies. As an African proverb says, cattle are born with ears—they grow horns later.

4. Open Secrets: The Religious Substratum of the Modern African Public Space

The portrait of the African church painted above challenges us to remember four things: First, it is important to enlarge the boundaries of our understanding of political engagement beyond overt activities such as political protest, party politics, and the electoral process. Second, we should be attentive to the magical substratum that underpins the political culture. The pattern of political engagement is determined by the political culture, and Pentecostal political response is embedded in the indigenous terrain and the religious foundations of the political culture. As Daniel Smith put it,

> The Pentecostal critique of politics, power, and inequality in contemporary Nigeria draws on a much longer African legacy in which the accumulation of wealth and power is explained in terms of witchcraft and the occult. As in the past, contemporary inequalities in sub-Saharan Africa, including southeastern Nigeria, have been articulated and publicly debated using idioms of the supernatural. Traditional African responses to inequality explained by witchcraft often relied on invoking countervailing positive occult forces to protect against or reverse the effects of black magic. The Pentecostal construction of evil associates all forms of the occult with the work of the devil and conceives of the battle of good and evil in the human world as a battle between God and the devil.[25]

It is germane to reiterate that, in the African terrain, the pneumatological approach is key to understanding the Pentecostal political theology and practice. In this, the resilience of indigenous religion is a very important dimension. Third, that the vast differences within the regions and countries within the continent compel attention and comparative perspectives. Steve Ellis and

Gerrie ter Haar have pursued this theme in their book *Worlds of Power* by drawing upon examples from the entire continent. Here and in the next chapter, I shall use illustrations from various culture theatres in Nigeria to paint the religious substratum of the political culture.

Fourth, that the sacralization of political order and ethics in primal society informs the political culture in the modern public space. The political elite tap the resources of primal religion in their competitions in the modern space; they provide an enormous opportunity for primal religiosity to influence the dynamics of modern politics. A legitimacy crisis merely intensified the process in a religious space bedeviled with an occult explosion. Meanwhile, other religious forces are growing, with many political implications. A few studies are taking holistic view of the entire political field so that Pentecostal presence is perceived and analyzed comparatively. For instance, Rosalind Hackett argued that new spiritual science movements with political significance are forms of cultural invention, some deriving and all "consonant with the world-affirming and pragmatic orientation of traditional religious beliefs and practices."[26] Indeed, Pentecostals are implicated in the conflict generated by the Abrahamic religions in the political dynamics of Africa. It has been suggested that the Christian–Muslim conflict could be explained as the clash of two fundamentalisms. Pentecostalism must be studied within the broad range of roles played by religious forces beneath the political events in Africa. The implication is that Pentecostal theology and practice run deeply in its response to the religious undercurrents of the political culture. As van Djik concludes:

> Pentecostalism's fascination with horrific witchcraft stories plays a role in the construction of a critical politics of identity. It destabilizes other frameworks of identity production, such as the modern Malawian postcolonial state, seeking to enhance its dominion over its citizens through a specific project of nationhood.[27]

It was not only President Kamuzi Banda who danced with secret cults in the national stadium: President Jerry Rawlings of Ghana proactively resurrected indigenous cults while President Nicophore Soglo of the Republic of Benin declared voodoo as the national religion. Many African leaders espouse Christianity in public but dance with secret societies behind the scenes and commit ritual murders in secret. Kenneth Kaunda of Zambia patronized a shrine, The David Universal Temple, operated by an Indian guru, M. A. Ranganathan; President Bongo of Gabon belonged to the Bwiti and Ndjobi secret societies; and William Tolbert of Liberia served as both the president of World Baptist Alliance and the supreme *zo* of the Poro society. A host of others—including Houphet Boigny, Idi Amin, Sanni Abacha—used secret rituals to maintain their power.[28] Traditional religion ranked high as the dominant religion in eight West African nations. This is the backdrop for understanding Pentecostal political theology. Pentecostals look beneath the structures of the public sphere to address the spirits that govern them. This theme opens the possibility for examining how both the overt and covert dimensions of political engagement are equally important.

In Africa, the sacralization of the cosmos legitimates the political space and dynamics of the political culture. The rulers and the ruled often act from a sense of the presence and ultimateness of the spiritual forces. This fact is seen in the four models of social control (socialization, restriction, punishment and reward); the socialization process inculcates the acceptable norms of the community. Covenanting rituals, with what Victor Turner calls a "forest of symbols," bond the child with the spirits at the gates of the community. Van Gennep has examined the physical, psychological, and sociological dimensions of socialization. Shorter adds that the process continues into adulthood, imparting the wisdom of the ancestors, religious wisdom, and wisdom for living well and fully for one's own sake and for the sake of the entire community. The proverbs, riddles, songs, and dances exude moral guidance.[29] The ritual may involve withdrawal from the community and periods of exclusion and communion with the spirits of the land. The community restricts those who would flout its values with prohibitions, gossip, joking relationships, satire, and cultic action. Punishment crashes on the heads of the obstinate; the offended deities are then appeased with sacrifice and rites of purification. Those who uphold such values are rewarded with honor, a chieftaincy title, praise names, and an eagle's feather, all to the accompaniment of the flute and big drum. Political ethics in a traditional society are rooted in the social control models. The foundation is moral and sanctioned by the gods for the wellbeing of all. Truthfulness, decency, moderation, and wisdom are acceptable leadership values. There was no secular theory of obligation. To accede to authority roles, the individual must be "animated," imbued with a close relationship to the gods of the community. As a chief, the animation rites endow the "tongue of the tiger." This tongue is sharp and will judge rightly without favor or be swerved by patronage of the rich. Many studies have used the rituals surrounding the enthronement of rulers to buttress the religious roots of legitimacy in primal society.[30]

Our interest is not to mine the political structure of African cultures but to emphasize a certain ambience; namely, that modern political culture has sought to corrode primal ethics and yet the spiritual dynamics of the primal order have invaded modern politics. Traditional cults are used in modern public space without due moderation and boundaries because the modern space is supposed to be an unlimited and unbounded space. Rulers and the political elite act out their quest for legitimacy in the primal space without absorbing its values. For instance, in traditional society, the leader is a ritual agent even in the situations where there are priestly guardians of communal shrines. Priestly functions are invested in the paterfamilias, first sons, kinship heads, village, clan leaders, and female priestesses. Gerontocracy, the rule of elders, predominates because elders and ancestors are in close proximity. In any community, there would be ritual power nodes—diviner, seer, herbalist/healer, and witchcraft expert—who provide protective enhancement and destructive medicine, charms, and amulets. General practitioners may combine some of these roles; and an elastic structure enables the recruitment of spiritual forces from foreign communities for witchcraft detection and protective and achievement-enhancing medicine. Guilds and secret societies also coexist, sharing wisdom, craft, cult, and medicine. They mobilize around certain interests, including healing, wealth, influence, esoteric knowledge, mutual aid, and entertainment. In some communities, leaders can only emerge from among the members of the secret society.

The key theoretical frame here is the concept of three publics discussed in the previous chapter. The clientele character of patrimonial culture from the emergent public overwhelmed primal values under indigenous rule. The victory of the emergent value system is illustrated by the expectation of villagers that their kith and kin should go to the emergent public and claim their own share of the national cake by hook or, preferably, by crook. If a fraudulent public official were prosecuted, his village elders would go on a delegation to protest. Dishonest individuals can now take chieftaincy titles without fulfilling the moral prerequisites. The immoral ethics of the emergent public have debauched the salient values of the primal culture and provided fodder for power adventurers and predatory military rulers. Praetorian regimes both engender and exploit the collapse of the religious and moral force that propped up the society. A close look betrays the ironic "villagization" of the modern political space. Political actors pose as warriors from their villages to compete for national resources on behalf of their communities; therefore seeking legitimacy in the primal political base. They undergo rituals of empowerment by attaining chieftaincy titles and membership in cults and secret societies; they patronize ritual agents who provide protective charms and amulets. Thus "fortified," they are able to detect poison, ward off witchcraft spells, and operate with immense vital force. The emergent public is viewed as a place in which success can be achieved only with magicoreligious power derived from any efficacious sources. The preparation for the foray into the emergent zone starts from the village, which has the benefit of building grassroots support by showing the villagers that their political representative is one of them and shares their value system. One can appear as a champion of African culture, dance with the masquerade, and pose as a nationalist of no mean order!

In a context in which economic power is derived from political power, the elite utilize primal cult and spiritual force in self-aggrandizement. They assume titles which position them as the "the leopard which guards the village, the voice of the people, the light, the sun, the moon, the lightning that shows the way, the war leader" of the people. The imagery is a teasing cluster of money, power, and light on the darkened path of communities. Armed with village legitimacy, they offer themselves as a good investment for the military leader who is in the market for clients and ready to pay cash for some form of legitimacy. An intimacy of power is crafted. The parasitic relationship vitiates traditional institutions, robbing them of their values and disarming the rural masses of their will to protest. In the last five years, the inability of the political elite to withstand tyrants and protect the masses from the humiliations of poverty can be explained by the interconnection between the primal and emergent publics. The political elite proved to be the clay feet of civil society. The dynamics of our legitimacy crisis are rooted in religious culture.

Two further illustrations are taken from ethnographic data from two ethnic groups in Nigeria. These powerful cults emerged from primal religiosity to dominate the modern political space: the *Ogboni* from Yorubaland and the *Nyamkpe* from the Cross River basin in southeastern Nigeria. Both are powerful secret societies whose votaries ascended through rungs or degrees of initiation. The *Ogboni* cult controlled Yoruba society and could discipline a king. It became dominant because Nigerian contact with whites, traders, commissars, or missionaries first took place in the Yoruba environment. The indigenous people used their secret society as a means of mobilizing adequate responses to the new dispensations. Gradually, other Nigerians sojourning in Lagos found that the society conferred protection, access to wealth, power, and upward mobility in professions and politics. It became a transethnic religious force dominating modern sectors such as business, professions, and politics. The judiciary, civil service, military, government, and even top ecclesiastical posts were lorded over by *Ogboni* members. In 1914 an Anglican archdeacon, Venerable T. A. J. Ogunbiyi, founded the Reformed Ogboni Fraternity in an attempt to remove the "pagan" rituals and enable Christians to participate without qualms. He emphasized the benefits of bonding in the brotherhood. Each initiate swears to be "in duty bound to help one another in distress, to succor, in adversity to warn against danger and be charitable under all circumstances." Thus, the two *Ogboni* cults coexist as a powerful secret society from the primal religion and serve as a power node in the modern political space. Their secrecy, class, wealth, and bonding enable them to wield enormous influence.

Nyamkpe played a similar role among the communities of the Cross River basin but to a lesser extent. A cult of the leopard spirit, it served as the political force, adjudicator, and enforcer of customs among many ethnic groups in the region. It was of Ejagham origin but gained much prominence because of the role of the Efiks of Calabar. Calabar was the port of early commercial contact with the hinterland. It soon housed the provincial commissioner, new courts and educational institutions. The secret society was first used to choose local rulers, then served as a trade mechanism to galvanize indigenous traders and settle disputes, and finally functioned as a society for the wealthy and powerful class. The entry fee increased as the society became more important in both the colonial and post–colonial dispensations. Like the *Owegbe* cult among the Edo of midwestern Nigeria, secret societies became core instruments of political mobilization in Nigeria. As ethnic competition intensified, communities resorted to these mobilization systems. They served as pressure groups, secret enclaves where the fears and strategies of the community were discussed. They mobilized the elite, offering covenants of mutual support, wealth, cult security, and protection in dangerous terrains, as well as political clout. Recently, those engaged in developmental and environmental struggles among the Ijaw have formed secret societies imitating the *Sekiapu and Ekine* society among other Niger Delta communities. Thus, at the federal level, there is a mushrooming of ethnic identities suffused in cults of the primal publics, each struggling to serve its own narrow interests. Military dictators found the scenario easy to maneuver: "settling" some groups, recruiting others, and destroying any opposition that refused to be compromised. This explains the orgy of sycophancy around the dictator.[31]

This is a worldview far removed from Enlightenment rationalism. People still believe in the availability of spiritual forces that can be tapped for vital force and protection in the public space. This explains why the language of witchcraft is used loosely in an environment where night guards, politicians, police officers, civil servants, soldiers, businessmen, academics, and students could all go to native doctors and acquire the requisite medicine for protection, power, passing examinations, gaining promotions, making money, retaining good health, traveling safely, and winning in sports. Robbers seek bulletproof medicine and smugglers seek medicine that will make them invisible to anti-drug or customs agencies. The amazing thing is that there could be so much failure in spite of all the charms that people carry with them. As rational social structures collapse, there appears to be an increase in the penumbra religious zone. Politicians will hire traditional rainmakers to scatter opponents' political rallies with heavy rains. Primal religiosity is employed in electoral pranks instead of using hostile advertisements. In the early 1990s witches took out an advertisement in a newspaper to announce that they would be hosting an international convention in the ancient city of Benin. The leader of Nigerian witches started an annual prophetic declaration of major events of each new year—usually that a very important person would die! But the political focus of the prophecies reflected the disquiet in people's mind caused by the legitimacy crisis.

Rijk van Djik describes a similar situation in Malawi. He argues that the centrality of the diatribes against witchcraft in Pentecostal preaching touched a central nerve in the urban Blantyre: "Witchcraft made people disappear, it made people suffer; it made the ordinary township residents fall victim to the evil powers of nocturnal world, producing in the process one haunting question: are politics and witchcraft one of a kind?"[32] In the urban-dwellers' anxiety-ridden environment a wide range of conditions were explained by the prevalence of spirits from traditional religion: zombie scares, panics about the occult trade in human body parts, unemployment and hardship, failed enterprises, and lack of promotion.

The proliferation of secret cults in the public space started in the development of towns as many people gathered in one space with medicines and cults from different ethnic groups. Its force has merely risen in intensity. The Nigerian government outlawed formal secret cults such as Ancient Mystic Order of the Rosi Crucis and Freemasonry in the civil service and military with the Gazette of 1977. Perhaps the proliferation grew from the revival of indigenous religion during the civil war (1967–1970) and the intense competition triggered by the oil boom thereafter. In universities, it turned into a scourge of educated culture when students formed innumerable secret cults, each outdoing the other in violent crimes. These were not fraternities or peer-support groups as in North American universities, where the worst fate would be to drink oneself to death. Rather, the students visited native doctors, poured their blood into shrines, and established violent cults that intimidated fellow students (especially females) and faculty. The political dimension was soon obvious as the student cults rivaled one another to control the hall governments, students' unions, and the National Association of Nigerian Students. As they lacked in learning and morals, one could anticipate another blow on the vaunted civil society that would oppose predatory governments. They not only aided the disabling of the academic environment but, during the political mayhem of the years 1993–1998, many of the cult students became drug dealers, thugs for politicians, and mobilized student support for the military oligarchy's quest for legitimacy. Through them, primal cults ascended into the ivory tower with devastating consequences. It should also be added that as the legitimacy crisis intensified, both the savagery in the competition for resources and political power and the use of violence as a tool in politics increased. Thugs fortified themselves with charms, "powerful" prayers, concoctions, and incantations. Groups of thugs had ritual chaplains. Agents of social disorder were recruited in the competition for wealth and power. This is only a part of the story that will be continued in the next chapter.

II

Tembisa

Pentecostal Political Theology and Practices

1. Religion: Invention of Culture and Politics

One more block must be built around the substratum of African
political culture before we discuss how African Pentecostalism engages the modern public space or serves as a beacon of hope, or
tembisa. The contemporary African public space is a pluralistic environment imbued with growing religious forms that operate just under the radar of public view but control the political culture. Unlike
those discussed in the last chapter, some of these religious groups are
drawn from outside sources, or simply reinvented. Two religious
groups come to the fore in the analysis of the innards of modern
political culture: the first, the *Mami Wata* cult is rooted in primal
religion but is a good illustration of "invention of culture." It added
foreign elements in the emergent culture. As R. W. Hefner observed,
"the incorporation into a larger social order acts as a catalyst for re-
formulation of indigenous religion."[1] The other is completely foreign
but is utilized like the secret societies of primal culture and prolifer-
ates as a means of surviving in the emergent public. The rise of the
"Spiritual Science Movement" has not featured much in the academic
analyses of religion and politics in Africa. Rosalind Hackett, who
coined the terminology, was still confused about an adequate typology.
She noticed a proliferation of the movement in Calabar in the
1980s. The focus here will be only on two such groups that are size-
able and have considerable political impact: namely, the Ancient
Mystical Order Rosae Crucis (AMORC) and Grail Message.

In current literature, much interest is lavished on the *Mami Wata* cults of Africa because art historians are fascinated with the rich iconography and influence of goddesses in gender studies. It is a female cult. In the primal world-view, rivers were important. A world exists in the waters where goddesses preside. These goddesses of the river gave beauty, wealth, and fertility power. Women speak of dreaming that they went into the river during pregnancy and were given beautiful babies. Marine deities such as *Oshun* patronized divination, witchcraft, and sustained political power.[2] For power and wealth, people killed cows for *Idemili of Nnobi* and took the title of *Ogbuefi Idemili*, conferring a high social and political status. Communities built shrines and installed priestesses. Marine cults proliferated. Ifi Amadiume has shown in her study of the power of the goddess among the Idemili community in Igboland that when the river and its cult becomes crucial for the political life of the community, patriarchal ideology intervenes to place either a male priest or a husband over the female priest. The idea grew that there was a queen in the water whose beauty was surpassing, who did not give fertility, health, long life, or progeny, and did not act as mother; rather, she gave wealth, power in life pursuits, and sexual prowess. She was more of a lover than a mother, whom votaries sought for gifts that bestowed allure, beauty, and grandeur. She was outside any one social system and gave gifts with significance in the emergent culture; thus, people gradually associated her with European goods. Shrines were consecrated in the homes of ardent votaries. As the pantheon of water spirits expanded and the number of devotees grew, their ritual paraphernalia and icons became more elaborate, incorporating foreign cultic features. There are two nuances to be observed in this shift: first, the veneration has spread throughout sub-Sahara Africa and has been featured in much anthropological literature. Second, as Bastian observed, "most of this material, however, has emphasized the visual component of Mami Wata devotion-focusing in on what we might call Mami Wata style, a syncretistic mixture of west African iconography and western commodity fetishism."[3] The traditional version entangled with the lore of sailors. The notion that she traveled in a canoe was added. Cults burgeoned in which the priestesses would divine and perform rituals to connect an individual with a mermaid spirit who would grant riches, political victory, and high position. The person would promise to observe certain prohibitions and sacrifice something precious to the spirit. Many of the Nigerian political elite resort to these shrines on the river banks for the munificence of the mermaid. When professions such as engineering, architecture, and banking collapsed in the late 1980s, politics became the only means of making money or collecting the crumbs from the tables of military rulers. There could certainly be a connection between economic collapse and the proliferation of *Mami Wata* cults.

H. J. Drewal has argued that the cult was transformed from the traditional mode to serve the interest of the emergent public with the Euro-African commercial contacts in the fifteenth century.[4] This may explain dreams of a journey to a domain with white people, posh buildings, and all sorts of finery. But African contact with Indians has also been crucial. The material representation of the Mami Wata as a snake charmer grew from African interest in Indian prints of Hindu gods and goddesses and spirits. The lithographs of Buddha and other chromolithographs are of Indian origin. In the colonial period, magazines and catalogues of Indian charms, spells, rings, candles, talismans, and perfumes proliferated in Nigeria. They promised easy paths to wealth and success and protection more powerful and expensive than the traditional "medicine." The dangerous proviso was that if the devotee misused the directives, the person could become mad! Africans associated the success of Indian merchants with the potency of their religious cults. The impact of Asian and exotic cults in modern Nigerian life deserves research. It is a key factor in explaining the resilience of nativistic and vitalistic religious enterprises among the African Instituted Churches (AICs). Popular religion thrives on it. In an emergent culture, religion has always proved a resort for the desperate person who finds day-to-day survival in the urban setting rather traumatic. *Mami Wata* cults promise materials for use in modern living and money that can be used to purchase votes and power and enhance success in the modern political space. After this person dies, a squabble would often break out among his progenies and it is believed that all the wealth would be dissipated or "return" to the marine world from whence it came. *Mami Wata* must engage in recycling!

The evidence of the extent of this cult has emerged from the burgeoning literature on deliverance. For instance, during many of the monthly breakfast meetings of the Full Gospel Business Men's Fellowship International, a number of the elite give testimonies of their spiritual journey and their struggles to make money and gain power in the world. L. R. Rambo has discussed the impact of these biographical reconstructions in encapsulating the believer. Many of these are published in gory accounts of sojourns with marine cults.[5] In 1990, a prominent politician who rose to the post of a deputy governor of one of the states in southeastern Nigeria told the Full Gospel audience how he and many of his colleagues patronized a marine deity through whom they received occult materials from India. He said that they would place an order for candles and other ritual materials by writing the list on a piece of paper and burning it in a shrine located in his home after using the appropriate incantations. The ordered candles and items would then just appear in his personal shrine. His shrine became his route to the governor's mansion. Through the prayers of his wife, he became "born-again." He is now a preacher on the futility of the endeavor. The expense in setting up a viable shrine indicates that this is a game played primarily by the rich. The importance of this data is that it provides an internal Pentecostal critique against materialism, consumption, and the allure of modernity. Believers are warned that many of the couture fashions are produced inside the water and are designed to lure the believer into devotion to the marine spirits. A marine spirit afflicts her victims by promising them "modern" riches such as beautiful cars, jewelry, perfume, and computers but usually deserts them, leaving them afflicted with inexplicable diseases and death. People who once ate at the table now eat on the floor; many die as paupers. Marine spirit wealth is ephemeral. As a Pentecostal chorus intones, Mami Wata provides "*na yeye* power" (useless, empty power) in contrast to the transformative power of Jesus.

Similarly, the AMORC and Freemasonry are secret societies for the professional elite. They are much like *Ogboni*, except that they originate from the West. The AMORC, or Ancient Mystical Order Rosae Crucis, is an esoteric fraternal order founded by H. Spencer Lewis in New York in 1915. It claims continuity with an ancient Egyptian occult order and promises to help people discover the secret powers of inner vision and cosmic consciousness. The concern here is not with their "mystical philosophy," but with their political relevance. On the surface, they provide international linkage, a worldwide cultural fraternity, access to financial opportunities for the professional elite, and spiritual solace. They are bastions of political power in the state. At the cultic level, they constitute a similar invention of culture, and appropriate new spiritual modes to serve functions already articulated in the primal religion. The symbols are, therefore, differently attuned to the Western magical tradition. Studies on Sierra Leone, Liberia, and Cameroon exposed how the Lodge (Rosicrucian and Masonic) constitutes the nerve center of power in these countries. A thorough analysis of the intricate web of power and influence of the Lodge is provided by Abner Cohen's *The Political Culture of the Elite*, a case study of the Creoles of Sierra Leone. Lodges are popular throughout the West African coast. Nigeria, being rather too large and endowed with a centrifugal power structure, does not grant such important to these groups, but the Rosicrucians and Freemasons are very influential in the South.[6] Many Christian groups are concerned that many of their important members are also members of these two religious secret societies. The Catholics, Anglicans, and recently the Methodists have countered by giving elite members titles and bizarre uniforms and long parade swords within Knighthood Orders. On the surface it may appear that they do not appreciate the political and economic dimension to cult membership, but some say that the liturgy of the Knight Orders resembles those of the Rosicrucians and the political function is the same.

There are over a dozen groups within the Spiritual Science Movement; most of which sprang to life in the 1980s. One line of enquiry could explore the human conditions as a backdrop and ask why Nigerians appear to be so receptive to these spiritual groups. Some groups are from the West and many are Asian. The Masonic Lodges are prominent because they were founded in colonial times and served as a contact between the rising African elite and the Europeans. Among the new ones, only the Grail Message has acquired some modicum of social importance because its leader in Lagos, Eric Lawanson, was a rich professional and pitched a television campaign to the educated, professional elite. Emphasizing cleanliness in personal appearance and a quiet demeanor, they built temples that stood out because of their flowers, exquisite architecture, and elaborate landscaping. Their canon, *In the Light of Truth,* is a three-volume treatise on spiritual knowledge concerning human existence in creation. It was supposedly written by Abdurashin, though there is no such person; the founder of the organization was from Vienna. Some surmise the presence of ancient gnostic traditions within the movement; but there is secret knowledge that only the "sealed" know. The Grail Message has mobilized the highly literate and professional elite all over Africa, people with access to wealth that could be exchanged for political power.

This analysis has avoided a serious discussion of popular religion and focused, instead, on the magical substratum that influences political ethics and practice mediated by the political trends and practices of the rulers. This method prevents any religious tradition from posing as normative precisely because people are exploring and exploiting various religious forms at the same time. Each religion has both a formal node and an informal substratum or "supplementary religiosity" riddled with cult. Cult becomes the contested space in the pursuit of power and protection, a theme that the legitimacy crisis intensifies. The ethnographical data has focused on Nigeria, but there are multiple examples across the continent. The growth of Sufism in Islam and certain forms of AICs among Christians of the messianic, vitalistic, and na-tivistic types could be better explained from this perspective. David Maxwell's study of Zimbabwe in the post-liberation war period underscores the conten-tions here; during the war, there was a resacralization of ancestor cults. After the war, people agonized with guilt because people had died from false accu-sations, and dead relatives had not been properly buried. Spirit possession proliferated, and the social and psychological wounds of the war required healing. How did Pentecostal political theology and practice respond to this crisis? It is suggested that Pentecostalism has used the rich substratum of political culture to develop a critical rhetoric against power and authority in the state. Political leaders are portrayed as possessed and empowered by the spirits that they worship in secret. But the movement has ventured beyond political criticism; Pentecostalism has also been engaged in social activism.

2. *Tembisa*: Embedding Hope in the Public Space

Tembisa means hope. But it is also the name of a neighborhood in South Africa's East Rand, on the outskirts of Johannesburg. Tembisa was one of the neighborhoods surveyed by the Center for Development and Enterprise (CDE) in 2006. Over the past two years the CDE has been part of an international research project involving Professor Peter Berger (Boston University) and Professor James Hunter (University of Virginia). The purpose of this project is to explore the role of Pentecostalism in developing nations. A number of the surveyed neighborhoods are plagued by poverty, unemployment, and disease. For instance, the Hillbrow section of Johannesburg, which is a haven for immigrants from many African countries, has about a 30 percent unemployment rate and a high percentage of HIV/AIDS cases. The Harvest Bible Church is located in its midst. Soweto's condition is known to the whole world. Soweto is southwest township, the largest African township in South Africa and the home of goldmine workers. It bears the imprint of all the evils of the apartheid system. The neighborhood of Tembisa ranks even lower than these. It suffers from heavy crime, an 80 percent unemployment rate, a high number of HIV/AIDS cases, and a name that belies its real condition. A Pentecostal church is located in its midst, struggling to provide jobs, sustain families, and deal with the scourge of the disease. The CDE's survey report drew some astonishing conclusions: According to the census data in South Africa, the Pentecostalism movement grew from 4.6 million members in 1996 to 6.8 million in 2001. In many places, the movement had overtaken the famed Zionist movement. Significantly, many of those interviewed emphasized the role of religion in confronting poverty. They implied that religious values were neceassry for creating a new mindset that encouraged discipline, hard work, and self-reliance. The conclusion is that people were influenced by both traditional beliefs and the Pentecostal churches that were deeply engaged in poverty alleviation projects.

Tembisa is a shocking assertion that Pentecostalism exudes a proactive social consciousness and political theology. It is needless to add that soteriology is a means of tracking political engagement because the church confronts the powers and authorities by its actions. It presents a different way of being human and exercising one's power in a manner to assist other people to be truly human as well. Charity and solidarity are not substitutes for the responsibility of the state, but they are essential as pointers, which returns to the former argument that we should broaden the purview of the political field and differentiate between covert and overt political engagement. The link between Pentecostalism and Ethiopianism made it clear that Pentecostal presence and theology contained inbuilt political dimensions, such as nationalism, pan-Africanism, racial concern, and an antistructure attitude. But early Pentecostalism, like its cousin evangelicalism, tended to mute public political radicalism. The doctrine of the two kingdoms, or two keys, created a certain ambiguity. An eye to periodization is important. When the second liberation or democratization process of Africa started in the wake of the victory of capitalism—the end of the cold war and the collapse of USSR—the mainline churches played an active role in mediating the changes as dictators were forced out of office. This involvement was partially because of the youthfulness of the movement as a whole. The older churches had been involved in politics since the civilization project under the colonial canopy. The Pentecostal theology of engagement is a trend that became more visible and overt in the 1990s. It came in the wake of the recovery of holiness ethics, the disgrace of rabid prosperity preachers, the reappraisal of the Christian's relationship with the world, and the emergence of intercessory ministry.

Pentecostal political practice runs in four interlocking grooves:

1. rebuilding the individual, thus bestowing the power to be truly human;
2. a predominantly covert form of social activism, attacking socio-political and moral structures;
3. an increasing assertion for the rule of saints and the politics of engagement; and
4. building the new Israel by empowering communities to participate in the foretaste of God's reign. It thus breaks the dichotomy between the various categories—individual/society, private/public—using the resources of the gospel to weave a multifaceted and holistic response to the human predicament in the African ecosystem.

i. Rebuilding the Individual

Pentecostal reasoning is palpable in its explanation of causality. The movement argues that the pauperization of individuals and communities often manifests itself in physical (health), psychological (emotional), and material ways as people struggle to eke out a living while inflation reduces their purchasing powers. Political instability and the militarization of the society combine to create vulnerability, insecurity, and hopelessness. The first task of Christianity in such situations is to save people from hopelessness by creating new empowering tools of hope and new sources of security, not by repeating old excuses about the redemptive qualities being Christlike. Victims of predatory states are often great cynics; they see the gap, the shadow between the promises of the rulers and the harsh reality of their own living conditions. The Pentecostal message searches through God's assurances against poverty and sickness for signals of transcendence that contradict the speech of rulers. The idiom of prosperity goes beyond material wealth to embrace such matters as spiritual renewal of the relationship with God in Christ through the power of the Holy Spirit, the rebuilding of all forms of brokenness, the provision of health, the reversal of economic desolation, and the political and social well-being of individuals and communities.

Prosperity comes from repentance and the renewal of a relationship broken by sin and pollution; it is also a sign that healing has occurred. The process involves both repentance and the claiming of promises in the Bible. Objectors to the faith-word movement point to insufficient recognition of the sovereignty and freedom of God. God is not a coin box. Others point to the danger of pursuing material things as the Gentiles do, citing their ignorance of the spirit behind things and the allure of the material world. In certain African circles, the argument is academic because of the degree of poverty. Everyone is struggling to survive. Some flaunt their wealth, but many do not have access to even the most basic means of survival. To such people, a message that assists self-intergration and promotes survival is alluring.

Pentecostals encourage the individual to fight back, to refuse to accept defeat, want, failure, pessimism, or negativity. This would shape the person in the image of the rulers and the controllers of the wealth. In the Bible, Jabez, among others, strove to reverse the verdict of poverty, refused to accept defeat, and cried out to the Lord. The contours of the prosperity gospel will be discussed later; suffice it to say that it does not discourage the individual from applying managerial techniques or working hard. Much to the contrary, self-help aids are taught at special seminars during church outreach. Pentecostal students' fellowships provide extra lessons for members in various subject areas to avoid the shame of seeing born-again students fail their examinations. It is not a crossless Christianity, but it refuses to idolize suffering. Pentecostals typologize the sources or causes of sources: spiritual and natural forces, germ theory, individual or community sin and pollution, and suffering in the course of serving God. Each type requires a different mode of response. Quite often the discussion on why certain prayers are not answered leads back to sin, repentance, chastisement, and the patience taught by suffering. However, as the Pentecostal movement has broadened, some preachers, in the heat of competition, have moved into the realm positive thinking, urging members to repeat certain laws or principles and to claim material wealth and health.

Now, let me return to Tembisa. The report reproduces an interview with Rev. Basina who aspires to grow the church and encourage suitable members to assume careers in the field of ministry. Once they are educated, he said, he hopes to erect tents throughout the township that will act as satellite churches. He builds his membership base through home visits, and his response to the social problems is to exploiting the ethical resources of the Bible in very clear ways: opposition to the practices of promiscuity, homosexuality, and abortion are clearly delineated to potential members. In regards to the HIV/AIDS crisis, the church opposes the government's view on condoms and instead promotes abstinence (shifting focus on from the government's national anti-AIDS campaign: A (abstinence) B (be faithful) C (represents Christ rather than condoms). To fight the crime rate, he insists on ministering to those in prison and requests other pastors to visit the prisons, identify members of their churches, and work with them. The area in which he works is plagued by high crime rates, but he has not been affected by this. Reverend Basina is both pastoral and pragmatic:

> In terms of the views relating to healing and the AIDS pandemic, Rev
> Basina said that he can attempt to "lay his hands" on members in

order to heal them but he is aware of the limitations regarding that. He said that counselling is provided and that they offer services at clinics that provide counselling and encourage a move towards religion for HIV positive/AIDS patients. He actively promotes the church's views on monogamy and abstinence prior to marriage in the hope that it will play a role in prevention, however, counselling is provided given the extent of the pandemic. He chooses to avoid public discussions on AIDS so as not to make HIV positive members feel uncomfortable. At a subsequent workshop with CDE researchers, Rev Basina responded to a question on how he dealt with sin by saying that he left that to visiting preachers to deal with for him, effectively sub-contracting that part of the "business" to others.[7]

Ann Bernstein's core thesis is that the contributions of the growing Pentecostal movement are flying under the radar of social commentators and policy makers. The report showed that, in one neighborhood after another, the Pentecostals were involved in rebuilding the broken lives of residents by foraying into difficult social contexts and tackling issues such as robbery, crime, and health problems. The second key aspect is, therefore, the emergence of a theology of engagement that gradually rejects the binary view of the old political theory. We recall that missionaries first persuaded their converts to avoid politics, then sanctioned those who participated, mounted a religious version of passive revolution when the wind of change could not be contained, and finally embraced those members of their denominations who held the new reins of power. The regional factor is important because many of the conclusions in the instrumentalist discourse failed to have a continent-wide perspective.

ii. Redeeming the Land

A second strand of the Pentecostal rebuttal of the antipolitical posture is recovering a theology of land as both a gift and covenant signifier. The loss of Eden and the exile of Abraham's children become paradigms of the loss of a gift and the weakening of covenantal relationship through rebellion, neglected stewardship, idolatry, and pollution. The prescribed route for recovery is an intentional effort to create a new community of resistance that employs identificational repentance to deliver or redeem the land from the hostile occupiers or spirits at the gates of communities and that would intentionally bring a renewed covenant into being. Sometimes Pentecostals refer to this process as "building a new altar." They declare the mercy and grace of a covenant-keeping God who gives a second chance to the continent.[8] Psalm 24:1–2 says that when the land is returned to its owner, peace will reign and prosperity return. Certain themes, therefore, dominate Pentecostal political theology and practice:

rebuilding broken people and nurturing an army that will deal with the political substratum by exorcising the pollution caused by traditional rituals,
secret societies, and the cultic practices reinvented by the predatory elite. They
imagine spiritual warfare using the paradigm of Moses, whose staff swallowed
the magicians' serpent. They respond to the past and contemporary cultural
underpinnings of the public space with the resources of the canon. They pose
as the new Israel, using the Scriptures as a tribal history book to regain their
lost heritage. This strategy involves an example from the politics of Jesus as the
discourse for political engagement. These strands serve as the basis to overtly
intervene in politics by endeavoring to replace the missionary churches in the
corridors of power, by addressing issues of national significance, and by participating in the electoral processes. We shall now briefly examine these dimensions and thereby build a composite image of Pentecostal political thought
and praxis.

The key question is whether a spiritual perception of reality and diagnosis
of Africa's political stagnation—the acknowledgment of the ultimacy of God's
act in history or "spiritualizing politics"—denies the data from social sciences
and rejects social activism. It is important to understand three dimensions of
the concept of principalities and powers: the traditional notion of spiritual
beings floating in the sky, the denial of their existence, and the application of
the concept only to the dynamics of socio-economic and political institutions.
Ruth Fratani-Marshall insists that Pentecostal discourse on current economic
and legitimacy crises perceives power as being undergirded by a spiritual force
and entails a fairly bold attack on the state:

> In its engagement with local forms of knowledge and practice it
> develops an ongoing critical debate about government, one which
> not only indicts the immorality and inequality at the heart of domi-
> nation, but does this by using a language and imagery that reso-
> nates in the imagination of the dominated.... Pentecostalism is a
> political force not merely as a result of successful competition within
> the religious field–providing the spiritual and material benefits oth-
> ers did not. Its radical success in conversion has as much to do with
> the fact that it re–conceptualizes the moral order, claiming a re-
> demptive vision of citizenship in which the moral government of the
> self is linked to the power to influence the conduct of others. To
> align oneself with the wrong sort of supernatural and material
> powers, and to regulate one's conduct according to the wrong set
> of precepts opens up the space in which the failure of the nation is
> manifested.

She goes on to cite the rationale provided for the foundation of an organization
dubbed "Christians for the Regeneration of the Nation:" that says that without

spiritual change, no program will have its effect. The sin of the nation is based on the sin of the individual.[9]

3. Building a Beloved Community

As mentioned earlier, the Pentecostal movement is usually an ecumenical bonding, creating a new family; a caring, supportive group providing solidarity in the midst of the breakdown of old moorings. Those of the household of faith constitute a new identity for the Christian community, serving in ways that missionary denominations could not and buffering many in the midst of stagnation and economic collapse. This new community nurtures and builds a corps of human agency to work with the divine in the process of restoration. Within its ambits and spirituality, people receive the call to foray into the wider political arena. This is important because participation in the public space must be rooted in the conviction that God actually sent the person and, therefore will sustain and supply the resources for faithful participation. This the root of an ethic of *metanoia*, accountability and transparency. The values prescribed by the World Bank's policies could not be achieved through secularist ethics. Pentecostals quote the passage in Ecclesiastics 10:7 with great seriousness: I have seen servants upon horses and princes walking as servants upon the earth. This is declared to be an unnatural trend. As Jesus did with the woman who had a spinal problem, healing her and restoring her sense of worth as the daughter of Abraham, so do Pentecostals urge their members to know who they are in God's scheme of affairs. They are sons, daughters, princes, and citizens of the heavenly kingdom. They are to be heads not tails, to ride on horses rather than walk as servants. They should foray into the public sphere to recover their lost position (described as taking the chair back from Satan) through deliverance and intercessory ministries. The recourse to supernatural explanation holds demonic forces responsible for failed socioeconomic developements. Evil is imaged as a personal spiritual force that inhabits and manipulates in order to control places and systems. Deliverance includes expelling hindering spirits from individuals, places, and offices and from the affairs of people, families, and communities. It is more than an exorcism; it includes replenishment with new power for coping victoriously. Some believe that as soon as one is born again, one starts to gain victories in life-situations. Others argue that until the old covenants have been deliberately broken they are still operative, because Satan is very legalistic and has the authority to make demands on individuals and their communities.

It is believed that both individual and communal problems are the consequences from the pollution, disobedience, and iniquities of the fathers or leaders. A systematic response includes the redemption of space through rituals of land deliverance that restores the covenant relationship between God, man, and nature. When the land is handed back to its rightful owner, the political, economic, and social affairs of the community will begin to improve. The hindrances, or devourers, will be driven away and their authority withdrawn. The relationship between deliverance and politics sometimes arises from the diagnosis that some rulers hold the community in fearful sway through witchcraft or bewitchment. They use unwholesome power from marine spirits or other evil sources to secure themselves and their political offices. Brethren counter such powers through intercession, prayer walks, and deliverance rituals.

The import of this paradigm is that affairs of the earth can be changed through prayers. Political dissent and action can be pursued on one's knees, not only by carrying placards; in fact, the "worn knee" approach is considered more effective and salutary because it seeks the will of God on earth and gives the battle to the Lord. Human agency in consonance with divine activity is the surest means of gaining true victory. Humanistic projects are often tainted and may not always be undertaken for vicarious reasons, which explains why revolutions derail and often become more totalitarian than the system they replaced. To deal with the spirits of wickedness that possess rulers, Pentecostals apply fasting, prayer retreats, researches on the dominant spirits possessing the gates of the communities, and prayer actions. These efforts may also involve prayer walking, traveling throughout the community, speaking and calling into being the good of the community. Everyone can pray but not everyone has the gift of intercession; the Holy Spirit gives different gifts to different people. Thus, the first activity in interecessory ministries is to select and train participants. This phase is described as the Gideon's choice, that is, the ministry chooses only the committed who demonstrate signs of holy living, deliverance from ancestral curses, possessing a clear sense of call, and endowed with the gifts of the Spirit. The simple assumption is that one cannot fight the enemy if still in the enemy's camp. Pentecostalism changes emphasis often. In recent times, Urban Prayer projects have proliferated throughout Africa. This could be interpreted as the new manifestation of the move of God, or as attempts to deal with the rising level of frustration, unemployment, and crimes in urban settings. The police in such situations cannot be trusted, since they are likely to be participants in the criminal activities. Intercessors reassure themselves that God loves the city and has plans for the good of the city; that Satan has hijacked the cities through evil rulers and wicked people; that their sins have produced the famine in the land. Prayer warriors are delegated to key areas of the city—such as the markets, city hall, major industrial sites, and banks—with the mandate to recover those key economic and political sites from the powers that hold them in bondage. The group will denounce the evil spirits, order them to leave their strongholds, confess all the evils that have been perpetrated since the founding of the city, hand those areas over to God, and anoint the walls or soil with olive oil, signifying sanctification and the presence of the Holy Spirit.

4. Intercession as Political Praxis

The battle has been carried from cities to the entire country. The Intercessors for Africa have National Prayer Houses in each country; the one in Nigeria, for instance, is made up of young professionals who acquired a university education in the 1970s and have gradually gone into full-time intercessory ministry. Emeka Nwankpa is a barrister-at-law; he studied at the University of Ife and is coordinator for the Eastern zone. Steve Okitika, an electrical engineer, studied at the University of Ife and is responsible for the entire house. Kola Akinboboye is a medical doctor in charge of the Western zone. Uduak Udofia is a medical doctor and responsible for the Southeastern zone. Ntiensen Inyang, a computer engineer trained in the United States, is in charge of Lagos. The Nigerian body is linked to other national houses in Africa. Other countries have their leaders, such as Nandjui Dogbo Simon of the A.D. 2000 and Beyond Movement, Cote d'Ivoire; Sam Otu-Boateng, coordinator for Ghana; and Violet Ntegha for Abidjan. As the brochure for the Intercessors of Africa says: The Ministry is nondenominational but complements and supplements the Church as a service arm. Intercessors for Nigeria has a network of cells in many cities of the country and each day of the week a number of cells uphold the country in prayers according to Is. 62:6–7. Between God's prophetic abundance for Nigeria and its realization stands the intercessor to pray it into being. The Ghana Intercessors publish a teaching magazine, *Obrapa*.[10] Affirming the relationship between divine initiative and human agency, they apply prayer as a tool to combat the abuse of power and poverty. They do not ignore economic analyses, but use them as briefing data. Collecting such background information is called "spiritual mapping" and enables the intercessors to know what to pray for and how to refer the situation to God, whose throne is the court of first importance.

Pentecostals affirm the rule of the saints as essential for the recovery of the nation. This implies the church getting entangled in soapbox hustling. "Praying brethren" into offices is now a familiar endeavor because when a ruler is just, the people rejoice. The first aspect of this process is the trenchant criticism of the state, not only in words but in action. City projects, prayer tours, retreats at crucial moments in the life of the nation (so as to confess the sins of the leaders that brought God's anger on the land, the rulers, and the people) all constitute strategies of political dissent, an exercise of political power at the level of infrapolitics. For instance, during the Constitutional Conference of 1995 in Abuja, Nigeria, some Muslims proposed that the Nigerian flag should be redesigned by adding a red star. The committee was led by a powerful

Muslim traditional ruler. Adoption of the measure seemed imminent. The National Prayer House summoned about a hundred of its members to congregate at the Sheraton Hotel, Abuja, for three days before the plenary session vote. They prayed to God, telling Him that they realized that this change was a ploy to impose the Islamic symbol and that they were opposed to it. They implored God to intervene in spite of the high position of the chairman of the committee. On the fourth day, the matter was scheduled for a vote. Suddenly, a member of the Constitutional Conference stood up and declared that tinkering with the flag and the national anthem were diversionary wastes of the time of the honorable members. Other conferees yelled in support, and the motion was rejected, to the confusion of the big man. It could be that the members were concerned that the bill contained a provision for enlarging the powers of traditional rulers. But the jubilant prayer warriors only saw God's intervention; they thanked God and headed home. This episode indicates a new form of Christian political activism in the country. Without denying that Nigeria is a secular state, Pentecostals act with the vision of a theocracy, where Yahweh rules. Pentecostals are, therefore, heavily involved in the Christian Association of Nigeria, designed to promote the interest of Christianity in a hostile environment in which the Muslim rulers seek to dominate and use the Nigerian state in furthering the interests of Islam.

A Pentecostal Internet newsletter reported the large attendance from March 14 to March 15, 2002, when The Christian Coalition against Corruption met at the National Center for Women Development, Abuja, to discuss the theme: *Ridding Nigeria of Corrupt Practices.* The delegates issued a communique that attacked the doctrine of two kingdoms (heavenly and earthly), urged Christians to become involved in politics, and criticised the polluted political culture of Nigeria and other African countries. Its resolutions included the assertion that the Goliath of Corruption could be countered through a deep,reflective, transformed, and responsible Christianity empowered by the Holy Spirit; that the fight is the mandate for this generation; that the church must be a voice of transformation, and should change the ethics of the civil service through education. It searched the Old Testament for iconic figures of social transformation to hold up as models of the enterprise. I. M. Enwerem considered the new politics of engagement by Christians a dangerous awakening because they threaten the pluralistic ideology of the modern state and demonize Islam as the spirit of the bondwoman.[11] Coinciding with the rise of Islamic fundamentalism, it is argued that Pentecostalism has caused a clash of fundamentalisms, contributed to the surge of religious violence, and frustrated Muslims who are watching Christianity resurge in the preserved zone carved out by colonialism. This explains the 1994 Muslim protest that led to the cancellation of Reinhardt Bonkee's outreach program in Kano. The literature on the explosion of religion into the public space in Africa has burgeoned. The rise of the Pentecostal theology of engagement is a crucial aspect to these developments, as the 1997 Chalcedon Reports concluded with the example of Zambia. The irony, however, is that sometimes the Pentecostals use the image of Cyrus, from the book of Daniel, to move beyond sectarian lines when praying for a leader who will be guided by the hand of God. These radical politics have enabled Pentecostals to work with interfaith groups in the political arena in such places as Malawi, Kenya, Benin, and Guinea. But, as we shall argue in the next chapter, Pentecostals have failed to develope an adequate theology of dialogue.

5. Recovering Adam's Chair

In Pentecostal narrative theology, Adam had enormous spiritual and political powers. He had the authority to name all of God's creation and govern the garden. But he lost all of his authority. God sent a second Adam through Jesus Christ and Christians, as His disciples, have a divine mandate to work with the truine God to recover the chair that Adam lost. Thus, a crucial area for further research is the emergence a political theology of engagement among Pentecostals visible in the increasing contact between African politicians and Pentecostalism. Attention has been drawn to the relationship of Pentecostalism with dictators such as Arap Moi in Kenya and Jerry Rawlings in Ghana. The manipulation of religion has always led politicians to co-opt the church. Political theories usually explore contexts where history and culture contest the clear separation of church and state advocated in the constitution of the United States. In Africa, the bulk of the evidence points to a history of collusion between church and state; a notion enshrined by colonialism and its civilizing ideology. In the last few decades, the relationship between charismatism and political mobilization has intensified. Many presidents have declared themselves to be born-again; so have myriads of politicians who seek the powerful prayers and group intercessions of the Pentecostal and charismatic leaders and sodalities. There is a conscious use of charismatic mass appeal to build up potential voters for godly candidates. Since mission-founded churches have always sought the ears of rulers, the new Christianity wants to forge a link with any ruler who wants to yield to Christ. Many political parties use Pentecostal choruses as a sign that they are honest brokers. Pentecostal pastors such as Chris Okotie of Nigeria and Nevers Mumba of Zambia have run for the presidency. But some Pentecostal leaders reject the efforts to abandon the priestly role for the kingly throne, arguing that priests should speak, prophecy, and caution the throne. The mediatory roles of priests is to stand between the people, their earthly rulers, and God.

However, priests should encourage brethren to access top political posts and to act as Modercai did in the book of Esther. Pentecostal political theology has a very strong eschatological emphasis. The not-yet has intruded into the here and now. The foretaste of the not-yet should be increasingly experienced as the dynamic waiting period draws towards a close. Admittedly, Satan's reaction would increase and (as one pastor put the matter) there are two types of revivals in progress: the charismatic and the satanic. Therefore, political engagement is mandatory to ensure that the fruits of a victorious life are experienced. Human agency works with the divine through charitable institutions, refugee programs, financial investment institutions, and various forms of aid to those of the household of faith. Pentecostals run not only Bible schools but also nurseries. The Total Child Program is built around the model of Jesus' own development: He grew in body, spirit, and knowledge. A program of Christian education for children combining learning with Christian formation is carried out by the Children's Evangelism Ministry. This program attaches great importance to bringing up the children of the brethren in godly environments devoid of the foul spirits found among unbelievers. Family studies, clinics, and marriage counseling are other instruments used to build up the godly band. The family is the base of the state.

The Intercessors and other ministries in West Africa have, therefore, spent enormous resources assisting the Liberian refugees and churches in their post–civil war recovery projects. Many born-again Christians volunteered to serve as nurses, teachers, and doctors in Liberia, without remuneration. In Nigeria, for instance, a call went out at the National Prayer Conference, held in Onitsha in January 1996, for those who may have received ministrations from the Holy Spirit to take leave of absence from their jobs to serve in Liberia. Some ministries have opened financial investment houses and other businesses to assist members, provide jobs, and fund projects. But every ministry emphasizes charity as a virtue that God rewards; one's prosperity depends on how much one is willing to give back into the storehouse of the Lord to aid the brethren. Every member is encouraged to assist other members. Pentecostals intone that one is saved by grace alone for service to others. The exchange of material aid brings a foretaste of the reign of God to the present.

Thus mobilized, Pentecostals could move into the political space that was widening in the wake of the legitimacy crisis. From this perspective, the rise of Pentecostalism in Africa has more political import than has typically been realized by a narrow purview of what constitutes the political arena. This fact is not lost on many African leaders. For Pentecostalism, the political realm consists of discourse and activity on extraction and allocation of resources and services, providing the individual and community with spiritual and material benefits that the state promised but failed to provide. By creating a social order in which one can live a wholesome life with regulated, disciplined conduct, Pentecostalism mobilizes the multiple identities of citizenship. By first inventing and then redefining a transnational identity, it brings the wider world into the village. It responds to the needs of urban dwellers to deal with the problems related to their roots in the primal world of their villages. It challenges the doctrine of the *l'etat theologique* by revisiting the state's modes of organizing power, its institutionalized domination, its general principles of state and norms of behavior. This is an enormous shift: from a pietistic view of social activism as a means of restraining evil, to politics as a means of advancing the Kingdom. Pentecostals reconceptualize the moral order, claiming a redemptive vision of citizenship; and by reinstilling values in the family, they empower the vulnerable. Paul Gifford said that in Ghana,

> the appeal of these new churches is not only that they constitute new communities providing support no longer provided by dissolving traditional structures; or that they perform socail functions (like arranging marriages) that traditional procedures no longer accomplish; or that they give opportunity to the youth to exercise authority in gerontocratic society; or that they redress gender imbalance, or provide material assistance, employment, identity or opportunity, or bring colour (through their exuberant worship) to otherwise drab lives. They do not flourish primarily because they are a place to feel at home, or a homefor the homeless, or because they meet the quest for belonging. Undoubtedly many do these things in various ways and to various degrees, but they flourish mainly because they claim to have the answers to Ghanaians' existential problems and especially to their most pressing existentail problem, economic survival.[12]

He is partially right because he missed the most important aspect of the reshaped Christian culture namely, the religious revival that is blowing through Africa as the wind of God.

12

Child of the Bondwoman

Islam and Sharia in Pentecostal Rhetoric:
A Nigerian Case Study

1. Introduction

A major aspect of Pentecostal political theology is the lack of a viable
theology of dialogue in an increasingly pluralistic public space. This is
crucial because the rise of Pentecostalism is implicated in the dysfunctional role of religion in the public space. The democratization of
the public space has created an increased level of public participation, allowed many voices and vested interest groups to seek a hearing,
and nurtured a variety of political pressure groups wielding religious agendas. This enlargement of the public space has been worsened by the weakness of the state in controlling the unleashed
ferment. In all countries, political violence has increased. In the Horn
of Africa, as well as Tanzania, Malawi, and Kenya, Muslims are contesting the political system built in the 1960s. The intensified level of
religious violence around the globe and especially in Africa is a dis-
concerting dimension of the twenty-first century. Some argue that
religions have an innate affirmation of violence; that, in spite of the
many levels of meaning given to the word *jihad*, it demands the use of
force, and especially violence, to protect religion, and that Christianity's track record is no better in this aspect than any other religion.
This chapter will examine the various discourses, especially that of
the Pentecostal dimension, by focusing on the religious conflict between Muslims and Christians in Africa, using a Nigerian case study.
  Nigeria is a good case study because of the numerical strength
of the two Abrahamic religions, the clear geographical concentration of the populations of both religions, the importance of oil in

the new political realm, and its shared borders with other West African Islamic states. Nigeria was connected with the ancient states of the Central Sudan. The country has suffered from religious violence and has become religiously divided by the establishment of sharia states in the northern sector of the country. I will, first, explain the sharia in Muslim religion and life and, second, historicize Islamic politics in Nigeria by defining four phases from Islam's insertion to its contemporary democratic dispensation. The story of the emergence of Pentecostalism into the northern region of Nigeria has already been told. Therefore, this chapter will examine the discourses used by scholars to explain the rising crescendo of religious violence, the radicalization of Islamic politics amid the competition for dwindling economic resources, response to modernity, the dilemma of pluralism in a modern African state, and especially the "clash of fundamentalisms" induced by the insurgence of Pentecostalism and charismatic forces into Islamic strongholds. The reassertion of local identities and the manipulation of religion as a cultural signifier is reflected by the demonization of Islam in Pentecostal rhetoric.

2. The Sharia in Islamic Religion and Life

It is germane to understand what the sharia is in Islamic life. Sharia is the wool and weft of the Islamic faith and the core of its ethical system. Its intricacy lies in its two sources: divine and human. The divine constituent is manifested through the Koran and the Prophet's Sunnah. It contains revealed principles, exhortations, and laws. The Sunnah is the elaboration and exemplification of the content of the Koran. Thus, one can arrive at an ethical decision by asserting that it was done so in the time of the Prophet.

The human component derives from the writings of Muslim scholars and sages. There is a certain fluidity or flexibility (*muruna*) and evolution (*tatawwur*) to this component because it is not an inherited code that devotees merely apply to their lives. It has been possible for various communities to inculturate and craft codes to solve their problems as each seeks the best means of applying the divine aspects of the sharia. Sharia demands that judges should contextualize rulings (*mazahib*). The practice of the sharia in different contexts is compelled by people's self-understanding, peculiar circumstances, and changes in human conditions and experiences. It is not a fossilized code, but a dynamic process that enables ancient knowledge to be applied in a modern setting. This is what is called *itjihad*, a human activity, prone to error and subjectivities. Its binding nature is often limited to defined contexts, though its purview embraces all of life. Sharia law can be defined as both strict and flexible because while it is based on absolute principles, it responds to changing conditions and human experiences. It combines the seemingly incompatible twin impulses of primitivism and pragmatism; the ability to hold in tension otherworldly aspirations and this-worldly shrewdness. The primitivistic impulse or the idealistic side of sharia is the determination to return to first things; to be guided solely by Allah's will in every aspect of one's life. The pragmatic side is the willingness to work through social and cultural forces, which explains why it is practiced differently in various cultures. It could be argued that sharia evokes moral principles that are eternal and resonate with both Christian and secular principles. The perspective here is that major problems arise when sharia is not properly indigenized; when codes woven in some contexts are applied to others inflexibly and without local initiative.

Yet sharia is a prescriptive divine law rather than an existentialist ethic. It does not permit the relativist, liberal theology of Christians. Like the Talmud, its application is choreographed systematically through a maze of authoritative voices in an exegesis that uses human wisdom to explicate the divine without injury to the former. This explains devotees' frustration at the spate of protests. As the Grand Khadi and judges of the Sharia Court of Appeal, Sokoto, argued on March 25, 2002: "It is not allowed for a person to beg for another who has been brought before a court for the offence of theft or zina punishment. It is compulsory to punish them with Hadd punishment if they are found guilty. Even if they swear not to do it again; and they change to good people. Because the issue of Hadd, if it is before an Imam and the suspect is found guilty, this is *Allah's right*; it is not proper for a person to save another from Hadd punishment."[1] However, not everybody arrives at the same position and, therefore, there are at least four major schools of Islamic jurisprudence: the Hanafi, Shafii, Hanbali, and Maliki. Following the Zamfara examples, Nigerian sharia states opted to rely heavily on the Maliki School that had been designed in Arabia and introduced by the Almoravids; a situation fraught with problems that are both ideological and too intricately legal for our concern here.

Suffice it to say that sharia is an agent of social control that leaves the socialization process to the Koran and blends the restrictive and deterrent models with punitive instruments. The Sokoto judges argued that, through an unflinching application of *Hadd*, sharia would extol virtue (*ma'rufat*) and cleanse the society of vices (*munkarat*). Advocates claim the extirpation of prostitution, burglary, social violence, and hedonistic lifestyles; they say sharia may even be the antidote to the scourge of HIV/AIDS. The jury is still out on that claim.

3. Historicizing Islamic Presence in Nigeria

In constructing a historical portrait of Islamic presence in Nigeria, periodization is crucial because the face of Islam has changed through time. Islam in Nigeria is a part of the trans-Saharan movement of the religion after it captured the Maghrib in the seventh century A.D. Soon, Dyula traders followed the River Niger into trading cities such as Zaria, Kano, and across to the Borno-Kanem empire around Lake Chad. Thus, by the ninth century, northern Nigeria was woven into the tapestry of Central Sudanic culture.[2]

Islam appealed to the people of this region because of the magico-spiritual techniques displayed through its prayers and charms, social affability, the prestige of its international network, and its political and military clout. Its divination process soon absorbed the indigenous techniques. A key aspect of the pre–colonial history of the region is that nine jihads, or assertions of orthodoxy, occurred before the turn of the nineteenth century. Each involved state creation, as the Fulani reshaped the map of West Africa. The Uthman dan Fodio jihad that created the Sokoto Caliphate in Nigeria by 1804 was typical of the evolution of new administrative structures that followed the change of Islamic presence from quarantine through mixing to jihads.[3] Whenever the Muslims arrived in a community, they would live separately and gradually mix with the indigenous people through trade and other forms of relationships before resorting to a jihad to reassert orthodoxy if the mixing stage appeared to compromise a conservative practice of the faith or if the *umma* felt that it was oppressed by infidels.

This backdrop colors Islam's presence in the colonial setting. British co-lonial officers were intrigued by the sophistication of the emirate administra-tive structure of the Sokoto Caliphate that extended from northern Nigeria southward to northeastern Yorubaland. The British policy of indirect rule, compelled by lack of manpower, happily adopted the structure. A protectionist policy by "Christian" Britain ensured that Islam benefited from colonial pres-ence. Missionaries were barred from emirates; much lobbying modified this to a "one mission, one emirate" policy. Muslims utilized the railway and new communication facilities to trade in the South. The British, however, severely restricted sharia ethics to matters of personal law; criminal matters fell under the jurisdiction of their new judiciary and administrative structures. Indeed, by 1958 an internal debate that threatened the rump of the sharia, preserved by the colonial government, raged among Muslims in the pages of the *Nigerian Citizen* newspaper. The debate ensued in the wake of the abolition of Islamic courts in Egypt by Nasser. Three distinct positions emerged: Some argued that the interpretation was too conservative and lacked the spirit of the Koran; others argued that it was built on a syncretistic version that emerged through Almoravid cultural contact with the European legal system and was, therefore, not true to the Koran; and a third urged its retention on pragmatic grounds, for while the decision in Egypt was welcome, Northern Nigeria did not possess the manpower with the legal expertise to imitate Egypt.[4]

But the early independence period between 1960 and the end of the civil war in 1970 witnessed a vigorous attempt to implant Islamic consciousness and presence into the independent state. The lightning rod was the Premier of Northern Nigeria, the Sardauna of Sokoto, a grandson of Uthman Dan Fodio, a scion of the ruling dynasty in the Caliphate. He used the state apparatus to evangelize by enticing individuals and communities with monetary rewards and promotion in civil service. A political party, the Northern Peoples' Congress, was another useful instrument in this endeavour. His goal was to unite the entire northern region of the country under Islam. This is the *One North* program of the period, 1960–1966. The fact was, the Jihad of 1804 did not conquer all the communities in the north; in fact, many un-Islamized ethnic groups became Christian under the evangelical missionary impulse of the Sudan United, Sudan Interior Missions, and Dutch Reformed Christian Mission. The Sardauna imposed Muslim rulers on many of the unislamized communities and lured the elite of the Plateau and the Middle Belt zones. He initiated the use of money from Saudi Arabia to fund Islamization policies in Nigeria. Muslims felt insecure in the new amalgamation of ethnic groups called Nigeria. While they lacked mineral resources like oil as well as a seaport, they possessed a robust invented history and cultural pride.[5] Moreover, Islam perceives state power as central in promoting religion; thus, control of the Federal government remained a cardinal goal.

It could be surmised that oil wealth enabled Nigeria to recover from the devastating four years of civil war (1967–1970). It provided the resources for reconstruction efforts, but the oil boom had its dark side. The war created a new moral context; it gave bitterness, greed, and raw ethnic emotions a free space where they could easily be mistaken for ethnic or national varieties of patriotism. Ethnicity became the major harvest from the battlefields of the civil war, while corruption ate the innards of the sociopolitical culture. Meanwhile, the military dictatorship was controlled by Muslims and, with its unitary structure of command, vitiated federal polity and militarized the social space. The story of Nigeria, henceforth, would be dominated by the virulent competition for "the national cake." It became tempting for the elite to manipulate religion and ethnicity.

Under the military dictatorship between 1970 and 1999, the internal changes within Islam could be best illustrated in two distinct time frames: between 1970–1979 and 1980–1998. During the leadership of Sarduana, two power nodes controlled Islamic politics; the political party Nigerian Peoples' Congress and *Jamatu Nasril Islam* (Victory for Islam), an organization that operated as the religious vanguard of the Nigerian Supreme Council for Islam and was chaired by the Sultan of Sokoto, the spiritual head of the *umma*. A sufi brotherhood, Qadriyya dominated the interior of sunni spirituality. But opposition was rife. On the political front, the Tiv community led the rebellion against encroaching Fulani pastoralists while the rest of the Middle Belt elite sponsored a political party called the United Middle Belt Congress. In the city of Kano, opponents of the Caliphate preferred the Tiyaniyya sufi order under the charismatic leadership of the Senegalese Niass and formed their own party, the Northern Elements Progressive Union, led by the populist Alhaji Aminu Kano. His contention was that Uthman dan Fodio was a leader who cared for the poor, but that his scions had become elitist consumers who ignored the poor and were unworthy of the heritage of the jihad leader.

But in the post-civil war era, the hub of political activism shifted radically to youths and students. The Muslim Students Society (MSS), *Radiance* magazine, and Movement for Progressive Nigeria became radical critics of the elite. The young people perceived a gap between Muslim realities and Islamic ideals. They alleged that the Muslim elite did not observe the *ribah* laws, did not practice *zakat*, and had not used their political influence to install the true Islamic ethical system, the sharia. Meanwhile, other groups such as the *izalatu* and *Wahabis* were opposed to the occult misuse of the sufi orders. They became the conservative movements for the restoration of orthodoxy. All these groups became politically radicalized and forged a social movement for political action. Literature explains the phenomenon as an appeal to the socioeconomic background of Nigeria that acted as the template for the religious script from the late 1970s into the 1980s.[6]

However, the interior of Islam was not monolithic. Internal differences included the Shiite votaries patronized and radicalized by Iran. The *darika* and anti-*darika* emerged within the radical student body. The Sunni who dominated the government persecuted the Shiites.[7] Meanwhile, the level of rural–urban migration created new negative social forces. A band of youths emerged by the late 1970s, just as the oil boom turned into oil doom and coups and counter-coups betrayed the Nigerian military as being armed bands of power adventurers. These were the *yan almajiris*, unemployed followers of mallams. They begged, stole, and provided the personnel for riots, and served as thugs for politicians. Since the 1980s, the danger posed by the combined forces of radical students and unemployed youth has deepened as the face of Islam turned violent. Consistently from 1980 to date, all sorts of issues have caused riots and church-burnings. Inquiries into the unrest deployed socioeconomic analyses that argued that the softness of the state and the collapse of the economy created poverty and a great potential for rebellion among the unemployed.

Once, a charlatan preacher from The Republic of Niger named Mohammed Marwa led the rioters as a pied piper; at other times, fights would break out in secondary schools, polytechnics and universities, and engulf towns. Meanwhile, Islamic insurgents took a number of routes: Some promoted Qur'anic schools and education (*islamiyya*); others sought to bridge the gap between the North and South with Western education (*madrassa*); some forged deep contacts with patrons from Libya, Pakistan, Iran, Turkey, Iraq, and especially Saudi Arabia. Commercial relationships, banking, membership in the highly politicised OPEC (Organization of the Petroleum Exporting Countries) and Organisation of Islamic Conference cemented the obvious efforts to turn Nigeria into an Islamic state. The linkage of Islamic radical politics to international Arab geopolitics is a crucial dimension that explains the Islamic rhetoric, funding, and strategies, especially the diatribe against real or per-

ceived Western cultural influence and its modernity project. Islam views Christianity as a vestige of Western presence. At many points in time, the enactment
of sharia laws have served as the clarion call for uniting the centrifugal forces
within Islam. It is important to underscore that the politicization of Islam and
its violent tendencies created a populist type of Islam that sought to control the
elite, even when the elite pretended to hold the reins of power.

This is important for understanding the face of Islam in the new democratic dispensation from 1999 to the present. The return of democratic rule
created an enlarged public space for the free pursuit of religious and political
programs without fear of secret service harassment. It was now possible for
populist politicians to mobilize against wealthy Muslims and tap into the
radicalism of either students or *almajiris*. The "new breed" politicians lacked
restraint, discipline, and redemptive social goals.

The driving force in Islamic politics in this period focused on the threat
posed by the rotational presidency provision in the new Constitution, a provision that enabled a southerner to enter the Aso Rock in Abuja (where the
presidents of the country live and work). It appears that the Muslim military
leaders who built the complex hardly anticipated that a non-Muslim would ever
live there. Inside Aso Rock there are three mosques and no place for Christian
worship. Even the domestic allocation of space assumes that the occupant will
have at least four wives. At the back of the huge complex is a ritual space where
some mallams would bury live rams every day as sacrifices to maintain the
baraka (power) of the leader. It is public knowledge that huge amounts of
public funds were spent on this ostensibly public space, obviously along explicitly Muslim lines.

In conclusion, sharia provisions have always existed in the Nigerian Constitution and in practice. Allen Christelow argues that Emirate councils continued to implement the criminal prescriptions of the sharia under the colonial
rule until the last decade of the 1950s.[8] The major shift is that the new rulers
have expanded the boundaries of sharia to cover criminal processes (*Huddu*
and *Qisasi*) and invoked punishments from the Maliki legal structure. The
class factor is crucial in understanding the sharia. The masses want the sharia,
believing that it will help them in legal, social, and economic matters; to them,
the sharia ethics prescribe a humane and non-exploitative relationship among
social groups. Women believe that sharia laws protect their rights in matters of
divorce and ownership of land and property in a predominantly patriarchal
culture.[9]

4. Anatomy of Islamic Politics, 1970–2007

With the historical background delineated, the politics of religion can be analyzed starting from broad themes to specific discourses in the literature. First,

in the modern political space, religion has been resilient and ignored the predictions of its demise by prophets of secularism. Second, many of the contesting religious forms have historical backgrounds that make them innately dysfunctional forces in the modern public space. They are all religions of protest; they have operated separately with hostile perceptions of one another for a long time. Each is imbued with a vision and endowed with sacred texts, and competing claims of uniqueness prevent fruitful contacts while the patterns of insertion and modes of appropriation belie the rhetoric of peaceful religion.

Third, most of West Africa is Muslim with about Islamic 80 million devotees. A survey from 1992–1996 indicates that when ranked, West African states show a predominant level of the population (1), second-ranking (2) and third-ranking (3) of the population as follows:

Level	Muslim	Christian	African Traditional Religion
1	8	5	5
2	2	6	10
3	8	7	3

Out of the eighteen states in West Africa, most are Muslim and primal religion is still a strong force.[10] Thus, Nigerian Muslims want to act like other Muslim countries in the region. The political dimensions to OPEC, OIC, and ECOWAS (Economic Organisation of West African States) create further pressures. With a total population of more than120 million, Nigeria has the largest, and certainly the wealthiest, concentration of Muslims in the region, about 49 percent of the population. Thus, there is psychological pressure to demonstrate a Muslim character, with a perception of the Christians and the state itself as stumbling blocks. Geopolitics, therefore, explains an aspect of the Muslim insurgence.

One of the favorite theories is that contemporary Islam is compelled to respond to the emerging modernity symbolized by global cultural forces and the posture of secularity by imploding the power of the state and its use of liberal ideology. These forces collide with the predominant theocratic conception of power that informs Islamic domestic and public arrangements.[11] Therefore, there is a rejection of the separation of religion and politics because Islam covers *all* aspects of life; it is a total worldview. Even those who lean toward notional separation only mean to say that the religious sphere is non-identical, though still connected, to the political sphere. In their opinions, state power should still be used to provide the coercion that ensures religious integrity. It may not be safely assumed that Islamic political thought has been monologic. Some Muslim clerics are concerned about keeping enough distance between the crown and the turban to prevent the manipulation of the sacred by political entrepreneurs. All the nuances have been canvased as Islam struggles to respond to the challenges of modernity.[12] Fundamentalists stand out as sore thumbs because of their head-on attack on the modern confidence in political ultimacy and the futility of the state. The urge is always to create a certain environment for the *umma* where Islamic ethics and culture predominate, and to reject with violence any political arrangement that marginalizes the *umma*.[13] Within the democratic dispensation in contemporary Nigeria, Muslims have the confidence that the time has come to boldly create a vibrant Islamic cultural space. They do so while deploying anti-Western diatribes based on new forms of literature produced by the Muslim diaspora in the West. The measure, provenance, and message of this genre of literature invite study.

For some social analysts, the radicalization of Islamic politics brings the dilemma of pluralism to the fore. What happens to non-Muslims living under the sharia?[14] In a contested political space, less time is spent on cultivating dialogue.[15]

5. Discourses on Religious Conflict Transformation

i. Conflict Model

In Nigerian scholarship, there are five dominant discourses in literature: the conflict, instrumentalist, rainbow, competing fundamentalisms, and state models. Each has subsidiary dimensions, and it should be noted that these are not necessarily discrete categories.

The conflict model argues that religion has been a dysfunctional force in Nigerian politics and is the cause of instability. This model locates the source of the dysfunctional role of religion in the public space in the nature of religion itself:

1. Religious ardor/passion runs at deep levels of the human being and breeds loyalty; the depth of loyalty installs boundaries to exclude others who do not participate or share the same religion.
2. Religious prescription conjures certainty and assured reward. It is one source for nurturing difference and identification of the "other."
3. Doctrinal and theological interpretations sustain certain ethical practices. For instance, some canons offer rewards for using force to sustain religion, or instill the demand to do so.
4. The virus theory says that violence spreads like a virus, infecting others to create an environment in which the use of violence is an accepted option. Young people growing up in such an environment regard it as a perfectly acceptable response.

A combination of these factors engenders the wider politics of difference and compels devotees to do difference in avoidable ways.

Three more dimensions arise from the imperatives of religion:

1. Historical factors including territorial divide and ethnicity. The appeal to a prideful heritage and history could be used as an arsenal in the competition in the modern political space. But it hides fear and insecurity; modernity challenges the roots of such heritage, and it could become a burden that constrains the search of creative possibilities.

2. Religion as a marker of identity (either group or ethnic). David Laitin argues that while the Yoruba of southwestern Nigeria use land as a cultural signifier, the Hausa/Fulani use religion and specifically Islamic religion as a marker and group identification, especially when dealing with outsiders.[16] The recruitment of religion complicates the quest for transformation.

3. Intrinsic ethics of violence in boundary-maintenance within religions has drawn attention to the history of violence and conflict in Muslim–Christian relationship.

Thus, Toyin Falola studied the history of violence in Nigeria and subtly raised the question of whether religion innately contains a prescription for violence.[17] Does the binary worldview that divides the faithful from those proscribed to the sword instigate the use of violence for the preservation of orthodoxy? On the one hand, it argues that ad hoc responses to cases of violence ignore the consistent history of violence in religious matters; on the other, it distinguishes between the academic and popular understanding of jihad. Interpretations of the word *jihad* indicate that it not always used to invoke war, but also refers to thinking and self-reflection. It resembles the Greek word, *dialogos*. This academic exercise does not impress the common person. Popular belief and practice tends to privilege the declaration of jihad as a self-assertion that employs violence in defense of true worship. Jihad has always been an instrument for revolutionary change; and revolutionary change must, perforce, involve the use of violence.

Theories on the connection between violence and religion point to the fact that the twentieth century has been distinguished by "categorical violence"— violence directed against people on the basis of their membership in a certain group. Categorical violence has three distinctive features: excessiveness, a discourse on purification, and a ritual element. This recognizes the fact that nonreligious ideologies can also produce violence. Categorical violence can be powered by any metaphysical meaning that is embodied in the notion of the good and true. Destruction is thought of as divine and restorative; thus, the restoration of orthodoxy in the face of alleged corruption or desecration could be achieved through divine destruction.[18] This is similar to scapegoating, the impetus to identify an opposing group onto which we can project, and which provides an explanation of, the root problem. Scapegoating ritualizes violence. Thus, if America attacks Iraq, a Muslim in northern Nigeria could sacrifice a southern Christian as an scapegoat to restore purity and exact revenge for the Muslim blood being shed in Iraq.

However, the easy resort to violence in the post-1980 period and the excessiveness in religious violence in Nigeria may reflect the intricate weaving of religion into three other fabrics: a culture of violence, militarization of the society and decimation of the civil society. A culture of violence in the society reflected the militarization of society caused by years of military rule. Hassan Kukah argues that military rule denies access to other channels of organized opposition and imposes limitations on people's ability to negotiate with the state; thus, social dissenters find that violence is the only means of attracting the attention of military regimes that have little patience for discussion. During the long periods of military rule in Nigeria's history, there were neither parliamentary nor other viable institutional mediators between the people and the government.[19] The decimation of civil society muffled critical voices, and created the monologic state.

Another strand of this discourse argues that this period was characterized by a social breakdown and greater social suffering, therefore increasing the level of social violence. The oil boom was gradually giving way to oil doom. It has been shown that both the rates of armed robbery and the resort to cultism increased when the World Bank installed the structural adjustment programs as a consequence of economic failure and insisted that people should "tighten the belts" on their already lean waists.

In Nigerian Universities, forty-one cult groups emerged during 1980–1995. Cultism became deadly and vitiated the academic culture.[20] Violent cults in universities were funded by politicians; many are directly linked to traditional religious shrines. This fact should stimulate research into the resilience of indigenous religion in the public space, especially during times of social stress. People resort to indigenous cults or the use of "medicine" and amulets in religious conflicts. The line between reverence for and the magical perception of the Koran became blurred long ago among the less educated in popular religion.[21]

Finally, conflict theories adduce that there are three levels: the manifest, the underlying cause, and the ideological core in each conflict situation. Many argue that, in spite of the political and ethnic dimensions in religious violence, the specifically religious dimension should not be ignored precisely because religion looms so large at our ideological core, buried deep within the human psyche.

ii. Instrumentalist/Manipulation Model

The instrumentalist model identifies class as the underlying catalyst of conflict; in their view, it is competition and struggle among the elite that compels the manipulation of religion. Thus, many of conflicts are not even related to religion, specifically. The elite who pose as devotees and defenders of Islam are not what they pretend to be; they are driven by more mundane interests such as power embedded in the political arrangements, the strains in operating a federal structure, and the sharing of resources in a constitutional arrangement that allocates a great deal of authority to the center. Meanwhile, the economic collapse, the long period of military rule (that vitiated the federal structure by imposing the military unitary command), legitimacy crises, and the scourge of poverty increased the level of competition in the public space.

This model also argues that conflict has been engendered by the response of Muslim elites to the power located at the center of the federal structure. There are two subtle dimensions to this discourse: the first is the difference between the Islamic conception of power versus the practice in the modern African states; the second concerns Muslim response to modernity's structures and ethics. According to Lamin Sanneh, the Islamic concept of power asserts that the state's power should be used to serve and preserve religion. It denies the separation of powers and the ambiguous doctrine of two swords/two kingdoms entertained by Christians. Religion suffuses the whole of reality. The flip side, of course, is the danger that the state could use religion to gain legitimacy. Ancient Muslim sages cautioned against this and adopted a middle axiom that distanced the *seriki*, or turban, from the crown.[22] But many observers agree with Bala Usman, who alleges that religious leaders have already fallen into the embrace of the Muslim elite who manipulate them into mobilizing the masses to serve the ulterior interest of the elite. These leaders exaggerate political and social facts as devices to alert the masses about their presumed marginalization by infidels—a vindication for jihad and violent response.[23] As an aside, people have always wondered why violent activities follow the Friday *jumat* prayers.

The model further argues that with adequate economic resources, good governance, and just distribution of wealth, everyone would live happily together. The Mervyn Hiskett model focused on the *almajiri* as examples that unemployed youth provide the fodder for religious violence.[24] This is used to explain the incredibly violent Maitatsine riots that rocked Kano and other northern communities between 1980 and 1985. The *Yantsine* represents a populist genre of Islam that attacked both Muslim elites as well as Christian southerners in Kano, Maiduguri, Kaduna, Yola, and Gombe. The argument claims that social order could be secured by ensuring that these youths, attached to Muslim teachers or *mallams*, are given employment and saved from the indignities of religion-sanctioned begging. Some Muslim governors have recognized the force of this argument and installed programs to alleviate the fate of the *almajiri*. But some scholars demur against the demonization of the *almajiri*.

Moreover, the model fails to explain the anti–Christian riots in Kaduna and Zaria nurtured by university students who dreaded the possibility of a southern President for the Students' Union in 1987. The Muslim Students'

Society was formed in that university in 1977 and sought to turn it into a Muslim community. The Hiskett model does not explain the fact that the combination of ethnicity and religion caused over ten ethno–religious conflicts in Northern Nigeria between 1980 and 1992. A good example is what happened at Zango-Kataf when the un-Islamized communities upon whom the northern elite imposed Muslim rulers took the occasion to rid themselves of those leaders. Arguably, a sustainable environment may ease tension, but the socioeconomic argument does not adequately recognize the power of religion in fostering bigotry, superiority complexes, and conflict; or how reverence for the Koran spurs devotees to become protectors against desecration. Above all, it does not explain why poverty and unemployment do not elicit anti-Islamic violence in the southern region of the country.

Three groups of scholarship advocate the instrumentalist model. The first of these is the socialist-oriented scholarship that has long privileged this model, since they relegate religion to the periphery in their social analysis, caricaturing it as humbug. This school of thought was prominent in the conclusions of the government committee that produced *The Report of the Political Bureau: Federal Government of Nigeria, March, 1997*. This group prefers a public space entirely free of religious language and interests. The second group of scholars to embrace the instrumentalist model consists of internal critics within Islam—those educated Muslim youth who feel that the elite have neither been faithful to the doctrines of the religion or helpful to the masses. Prominent among this group is Sanusi Lamido Sanusi, a scion of the ruling family in Kano. He trained in the West as a banker but is also a recognized *mallam*. His trenchant critic of the Muslim elite has particular poignancy because of his class background.[25] Writing for the northern-based newspaper, *Weekly Trust* (June 22–28, 2001), Lamido observed that "whether it is in the name of religion, region or ethnicity, the Nigerian elite everywhere strives to keep people in perpetual ignorance of their real enemies." There are two underlying themes to Lamido's position. The first is a theological root that argues that Islam is about delivering justice, not a tool of simplistic politics of identity and definitely not a tool for self–seeking agendas. A second dimension is his concern about the internal disunity among Muslims caused because the *izalatu*, Wahhabbist fundamentalists are violently opposed to the *tariqas* or sufi orders whom they accuse of engaging in doctrinal abuses. Acting as youthful advocates for purity, Wahhabbist fundamentalists decry the compromises among the elite who no longer obey the *ribah* laws, care for the poor, or encourage learning among the *umma*. The goal of the *izalatu* is to restore the pristine traditions of Islam. The protagonists in the sharia controversy tend to employ Wahhabist rhetoric. According to Lamido, neither the appropriation of religion as the referent for political identity by the northern Muslim elite nor the violence of the extremists augurs well for genuine Muslim interests. The third strand of scholarship embracing the instrumentalist model consists of secularist commentators who appeal to modernity discourse and borrow from an Enlightenment worldview.

iii. The Rainbow Model

The rainbow model contains at least four subsets that urge inherent doctrinal resonance, the primacy of pluralism, the need for religious toleration, the nationalist goal for indigenizing the world religions, and even the acceptance of secularity in creating a free public space for the practice of religion without the trammels of state restrictions. The first position argues that each religious tradition already has models for peaceful coexistence built into their doctrines. They both preach peace, love, the sanctity of human life, and other salient ethics, say these scholars; and the interiors of the faith traditions can be mined to identify and promote religious transformations through these pathways. The richness and diversity of these religious traditions can be compared to the colors of the rainbow that enhance the cultural life of the nation. The rainbow model appeals to the shared origins and ethical resonance among the Abrahamic religions. It is built on the prominence of Abraham, Moses, the patriarchs, and Jesus in the Koran, as well as cultural ingredients, and feast and fast periods. It goes on to argue that respect for human dignity should build a bridge for coexistence. This was the staple in conferences of the Nigerian Association for the Study of Religion through two decades, from the mid-1970s to early 1990s. The Abiola Foundation funded the Association to research in this area in the 1980s. Perhaps Abiola typifies the irony in this posture: To garner Muslim support for his political ambition, he built mosques and Muslim schools; to build a broader political base, he gave money for research on peaceful coexistence; he mediated the implosion of international Islamic influence in the country and still did not enjoy the full confidence of the northern Muslims because of his lack of an Arabic pedigree.

But a variation on this model propagated by secular-oriented/reformist Muslims subtly emphasizes the indigenization of religion. It argues that both Islam and Christianity came into the nation at certain points in time and bear the traditions and cultures of their religious messengers, that the Arabs were just as hegemonic and racist as the Western change agents, and that these religions need to be inculturated and translated to answer the needs of specific African peoples and environments. Some argue that the Muslim laws that emerged in ancient Arabic contexts differ prominently from the needs of contemporary Nigeria. Wahhabism, which represents an extreme minority sect among the *sunni* Muslims, was rejected in Saudi Arabia at an early period, and many Muslims continue to reject it. This response delayed the introduction of the sharia in northern Nigeria, though the Saudi rulers later found its conservative cultural practices to be useful for their own political goal. They adopted the ideology, and have since propagated it as if it was the core of

Muslim orthodoxy. The nationalist perspective points to the external factors in the escalating religious conflict and believes that a proper historical understanding of Islam might create a wholesome social space.

The argument is that, if left alone, Nigerians could solve their religious problems. It has been the external enemies of the nation funding religious conflict in Nigeria, they argue, and these forces attempt to destroy national unity by recruiting indigenous Nigerian agents to serve as conduits for foreign Muslim countries that have increased their investments in Nigeria. This discourse points to the fact that since the mid-1980s Arab countries have intensified their funding of mosques, Islamic education, and charitable infrastructure in Nigeria. In 2004, the Nigerian government accused some Arab embassies of using their mosques to mobilize dissidence. The government alleged that some affiliates of the al Qaeda movement had started operations in northern Nigeria in 2001 as charitable nonprofit organizations.

Without resorting to statistics, it is arguable that Islam has grown rapidly in Nigeria because of the adaptability of Islam to local cultures and its capacity to tolerate popular practices that arise out of ignorance of the religion. The absorption of Ifa divination into Muslim divinatory process is a good example. Attention has been drawn to the impact of the fact that the Koran cannot be translated from the Arabic. This insistence on the use of Arabic language explains the varieties of Islamic practices among many communities because it depends on a high level of literacy in the Arabic. Ignorance of the provisions and informed interpretations of the canon is the bane of all religions.

However, apologists argue that Islamic ethics against drinking alcohol produced better, disciplined communities. It was not only that Christians permitted the consumption of alcohol; "Christian" European traders promoted the gin trade and, as a result, coastal African communities became vulnerable to moral instability. The sharia is buttressed on its capacity to promote a higher level of individual and communal morality and physical security.

From here, the model has progressed in different directions: some, like Simeon Ilesanmi, deploy the concept of religious pluralism.[26] The weakness of the discourse on this school of thought is the scant attention paid to the three dimensions of religious pluralism:

1. In some contexts, there are possibilities for cooperation in public life, constructive encounters, and open witness. All stakeholders must endeavor to maintain the peaceful environment.
2. In other contexts, there are tensions growing where there used to be harmony. People respond to this deterioration in diverse ways; some determine to build bridges, while others are confirmed in prejudices and negative perceptions.
3. In some contexts the relationships between people of different faiths are openly hostile.

The practice of religious pluralism requires a clear identification of the context because each context requires a different strategy and response. All religions are growing, and the salience of religion in the political space of the Third World has become quite alarming, according to Jeff Haynes.[27] Therefore, conflict arises from the competition by multiple religions each clothed in its invented history and unique claims. The older ones seek to establish a dominance that is stoutly resisted by new religious movements. Market and rational choice theories tango here. Pluralism is portrayed as the enlargement of sacred space that increases the level of competition and, in an African context, is somewhat different from the Western experience of the concept. Thus, Ruth Marshall-Fratani points to the peculiarity of pluralism in Nigeria that means "a plurality of citizenship, each with its own moral vision, invented history, symbolic forms, models of power and authority, and institutional expressions, all interacting in the context of an authoritarian power whose control over public goods and accumulation is constantly under the pressure of their claims, and whose legitimacy is challenged by their alternate vision."[28] Faced with the dilemma of pluralism, political scientists such as Jibrin Ibrahim argue in favor of secularity of the state ideology. Often, the secularist argument is blurred by the plea for toleration but it holds to the old argument that only the separation of church and state will protect minority religious groups.[29]

iv. Competing Fundamentalisms

This model argues that the increasing conflict may be a result of "competing fundamentalisms." Paul Gifford in his *The New Crusaders* (1991) presents both Pentecostalism and radical Islamic groups in Africa as fundamentalists.[30] Commentators connect the violent response of incensed Muslims in the last two decades with the implosion of Pentecostal-charismatic spirituality. Since the mid 1970s, charismatic evangelical activities have intensified in the northern regions that had been preserved Muslim enclaves. A good example is the crusade by the German-born Reinhard Bonnke in the ancient city of Kano in 1990. For one week, over a million people gathered every night in the stadium. He sent vans through the city to bring the blind, deaf, and street beggars. It is claimed that he healed many, but when he planned to return two years later, a riot broke out to signal Muslim resistance. Muslim youths have, during this same time period, come under the ideological influences of international Muslim radicalism. The conjuncture of the two trends (the rise of youthful Islamic radicalism and youthful charismatic/ Pentecostalism) may have intensified the violent atmosphere.

It should be emphasized that the demonization of Islam in Nigerian Pentecostal rhetoric and the lack of a dialogical theology and praxis among this rapidly growing form of Christianity may have caused much harm and hindered conflict transformation.[31] But Pentecostal political ethics must be understood from the dynamics of the political culture. The *d'awaah* and the great commission are like hypnotic drums calling followers to a modern form of a crusade. The demarcation of Nigeria into sharia and non–sharia states is an intentional territorialization of Islam, a veritable attempt to demarcate sacred spaces and boundaries against infidels. But charismatic spirituality rejected the compromises of the old mission-founded churches, and demonized "the religion of the bondwoman." Southerners have turned the strangers' quarters in the Muslim North into Zion cities bustling with economic pursuits and charismatic Christian activities. They organize evangelistic tours to heal and convert Muslims. They see no reason why Muslims should only operate freely in the south while Christians are restricted to the north. Some Muslims detect a disgusting whiff of Zionism in their doctrine. The Christian Association of Nigeria that Enwerem discusses in his *Dangerous Awakening* counters the leadership of the *Jam'atu Nasril Islam* (Victory for Islam) and the Nigerian Supreme Council for Islamic Affairs led by the revered Sultan of Sokoto (heir of the Sokoto Caliphate).[32] The new, and daring, Christian stance elicits violent responses.

An interesting aspect of the new religious landscape has been the emergence of highly visible Christian spaces in the northern regions of Nigeria. In every northern city, space is divided between the ancient sites and the strangers' quarters on the outskirts, known as the *Sabon Gari*. As the southerners developed commercial power, these areas gained a distinctive southern, Christian identity that charismatic groups constructed as redeemed spaces. In Kaduna, for instance, the Christian habitat situated across the river from the ancient city that was a part of Central Sudan in the medieval period, is known as "New Jerusalem." Somini Sengupta's report for *The New York Times* points to the power of identity and otherness embedded in that name and how it conjured negative responses from Muslims.[33] Many worship centers dot the interstices between bustling shops and industries. This profile attracted hostile attention from Muslims; it was as if Christians had seized holy land on which to practice their infidel activities. In Bauchi town, for instance, the local officials decided to relocate all churches to one site on the outskirts of the town as if to quarantine them. Muslims who had been protected from Christian proselytes by colonial officers in years past were horrified at the boldness of the new Christian entrepreneurs.

v. State Discourse

Another index of the hostile environment is the rise of an intense rivalry over the appropriation of the modern media as a propaganda tool. Muslims countered the charismatic insurgence by imitating the propagation techniques of the Christians who employed radio, TV, tracts, and cassettes. The attraction of the media for the Pentecostal groups has become a major area of research.[34] In response, Muslim vendors invaded the motor parks and public places with cassettes blaring Muslim songs and sermons. The *da'wah* call compelled Islamic evangelism to surge from the mosques into the larger public space. The geography of religious expression became important in understanding the new face of religion in Nigeria. Competition in the religious market intensified, which explains the easy resort to violence. In the new democratic dispensation, northern, non-Islamic ethnic groups started to assert their autonomy, recover years of battered identity, and reject the politics of cultural domination and exclusion. They adopted Christianity as their cultural signifier and mark of identity, just as their opponents employed Islam. A number of issues became flash points: chieftaincy matters, pilgrimages, equal allocation of time and space in state-owned media, and the share of political offices all caused much debate. The unislamized communities revisited the imposed concept of *One North* and insisted that Muslim leaders would no longer govern them. In the case of Zango Kataf, a violent encounter ensued when the Muslim Hausa rulers balked at the cultural renaissance.

Another sore point is that the federal government of Nigeria participates in and sponsors Islamic pilgrimages to Mecca; it not only set up a Pilgrims Board, it sends an official delegation. At a certain point in time about fifty thousand people went on the hajj in one year, though Saudi Arabia has since forced a reduction of such large numbers. The pilgrims enjoyed a subsidized foreign currency exchange; many could afford to engage in trade and other profitable non-religious activities. Christians insisted that they should receive sponsorship for pilgrimages to Jerusalem and Rome. In Nigeria, those who perform the hajj are called *Alhaji/Alhaja*; Christian pilgrims who have journeyed to the holy land have started to write *JP* or Jerusalem Pilgrim after their names. Roman Catholic and Anglican patrons conduct a lucrative trade in bottles of water from Jordan and crucifixes that have been blessed in the holy sites on Mount Olive and the Holy Sepulchre in Jerusalem.

The environment became volatile because the youths in schools were recruited to serve as the vanguard. Conflicts boiled over in many secondary schools, polytechnics, and universities. At the tertiary levels, elections into student union positions took on the character of religious battles. The unemployed, artisan apprentices, houseboys, and street urchins supplied the fodder for these battles. A certain theology among the Christians that could be dubbed the "third slap doctrine" sustained the new determination to avenge violent attacks: They argued that when the Bible encouraged them to turn their cheek, it provided for only two slaps. After the second slap, the Bible is silent and, therefore, one could avenge oneself on the basis of that silence. There shall be no comment on this piece of exegesis. Suffice it to say that many Christians decided that they would defend themselves under attack.

6. Child of the Bondwoman: Demonization of Islam in Pentecostal Rhetoric

Pentecostal rhetoric borrows heavily from the Old Testament though the same story is told differently in the Bible and Koran. First, "the child of the bondwoman" concept was used to critique the state and the dominance of Muslims in the governance of the country. It was pointed out that the book of Ecclesiastes said that it was a strange sight when "Folly is set in great dignity, and the rich sit in low places. I have seen servants upon horses and princes walking as servants" (10:6–7). So, years of Muslim control of the governance must be unnatural; it was time for Christians to regain their lost saddle. They are the children of a rich potentate and should sit in the high places and ride on horses. A second strand of the motif treated Ishmael as being outside the covenant, thus making Islam the illegitimate religion of the bondwoman. As Ishmael's descendants constituted a threat to the children of Isaac, so does Islam constitute a threat to Christianity. This particular threat was a punishment because of lack of faith; Ishmael was born out when Abraham's own impatience tried to help God. This perspective was the standard fare of the nineteenth-century evangelical missionary era, in spite of E. W. Smith's attempt to rescue Islam from hostile perceptions.[35] The favorite sermons among Pentecostals in those days harped on the centrality of this political theme.

Third, from here the doctrinal assault would climb to what Muslims would regard as blasphemous heights—querying the identity of Allah. Allah, it is claimed, was one of the 360 gods in the Ka'abah in the pre-Islamic period of Arabia and survived the reorganization of this temple after Mohammed's victory simply because his father was the priest of that particular deity before he died. Pentecostal rhetoric condemns the idolatry in Islamic divination, magic, charms, amulets, sufi rituals, and potions (including the water from washing the Qur'anic tablet). Pentecostal cosmology demonizes the core symbols of Islam, such as the moon and star, as well as their rituals of power. Pentecostal cosmology is constructed upon a three-dimensional perception of heaven: The highest heaven, or the third heaven, is where God dwells though it is agreed that the "heavens of heavens" cannot contain him. The second heaven below is where Satan and his cohorts were demoted after their unsuccessful rebellion. From there, they control the first, and lowest, heaven that holds the sun, moon, and stars—Orion, Pleiades, Arcturus, and Mazzaroth (Job 38:31–32). The principalities and powers in the second heaven use the powers located in the constellations to control the destinies of individuals and communities. Early morning calls from the minarets are perceived as invocations to the princes of the air that control the second heaven, and as incantations for receiving power from the first heaven to control the destinies of cities and the nation. Such prayers are actions in the political struggle for the soul of the nation. Pentecostal preachers urge the born again Christians to counter the powerful pronouncements instead of "being at ease in Zion." Participating in all-night vigils or tarrying on prayer mountains, and the practice of early morning shouting serve as viable rebuttals in the competition for controlling the air space and destiny of Nigeria.

Fourth, the demonization of Islam in Pentecostal rhetoric and practice moves ineluctably into the international political arena. The concept of Christian Zionism is crucial. A favorite text of African Pentecostals describes David constructing Jerusalem as the Lord's delight and premier cultic center. He encouraged all to

> Pray for the peace of Jerusalem:
> They shall prosper that love thee;
> Peace be within thy walls: and prosperity.... (Psalm 121:6–7)

Pentecostals pray for the well-being of Jerusalem and support Israel. At the religious level, this yields blessings. But this politics of difference contests international Islam. Christian Zionism takes different shapes and dynamics in different contexts. In Nigeria, there are indigenous cultural roots, for many ethnic groups trace their origins to Hebraic sources. Johnson's *History of the Yoruba* of southwestern Nigeria did so in the nineteenth century; G. T. Basden's *Niger Ibos* repeated this for the Igbo of the southeast in 1937.[36] Scholars and missionaries have illustrated the attraction of the Old Testament to Africans. The myths of origin utilize the resonance in cultural, ritual, and cultic symbolic forms between Hebrew and Nigerian ethnic groups. Christians begin from their self-perception as the New Israel and tap into the rich symbolic and cultural resources.

The ideology moves from here to the African renaissance discourse in political analysis that reconstructs Africa's destiny by rejecting the discourses on "new realism" and "African pessimism" propagated by Western scholars. It rejects the pejorative Hamitic theory that alleges a curse on Ham's descendants. To the contrary, the Bible did not say that Noah cursed Ham. Africans are not descendants of Canaan. Africans or black people are able to tap into the ancestry of the early Jewish patriarchs because Abraham and Moses married black women. Many Pentecostals watch videos and read books by John Hagee's ministry that unabashedly support Israel and subscribe to a magazine produced by a Zionist group, *Israel My Glory*. It should be stressed that this ideology itself is not outsourced from America but, rather, is validated and reinforced by American sources. The Yoruba and Igbo claim that they are the lost tribes of Israel. Within this perspective, Pentecostals image the introduction of the sharia as a component of an insidious project to Islamize Nigeria and declare the Maghrib as being Arab instead of part of Africa. Pentecostals are reclaiming the force of "Ethiopianism" and African religious and cultural nationalism of the nineteenth century to weave a black theology of engagement.

Pentecostal rhetoric is built on the conspiracy theory that Muslims completed a grand design in which they planned to make Africa a Muslim continent by 2005. This was the key concern of the Seventh International Ministers and Christian Leadership Conference and Prayer Retreat at Port Harcourt in 2003. Speakers "exposed" how Gaddafi, the president of Libya, used money to trap African leaders and how Muslims were setting up Islamic schools and buying property in the continent. Key target countries for Muslims included Nigeria, Ghana, Kenya, South Africa, and Zimbabwe. In the report, it is alleged that a "world renowned missionary to Muslims, Dr. Bahjat Bataresh exposed the details of the plot."[37] The economic dimension to Pentecostal rhetoric is that the sharia project in Nigeria affected southern businesses very badly, though the irony is that these businessmen controlled the sale of alcohol and the hotel, entertainment, and tourist business. However, the sharia threatens the southerners, as the alkali court judges might be biased against stranger elements.

Muslims perceive Christians as supporters of the view of Nigeria as a secular state, an idea that is Western. The Christians employ enough of a liberal arsenal to support the state on the front of secularity known as partial separation. They do not see the concept as in any way diminishing God's control over history. A significant factor is that Christians in Nigeria have moved rapidly from political apathy into a theology of engagement. They are willing to criticize the government, yet work with it. Christians want to supply rulers because, where the righteous rule, the people will be happy. This is a far cry from the politics of the mission churches that encouraged Christians to whisper behind the throne. The concept of land deliverance is a policy to reclaim lost covenant opportunities for the nation and to claim a command position to work with God in the end times. The force of the concept is to lay claim to the whole of Nigeria, including Muslim strongholds.[38] A new program, known as SALT—Christians are the salt of the earth—has joined the fight against corruption by holding leadership workshops for civil servants and top government functionaries. This threatens Muslims who have long held command posts in the civil service and military as birthrights. Pentecostal theology and practices have many strands borrowed from many sources but all conclude that there is a responsibility to improve the moral basis for leadership. Some argue that saints should go into politics. Some pastors have transformed pulpits into soapboxes, urging Pentecostal congregations to register as a voting block, and many pastors attract the patronage of the political class asking for either the prayers or votes of the congregations.[39]

Christian resurgence through charismaticism has enabled the mainline churches to become keenly aware of Islamic efforts to capture the public space. When a Muslim military leader surreptitiously registered Nigeria as a member of the Organisation of Islamic Countries in 1986, the uproar mobilized by the Christian Association of Nigeria forced its withdrawal.[40] This insurgence has inspired Muslim violence. This has raised the old question of whether religion is a dysfunctional force in the modern public space, especially when politicised.

Certain theological strands within world religions reinforce the rejection of pluralism, especially when they combine with a streak of conservatism. The Pentecostal combination of the uniqueness of Jesus' claim and the urgency of His mission blocks the development of an interfaith theology of dialogue. Few accept the possibility of being firmly rooted in one's belief system and still being open to others. This explains the frustration of Muslims towards radical Christianity and the tendency to encourage violence as a means of coercing others, in spite of the claims to shared Abrahamic roots and moral concepts. In contesting for control of the public space, both face the dilemma of implementing religious laws and ethics into a contemporary state.

Multiculturalism may be more feasible in worldviews that delimit religion to the periphery.[41] It is quite notable how global information technology creates multiple centers of conflict; the events in one center are brought vividly home in other locations thanks to this technology. Muslims in Kano can burn churches because they watched the televised American attack on the Taliban in Afghanistan. Indeed, when the world protested over the sharia stones punishing adultery (*zina*) and the key of Rome was given to a woman who committed *zina*, Muslims were incited and frustrated because these actions ridiculed Islamic ethics as barbaric. Global processes intensify local identities. Equally, the religious conflict in Nigeria is home-grown in response to the declining resources and softness of the state. Sharia is a complex matter and the Nigerian Pentecostals will need to develop a concept of dialogue for the sake of a stable public space. The conjuncture of radical impulses in time (1970–1980), space (northern Nigeria), and context (among the youths) within Islam and Christianity has turned religious politics in Nigeria into shark-infested waters.

PART IV

Pentecostal Words and Worlds

13

Standing on the Word

Pentecostal Theologies

1. Introducing the Religious Discourse

Pentecostalism is not a manqué social movement just because it meets some of the criteria: containing a numerically significant number of individuals who are united, mobilized, and committed around a cause. Rather, it is basically a religious movement, a genre of Christianity that should be understood both by what it says and does. Pentecostals believe that they have a message for contemporary communities, a message that contests the interpretations of the canon by the older mainline churches. The religious discourse enables historians to show that Pentecostal theologies vary in their explanation of the growth of the movement because the messages attract devotees. Though opponents claim that Pentecostals avoid theology as a tramp avoids a bath—that they are, in fact, defined by their anti-intellectualism—Pentecostals rebut the theory that they prefer the oral theology that Jesus practiced and reject philosophical theology and the gymnastics of high and low critical methods. The religious discourse enables a phenomenological, eidetic exploration, especially since the concept of a systematic theology has been thrashed in the postmodernist discourse. Theology is no longer a reified enterprise, but simply human reflection on the relationship of God-in-Christ to human beings and to the world of nature through His love and the power of the Holy Spirit. Every theology reflects its contextualized location. The resources of the reign of God are being experienced among us, but the fullness has not yet been revealed; each generation and each cultural context continually reflects on the meaning of the presence of the reign of God among the human communities. Pentecostals perceive themselves as the beneficiaries of increasing revelations of divine wisdom and resources. Each receiving context must examine and question the validity of the given "truth" that the missionaries proffered.

Some African Pentecostal theologies are borrowed from external sources; others are homegrown. Still others are derived from external sources and adapted to fit local contexts. The debate among scholars is often about the degree of foreign derivation. Some hold that global forces either catalyze the revitalization of local religious movements or thicken the pluralistic religious environment in which creative synthesis occurs. Others argue that the dependency syndrome in the political sphere is replicated in the religious space. How the new Christianity theologizes the concepts that were prominent in the indigenous religions is critical; and it does so against the backdrop of missionary theologies. Why are people excited about the new ways in which old things are said and done? Why do they flock to the stadia and outreaches? How do Pentecostal theologies connect the conception of salvation with issues of contemporary significance like poverty, wealth, prosperity, health, healing, and the reconstruction of daily life? Is African Pentecostalism a genre of fundamentalism? Finally, how do Pentecostals read and preach the Bible and claim the enduring, archaic power of its oral nature?

2. Pentecostalism and Fundamentalism

Commentators brand southern Christianity as conservative and fundamentalist.[1] Therefore I shall clear the underbrush about the relationship between African Pentecostalism and fundamentalism. In the West, there was a specific historical movement branded as fundamentalism. It was called that because it insisted upon a number of doctrinal positions that it considered as the basic fundamentals of Christianity that needed to be reaffirmed in the midst of corrosive change and theological liberalism. The doctrines included verbal inerrancy of Scripture, the virgin birth, substitutionary atonement, the physical resurrection of Jesus, and the bodily return of Christ. Chronologically, fundamentalism appeared after the Pentecostal movement in the 1920s. In fact, fundamentalism considers Pentecostalism a deviant form of Christianity because of major structural differences: Pentecostalism represents a paradigm shift that unshackles theology from rationalistic/scientific ways of thinking and expands the understanding of the spiritual dimensions of reality and the operation of the invisible world. It posits that there are three different ways of knowing—intellectual, observational, and experiential—and accords new emphasis to the realm of human experience. It says that the power of the Scriptures does not reside in the letter; rather, God is behind the law. Christ delivers His followers from the sin and allure of the world, and that atonement leads to salvation, baptism of the spirit, and healing. Therefore, the power of God continues to raise the dead beyond a single resurrection; miracles are still possible.

Fundamentalism deployed cessationism to reject the present reality of the *charismata*, saying that the spiritual gifts belonged to an older generation and had ceased to be relevant. In 1928, the World's Christian Fundamentals Association adopted a resolution: "Be it resolved, that this convention go on record as unreservedly opposed to modern Pentecostalism, including the speaking in unknown tongues, and the fanatical healing known as general healing in the atonement, and the perpetuation of the miraculous sign-healing of Jesus and his apostles, wherein they claim the only reason the church cannot perform these miracles is because of unbelief."[2] Admittedly, the hostility mellowed by the 1940s, but many Pentecostals still reject the branding of their movement as fundamentalist; others accept the label, but understand its meaning differently. Fundamentalists are not anti-intellectual, but are enlightened apologists who counter liberal theology and skepticism by applying the same philosophical method and high criticism as their opponents. As Russell Spittler put it,

> In contrast to fundamentalists and neo-orthodox Christians, Pentecostalism profoundly distrusted the intellectual enterprise. The Pentecostal critique focused not so much on diluted theology as upon withered piety. The fault lay not in wrong thinking so much as in collapsed feeling. Not the decline of orthodoxy but the decay of devotion lay at the root of the problem. It was not merely that the church was liberal, but that it was lifeless. What was needed was not a new argument for heads but a new experience for hearts.[3]

But fundamentalists espouse certain shared doctrinal positions inherited from old evangelicalism: the defense of the faith once delivered to the saints through a doctrine of biblical inerrancy; opposition and condemnation of modernizing trends by linking them to a perceived increase in worldliness; and the construction of a dualistic theological paradigm in which the forces of evil are perceived as being behind various manifest, systemic, and spiritual phenomena. The movement suffered a decline after the ill-fated, Pyrrhic victory in the monkey trials to uphold the teaching of intelligent design. Its cessationist posture equally buckled, and the chief protagonists homogenized and gradually passed off the stage.

Decades later, the usage of the term fundamentalism had an extreme makeover. Pentecostalism and Muslim fundamentalism became birds of the same feather by opposing modernity and stressing the inerrancy of their respective canons, nationalism, opposition to modernity, and minority consciousness. They both claim to be the authentic expression of their respective traditions; place stress on distinctive elements, activism, moralistic puritan ethics, and a combination of both intellectual and popular strands; and disagree with the supremacy of reason over revelation, de-emphasis of the supernatural, and the permitting of relativistic, universalistic ethics.[4] The American Moral Majority, that actually emerged when evangelicalism re-invented itself in the post–Second World War era, became the signifier of this movement within Christianity.

The term fundamentalism thereby acquired a broader provenance that unmoored it from its origins in the 1920s and made it elastic enough to be capable of wider application. It coursed within the brand of evangelicalism that rebuilt its ramparts in the midst of the cold war by mixing themes of patriot-ism, anti-communism, and anti-modernity. As an aspect of Protestant imag-ination, it rejected new technology as an extension of cultural innovation, materialism, and worldliness. Note Bryan Wilson's study of the opposition mounted by Pentecostals in Britain against radio, television, and new cultural fads like theaters and dance halls in the post–Second World War era.[5] This broad characterization of the term has survived into our contemporary period, torn from the original movement, and is used to describe a cluster of attitudes, theological positions and cultural values.[6] Martin Marty and Scott Appleby pinpoint five characteristics of contemporary fundamentalists: they are against secularism, for the preservation of their identity and way of life, and utilize weapons selected out of tradition against those seen as enemies to their godly cause.[7]

Fundamentalism became less of a movement and more of a worldview, a mindset; a subculture embracing exclusive truth claims and a strong sense of identity, reacting to the ravages of modernity (with its support of skepticism, liberalism, and pluralism) and restorationists. It focused on the attempt to regain the lost paradise of the old values and sense of community being at-tacked in times of rapid social changes. As James W. Sire argues in his book, *Name the Elephant*, the concept of a worldview is supple enough to be used in analyzing self, culture, and social trends; it can be used existentially and in-tellectually in reconstructing life stories.[8] Stephen Hunt uses the concept to analyze fundamentalism as a cultural force and to show how the fundamen-talist worldview bestrides both the religious and political spheres. It is, he argues, particularly attentive to matters of power (both secular and religious) because it perceives private morality to be intrinsically linked to the collective public good. Its strong religious dimension consists of core doctrines that are theologically conservative, espouse a biblicism that enables it to be backward-looking, and favor the constant experience of the supernatural. It responds to the exploding new world by constructing boundaries and support networks to insulate it from the dominant beliefs of the surrounding social milieu. The fundamental worldview participates in the culture wars from three different stances: one band of pessimistic premillenialists takes the sectarian high road by entirely rejecting society and politics (e.g., Jehovah's Witnesses). But an activist branch of the same pessimistic premillenialists confronts the public space and its culture wars with a moralistic "domination theology," just as the optimistic postmillenialists do. Hunt uses this strand of theology as a thread to weave Pentecostalism into fundamentalism. Domination theology has certain elements—an imperative to hasten the kingdom of God and push back the powers of darkness, as could be found in the 10/40 window-Muslim eastern countries and northern Africa; the ability to reimagine secular powers as heavily demonized principalities and construct a hierarchy of the spiritual forces, then respond through a number of strategies including spiritual mapping, intense prayer activities (prayer warriors, prayer chains, and prayer walks)—that counter territorial, occult, and ground-level spiritual forces. Domination theology uses prophecy and eschatological sign-watching to monitor geopolitical forces. The espousal of Zionism and the rejection of other religions in a pluralistic environment ensure that Pentecostalism is sanitized and prepared for the end of ages.

Hunt's real goal was to explain how Pentecostals objectify and project the concept of evil; how they mirror opposition to fundamentalism as evil, personified as Satan; and how they deploy deliverance as a strategy for confronting such anti-Christian thoughts and behavior patterns. An intense consciousness of the demonic becomes a key fundamentalist streak in Pentecostalism and the core template of its theology. Therefore, the movement allegedly constructs a belief system around rituals and symbols of spiritual warfare, viewing signs and wonders, charismatic healing, prophecy, and glossolalia as both spiritual weapons of warfare and proof of God's immediacy, presence, and power. Critics conclude that Pentecostalism gives the devil more than his due!

These critics argue that religious fundamentalism provides a powerful moral system to its adherents because it demands complete allegiance to a totally authoritative text and is able to provide a unifying philosophy of life and personal sense of coherence. They draw examples from Pentecostals, the Amish, Islam, and even a snake-handling sect. Hunt's fundamentalist worldview is a religious bricolage that contributes to the debate raised by Harvey Cox in the last chapter of his book, *Fire from Heaven*. Hunt rejects Cox's distinction between fundamentalist and Pentecostal spiritualities, which argues that the emergence of postmodern religious expression is becoming polarized into forms of fundamentalism and experientialism—the cerebral versus the intuitive, the literal versus the analogical, the analytical versus the immediate, belief systems versus personal experience—in response to the failure of ossified conventional religion to provide meaning to the masses. People are attracted to archaic and mystical modes of perception and inductive ways of thinking.[9]

Cox used the example of glossolalia to map the Pentecostal contribution to postmodern spirituality. Glossolalia serves as a signal of the intense, immediate, and interior level presence of the Holy Spirit; it delivers the devotees from the iron cage of grammar and strengthens their connection and communication with the supernatural; it becomes a mystical-experiential protest against existing religious language, and a form of cultural subversion that upholds the new religious subculture and worldview. Cox was actually arguing that the old character of Pentecostalism has been further valorized in spite of its resemblance to contemporary forms of fundamentalism because it has been adopted by many Evangelicals. Pentecostalism has continued to urge the enhancement of personal religious experience despite becoming willing to examine its belief system and shed much of the literalism of yesteryear. Even if the texts still jump from biblical pages into applications in popular preaching that fuse different historical horizons, Pentecostal scholars are sensitive to the diversity of the New Testament and the distance between historical meaning and contemporary significance, and deploy a hermeneutic, indebted to post-modernity, that sees biblical interpretation as a conversation between reader and text.

The key question is whether African Pentecostalism can be branded with the iron of fundamentalism. There are at least seven reasons to revisit the label. The character of African expressions of Christianity is often branded as con-servative, but the meaning of the terminology remains ambiguous. Cox is right in imaging the movement's focus as experiential and charismatic-driven. This enchanted worldview has shaped the concerns and character of African Pen-tecostalism. Put differently, its recovery of the pneumatic resources of the Scriptures has reshaped the religious landscape, catalyzed the charismatiza-tion of the mission-founded churches, and thereby transformed ministerial formation strategies. Moreover, the variety of theologies and practices within a movement that is notable for its diversity defies easy labeling. Even more notable is the movement's lack of ideological militancy, whether in social or political spheres. There is no evidence that African Pentecostalism is imbued with the political militancy and cultural ideology of the American Moral Ma-jority. I have argued that Pentecostal presence has great political import, but it has never promoted a strong political agenda. This is quite crucial because, as George Marsden argues, "the most striking feature of fundamentalism since the 1970s that distinguishes it from its forebears is its deep involvement in mainstream national politics . . . Fundamentalism has always had political implications. One of the several dynamics shaping early fundamentalists was a sense of alarm over the demise of a Christian culture. National revival, they urged, was the only adequate response. Salvation of souls, they affirmed, would restore righteousness to the culture. Born again people, they at least implied, would choose upright leaders who honored God's laws."[10]

The concept of spiritual capital in understanding religious movements is even more intriguing. It is argued that spiritual capital refers to the power, influence, knowledge, and dispositions created by participation in a particular religious tradition. The crucial question goes beyond the mere existence of spiritual capital and examines the specific values that it promotes and the ends to which its associated networks are used. Islamic and Hindu religious capital are directed toward a different trajectory than that of the Pentecostals. Underlying Hunt's interpretation is an ambiguous attitude towards Pentecostal charismatism, especially the claims on prosperity and healing by the Faith ministries. He alleges that they are reinventing "magical moments," thereby raising the issue of how best to interpret magic itself: Does the intellectualist discourse used by Robin Horton work better than the functionalist-symbolic discourse that images magic as an unreal pretension?[11]

In conclusion, critics argue that Pentecostalism has been implicated in fundamentalism because of certain shared doctrinal affirmations; literalist use of the Bible; and a preoccupation with economic, social, and political power. Thus, its emphases on church growth, winning converts, healing, deliverance, signs and wonders, and other expressions of divine power reflect a certain worldview that explains the Pentecostal response to the created order. The puzzle is exactly how its temper is reflected within the broad spectrum of African Christianity. Are all African Christians a bunch of fundamentalists?

3. Abraham's Blessings: Poverty and Prosperity

i. Prosperity in American Theology and the Bible

In the literature on African Pentecostalism, few issues have attracted as much attention as the source, implosion, message, and impact of prosperity theology. It is used to demonstrate the force of American influence and the shallowness of African Pentecostalism. Allegedly, extensive media use is to blame. I shall do two things here: show the origins and contours of the discussion in the literature, then examine how Africans understand and apply the theology itself. An issue of *Time* magazine in September 2006 carried an article entitled, "Does God Want You to be Rich?" It is illustrated with a humorous version of Michaelangelo's famous creation painting; God stretches His hands toward Adam, offering him a wad of American dollars. Prosperity theology emphasizes that God's promised generosity, as demonstrated with Abraham, is available for every believing Christian on earth today. As the covenant was a legal contract, so is the promise part of a spiritual contract. Each believer has the ability to access it, claim it, and possess it.

The theology points to faith as the route to prosperity. True faith is defined beyond mere belief; it is acting on the word, speaking into reality what does not exist, and dreaming and envisoning the desired goals. There are different strands in the theology. One genre focuses on how faith shapes prayers and how different types of prayers should be used to access different types of prosperity, for using the wrong tool for the wrong purpose courts failure. Prayers of faith, prayers of agreement, intercessory prayer, prayers of dedication, and anointing are only efficacious when used appropriately to access the blessings once promised to Abraham. Another genre teaches that one must invest before reaping any dividends; that one must sow before harvesting. The quantity of harvest is a function of the size of acreage cultivated, so believers should sow tithes and offerings. Some of the exhortations use the imagery of agriculture and the natural world, others sound like business management strategies and motivational recipes designed to inspire people and restore hope. As a preacher once intoned, no one wants to muddle through to heaven broke and ugly. Rather, atonement contains the promise and reality of abundant life. It is an aspiration for the poor and a message that unites people across racial, ethnic, and class boundaries. Prosperity gospel, therefore, runs in different grooves; ranging from crass, "sky-is-the limit" doctrines to God-fueled self-help varieties. After stumbling from several scandals in the 1980s, the message has been repackaged into a lighter model nicknamed "Prosperity Lite" (derived, incongruously, from beer brewing terminology). The general impression is that the message is basically an American invention.

Responses have been prolific and sometimes vitriolic. Some allege that the theology engages God in a spiritual *quid pro quo*; lurches toward full-blown American materialism; bows to the American dream and mainstream culture; and makes God little more than a celestial ATM, a means to an end instead of the end itself. They claim that prosperity gospel tilts on the brink of heretical, ethical, and heological errors; soft-pedals the implications of the fall (sin, pain, death), Jesus' atoning sacrifice, and the importance of repentance; lacks the fear of the entrapment by worldliness; and indulges in positive thinking. Each negative criticism has been proof-texted just as the rebuttals. Each side drinks from the same biblical well.[12]

ii. The Origins

It is clear that, although the prosperity gospel became massively popular in the 1980s, it has a much longer history. H. T. Neuman follows McConnell's *A Different Gospel* (1988) to allege that the theology of prosperity is built upon the same bedrock of faith/positive thinking that Kenneth Hagin plagiarized from E. W. Kenyon who, in turn, took the idea from the Unity School of Christianity. Some scholars, however, observe that faith teaching had its roots in second-century Gnoticism and has bobbed up throughout church history ever since. In the nineteenth century it flourished in the writings of Ralph Waldo Emerson, the Unity School of Christianity, and Philias Parkhurst Quimby. In a very balanced analysis, Robert M. Bowman says that the faith gospel could be found in the nineteenth century Higher Life and early Pentecostal movements that both influenced Kenyon's theology. He contests the Kenyon-Emerson connection by insisting on Kenyon's theological distance from Emerson's metaphysical New Thought teachings. He identifies the early proponents of the doctrine as William Branham, Oral Roberts, and Kenneth

Hagin during their healing revivals in the post–Second World War era. Perhaps one could also include the impact of F. F. Bosworth's book, *Christ the Healer*, in this background. A number of American evangelists spread it throughout Africa through evangelistic crusades and sending many young born-again leaders to Bible schools and summer conferences in the United States. The Fire Convention in Harare in 1986 becomes crucial as an example of prosperity theology's insertion point into Africa, and Benson Idahosa's flamboyant career certainly made it visibly fashionable. His scholarship awards to African students in his All Nations' Bible Seminary, Benin City, served as a breeding camp for adherents of the prosperity gospel. Different genres of the teaching percolated within the continent, especially in the 1980s when foreign books were still affordable and composed the reading list of many born-again Christians. Soon, shifts emerged within the theme; some harped less on faith, but aggressively urged believers to claim their desires. Yonggi Cho's book, *Fourth Dimension*, added another aspect that promoted the power of imagination, visualization, and utilizing the right word in the form of incantation. This struck cords with the interior of African indigenous spirituality.

iii. Content Analysis

The content of the theology is based on a certain way of reading the Bible and it is useful to reaffirm this before throwing the baby out with the bath water. First, it accepts the explanation for poverty given in the Old Testament. The prophetic tradition has a detailed typology of poverty and its causes. There are six broad causes present in the Hebrew tradition: the oppression of the rich, religious apostasy, social alienation, ecological causes, human factors, and self-alienation or lifestyle. Religious apostasy includes rebellion against God's will, sabbath-breaking, the neglect of cultic responsibilities, and failure to tithe. Social alienation includes war, bad governance, bureaucratic and fiscal irresponsibility, excessive administrative costs, and burdensome taxation. Ecological causes include famine, drought, hurricanes, tornadoes, lightning, earthquakes, volcanic eruptions, and other forms of natural disasters. It includes public health matters: plagues, death, illness, and poor sanitation, which could be caused by beings like insects, locusts, and such. Human factors include emigration, environmental ethics and pollution, agricultural practices, the depletion of natural resources, and a lack of ethics of replacement. Self-alienation is a major consideration in the wisdom collected in the book of Proverbs: poverty is linked to laziness, sloth, drunkenness, a wasteful life style, extravagance, the love of wine and women, disobedience to parents, immorality, sexual orientation, and fraudulence.[13]

The Old Testament's diagnosis of poverty draws a distinction between external, internal, and moral causes. Individual responsibility is still as essential as the external causes. Poverty did not only result from a lack of money but also from the breakdown in the moral order. Poverty-alleviation strategies included a wide range of efforts: community support, cure through exorcism, resocialization, and the renewal of consciousness (or psychological therapy). Prosperity was viewed as the full range of God's *shalom* and included equity, justice, righteous acts, and responsible governance. It covered the entire spectrum of the God-human-nature circle of relationships. The promises were composite parts of the covenant and, therefore, the Heritagist claims that the children of the patriarch had inalienable rights to the blessings unless rebellion intervened. This explains how Kenneth Hagin could use Mark 11:23 to argue that possession comes prior to belief. Within the ambit of the covenant tradition, tithing is less about money and seen more as a signal of obedience to and reliance on God. The identity conferred by the covenant informed the notion that the wealth of the Gentiles could be magnetically drawn to the barn of the believer. The Pentecostal identification with the biblical saga bridged the appropriation of Israel's heritage.

In the charismatic ministry of Jesus, a number of dimensions were added to the explanations of poverty, especially demonic causes. Jesus responded to hindrances caused by demonic forces and delivered bondaged persons, thereby showing an example of poverty-alleviation and a method for accessing prosperity. Faith, prayer, and repentance (the admonition to sin no more) served as instruments for accessing and retaining prosperity. While the power of the word accomplished much, Jesus still encouraged the believers to seek, knock, and ask (translated as *claim*) while suggesting the possibility of delay and the value of perseverance and hope. Jesus also provided prerequisite qualifications like repentance, abiding in the word of God, and a committed relationship. These prerequisites are important for accessing the promises. Jesus also shared some caveats; he said much against the love of money and love of the *kosmos* and cautioned against the hubris often found in prosperity. His ascetic lifestyle and the centrality of suffering, self-outpouring, and generosity challenged the simple understanding of poverty and prosperity. But the moral explanation of poverty cannot be avoided and the appeal to the supernatural causality is palpable.

Paul and the apostles provided the most extensive teachings on faith, spiritual gifts, the role of the Holy Spirit, and the power of the word as sources of wealth creation. They encouraged believers to give generously because giving would bring earthly and heavenly returns and promote evangelization. They crafted the language of power that later informed the different strands of the prosperity gospel. For instance, Paul's use of an anointed handkerchief, James's teaching laying on of hands by the elders, the use of olive oil, and a host of such methods have been adopted since, some in crass ways. As Bowman argued, the theological critical task is to examine the roots of the teaching in biblical anthropology (trichotomy versus dichotomy): the nature of faith and gifts of faith, the nature of Satan, the Christology of the early Jesus movement, the implications of *imago Dei*, the concepts of "little gods" and "spiritual body" of God, faith confession, and prayer. In the end, he concludes that while the word of faith is sometimes "suborthodox and aberrant," and while some teachers have advocated heretical ideas, the movement as a whole is within the stream of orthodoxy.[14] Individual teachers have added elements that they claim to have received from divine ministrations. For instance, Oral Roberts said that God asked him to buy a bunch of tomatoes on his way to the television studio and use these to teach the law of sowing and reaping illustrated by Paul in his letter to the Corinthians. Others added more strands, such as thinking of "wealth as God's will and blessing and poverty as curse," the Christian's authority to reject poverty and suffering, wealth-creation as a divinely ordained task, and other eclectic pieces of a complex doctrine. Often, the core of the issue is not proof-texting, but exegesis.

Now, we can pose the question of why the doctrine became popular in Africa, especially during the 1980s. We have already shown that there was a large increase in the numbers of foreign ministries and evangelists that came into Africa in this period; that the Fire Convention held in 1986 by Reinhard Bonnke in Harare was a watershed; and that the face of African Pentecostalism was changing as a new culture emerged characterized by easy access to electronic and print media, numerous national and international seminars for African church leaders, large outreaches, megaprojects, international networks, ethics of muscular evangelization, and a new emphasis on the growth and size of ministries. This spirituality combined a liturgical atmosphere of joy with the pursuit of miracles. Meanwhile, the glitz of televangelism repackaged the image and lifestyle of the pastor to match the large claims of his teachings. The socioeconomic and political backdrop that was characterized by soft states, abuse of human rights, and psychological disquiet is also quite important. It spoke to the contemporary experiences and challenges caused by pressures from economic collapse, a new type of ravaging poverty in new economies, militarized political cultures, and the explosion of global processes. These factors created conditions ripe for prosperity and the lens through which to read the Bible. The gospel speaks to people where they are.

It should be pointed out that the prosperity message flowed into Africa from many places besides the United States. Preachers from Southeast Asia, the West Indies, and the United Kingdom also generated versions of the teaching. Each offered their own variety of the prosperity gospel to an avid consumers' market. Some African pastors propagated it within the continent through Bible schools that offered scholarships to a number of African students. I will now argue that the popularity of the message was buttressed in its resonance with African indigenous concepts of salvation, abundant life, and goals of worship.

4. Nkwa: Prosperity in African Imagination and Theology

The importance of the achievements by three young Ghanaian scholars—Kingsley Larbi, Emmanuel Anim, and Kwabena Asamoah-Gyadu—lies in their interpretation of the prosperity gospel from the concept of salvation.[15] The concept takes its name from a military term signifying liberation from an inimical and life-threatening situation and the freedom to live an authentic life. Asamoah-Gyadu defines it as suggesting two fundamental emphases in Pentecostal soteriology: conversion and transformation through empowerment. African Pentecostals teach a doctrine of sequential three-fold conversion: believers move from "leprous anointing" (repentance from sin and initial acceptance of Christ), to "priestly anointing" (spirit baptism, sealed and seated with Christ, and the manifestation of charismatic gifts of the Spirit), to "kingly anointing" (or capacity to engage in a power encounter with forces of darkness). While a few groups teach total sanctification, the majority define sanctification as a process that yields more and more fruits of the Spirit. The debate about tongues as an initial sign of the spirit exists, but does not rage as fiercely as it does in the western world. Born-again Christians are encouraged to "covet" the gift, less as evidence of their faithfulness and more as a useful instrument for effective prayer. The spiritual tongue is said to be the language of the angels that confuses Satan. It becomes a weapon in the warfare imagery of both salvation and the security of Christian life. It is linked with a premillenial eschatology.

The gift of speaking in tongues can be received either by the laying on of hands or by the power of the pastor who asks people to open their mouths at the altar and start saying something loudly without worrying about what they are going to say. Each stage of anointing is followed by testimonies to acknowledge that the encounter with Christ has transformed the person from the inside, liberated them from the power of evil ways of life, and empowered them with the capacity to live a godly life. Repentance and bridge-burning acts demonstrated by answering the altar call become the signs that conversion has occurred. In this scenario, Spirit baptism initiates a deeper level of commitment that increases the sanctification of the believer and their accession of spiritual gifts. It is suggested that many people accept Christ but do not progress to the level of "kingly anointing;" without this endurance, believers often backslide and become benchwarming Christians. A large part of the Pentecostal diatribe against established churches is that they fail to empower believers. Asamoah-Gyadu puts it aptly: When outsiders see the exuberant aspects of Pentecostal behavior, they lose sight of Pentecostalism's central affirmation that the experience of the Holy Spirit transforms human life.[16]

There are three emphases: salvation means to be liberated, as if in warfare, from a vulnerable position or defeat, perhaps by evil forces and sinful habits, to regain a lost position in Christ, and to live happily. Pentecostals imagine and objectify the persistence of the sinful drive as externally originating from Satan, who hinders and attempts to destroy the ability of a Christian to run a good race. Salvation manifests itself in the transformation of material, physical, and psychic wellbeing. In traditional religion, such objectification existed. Witchcraft provided the idiom for articulating it. A person could be born as a witch and may not even know it; it was as if they were possessed. They could, however, be liberated through a ritual process. This is different from sorcery, when a person deliberately acquires the capacity for hurting others through charms and medicine. Either way, a force exists that confers the power to harm others. Individuals try to acquire antidotes and gain a countervailing power that enables them to progress or enhance life force, maintain psychic equilibrium, and resist those who may wish to harm or diminish their coping capacity. The African cultural idiom provided a pathway to resignify that unspecified power as Satan by utilizing biblical language and symbolism. Todd Vanden Berg demonstrates this by examining the Logunda community in central Nigeria to show how the indigenous concept of evil has been reconfigured through a process of "grounded integration," rooted in traditional beliefs about evil.[17] Personal responsibility and personal sin are never denied, but healing is both communal and derived from the interaction with spiritual power. Peace, and personal and communal integrity are restored through religious rituals that tap into supernatural power. Francis Young captures this in his study of salvation in the New Testament: "Salvation . . . is God's rescue operation, recreation, the restoration of a wholeness which involves transformation into 'Christs,' into bearers of the divine image."[18]

Prosperity theology, therefore, emerges from covenant theology, the concept of salvation, and the atoning death of Christ. Kinsgsley Larbi has deployed the etymology of the concept of "wholeness" among the Akan to underscore its resonance with the biblical view. African anthropology emphasizes vitality of life and abundant life as the chief goals for daily living. These are the ends of every religious ritual: to preserve, enhance, and protect life. Abundant life among the Akan resonates with the Hebrew concept of *shalom*, denoting total wholeness that is physical, psychological, spiritual, and social. For the African, it describes peace with God, the gods, ancestors, fellow human beings (family and community), and the natural world. Natural forces cooperate by yielding their fruits or "increase."

Many African communities share the understanding that prosperity and wealth are not material, but reflect inner peace, satisfaction, contentment, and the maintenance of social networks. The Igbo of southeastern Nigeria have a proverb that says that anyone who does not possess the support from a kinship group is a vulnerable human being. When a missionary vividly described how Jesus was tortured and beaten, a chief inquired about the response of his kin group. If his relatives had permitted the horrendous punishment without fighting back, Jesus must have been a bad man!

The Akan of Ghana use the concept of *Nkwa* to denote abundant life. *Nkwa*, says Larbi, includes the enjoyment of *ahonyade*: possessions, prosperity, and riches including children. It also embodies *asomdwei*: a life of peace and tranquility, especially peace with God, the spirits, kinsfolk, and neighbors. These are the contents of liturgies and concerns expressed in libations. As far back as 1974, Christian Gaba's *Sacred Scripture of an African People, the Anlo* dealt more elaborately with this. From here it is a short step to responding to forces that could thwart a person's *nkwa*. Such forces could be external and supernatural: *abayifo* (witches), *akaberekyerefo* (sorcerers), *asummantufo* (charmers and bad medicine men), and *awudifo* (wicked ones). They could also emanate from internal, moral faults or from polluting the land through criminal acts, misdemeanors, and the flouting of prohibitions. In this worldview, offences against spiritual forces have consequences that manifest themselves as hardship and afflictions in the physical realm. People consult ritual agents who diagnose the cause of their suffering and offer the proper processes for ritual cleansing, propitiation, and restoration. The agents acknowledge that they act on behalf of *Nkwagyefo* (in common parlance, *agyenkwa*), the one who saves, protects, and preserves life. This strand of indigenous knowledge opened the pathway for inculturating the Jesus figure as the one who rescues, redeems, and delivers us from danger. Mercy Amba Oduyoye says:

> The *Agyenkwa* means the one who rescues, who holds your life in safety, takes you out of a life–denying situation and places you in a life affirming one. The Rescuer plucks you from a dehumanizing ambience and places you in a position where you can grow toward authentic humanity. The *Agyenkwa* gives you back your life in all its fullness.[19]

Pentecostal prosperity theology, when properly exegeted, is rich in its capacity to re-imagine the gospel from an indigenous idiom. Pentecostal theology does not encourage people to fold their arms and wait for manna to drop from the skies; rather, poverty-alleviation strategies in indigenous communities are far more nuanced. The Igbo people say that *"onye kwe, chi ya ekwe"* (when one affirms, the personal god will confirm). *Chi* is the personal spirit that a person inherits and that determines their fate and destiny in life's pilgrimage. This proverb attributes poverty, or its absence, to both supernatural and human agency. The individual's willpower and the strength (power of the right hand) that is represented by the icon, *ikenga* and their attention to the moral dimensions of life can yield an escape. Often, the person's relationship with the *chi* is queried: Did the person inherit a bad *chi*, or fail to give kola nuts to the *chi*? Poverty alleviation, therefore, involves the ritualized stabilization of relationships between the human being, the divine, and the natural world.

Restoration of moral order ensures that human activities succeed and evil is warded off. All things that are seen are made of things that are unseen. Alleviation is not merely achieved by intensifying human activities, but by first restraining the capacity of negative moral forces to ruin human projects. When moral order is abused, the gates will be opened for poverty to enter the domains of individuals, families, and communities.[20] Therefore, Pentecostals provide the power of Jesus as the *agyenkwa* who rescues. This is the solution that people seek in the stadia of Africa.[21]

5. Healing as the Children's Bread

Jesus said that the power to be healthy is as easily available to believers as the children's bread. Indeed, the word for "health" and "salvation" in Greek is the same: *soteria*. But the simplicity of the statement becomes a problem for human beings and is often a point of contention in Pentecostal theology for which the Bible is paradigmatic. Critics of Pentecostalism wonder whether there is a place for redemptive suffering. The issue of health and healing is a very important aspect of religious life in Africa, and the explanation of the growth of both AICs and Pentecostalism in the continent. Healing is the heartbeat of the liturgy and the entire religious life. It brings the community of suffering together; it ushers supernatural power into the gathered community and enables all to bask together in its warmth. It releases the energy for participatory worship that integrates the body, spirit, and soul. I watched the healing of a deaf and dumb boy in a Pentecostal gathering that met in a schoolhouse in Monrovia, Liberia. Apparently, most of the congregation knew the boy. Dancing and praise took over the rest of the service. The din was so loud that the neighborhood gathered and, instead of complaining about the ruined peace on a Sunday afternoon, joined in the celebration.

But healing is a hot topic: What exactly do the churches mean by healing? Can healing always occur? Can healing occur without physical cure? Are the claims sustainable or fraudulent? Some churches emphasize divine healing without any resort to modern medical facilities. Others perceive them as being complementary. It is surmised that the popularity of divine healing in Africa arises from the poverty in the communities that are plagued by the collapse of health care delivery system. And the use of olive oil and local symbols heightens the possibility of manipulation and emotional control in the healing process.

A closer look betrays a dialogue among the deaf, where people talk past one another or deliberately emphasize one of the many aspects of health and healing: type, cause, diagnosis, therapeutic method, cure, and suffering. For instance, some pastors ascribe all causes of physical suffering to evil forces and to supernatural powers; others privilege natural causes, matters of hygiene, and germ theory. The most contentious aspect of Pentecostal theology is the causal connection between personal sin, the sins of ancestors (or "iniquities of the fathers"), and the health of a patient. Critics aver that this connection turns the victim into a scapegoat and evades personal responsibility of the sufferer. Pentecostals counter that Job's insensitive friends asked him whether rushes (reeds) can grow where there is no marsh because they believed that when fathers eat sour grapes, their children's teeth will be set on edge. Walter Hollenweger argues that, while it is true that God's faithfulness and promise to heal are eternal, God has the freedom to choose how, when, and whether to act. Therefore, the causal connection to sin is *expressis verbis* rejected by the gospel; there are healthy sinners and sick saints. Critics from the mainline churches reject the claim that faith automatically leads to health or unbelief to sickness, or that faith is a necessary condition for healing. Pentecostal healers, they allege, may unjustly judge the victims, indulge in self-salvation, parade the illusion of control over evil, collude with witch finders to usurp the role of God, and strengthen people's fear of witches and belief in magic. Hollenweger admonished Pentecostal virtuoso healers against trumpeting their healing successes because doing so confuses success with blessing and failure with curse. Healing should occur in a worshiping community and be incorporated into liturgy. Pentecostals retort that not everyone has that special charisma; spiritual gifts differ. Hollenweger, however, admits that the challenge posed by Pentecostalism to contemporary Christianity is the recovery of the perception of the church as a healing community.[22]

In South Africa, the Christian concept of *Amandla* in the Zulu language signifies the authority and power of the Holy Spirit over all types of oppression. It evokes the extra power and grace through which the Holy Spirit diagnoses, heals, and revitalizes believers. God's spirit is a vitalizing energy, a flowing and outpouring of power. Pentecostal pneumatology emphasizes that faith (whether of the patient or others) acts on the word and is essential for the healing process. The Pentecostal theology of health and healing uses the examples of Jesus and the apostles to demonstrate the explanation of causality, different styles of diagnoses, and healing/therapeutic methods. Christians are called to imitate Christ. People are given their gifts for the benefit of the community. From this perspective, gifts of the word of knowledge (discernment), tongues, and prophecy are diagnostic tools; while the gifts of faith and healing achieve the transformative purpose. Healing is not simply a physical cure. Healing camps have sprouted up all over the continent, as suffering and sometimes healing occurs under the glare of television cameras.

The Pentecostal theology of health and healing recognizes that coping-healing practices are mediated by the surrounding culture, worldview, symbolic system, and healing myths. Laurenti Magesa aptly describes this: "If the instinctive cultural impulse of most Africans leads to the belief that being community or in community is healthy, then it also implies that any lack of community harmony is 'dis–ease.' Specifically, lack of physical health is often understood to be symptomatic of a lack of spiritual, emotional or moral health; it is physically and spiritually harmful to the society and the individual concerned."[23]

Within this perception, sickness could be physical, psychological, socio-economic, or political. Health is achieved through reconciliation among human beings as well as by restoring the integrity of creation. Thus, a tree-planting eucharist service is a healing, reconciling process. The language of health in many African communities connects health to life and harmony, rather than built around the germ theory. A "walking corpse" is someone who is alive and physically well but living in conflict with family, neighbors, or community. It resonates with the biblical characterization of Zacchaeus: he was wealthy and physically well, but he was morally deficient or short as the Greek word, *helikia*, suggests. He did not have much character and was despised by the community. The text used the word *zeteios* to say that he was a seeker, someone who was materially wealthy and had all the trappings of external wholeness but was, in fact, empty inside and needing help. He was everything other than what his name, *ZaKaI* (pure, innocent) might suggest.

Unfortunately, Pentecostal preachers and their followers can put a premium on healing as a physical cure. When the cure does not happen, or people relapse, spiritual and credibility crises follow. By confining the practice of healing to only physical cures, they have lured opponents to debate the authenticity of such claims, and point out the possibility of malpractice and fraud. However, discussions of suffering often fail to explain the source and type: Is the suffering being cause by wrong choices, a dangerous lifestyle, an accident, or has it been encountered in the course of promoting the gospel? Suffering cannot be romanticized. Indeed, some Pentecostal groups draw a distinction between healing and divine health, which is imaged as a healthy life derived from a close spiritual walk with God. They also aver that healing can occur immediately or gradually manifest in due course. Both are miracles. A twist is that God will sustain the health of those engaged in His service. Therefore, while modern medical practices can be used as an instrument of healing by God, there is a danger in the over-reliance on modern medical practices and its use of chemicals; there is no technology for overcoming death.

Healing is about liberation from all that dehumanizes; it is the restoration of life. As Jacques Matthey said in his summary of a consultation organized by the World Council of Churches in Accra, Ghana: "to experience healing is not just to experience freedom from sickness and illness, or problems and suffering. Healing is a sign of what the Old Testament calls "shalom" (peace, salvation) as the establishment or restoration of right and reconciled relationships, now and at the end of time."[24] Pentecostal theology is constructed on the grounds that healing is the sign and witness of the presence of God's reign among God's people; that God's healing power is as easily available to believers as the parental obligation to put bread on the children's table.

6. Rightly Dividing the Word: Hermeneutics and Homiletics

Pentecostals claim that they boldly, tenaciously, and rightly "divide" or interpret or reveal the inner truth in the word of God. But their critics have a different "systematic" manner of dividing the word. Certain features are required of practioners pursuing the hermeneutical task: reading the text carefully (descriptive task), placing the text in canonical context (the synthetic task), relating the text to our situation through a certain mode of appropriation and through appeal to other authorities, and finally engaging the pragmatic task of living the text. Many theological enterprises tend to differ on the appropriation level; some lean heavily toward the pragmatic task. For Pentecostals, the pain of the human condition is too excruciating to allow them to indulge in involuted exegesis. Philosophical niceties seem like a luxury. The lens used in interpreting the word betrays the interpreter's attitude to the Bible as canon, the place of tradition, as well as the Trinity and other sources for reconstructing reality. The Pentecostal "bumper-sticker" hermeneutical method has attracted much debate; as a car sticker proclaimed, "This is the Word of God, I believe it and that is final." They bring a new approach that circumvents the crises in the art of interpreting the Bible that change with shifts in the theory of knowledge. Enlightenment and liberalism, fundamentalism and evangelical neo-orthodoxy—each has left imprints on hermeneutics. Pinnock has delineated the differences in hermeneutic principles of these groups.[25] Even within the Pentecostal movement, hermenutical practice has changed over time. In early Pentecostalism, the Bible was the word of God and understood at its face value. The operative principle of interpretation was the conviction that exegesis was best when it was as rigidly literal as it could credibly stand. The horizons of the past and present were fused with a pragmatic hermeneutical leap. Allegorization eased appropriation of the text, and preaching was spontaneous but not relegated to professional clergy.

In Pentecostal churches, the participation of the congregation in liturgy does not wane during the hearing of the word. The congregation responds, as the sermon reaches for an immediate experience for the listeners. The altar call is the climax. Admittedly, modern Pentecostalism is more open to studied and nonliteral exegesis, but the general attitude remains much the same. The truth must be fulfilled in life experiences. The language of God in African Pentecostal liturgy buttresses this fact. Pentecostals explore the language that communities use in addressing their sustaining divinities, ancestors, and Supreme Being and use these to describe God and Christ, showing that the

Godhead is superior to all powers available in the people's map of their universe. The reconstructed world is brought home to individual lives and circumstances by applying "bumper sticker" hermeneutics or "experiential literalism." Cheryl B. Johns said that Pentecostal hermeneutics is praxis-oriented, with experience and Scripture being maintained in a dialectical relationship. The Holy Spirit is what maintains that ongoing relationship. Lived faith is the result of knowledge of the Scriptures.[26] The emphases are on the experiential, relational, emotional, oral aspects of faith; the immediacy of the text; and the freedom to interpret and appropriate the multiple meanings of the biblical texts. It recognizes a spiritual kinship between the authors and readers and ongoing continuity with the New Testament church by pneumatic illumination. Personal and corporate experiences are woven into the hermeneutical task. This is the dialogical role of experience.

There is an emphasis on the narrative texts. As the reader gives authority to narrative sections of the biblical text, the text becomes a part of that person. Steve Land calls the Pentecostal view of the Scriptures as "Spirit-Word"; Cheryl Johns describes this approach as "knowing in active relationship." Johns has developed a four-part process by which the study of the text becomes a means of conscientization: First, the Christian story serves as a source of critique for the present. Then, there is a movement from present praxis to the story, bringing its own consciousness and needs to the appropriation of the story. Next, there is a dialectic between the vision that arises out of the meaning of the story and our present praxis. Finally, the vision shifts from the present praxis to the future being shaped by our appropriation. As W. Iser would say, reading the Bible is not just a cognitive experience, but an affective one as well. The text requires the reader to complete the circuit of communication. Pentecostals put revelation before cognitive understanding. Their ears itch for the new "piping hot revelation" the Holy Spirit just gave to the pastor. They practice hermeneutics of trust or fidelity instead of the hermeneutics of suspicion characteristic of liberal theology.

Years ago, Schleiermacher drew a distinction between "masculine readings" of Scriptures, which analyze the original meaning while keeping a historical and critical distance, and the "feminine reading" dominated by creative intuition and a sense of immediacy with the text. Pentecostal hermeneutic is feminine, eschatological, and organic, and helps the audience recognize the signs of the times and discern what God is doing in today's world. This becomes empowerment for a "counterworld imagination." The danger could be an eclectic reading that ignores the descriptive and synthetic levels of reading the text. In some cases, a misappropriation or misuse of scripture may occur in the hands of an ill-trained leader. Indeed, there is a move within the camp to systemize Pentecostal theology. For instance, a preacher used Isaiah 45:11— "Ask me of things to come concerning my sons, and concerning the work of my hands command ye me"—as the authority to teach that believers could use their faith to *command* that situations like threatening rain stop. There are many examples of incautious Pentecostal exegesis in circulation, creating an air of popular religiosity. But this does not detract from the benefits of a new, conscientizing, empowering hermeneutic that brings the gospel home.

S. A. Ellington has explained the Pentecostal approach to doctrine about the Scriptures. He says that Pentecostals understand and utilize doctrines in a fundamentally different way than those traditions that are more thoroughly grounded in rationalist models of considering the authority of Scriptures. "For Pentecostals," he says, "doctrine is not essentially generative in function but rather descriptive." It is used to verbalize lived experiences. "Beliefs are not derived from understanding but arise from intense experiences of encountering God." This knowing in relationship precedes articulation of experiences in normative doctrinal ways. As Brueggemann put it, "it is enough to acknowledge, be awed and delighted" in the assertion that all that exists is wrought by the extravagant generosity of God. The word is embodied in the community and, therefore, the text is read eschatologically as the intrusion of the kingdom of God into the present and as empowerment in living out its promises.[27]

To illustrate how the hermeneutic is given wings by the homiletics, we take the pericope in Luke 13:10–17 where Jesus healed the crippled woman. An African Pentecostal preacher would first describe the sad fate of the woman so that everyone would recognize a similar case in the neighborhood or village. There might be an interlude with a plaintive song from a traditional dirge or folk-tale. Then, Jesus' entry into the context would be portrayed in such vivid colors that each person would feel His awesome presence. The past is given life in the present. The healing would occur as the whole congregation stands to sing that "in the word of God, there is power; in the name of Jesus, every knee shall bow." Other victory choruses would follow before the main coup in verse 16. Jesus calls the woman, "the daughter of Abraham," that is, one in whose body the promise of God and enduring covenant was powerfully at work. Her social context had constructed her otherwise—crippled, ugly, dysfunctional, and worthless. For years, she accepted this verdict for her life. Jesus renames her and imbues her with a sense of being much different. She accepts his counter-verdict, "stood up straight and began to praise God." Jesus roots himself in the enduring covenant of God and refuses given manifests; He voices a different reality than that which is borne on the countertext in Genesis. Pentecostal hermeneutics surf God's counter-verdicts and use them to conscientize the people of God in the midst of life's debilitating contexts.

Answering the altar call is like a degradation ritual that ensures that the respondents can now act differently and perceive the world in a different way. The homiletics craft language in a transformative manner so that the believer would begin to speak differently and soon, through biographical testimonies, share and validate the religious belief system being advocated. The process of turning text into oral and experiential models is a recovery of what the Bible originally was. Pentecostal hermeneutics provides an altered view of self - identity change, bridge-burning, and cognitive restructuring.

Hermeneutics underscore the Pentecostal emphasis on the power of the word in spiritual formation; the word resists forces that could lead one to backslide, reverses curses, provides deliverance, and claims the things that the Lord has made. This is why the brethren arrive for Bible studies and Sunday worship with notebooks, to take down the message or "revelations" that should be applied during the coming week for victory. This is the practice of victorious living. Everyone is urged to be an overcomer and "demon destroyer." Preachers reproduce teaching tapes and videos and believers are encouraged to read devotional literature instead of "jezebelian" or secular novels. Ministries produce magazines full of biblical teachings. This is a far cry from the liberal critical tendency to discount the speech of God as mere rhetoric and metaphor.

The hermeneutics for conscientization is choreographed with a vigorous homiletic that mines the people's experiences, dramatizes them, supports them with "real-life" testimonies, and brings the promises in the Bible so that no one will leave bearing the burdens of yesterday. A pastor would tell the story of a woman who was carrying a heavy load. A car stopped and offered to assist the woman; she accepted the offer and got into the car, but continued to carry the load on her head instead of setting it down. The congregation would indicate that it was a foolish thing to do. Rambo argues that[28] audience participation, singing, dancing, and yelling aids believers to perform religiously before rationalizing the process. Such rituals offer knowledge in a distinct form that enables the believer to understand, experience, and embody the new way of life. Pentecostal leaders bring together materials from both internal and external sources in a manner that the unlettered can understand; because, behind the macroeconomics, of the global market is the divine will. Pentecostals urge members to avoid judging by sight but to judge by revelation, so as to discern which spirits are operating behind manifest events. Pentecostal homilectics inspire action and social engagement.

For instance, land deliverance is only one of the strategies employed. It is sometimes subtle and avoids overt iconoclasm: believers "walk" around shrines as hostile, polluted ground and command the spirits to leave. Sometimes, during emotional crusades, those with authority over the land and affairs of the community will be asked to confess the iniquities of the fathers being visited upon their progenies and hand over the land to the authority of Jesus. This symbolic action will ensure prosperity for all the people. In these ways, the born-again brethren in Africa are bringing a spiritual solution to the great issues of the day; taking the context, the worldview, and the ecology of their communities and bringing them within the gospel mandate.

14

Reverse Flow

*Pentecostalism and Immigrant
African Christianity*

1. Oases of Christian Faith: Defining Reverse Flow

In many countries of the global north, much attention has focused
on the religion of immigrants that reshapes northern religious
landscapes. It is surmised that immigrants come with a more conservative theology and practice, insist on using their own languages
and cultural expressions, prefer to import their own priests, and
challenge the authority of traditional hierarchy. In their resistant seg-
mented assimilation, they breed conflict and scramble the religious
structures. The influx of Christian leaders from the global south into
the north is described by the concept of reverse flow. *The Seattle Times*
of March 26, 2006, carried a headline declaring the upsurge of
"Christianity's Second Wave." Based on the data from the Center
for the Study of Global Christianity at Gordon-Conwell Theological
Seminary, South Hamilton, the newspaper pointed fingers toward charismatic and Pentecostal movements as the agents of the
second wave. The newspaper echoed the first page of *The New York
Times* of April 18, 2004, that blazoned its own caption as a statement: "In New York, Gospel Resounds in African Tongues and Pulses
to the Beat of Congas." The author, Daniel J. Watkins, posed the
problem in a broader perspective:

> Every Sunday, in more than 100 churches across New York,
> pastors preach the Gospel in languages like Ibo, Twi, and Ga.
> Conga drums drive songs of praise. Swaths of kente cloth
> cover bodies swaying in the pews. An explosion of African

immigrant churches in the past 15 years has helped reshape religious worship in the city. The surge is creating oases of Christian faith for newcomers from Nigeria, Ghana, Congo, Ethiopia and other countries and fueling an evangelical movement long the province of Latinos and African Americans.

Watkins surveyed a wide range of church types and contradictory explanations. A historical excursus demonstrates that reverse flow was not an invention of Pentecostalism. It originated in the mainline churches. In the nineteenth century, a forward-looking missionary anticipated a "blessed reflex" when the sending-churches of the West would be challenged and renewed by the churches then springing up in Africa, Asia, and Latin America.[1] This terminology was reinvented as "reverse flow" in missiological discourse in Africa during the late 1970s as a part of the debate on indigenization, moratorium, and the decolonization of the African church. The process of political decolonization occurred earlier than the decolonization of the churches and had varied impacts on church groups based on certain indexes: the size and ecclesiastical organization, the vertical spread and social quality of adherents, the inherited pattern of colonial relationship, and the theological emphasis and international relations. These impacts also depended upon the manner of disengagement from the mainline churches, the weave of neocolonial fabric, and the dosage of Marxism in the political mix.

Any of these issues could aid weal or woe depending on the context. For instance, in the Democratic Republic of Congo, General Seseko Mobutu perceived the Roman Catholics as a danger to be demolished, because gods do not brook competition. Faced with the challenge from indigenous intelligentsia and the new African states, the core of godly, passive revolution depended on the rearguard actions to retool in order to maintain influence using indigenous personnel and resources. This was the main thrust of the missionary policy of indigenization. However, there were at least a dozen measures of indigenization including initiating manpower development, restructuring internally through church unity and ecumenism, balancing aid and selfhood in funding in order to cure dependency and nurture stewardship, revisiting cultural policy through adaptation and thereby catalyzing a controlled initiative in art and liturgy, realigning the church-state relationship by involving more Christians in politics, encouraging theological reflection, and installing a new model of relationship that uses the idiom of partnership to camouflage paternalism and thus essaying to maintain social services along the old lines. These cumulatively would remedy the after effects of the excessive control of the past by preserving the core of missionary structures while broadening African participation to respond to the challenges created by the insurgent nationalism of the new African states.

This counterinsurgence was aided by a paradigm shift in the ecumenical movement that became visible at Uppsala in 1968. Konrad Raiser termed it "the expansion of the ecumenical perspective universally to all humanity."[2] The new ecumenical paradigm raised a new understanding of mission, defined in relation to the challenges of modernity, science, and technology, dialogue with other faiths, and issues of justice and race. The support for freedom fighters stirred an internal debate that only began to subside at the World Council of Churches (WCC) Assembly in Nairobi in 1975. Similarly, Vatican II, which had only 61 Africans bishops out of a total of 2,500 bishops, was a watershed in redesigning the Catholic Church's policy in mission and social service. It released African energy in the Church as a number of papal pronouncements appeared to speak to Africans in a new voice. In 1969, Pope Paul VI made the famous declaration that "you must have an African Christianity. Indeed you possess human values and characteristic forms of culture which can rise up to perfection so as to find in Christianity, and for Christianity, a true superior fullness and prove to be capable of a richness of expression all its own, and genuinely African."[3] Pope John Paul II's call for inculturation and enrichment brought much hope before people realized that curial control and liturgy within Roman rites shortened the ropes. Nonetheless, the renaissance of Christian art left an enduring mark as Father Kevin Carroll in Nigeria, Ethelbert Mveng in Cameroon, and John Groeber in southern Africa mentored a number of young artists.[4] Equally impressive was the depth of liturgical renewal in music, dance, use of native languages, radicalization of the block rosary, and formation of associations around new liturgical practices such as vigils, retreat centers, and such sprung up, to the consternation of missionaries.

The details of these strategies will not bear repetition. Suffice it to say that the level of ministerial formation galloped forward from the 1960s. Theological education had an enormous boost with the formation of regional and continental associations that encouraged theological reflection and revision of curricula in Bible schools. Many churches experimented with Theological Education by Extension while the genesis of the Ecumenical Association of Third World Theologians (EATWOT) brought together many from those regions of the world where the pressing question was "Eat what?" In the rainy season of 1973, the WCC met at Ibadan to explore how to readjust the funding of African churches in order to encourage them to learn the art of giving. When the Board of Faith and Order of the WCC met at Accra in August 1974, there were more church union talks going on in Africa than in any other continent. The leaders of the Church of South India and those from Ceylon toured Africa to provide advice. Except for the case of Zambia, all other negotiations for church unity/ union collapsed. To use the case of Nigeria as an example, theological and nontheological reasons colluded to thwart the dream of the united church among Protestants. The scions of the faith churches dismissed the constitution of the Union as lacking an adequate dosage of spirituality. Other minor doctrinal matters caused concern, but the real weighty issues were personality clashes and rivalries, denominational hostilities that had not healed, competition for the bishoprics, and ethnicity. Finally, some Methodist congregations took the Union committee to court while the civil war (1967–1970) scattered the litigants.[5] Studies from eastern Africa have confirmed how the same factors that destabilized African nation-states wreaked havoc in Christian circles.[6] Admittedly, many of these could occur in any other context beyond Africa, but the key difference was that Africans felt that church unity was imposed from the outside.

Could the retooling strategies be interpreted as passive revolution? J. V. Taylor, who served as general secretary of the Church Missionary Society in those heady 1960s, gave an unvarnished evaluation of the indigenization process. He observed that it had become fashionable for white men of his generation to join "in the chorus of disparagement against the Gothic churches and pietistic hymn tunes that have everywhere stamped the church as a foreign import" in Africa. Worse, indigenization had failed because the indigenous people believe that "we are playing at it" while holding to orthodoxy, fearing the dangers of syncretism, acting with "mixed motives" and unduly moralistic ethics. "Instead of waiting humbly to discover what kind of leadership the Lord is raising up for His church in Africa or Asia, missionaries have been busily engaged in grooming successors to themselves...reproducing their stereotyped kind of leadership."[7]

In a way, this was a truism, having been the goal of missionary education and elite formation. The strategy was sharpened for new ends. But Taylor reveals that decolonization caused much soul-searching about the meaning and goal of mission. Attention turned briefly from the abilities of Africans to keep away from the warm embrace of witch doctors. Lars Thurnberg called it "the redemption for the wrongs of history." Lesslie Newbigin imagined a context where sending churches would become "bridge-builders" serving at "mission points." The Lutheran World Federation experimented with "reverse flow in which African ministers were posted to German congregations where everybody treated them with cold civility.

The African story in the decade 1965–1975 is that people increasingly found the missionary version of indigenization to be unsatisfactory and restrictive. Yet Christianity was attractive and grew tremendously as the charismatic spirituality of the *Aladura* or AICs (African Instituted Churches) was absorbed into the mission churches. Liturgical experimentation caused disquiet in many places as "traditionalism" impeded progress. There was also an increasing laicization of the church. Many reasons for the disquiet are adduced. These include increased use of the Bible and vernacular as Vatican II released people from the restrictions of yesteryear, and enabled the Africanization of the liturgy; the government takeover of schools and hospitals, which jolted the ascendancy of the churches, compelling them to turn to their true calling; the growing competition from the Christian left-wing or AICs; and the deliberate policy to encapsulate the elite and the impact of a new crop of trained clergy and theologians. The laicization of the church was particularly significant because the churches wanted their people to use their powers and good offices to act as *"defensores fidei."* Knighthood Orders were designed to attract members. These orders, in turn, found the church members to be assured political voters.

Soon, lay social and financial influence became more important in church affairs and decision making than was anticipated. The "nationalism" of the new theologians harped on the vestiges of missionary structures and the predicaments of an unindigenized church. New terminologies were canvassed such *contextualization, traditionalization, incarnation,* and *inculturation* as Africans wanted a new type of church or renewed body of Christ and a new relationship with the West. Celibacy was challenged in the Roman Catholic Church just as some Protestants wanted to celebrate the commensality of the Eucharist with palm wine or kola nut. The Bible supplied precedents proffering the possibility that the spirituality of primal religion did not always conflict with the canon. There was much ferment in the churches as well as efforts to sabotage the limited indigenization project from the inside.

Outside the church, the growth of the African state in this period was significant by causing political instability, human rights abuses, environmental degradation, and economic collapse. New states imaged their goals—such as national redemption, economic salvation, political justification, national regeneration, and sanctity of the state—in Christian garb in obvious attempts to bowdlerize. Many became one-party states, others praetorian, while some took to Marxism. The churches became alarmed over the single-party nature these states were embracing. The Catholic Church assigned the Jesuit veteran missionary J. C. McKenna to study the problem. He found that out of forty-four sub-Saharan nations, fifteen leaned in the one-party direction soon after independence. On a closer look, none was purely Marxist, since the cold war attracted a variety of leftist ideologies from the USSR, China, Cuba, Latin America, and Europe. Africans responded with homegrown breeds as Conscientism, African Socialism, humanism, centralized democracy and so on. In spite of Ratsiraka's catechism of socialist ideology in Madagascar, the *Red Book* the churches thrived. Soon, the hostility in former Iberian enclaves diminished. Renamo flirted with Pentecostals, and National front for the Liberation of Angola (FNLA) with Baptists even as peace was brokered in the civil war in Angola by lay Catholics of the Communita di Sant'Egidio in Italy. In Angola and Zambia political rhetoric did not hurt the churches as much as the bad economic policies and disease.[8] On the whole, the power adventurism of the states forced major changes on the pattern of Christian presence in Africa.

All these chickens came to roost in the moratorium debate from 1971–1975. "Moratorium" was a more strident and different form of the indigenization project. It reflected African impatience with the nature, pace, and results of mission-initiated indigenization. Africans suspected a hidden agenda to embroil them in cosmetic changes while the same people retained real power. John Gatu, the secretary-general of the Presbyterian Church in Kenya, initiated the call during a visit to the United States in 1971. He embarrassed his hosts by declaring that he had not come to beg for money or personnel, but to request that missionary aid in money and personnel should cease for at least five years so that the short man could learn how to hang his knapsack within reach. Earlier, he led his church to produce a document stating what it believed, which raised the issue of doctrine. Burgess Carr, the secretary of the All Africa Council of Churches (AACC), Nairobi, was equally enamored of the moratorium call, proposed it at Lusaka, and invited African churches symbolically to Alexandria to draft an African confession of faith. By 1974, E. B. Idowu, the new leader of the Methodist Church in Nigeria, who for the last decade had spoken about the predicaments of an un-indigenized African church, moved the boundaries to matters of polity by proposing a patriarchal polity in consonance with the early church in North Africa. Were these romantic moves or sabotage?

Many Western mission bodies saw red and responded in a number of telling ways as a debate ensued in seminars, conferences, and journal pages. The argument here is that in the course of the debate the impulse and character of reverse flow were articulated. It was argued that *theologically*, moratorium was unacceptable because of the Pauline imagery of *soma*, that we are one body and one part cannot prevent the other from performing a mandatory task. Mission was the raison d'être of the church, a command from the Lord. The converse would apply that Africans had the mandate to do cross-cultural mission. *Ecclesiastically*, it was dangerous to become a national church. Becoming a national church threatened catholicity; the pilgrim and the indigenous principles must be held in tension. Interestingly, this served as a compelling reason for Africans to reverse the flow. *Logistically*, missionary organizations from the global north argued that it would be impossible to dismantle the mission structures that had been built for over a century. This would imply that Africans must build and sustain their own structures for cross-cultural mission. Then, there was the gut reaction of those who presumed that the Africans had proved ungrateful after years of sacrifices by missionaries. Eliott Kendall, who took over from T. A. Beetham, secretary of the Conference of Missionary Societies of Great Britain and Ireland has documented the overt and subtle pressures mounted on African church leaders.[9] Dissent was punished with denial of funds and low-intensity operation or underhanded strategies to foment local rebellion against nationalist clergy who supported moratorium, since moratorium was perceived as sabotage. The strategy of punishment would backfire by fostering nationalism as a plank in the reverse flow platform.

Initially, it did not take long for African ranks to break among the mainline churches: Some leaders preferred receiving aid rather than suffering as freedom fighters. Carr lost his job while Idowu became embroiled in schism; and the AACC languished until everyone forgot the spelling of moratorium. Avoiding the cardinal sin of monocausality, there was more to the fates of these men, but the debate about moratorium was crucial. Moratorium exposed the character of African relationship with the West: Extraversion appeared to be built into the pattern of African relationship with the West as an essential ingredient to maintain "eternal juniority." Even the support among white liberals proved ambiguous as some Protestant missions took the opportunity to abandon missionary engagement. However, these missions have found that the collapse of their missionary involvement diminished both the volume of local funds received and their sense of importance in their churches, so they are now forced to create new network patterns. Moratorium and African liberation struggles influenced the shifts in the strategy for decolonizing the African churches. When the WCC General Assembly met in Nairobi in 1975, the themes indicated a new mood that accepted African Christian maturity in ways hardly planned by the missionaries.

As a part of the moratorium debate, it was loudly wondered whether cross-cultural mission was a biblically mandated monopoly of the whites. Is it possible that Christians from the global south also possess the mandate to evangelize the global north? The Lutheran World Federation sent five Tanzanian clergymen to European churches to experiement on the reverse flow model. As they reported in 1982, they were received patronizingly. The experiment failed because the Tanzanians did not articulate a theology and ideology for mission, did not build and sustain their own structure, did not express a strong nationalist passion as that which inspired the white missionaries, and did not sponsor themselves. They were like visitors doing field placement in white churches. Africans in the mainline churches who started the reverse flow concept fumbled the ball near the goalpost. This is where the burgeoning numbers of Pentecostals came into the picture in the 1980s when the reverse flow initiated by mainline churches was throttled by the unresolved problem of racism. Before then, one could trace a few cases of African missionary enterprise in Europe, such as Daniel Ekaette's work in Liverpool in the 1930s. He served as a houseboy to Scottish missionaries in Calabar and was much inspired by Mary Slessor, a Scottish lady who cared passionately for the indigenous people, rescued many babies, and served as beacon of justice in the early 1900s. Later, Ekaette went to England as a seaman in the false belief that every British citizen was a Christian endowed with Mary Slessor's heart. To his shock, he was confronted with the destitution of Africans and many mulatto children. He started a church and a charitable institution, but racism snuffed the enterprise.[10] The AICs were the more successful organizers of alternative, African worship places because their spirituality was too exotic to fit into the churches in their new emigration homes.[11] Ordinarily, when Africans migrated to the global north, they would locate the worship places of the missionaries who evangelized their homelands. Most often, they won the acceptance of their hosts who showed them off as trophies of the successful missionary works. The first to start congregations based on language and ethnicity were Koreans and Taiwanese. But these grew as ethnic enclaves within northern denominations. Since Africans tended to migrate toward the colonial metropolis, language did not constitute an insurmountable barrier, although Frantz Fanon's *Black Skin White Mask* describes a pathetic picture of dependency syndrome choreographed by an African immigrant standing in front of a mirror in France practicing how to roll his tongue for the correct pronunciation.

This historical excursus was necessary because the background of moratorium must be clearly appreciated. Moratorium generated the reverse flow concept, and grounded its rationale and its characteristics. But moratorium also created confusion over its original meaning. Does it consist of mission from the global south to the global north, from the former missionary-receivers to former missionary-sending contexts? Or does it represent the outflowing of missionary impulse from the global south to all parts of the world? The first is a narrower perception of reverse flow and the second is a broader view that traces the south-south as well as the south-north linkages. When set within the broader perspective, the missionary impulse from the global south is sometimes directed south-south rather than south-north. For instance, South Korea sponsors more missionaries than most other countries (about twelve thousand in 2005) and targets a wide range of countries in the global south. Indeed, more than 45 percent of Korean missionary activities are in the southern hemisphere.[12] Though lacking in statistical data, African missionaries are found in many Asian countries just as Latin Americans and Asians are doing mission in Africa. The Haggai Institute has been a connecting link between African Pentecostals and the Southeast Asian mission field. Commerce also created a path because some African traders remain as suppliers to those who come from home. They link with the Chinese middle-class entrepreneurs who constitute the main Christian population. This is a research theme that is opening up and should defuse the intense concentration on mission to the global north that has raised a debate generated by the culture wars within the north. For many in the global north, the issue is not the decline of Christianity in the global north under the impact of secularism and the attendant culture wars, but the security concern that terrorists may infiltrate into the northern countries through religious groups, or that immigrant religions could bolster the ranks of conservative politicians against the enlightened liberal project.[13]

Certain issues are germane here: The volume of the missionary impulse from the south is increasing at the same time that the northern missionary impulse is declining in its intensity but showing a measure of resilience and diversification of its strategy. As Robert Coote has shown, when the North American Protestant data is read closely by removing the large number of short-term missionaries, there is a measure of decline among North American

Protestant missionary bodies. But a new trend is emerging among Evangelicals: Thousands are connecting with the new Christian centers in the global south as visiting and short-term missionaries because a number are turning away from domestic issues (abortion and sexual orientation) to global social concerns over ecology and HIV/AIDS. More cogent is the impact of immigration policies in the global north that opened up a larger space for Africans and thereby reshaped the character of the immigrant population. We should explore the contours of this enlargement of scale.

2. The Character of the African Immigrant Community

> His name is Themba
> He lives in Soweto
> Every morning he goes to the airport
> To watch the planes come and go
> He has changed his African name
> To a western one
> 'Cause he doesn't know how it hurts
> To have a name you can't be proud of
> He hopes that one day, one day
> One of these birds of the sky
> Can take him
> To a very very far land.

This is a touching ballad on a scorching phenomenon by the South African reggae artist Lucky Dube. As someone ruefully observed, "Everybody in my village wants to go to America." Every day, thousands of able-bodied Africans like Themba leave their roots in search of very faraway lands. For many, it is like an odyssey that spans years of tortured existence in transit. The pattern is multidirectional and the pace of the exodus is increasingly intense.

The statistical scope of the syndrome of departure is hard to confirm. The U.S. Census Bureau shows that in the United States in 1997, African immigrants had the highest educational accomplishment of all immigrant groups. In the age group of those twenty-five and older, 48.9 percent of African migrants had a bachelor's degree and above, compared with Asians at 44.6 percent, Europeans at 28.7 percent, and Latinos at 5.6 percent.[14] It is reported that more than ten thosand faculty members deserted African universities in the last decade of the millennium. A generational analysis points to the fact that the first generation of African scholars trained overseas under the ideology of questing for "the golden fleece," returned and trained others. A second generation studied for undergraduate degrees at home and traveled out for postgraduate specializations. They were more likely to stay abroad, and if they returned, did not stay long. This shift was driven by limited upward mobility, economic crises that affected incomes, and widespread political repression that constrained academic freedom. A third generation has suffered from the stringent limitations of changing immigration policies by Western nations and a lack of scholarships from Western institutions; they are more likely to be trained in the national universities under extremely difficult conditions, without the guidance of senior scholars, and without adequate books and laboratories.[15] Thus, while it may be useful to revisit the stirring examples from the era of African nationalism when the educationist K. E. Aggrey, the journalist Nnamdi Azikiwe, and the charismatic orator, Kwame Nkrumah, demonstrated African pride for the motherland, it must be recognized that the desire to emigrate is a syndrome determined by generational, ideological, and contextual shifts. Thus, incentives, governance, political culture, and policies on capacity development, quest for meaning, and self-development have triggered the syndrome, or desire to emigrate.

Some analyses place the syndrome in wider perspectives, arguing that migration is an endemic dimension to human life: Interpersonal conflicts and other internal problems have catalyzed migration in the past, while external factors such as war, incursion of other groups, culture contacts, and such have also forced some people to migrate. Buoyant economies tend to create osmotic pulls on lower economies. Rural-urban pulls always catalyze minor migrations. Paul Zeleza argues that the causes, courses, and consequences of contemporary international migration are tied to complex social networks that have arisen as a result of the long processes of globalization. Global migration in the twentieth century indicates that international migrations have intensified, as asylum seekers, refugees, and occupational migrants have moved to the West. The January 2000 issue of *La Monde Diplomatique* used the calculations by United Nation High Commission for Refugees (UNHCR) to describe the rising tide of refugees, especially from Africa, the Balkans, and Middle East.[16] Skilled migrants have assumed a greater importance to their native countries. The intensified south-north pattern has generated the racialization of migration, increased the number of illegal immigrants, and even introduced the possibility of dual citizenship. Analysis must balance the internal and external impulses.

In this period of human history, it has become an Africa-wide problem. Drought, military coups, and civil wars have created massive population shifts within the continent. We are experiencing push, or compelled desertion of homelands, rather than mild pulls. It is as if the continent is spewing out its people. Every year, thousands of Africans desert the soft states of Africa, the failed economies, and corrupt political environments. But sometimes, the reasons are more psychological than economic. From May 18, 2004–July 18, 2004, the British Broadcasting Corporation ran a five-part series entitled *Guinea: Unstoppable Exodus*. The writer, Joseph Winters, traced an African migrant, Mamadou Saliou Diallo, whom he encountered in Europe, to his village in the lush, picturesque, rolling hills of the Fouta Djalon region of northern Guinea. Winters concluded that though "the soil is so fertile, no one is starving but the younger generation is no longer content with mere survival and a way of life which has hardly changed for generations."[17] The ideological slant that images the cause of migration as a treasure hunt was incomplete since this better explains European migratory patterns of yesteryear. The contemporary situation in Africa was complex. Winters pointed to psychological roots as the reason many sought to emigrate to the West. For instance, African children were taught that Santa Claus lives in France, and young Africans internalized images of Europe, its way of life, and material goods as being most desirable. The African elite who flaunt Western materialism encrusts the image and fosters this form of mental slavery.

As Zeleza argued, Africans do not constitute the largest migrant population, although their share increased at a faster rate, from 10.6 percent to 13.1 percent in the period between 1965–1990, and even faster in the last decade of the millennium. Initially, it followed the paths of colonial heritage and linguistic trails. Thus, the French assimilation policy attracted migrants from their colonies. France had the largest concentration of African migrants: 33 percent of the foreign population in 1990. But the pattern became diffused as the United States became an attractive destination from the 1970s, and Germany, Canada, and northern European countries became friendly in the 1980s. Suffice it to argue, however, that the size and the trend of migration are determined by the changing immigration policies of the northern globe and are exacerbated by the decimation of both the civil society and the middle class by predatory, authoritarian regimes, whether *prebendary* (where the ruler treats the nation as his farm) or *praetorian* (where rulers mistake the nation for a military barracks). All employ clientele strategies, and manipulate ethnicity and religion in sharing the national resources in the politics of exclusion. The discourses in the literature, therefore, emphasize power relationships as determinants in understanding migration patterns: The neoclassical economic perspective privileges the demand and supply of labor; migration systems analysis argues that migrants follow linkages based on colonization, trade, cultural, and political influences; while the social capital discourse examines the internal networks that facilitate immigration toward certain regions. All rely on the principle of osmosis that has long been deployed in understanding rural-urban migration: the push created by declining resources and the pull toward stronger economies.

However, in understanding the immigrant community, the vagaries of the developed world's immigration policies have further scrambled the characteristics. African professionals are now working all over Europe driving taxis, picking grapes, looking after old people, working in brick-making factories, or packaging chewing gum. It is important to indicate that the professionals who migrate do not necessarily find employment in their fields of specialization. Some retrain into new professions; others barely survive. The immigrant condition is riddled with hope, hardship, broken dreams, and measures of success. Immigrant Christianity serves as a balm in the entire process, ranging from why and how the immigrants came to their new countries, to how they cope in the new homeland. The journey begins with prayers in Pentecostal churches and prayer camps for travel visas, to prayers in immigrant churches for everyday survival needs such as working permits, employment, and money for rent mortgage, health insurance, and other bills. There is also the added pressure to accumulate money and goods to transfer home.

3. An Anatomy of Immigrant Christianity

i. Methodology and Typology

Scholars have studied immigrant churches from different perspectives. The broad view understudies all types of religions practiced by immigrant African communities: the resilient indigenous religious practices that have flowed into the diaspora African religions that came from Central America, the increasing size of African Islamic presence, the aroma of spiritualism, the rich Afrocentric liturgy of AICs, and the growing presence of various brands of Christianity, especially charismatic and Pentecostal spirituality. This perspective has benefited from studies on diaspora religions (describing the global scattering of Africans outside the continent of Africa) though the adequacy of the concept has been contested. As Gerrie ter Haar observed, the word *diaspora* is used in three ways: to refer to the process of becoming scattered, to the actual community that has been scattered, or to the place of scattering. It may include African Americans, West Indians, and black South and Central Americans.[18] While Kehinde Olupona studied a broad range of the religions of African immigrants in the United States, Afe Adogame examined the relationship between African migration, experiences, religious practices, and the globalism discourse.[19] Ezra Chitendo draws attention to the research problem about voice, the insider's or the outsider's. Frieder Ludwig asserts that Philip Jenkins's simplistic categories about the liberal Christian north and neoconservative global south are good examples of how a distant location could distort an image. Fouad Ibrahim uses the Coptic diaspora in Germany to illustrate that immigrant attitude toward both their religion and the new home change through time. After early efforts to assimilate failed, Egyptian immigrants are rediscovering their identity through Coptic spirituality and practices in the face of a hostile, marginalized, social environment. In Israel, Galia Sabar identifies those who face quadruple marginalization: They are black, undocumented, Christian, and socially peripheral. Arab Christians discriminate against African Christians. The reality in the Holy Land jars prominently against the dreams of the Holy Land. Thus, the complexity in studying African immigrant religions is connected with the changing patterns, size, and experiences of a wide range of immigrant populations.[20]

Some studies have narrowed the focus on Christianity. Among these, most have focused on charismatic Pentecostal churches, while a few have paid attention to the burgeoning presence of African mainline churches. The Pentecostal studies have tended to profile megachurches such as Church of the Pentecost from Ghana, Redeemed Christian Church of God from Nigeria, and successful European churches such as Kingsway International in London, and Embassy of the Blessed Kingdom of God in Ukraine. Thus, there is an imbalance in the regional coverage biased narrowly toward West Africa. Outsider perspectives tended to essentialize and narrow the focus on the character and import of religious practices on diaspora communities. Ghanaian immigrant communities have had more than their fair share of scrutiny. This raises the question of whether the immigrant churches are studied as ethnic churches in foreign sites—a veritable image of oil on water—or as a part of the new religious landscape of European Christianity.

Most studies focus on the last three decades and pay little attention to the long view about African religious presence in the northern globe partially because the explosion of charismatic and Pentecostal movements attracted attention to the phenomenon of Christianity and African migrant labor in the northern globe. These churches serve immigrants in zoned sites of European cities. This African religious presence intensified from the 1980s and was characterized by the emergence of a new generation of leaders that was more educated and enjoyed increased contacts with northern Pentecostalism through outreaches, leadership training programs, and media. Naturally, the scholarship focused on contemporary African Pentecostalism that could be studied with the current fads such as modernity, externality, and globalization discourses. The scholarship focusing on a few megachurches as being indicative of the character of contemporary reverse flow runs the risk of missing the depth and nuance of the situation. Many immigrant churches struggle with low attendance and an inconsistent membership made up of people who work shifts at their low-paying jobs. Stories abound among frustrated pastors whose members sometimes deny the congregation the use of their electronic keyboards because they had to take the keyboards with them when they left to go to work.

A further danger lurks within these thick descriptions of the successful few because the descriptions hide larger questions about the impact on sending and receiving contexts or host perceptions. Pentecostal rhetoric may avoid the fact that the hosts consider these successful few as exotic and may be hostile. As a process of reverse flow, have these churches succeeded in attracting a wider band of population outside their ethnic and national bases? For instance, the Redeemed Christian Church of God is as predominantly Yoruba as the Church of Pentecost is Twi. In Toronto, Canada, the Church of the

Pentecost has two branches, the larger one, with over three thousand members, is Twi, while the smaller branch with one thousand members has some non-Ghanaians. All the other branches in Ottawa, Montreal, Hamilton, and Victoria are predominantly Ghanaian. Samuel Adelaja's Embassy of the Blessed Kingdom of God is unusual for being Ukranian. Kevin Ward's analysis of Ugandan Christian communities in Britain is interesting because the Ugandan immigrant communities reflect the deeply contested nature of ethnic divisions in their homeland. Many join Anglican and Catholic churches because of the deep political loyalties carved by these churches in the history of Uganda. A few Ugandan priests serve both Anglican and Catholic churches in Britain. Within the *biwempe* or the Pentecostal camp, the Baganda predominate in seven Baganda congregations in London, and one uses Luganda vernacular. Religious affiliation is used to reinforce ethnic identity, solidarity, and to develop survival skills.[21]

There are different types of African Christian presence based in the global north but primarily serving African immigrants. As observed earlier, the AICs were the first to establish their presence by catering to members who emigrated. In the United States, their ritualistic liturgy that combined many indigenous elements attracted Afrocentric African Americans who were attracted to what they regarded as authentic African Christianity. The AICs remind them of the spirituality in Ethiopianism. The relationship between African migrants and West Indian churches that became an identifiable feature in the United Kingdom from the 1950s has not been fully examined. Between 1997 and 1999, six conferences were held on the burgeoning African churches in Europe, estimated to total three million members in 1999. In all the gatherings, participants deliberated on the high level of marginality and racism suffered by African and Caribbean congregations in European Union–member countries. This forced Africans and Caribbean Christians to band together, and led to a meeting of African Christian leaders from five European countries at Notre Dame de Justice, Rhode Saint Genese, Belgium, on December 5, 1999, where leaders formed the protective umbrella known as the Council of African Christian Communities in Europe, a pressure group and strategic partnership of vulnerable immigrant churches.

The situation is very different in the United States where African churches meshed neatly into African American and Latino/a spirituality. It has been argued that these three groups have slowed the retreat of Christianity in North America. Reginald Bibby's book *Restless Gods: The Renaissance of Religion in Canada* makes a similar argument for a North American exceptionality. Thus, three forces pull these churches in different directions: First, common socioeconomic and political problems compel united responses by immigrants. However, the condition of marginality induces ethnic cohesion. Second, the recruitment strategy that follows the warm lines of family, friends, and members of one's ethnic group or former members of one's church in the home country creates the tendency toward the formation of ethnic/vernacular churches. Third, a missiological ideal to evangelize the whole world motivates some congregations to reach for multiracial and multiethnic status. In Nuremberg, Germany, I was intrigued by the liturgy in the Church of Pentecost. They read the Bible in three languages, German, Twi, and English. Many of the Africans are married to Germans. But multiethnicity is pursued by many immigrant congregations because they originated from interdenominational house fellowships and grew into independent churches founded by immigrants, some of whom may be compelled by the exigencies of the political economy to huddle in separate worship centers as safe zones. In Sweden, for instance, members of African churches are joined by other immigrants because of restrictive state policies that are not publicly articulated in an environment that pretends to create open spaces understood as conducive, free environments where different social and religious groups could operate without hindrance.

Most African immigrant churches start with lay immigrants. The laicization of African Christianity that followed decolonization has come full circle. The group may link with a Pentecostal church in the home country or bloom from its own resources. Some of the founders may later acquire theological training or request a trained pastor to oversee the operation. Many combine pastoral work with their secular profession. Indeed, the Christ Embassy (Port Harcourt, Nigeria) insists that all pastors in the international sector must earn their wages through secular employment. This reduces friction over financial matters, cuts operational costs, and enables the congregations to expand their facilities faster. Lay power encourages rapid expansion. Polity is important because the linkage may invite control from the international department of the church located in the home base. The old problem between the home board and missionaries in the field may rage unabated, especially since many Pentecostal churches centralize the posting of pastors to international congregations from the home base. A few establish international and regional offices that post pastors to congregations in specific regions of the country. Centralization intensifies virulent church politics, nepotism, abuse, and conflict.

Some immigrant congregations are branches of churches in Africa. These are deliberately founded by the leaders in the home base as extensions/overseas branches. An affluent congregation in Africa may sponsor an overseas branch as a mission project. From the 1990s, many mainline churches in Africa founded such international congregations. Pentecostals and Evangelicals have intensified efforts in this direction. Reasons for these efforts vary, but they are usually begun either to mobilize members who could contribute to the church's projects at home, or for prestige. Quite often this church planting has been motivated by immigrants. For example, a Presbyterian pastor completed his education abroad, stayed in his adopted country, and founded a congregation before inviting the church in his home country to bless it as a branch.

The main problem was in deciding whether it was a congregation of the Presbyterian Church USA or a congregation of the Presbyterian Church in the pastor's home country. Many African churches are opting for the latter affiliation. It is now a common sight to witness dedication ceremonies by senior church officials from various African countries. A number of ministries founded by Africans outside Africa choreograph their own reverse flow by founding congregations in the home countries. Some start by holding outreaches that mobilize a number of indigenous ministries, but gradually create resentment by starting their own branches. Permutations abound. There is the case of an Assemblies of God pastor from Kenya who was sponsored for theological training in the United States. When he returned to Kenya, he teamed with his wife to start a ministry linked to the support from a house fellowship that he served in the United States. Sometimes, a pastor or a leader in an African Pentecostal church would migrate (perhaps by winning the lottery or marrying someone with a green card) and find employment by gathering a congregation. Thus, many immigrant congregations are small and nearer to the grain of immigrant life.

The complexity in studying immigrant Christian presence arises from two other factors: the activities of itinerant evangelists, and the growth of house/ prayer fellowships among immigrants. A large number of ministers from Africa visit the northern globe as itinerant evangelists. Some visiting pastors minister to African churches and house fellowships, a feature of immigrant Christianity that has burgeoned. Many Africans belong to house prayer fellowships that hold meetings on Saturdays in private homes or church buildings so they won't compete with members' allegiance to churches. For instance, in Edinburgh, the African-Caribbean Christian Fellowship is hosted on Saturday evenings by an Elim Pentecostal church. Many African visiting evangelists share pulpits in African American churches, while still others hold special programs in white churches or in a network of churches. They would, in return, give their pulpits to the foreigners who hosted them. Pulpit sharing has enabled a wide variety of ministries to do cross-cultural mission and has enabled African American ministries to engage in the evangelization of the motherland. Some African pastors have regular itineraries garnished with prescribed seasonal schedules as if these are preaching outposts for the home church. Others visit occasionally whenever a ministration could be organized. Certain conclusions about cross-cultural mission are possible: The volume and variety of cross-cultural mission among African Pentecostals is extensive. Other churches and religious groups have recognized the potential that is related to the growth of the African immigrant population whose salience is recognized based on their religious zeal, propensity to use religion as an identity-shaping and survival force, and financial capacity. Mission to immigrant communities has become a core aspect of all brands of contemporary African Christianity. An ethnic-based Roman Catholic presence has been mobilized, perhaps in imitation of Latino Catholicism. Witness, for example, the burgeoning Nigerian Catholic congregations in various cities in the United States.

ii. Religion as an Identity-Shaping Force: A Functionalist Analysis

It intrigues Europeans that a majority of Africans are drawn to enthusiastic religion instead of adapting to secular Western ways. Many scholars deploy the instrumentalist discourse by emphasizing the functions of the religious groups to a population in transition. It is argued that these religious communities cater to the African psyche that is deeply religious; that these churches provide a home away from home; buttress identity; empower immigrants; provide coping mechanisms, social networks, security, employment, and legal and financial aids; and many social services and counseling on how to engage the new society with success. Churches in the United Kingdom are more likely to become involved in social services in the neighborhoods than are those in the rest of Europe where there is a "system" that is supposed to work on its own efficiency. The capacity to provide these services serves as the attraction, recruitment, and encapsulation strategy. People are attracted to bigger organizations because of their capacity to shield the individual against the hostile winds in a strange land. Galia Sabar and Shlomat Kanari paint a very touching portrait of African communities in Israel where music becomes a key force of survival. Some of the leading musicians could use this as an instrument to rise from their marginalized existence and may acquire the capacity to travel to other parts of the world.[22]

The immigrant churches in England make the extra effort to be seen as social service centers. The moral system among the born-again Christians helps the new migrant to be frugal, hardworking, focused, able to internalize the Western value system, and willing to eschew wasteful lifestyles. As moral havens, immigrant churches have economic, ethical, and social implications. Pastors stand between the immigrant and the police and, therefore, these churches help the immigrant to be law-abiding. In some cities, security officers recognize churches' potential as mediators and deliberately forge relationships with churches. The psychological refitting of the individual personality within the Western context is a major aspect of the tasks facing an immigrant church. This explains why some churches package their infrastructures to resemble corporate structures and deliberately refer to themselves as "connections," because they connect people to God, to other people, and to coping resources. As Rijk van Dijk says of the Dutch context: "At the level of externally oriented relations, Pentecostal leaders both in Ghana and in the Netherlands tend to act as brokers. They link information and interaction flows between different cultural contexts, and they fulfill an intermediary role between their networks and the larger society. They alleviate and accommodate some of the adverse effects of strangehood."[23]

Immigrants perceive these churches as cultural refuges where they can transmit their indigenous cultures and values to their children and thereby deal with the trauma of rearing children in the Western culture whose values clash prominently with the immigrants' indigenous values. Cultural clashes have the strongest impact on the structure of the family, where work, money, sex, child rearing, and authority patterns become contested grounds. Thus, pastors are compelled to intervene in marital problems by posing as "family heads." Immigrant communities are particularly fractious under the weight of new values, the stress of the new political economy, and the burden of their own old, village values. Marriages flounder and bitter divorces ensue because the antipatriarchal sexuality in Western culture jars.

But we must not lose sight of the religious dimensions of these churches. Immigrants still hold to the spiritual worldviews of the primal cultures and find the charismatic churches attentive to their deeply felt needs. Many itinerant evangelists travel around the globe to perform deliverance rites for African immigrants. Such powerful prayers are supposed to open the gates of "hard" nations for the benefit of the immigrants. As an immigrant prayer puts it: We did not come here for work because there is much work at home. We came for money and resources to improve our lot. So we pray for the doors and gates to open. Powerful healers and prayer warriors attract large numbers of votaries. For the immigrant, the liturgy feels like home, and buttresses the spiritual dimension. A full day of worship reconnects an individual to the spirit of the human community that exists in the homeland. As a perceptive member observed, the temperature at a church service might be too hot and the service itself might last too long for a non-African. But one hopes the sense of community, hospitality, and the recovery of the pneumatic resources of the gospel may contribute to the ascendancy of Christianity in host communities.

In Pentecostal rhetoric, many pastors reclaim the mandate to cross-cultural evangelization. This could become a sign of maturity with a tinge of nationalism. The cry goes beyond the black manifest destiny to evangelize Africa to the ultimate mandate to rescue the global north where Christianity is declining. Many of the African churches in southeastern Asia serve non-African congregations, and the pastors testify about visions that led them to hostile Malaysia and other such places. For example, a pastor traveled to New York to study in a Jewish establishment because the Lord called him to leave medical studies to prepare for witnessing to Jews. The dream may be a long shot but the passion is indubitable. For some churches, engaging the outside world enhances their prestige and makes the church an international organization like the "Anglican communion" or the universal Catholic Church. The quest for an international character and for external linkages could be interpreted as signs of modernity and globalization. But these are moot points precisely because the immigrants are already immersed in modernity and are crying for premodern forms of worship. Some churches fund large projects in the homeland through funds raised from outside. Some pastors support themselves through the goodwill of African immigrants who benefited from the pastors' ministrations, and so they can boast like Paul that they labor for Christ without salary from their churches.

What are the implications for global mission in the twenty-first century? At one level, the old system has been scrambled. New faces have emerged and the prophecy about a blessed reflex has been fulfilled. The true meaning of reverse flow is recognizing that the Great Command is a mandate for all believers, both individually and corporately. Each is called, each is sent. As Andrew Walls put it,

> Christian faith is now more diffused than at any previous time in
> its history; not only in the sense that it is more geographically,
> ethnically and culturally widespread than ever before, but in the
> sense that it is diffused within more communities. The territorial
> "from-to" idea that underlay the older missionary movement has to
> give way to a concept much more like that of Christians within
> the Roman Empire in the second and third centuries; parallel pres-
> ences in different circles and at different levels, each seeking to
> penetrate within and beyond its circle.[24]

The implication is that the paradigm shift has had an impact on both the global south and north. The north needs the humility to reassess its role and meth-ods, to probe the true forms of partnership as shown by Pentecostals, who share pulpits and reshape missionary presence into learning encounters like nongovernmental organizations engaged in rural development. The gospel is never planted but is given and received in dialogue. The global south must avoid hubris because the old problems of mission still require answers. In October 2006, I spent some time with twenty Korean pastors in Seoul. A pastor observed that doing cross-cultural mission invigorates his congregation and causes growth. But as I probed these active, missionary-sending pastors more about their problems, a catalog of issues rolled out that resonated with the problems in the nineteenth-century enterprises: rivalry and competition; funding; care of personnel; overemphasis on quantity, numbers, and size; imitation of models crafted by Western agencies; administrative and logistic problems; poor conflict resolution facilities; and the inability to create innova-tive strategies. Someone then drew attention to the need to recover the king-dom of God vision and model. This encounter was significant in outlining the problems of mission because the African practice of reverse flow has to be attentive to structural and missiological problems.

Conclusion

In conclusion, African Christianity, spurred by the charismatic and Pentecostal movements, has made its presence felt around the globe with an identifiable missionary character. As Roswith Gerloff put it,

African missions do not distinguish between spiritual and
the material. They base evangelism on spiritual empowerment,
as well as on social care for people. Different from European
style linear structures, African missions travel along a pre-existing
social relations such as family, friendship, village or island community, and trade and work comradeship. They rest on charismatic leadership, communicate in songs and signals, and understand the human person in his or her relationship to community. Therefore faith becomes the light, reliable and comforting
baggage in the process of migration and crisis. It testifies to a
God who wanders with people through the wilderness. It believes
in mutual respect and sharing. It turns the personal commitment of witnesses into a vehicle for being the gospel to be
proclaimed.[25]

The moratorium debate in the early 1970s evoked consternation among the
white missionary agencies that dismissed it as preposterous. Ironically, their
rebuttals provided the impetus for an African Pentecostal missionary enterprise. Within thirty years the movement achieved the goals that the mainline
churches failed to consolidate. Pentecostals have constructed a viable theology
of mission in which Africans can foray into the whole inhabited earth, and an
ecclesiology that can avoid the danger of being a national church. Pentecostal
outlook is notoriously international. Many African Pentecostals have built up
the logistical support to sustain the enterprise of missions, and the guts or
passion to challenge the northern monopoly by reversing the flow. By this achievement, African Pentecostalism has energized the scions of the mainline
churches to regain the vision of being a missional church. All projections point
to the southern concentration of Christianity through the next few decades and
the surging forth of southern Christianity into the global north that is suffering
from a massive retreat palpable in the nature of its cultural wars. Alasdair
Crockett and David Voas analyzed the major British social surveys and concluded that the decline is overwhelmingly generational in nature, rather than a
product of particular periods such as the Second World War or the 1960s; that
measures of religious affiliation, regular attendance at worship, and religious
belief show nearly identical rates of intergenerational decline. Two potential
modulators of decline were identified: immigrant population and the fertility
rate of the religiously active sector of the population. Crockett and Voas concluded that only the former was significant, that the nonwhite ethnic-minority
immigrant population is far more religious than the white population and has
higher fertility rates.[26]

To put contemporary African Pentecostalism in historical perspective, it is
reshaping the face of global Christianity and fulfilling the dreams of the
Ethiopian movement, as captured by Wilmot Byden's prediction:

Africa may yet prove to be the spiritual conservatory of the world. Just
as in the past times, Egypt proved the stronghold of Christianity
after Jerusalem fell, and just as the noblest and greatest of the Fathers
of the Christian Church came out of Egypt, so it may be, when
the civilized nations, in consequence of their wonderful material development, have had their spiritual perceptions darkened and their
spiritual susceptibilities blunted through the agency of a capturing and absorbing materialism, it may be, that they may have to resort
to Africa to recover some of the simple elements of faith; for the
promise of that land is that she shall stretch forth her hands
unto God.[27]

The effort has been made to retell the story of African Pentecostalism by
paying attention to space, time, themes, and various scholarly discourses. The
overarching conceptual scheme indicates that African Pentecostalism emerged
from African indigenous religious and cultural responses to the gospel message. It has been shaped by the same ideals that informed the responses of
the antistructural Ethiopianism movement, some of whose leaders exited
from the missionary structures to found native African churches. These confronted the structures created by colonial regimes and churches. The early-
educated elite, who had just regained freedom from slave trade, suffered
innumerable humiliations from cultural despisers of the age. They sought to
rebuild the African's battered image and identity through religious and cultural power. It has been a mistake to interpret the movement as mere cultural
nationalism. These elite articulated the deepest concerns of the gospel about
the meaning of the reign of God in the midst of asymmetrical power relationships and the monopoly of the interpretation of the Word of God. The
Word ceased to be spirit and life because its meaning was hedged to legitimize
structures of overrule. Some showed subversive loyalty, others gave voice to
racial discontent, while others liberated the Spirit in the Word through their
exit. The pneumatic challenge was posed more boldly by African prophets,
Aladura, Zionists, and Abaroho. The fruits of vernacular translation of the
Bible included the validation that the Spirit healed just as it did in the African
religious traditions. Pentecostals took the challenge many steps further precisely because they operated from the same premises as the radical Evangelicals among the whites. They showed a healthy sense of pragmatism in utilizing
the tools of modernity, and have moved to reverse the flow of missionary
processes because, once upon a time, African theologians shaped the doctrine,
polity, liturgy, and ethics of the early Jesus movement. African scholars such as
Origen, Augustine, and Tertullian were in demand throughout the Christian
world. Origen's method, Pachomian monastic rules, informed the Cappado-
cians and the European Benedictine orders. Today, African Pentecostalism is
daring to recover identity through religious power.

Notes

CHAPTER 1

1. Cephas N. Omenyo, *Pentecost Outside Pentecostalism: A Study of the Development of Charismatic Renewal in the Mainline Churches in Ghana* (Zoetermeer, Netherlands: Boekencentrum, 2002).

2. Paul Gifford, *Ghana's New Christianity: Pentecostalism in a Globalizing African Economy* (Bloomington: Indiana University Press, 2004), 23–24.

3. Donald Dayton, *Theological Roots of Pentecostalism* (Metuchen, N.J.: Scarecrow, 1987).

4. J. Kwabena Asamoah-Gyadu, "Born of Water and the Spirit: Pentecostal/Charismatic Christianity in Africa," in *African Christianity: An African Story*, ed. Ogbu U. Kalu (Pretoria: University of Pretoria, 2005), 395.

5. Peter D. Hocken, "A Charismatic View on the Distinctiveness of Pentecostalism," in *Pentecostalism in Context: Essays in Honor of William W. Menzies*, ed. Wonsuk Ma and Robert P. Menzies (Sheffield: Sheffield Academic Press, 1997), 103.

6. "Concerning This Movement," *Seattle Apostolic Herald* (October 1909), 3.

7. D. William Faupel, *The Everlasting Gospel: The Significance of Eschatology in the Development of Pentecostal Thought* (Sheffield: Sheffield Academic Press, 1996); and Edith Blumhofer, *Restoring the Faith: The Assemblies of God, Pentecostalism, and American Culture* (Chicago: University of Illinois Press, 1993).

8. Velli-Matti Karkkainen, *Pneumatology: The Holy Spirit in Ecumenical, International, and Contextual Perspective* (Grand Rapids, Mich.: Baker, 2002).

9. David Maxwell, "Witches, Prophets and Avenging Spirits," *Journal of Religion in Africa* 25, no. 3 (1995): 309–339, see esp. 314.

10. Kingsley Larbi, *Eddies of Ghanaian Pentecostalism* (Accra: CPCS, 2001), 278.

11. Gordon Fee, "Towards a Pauline Theology of Glossolalia," in *Pentecostalism in Context*, ed. W. Ma and R. P. Menzies (Sheffield: Academic Press, 24–37); Simon Chan, "The Language Game of Glossolalia or Making Sense of the Initial Evidence," ibid., 80–95, see esp. 93; Frank Macchia, "Tongues as a Sign: Towards a Sacramental Understanding of Pentecostal Experience," *Pneuma* 5 (1993): 61–76; and Luke Ndubuisi, *Pauline Concept of Charisma in 1 Corinthians 12* (Frankfurt: Peter Lang, 2003).

12. Allan Anderson, *An Introduction to Pentecostalism: Global Charismatic Christianity* (Cambridge: Cambridge University Press, 2004), 24.

13. Ogbu U. Kalu, "The Third Response: Pentecostalism and the Reconstruction of Christian Experience in Africa, 1970–1995," *Journal of African Christian Thought* 1, no. 2 (December 1998): 1–21.

14. Harvey Cox, *Fire from Heaven: The Rise of Pentecostal Spirituality and the Reshaping of Religion in the Twenty-first Century* (Reading, Mass.: Addison-Wesley, 1995 and David Martin, *Pentecostalism: The World Their Parish* (Oxford: Blackwell, 2002).

15. David Maxwell, "Witches, Prophets and Avenging Spirits," 320.

16. W. J. Hollenweger, "After Twenty Years of Research on Pentecostalism, *International Review of Missions* 75, no. 297 (January 1986): 3–12; and Grant Wacker, *Heaven Below: Early Pentecostals and American Culture* (Cambridge, Mass.: Harvard University Press, 2001).

17. David Martin, "The Global Expansion of Radical Primitive Christianity," *The Princeton Seminary Bulletin* 26, no. 1 (2005): 111–122, see esp. 114.

18. Peter L. Berger, "The Cultural Dynamics of Globalization," http:// speakingoffaith.publicradio.org) (Feb. 13, 2006).

19. For fuller treatment see Ogbu U. Kalu, "Globecalisation and Religion: The Pentecostal Model in Africa," in *Uniquely African?* ed. J. L. Cox and G. ter Haar (Trenton, N.J.: Africa World, 2003), 215–240; and Simon Coleman, "Charismatic Christianity and the Dilemma of Globalization," *Religion* 28 (1998): 245–256.

20. Paul Gifford, *The New Crusaders* (London: Pluto, 1991); and Steve Brouwer, Paul Gifford, and Susan Rose, *Exporting the American Gospel: Global Christian Fundamentalism* (New York: Routledge, 1996).

21. Paul Gifford, *African Christianity: Its Public Role* (Bloomington: Indiana University Press, 1998), 322, 47.

22. David Maxwell, "Delivered from the Spirit of Poverty: Pentecostalism, Prosperity and Modernity in Zimbabwe," *Journal of Religion in Africa* 28, no. 3 (1998): 350–373; and Kwame Bediako, "Christian Witness in the Public Sphere: Some Lessons and Residual Challenges from the Recent Political History of Ghana," in *The Changing Face of Christianity: Africa, the West, and the World*, ed. Lamin Sanneh and Joel A. Carpenter (New York: Oxford University Press, 2005), 117–132.

23. Lamin Sanneh, *Whose Religion Is Christianity?* (Grand Rapids, Mich.: Eerdmans, 2003), 22; and Ruth Marshall-Fratani, "Mediating the Global and the Local in Nigerian Pentecostalism," *Journal of Religion in Africa*, 28, no. 3 (1998): 278–315.

24. Allan Anderson, *An Introduction to Pentecostalism*, 19–38, see esp. 24; Ian Randall, *Evangelical Experiences: A Study in the Spirituality of English Evangelicals, 1918–1931* (Carlisle: Paternoster, 1999); and William Kay, *Pentecostal Britain* (Carlisle: Paternoster, 2000).

25. Dale Irvin, "Pentecostal Historiography and Global Christianity: Rethinking the Question of Origin," *Pneuma* 27, no. 1 (2005): 35–50, see esp. 44–45. On the "logic," compare D. W. Dayton's quadrilateral in *Theological Roots of Pentecostalism* with W. J. Hollenwenger's *notae bene* in "After Twenty Years of Research on Pentecostalism": 3–12.

26. Karla Poewe, ed., *Charismatic Christianity as a Global Culture* (Columbia: University of South Carolina Press, 1994), 17.

27. Dale Irvin, "Ecumenical Dislodgings," *Mission Studies* 22, no. 2 (2005): 187–205, see esp. 189.

28. Allan Anderson, "The Dubious Legacy of Charles Parham: Racism and Cultural Insensitivities among Pentecostals," *Pneuma* 27, no. 1 (2005): 51–64, see esp. 58–61.

29. David Maxwell, "Witches, Prophets and Avenging Spirits," 309–339.

30. Robin Horton, "African Conversion," *Africa* 41, no. 2 (1971): 85–108; M. Engelke, "Discontinuity and the Discourse of Conversion," *Journal of Religion in Africa* 34, nos. 1–2 (2004): 82–109.

31. Kevin Ward, "Obedient Rebels: The Relationship between the Early *Balokole* and the Church of Uganda," *Journal of Religion in Africa* 19, no. 3 (1989): 194.

32. Mathias Mundadan, "The Changing Task of Christian History," in *Enlarging the Story*, ed. W. R. Shenk (Maryknoll, N.Y.: Orbis, 2002), 22–53, see esp. 23.

33. W. Shenk, ed., *Enlarging the Story: Perspectives on Writing World Christian History* (Maryknoll, N.Y.: Orbis, 2002), xi.

34. Paul Emeka, "Benson Idahosa Factor in Nigerian Pentecostalism" PhD thesis, University of Nigeria, Nsukka, 2001.

35. Paul Gifford, "Africa Shall Be Saved: An Appraisal of Reinhard Bonkke's Pan African Crusade," *Journal of Religion in Africa* 17 (1987): 63–92.

36. Emeka Nwankpa, *Redeeming the Land* (Accra: Achimota, 1995); and Cephas N. Omenyo, *Pentecost Outside Pentecostalism: A Study of the Development of Charismatic Renewal in the Mainline Churches in Ghana*. Zoetermeer, Boekencentrum, 2002; and Mika Vahakangas and Andrew A. Kyomo, eds., *Charismatic Renewal in Africa* (Nairobi: Acton, 2003) contain reflections on the theme of the charismatization of African churches by some African scholars such as Cephas Omenyo, Laurenti Magesa, Faith J. Lugazia, Mika Vahakangas, Evaristi Magoti, Jesse Mugambi, Andrew Kyomo, Ronilick Mchani, and Auli Vahakangas. The data cover Kenya, Ghana, and Tanzania. See also Abamfo O. Atiemo, *The Rise of Charismatic Movement in the Mainline Churches in Ghana* (Accra: Asempa, 1993).

37. Edward Rommen, ed., *Spiritual Power and Missions: Raising the Issues* (Pasadena, Calif.: Wm. Carey Library, 1995); see *Pneuma* 13 (1991). The entire volume was devoted to the debate on spiritual warfare; Michael Reed, *Strategic Level Warfare: A Modern Mythology?* (Fairfax, Va.: Xulon, 2002); C. Peter Wagner, *Breaking Strongholds in Your City* (Ventura, Calif.: Regal, 1993); Kwabena Asamoah-Gyadu, "Mission to Set the Captive Free: Healing, Deliverance and Generational Curses in Ghanaian Pentecostalism," *International Review of Mission* 93, nos. 370–71 (July/October 2004): 389–406; and Opoku Onyinah, "Contemporary Witchdemonology in Africa," *International Review of Mission* 93, nos. 370–71 (July/October 2004): 330–345; W. J.

Hollenweger, "Healing through Prayer: Superstition or Forgotten Christian Tradition?" *Theology* 92, no. 747 (1989): 166–174.

38. Harvey Cox, *Fire from Heaven*, 213–241.

39. J. R. Goff and G. Wacker, eds., *Portraits of a Generation: Early Pentecostal Leaders* (Fayetteville: University of Arkansas Press, 2002), 87–104, 123–142.

40. Lee Young-Hoon, "Korean Pentecost: The Great Revival of 1907," *Asian Journal of Pentecosalt Studies (AJPS)* 4, no. 1 (January 2001): 73–83; Stanley Burgess, "Pentecostal of India" *AJPS* 4, no. 1 (2001): 85–98; A. C. George, "Pentecostal Beginnings in Travancore," *AJPS* 4, no. 2 (2001): 215–237; G. Burgess, "The Calcutta Revival of 1907," *AJPS* 6, no. 1 (2003): 123–143; G. Burgess, "Latter Rain Falling in the East," *Church History* 68 (September 1999): 648–665; Allan Anderson, "The Contextual Pentecostal Theology of David Yonggi Cho," *AJPS* 7, no. 1 (2004); Kang Chang-soo, "Resources for Studies of David Yonggi Cho," *AJPS* 7, no. 1 (2004); Boo-Wong Yoo, *Korean Pentecostalism: Its History and Theology* (New York: Peter Lang, 1988). See also David Smithers's accounts of the Korean revival in www.watchword.org/smithers/ww45c.html (May 20, 2002).

41. R. I. J. Hackett, "New Directions for African and Asian Charismatics," *Pneuma* 18, no. 1 (1996): 67–77; Matthew Ojo, "The Dynamics of Indigenous Charismatic Enterprises in West Africa," *Missionalia* 25, no. 4 (1997): 537–561; G. ter Haar, *African Christians in Europe* (Nairobi: Acton, 2001); and C. Omenyo and David Choi, "Korean Missionary Enterprise in West Africa, 1979–1999," *Exchange* 29, no. 3 (2000): 213–229; and Opoku Onyinah, "Pentecostalism and the African Diaspora," *Pneuma* 26, no. 2 (Fall 2004): 216–241. The entire issue of *International Review of Mission* 89, no. 354 (July 2004) is devoted to "The African Christian Diaspora in Europe and the Quest for Human Community." See articles in the *Review* by Roswith Gerloff, Afe Adogame, Kevin Ward, Fidelia Onyuku-Opukiri, Emmanuel Tshielenga-Kabala, and M. Louise-Pirouet.

42. J. K. Asamoah-Gyadu, "An African Pentecostal on Mission in Eastern Europe: 'The Church of the Embassy of God in Ukraine'," *Pneuma* 27, no. 2 (2005): 297–321; Ogbu U. Kalu, "Elijah's Mantle: Ministerial Formation in Contemporary African Christianity," *International Review of Missions* 94, no. 373 (April 2005): 263–277; and Gerrie ter Haar, *Halfway to Paradise: African Christians in Europe* (Cardiff: Cardiff Academic Press, 1998).

43. David Martin, "The Global Expansion of Radical Primitive Christianity," *Princeton Seminary Bulletin* 26, no. 1 (2005): 111–122, see esp. 121.

44. Lamin Sanneh and Joel Carpenter, *The Changing Face of Christianity: Africa, the West, and the World* (New York: Oxford University Press, 2005), 4.

CHAPTER 2

1. Max Warren, *Revival: An Inquiry* (London: SCM, 1954), 54.

2. R. L. Wilshade, *Sectarianism in South Nyasaland* (London: Oxford University Press, 1965).

3. Warren, *Revival*, 57.

4. Allan Anderson, *Moya: The Holy Spirit in an African Context* (Pretoria: University of South Africa Press, 1991).

5. Efraim Andersson, *Messianic Popular Movements in the Lower Congo* (Uppsala: Studia Ethnographica Upsaliensa, 1958), 101; Carl Sundberg, *Conversion and Contextual Conceptions of Christ*, Studia Missionalia Svecana 81, (Uppsala: Swedish Institute of Missionary Research, 2000), 133.

6. In Richard Elphinck and Rodney Davenport, eds., *Christianity in South Africa* (Oxford: James Currey, 1997), 68.

7. Rijk van Dijk, "Young Born Again Preachers in Post-independence Malawi," in *New Dimensions in African Christianity*, ed. Paul Gifford (Nairobi: All Africa Conference of Churches, 1992), 55; and André Corten and Ruth Marshall-Fratani, eds., *Between Babel and Pentecost: Transnational Pentecostalism in Africa and Latin America* (Bloomington: Indiana University Press, 2001).

8. Andrew F. Walls, *The Cross-cultural Process in Christian History* (Maryknoll, N.Y., Orbis, 2000), 135–154.

9. Tony Chafer, ed., *Promoting the Colonial Idea: Propaganda and Visions of Empire in France* (New York: Palgrave, 2002).

10. J. Mutero Chirenje, *Ethiopianism and African Americans in South Africa, 1883–1916* (Baton Rouge: Louisiana State University Press, 1987); and Gyraud Wilmore, *Black Religion and Black Radicalism* (Maryknoll, N.Y.: Orbis, 1998), chap. 10.

11. G. O. M. Tasie, *Thoughts and Voices of an African Church: Christ Army Church, Nigeria* (Jos: Connack Nigeria, 1997); David Shank, "The Prophet Harris, the Black Elijah (Leiden: Brill, 1994).

12. Adrian Hastings, *The Church in Africa, 1450–1950* (Oxford: Clarendon, 1994), 449.

13. C. G. Baeta, *Prophetism in Ghana* (London: SCM, 1962), 15.

14. Hastings, *Church in Africa*, 489.

15. Shank, "The Prophet Harris," 147n1.

16. Braide's fame caused him to clash with the colonial authorities because his diatribe against the consumption of liquor struck at the heart of the economy and caused a decline in the amount of tax revenue collected from the sale of liquor. He also caused unemployment in the courts because he adjudicated cases among the communities. People trusted his fairness.

17. M. A. Kemmer, *Niger Delta Chronicle* (1909). In L. Lugwuana, "Medicine, Spiritual Healing and African Response," *Africa Theological Journal* 23, no. 1 (2000): 27.

18. O. U. Kalu, "Waves from the Rivers: The Spread of the Garrick Braide Movement in Igboland, 1918–1939," *Journal of the Historical Society of Nigeria* 8, no. 4 (June 1977): 95–110.

19. See Frieder Ludwig, "Elijah II: Radicalisation and Consolidation of the Garrick Braide Movement, 1915–1918," *Journal of Religion in Africa* 22, no. 4 (1993): 298–315.

CHAPTER 3

1. Ogbu U. Kalu, "Doing Mission through the Post Office: The Naked Faith People of Igboland, 1920–1960," *Neue Zeitschrift fur Missionswissenschaft* 54, no. 4 (2000): 263–280; John D. Y. Peel, *Aladura* (London: Oxford University Press, 1968);

Christine Leonard, *A Giant in Ghana: The Story of James McKeown and the Church of the Pentecost* (Chicester: New Wine Ministries, 1989); and Abi Olowe, *Great Revivals, Great Revivalist: Joseph Ayo Babalola.* (Houston: Omega Publishers, 2007).

2. This account has been based on the following: E. Musembe Kasiera, "The Founding and Development of Nyang'ori Mission, 1909–1924," seminar paper, Department of Philosophy and Religious Studies, University of Nairobi, Feb. 20, 1980; see also Kasiera's PhD thesis, "Development of Pentecostal Christianity in Western Kenya," University of Aberdeen, 1981; Z. W. Samita, "The African Church of the Holy Spirit: Origins and Advent in Kabra Division, Kamenga District," *TransAfrican Journal of History* 25 (1996): 123–145; Ane Marie Bak Rasmussen, *Modern African Spirituality: The Independent Holy Spirit Churches in East Africa, 1902–1976* (London: British Academic Press, 1996); J. M. Lonsdale, "European Attitudes and African Pressures: Missions and Government in Kenya between the Wars," in *Hadith 2,* ed. B. A. Ogot (Nairobi: East Africa Publishing House, 1975), 229–242; A. J. Temu, *British Protestant Missions* (London: Longman, 1972)

3. Willy de Craemer, *The Jamaa and Church: A Bantu Catholic Movement in Zaire* (Oxford: Clarendon, 1977).

4. Carl Sundberg, *Conversion and Contextual Conceptions of Christ.* Studia Missionalia Svecana 81 (Uppsala: Swedish Institute of Missionary Research, 2000), 129.

5. Ibid., 131.

6. E. Musembe Kasiera, "The Founding and Development of Nyang'ori Mission, 1909–1924," Seminar Paper, Department of Religious Studies, University of Nairobi, February 20, 1980.

7. Allan Anderson, "The New Jerusalem: The Role of the Azusa Street Revival in the Global Expansion of Pentecostalism," Paper delivered at the 35th Annual Meeting of the Society for Pentecostal Studies, Pasadena, California, March 23–25, 2006.

8. Roberts Liandon, *John G. Lake: The Complete Collection of His Life and Teachings* (Laguna Hills, Calif.: Roberts Liandon Ministries, 1999); and Kemp P. Burpeau, *God's Showman: A Historical Study of John G. Lake and South African/American Pentecostalism* (Oslo: Refleks, 2004).

9. David Maxwell, *African Gifts of the Spirit: Pentecostalism and the Rise of a Zimbabwean Transnational Religious Movement* (Oxford, James Currey, 2006):41–45.

10. W. L. Williams, *Black Americans and the Evangelization of Africa, 1877–1900* (Madison, University of Wisconsin Press, 1982), 90.

11. H. Lewis, "Black Episcopalians as Missionaries to Africa in the 19th Century" In L. Price, J. Sepulveda, G. Smith, eds. *Mission Matters (*New York, Peter Lang, 1999):21–34.

12. M. F. Mutshi, and S. Bartlett, S. eds *African Americans in Mission: Serving the Presbyterian Church from 1883 to the Present* (Louisville: Office of Global Awareness and Involvement, 2000); D. Antwi, and Paul Jenkins, " The Moravians, the Basel Mission and the Akuapem State in the Early Nineteenth Century." In *Christian Missionaries and the State in the Third World.* eds., Hansen, H. B. and Twaddle, M. (Oxford, James Currey, 2002):39–51.

13. Herman L. Greene, *UPCAG–The First 90 Years: Volume I:1919 to1945* (Sussex, N.J.: Geda Publications, 2005),11.

14. J. S. Mills, *Mission Work in Sierra Leone, West Africa* (Dayton, Ohio: UB Publishing House, 1898), 116.

15. Fully discussed in Ogbu U Kalu, "Black Missionaries and White Abolitionists: Joseph and Mary Gomer in the Good Hope Mission, Sierra Leone, 1871–1894" *Neue Zeitschrift fur Missionwissenschaft*, 59, 3 (2003):161–174.

16. Herman L. Greene, *UPCAG–The First 90 Years, 1919–1945* (Sussex, N.J.: Geda, Publications, 2005).

17. Charles H. Pleas, *Fifty Years' Achievement, from 1905–1956: A Period in History of the Church of God in Christ* (Memphis: Church of God In Christ, 1956).

18. Elder J. W. Denny, *A Nostalgic Look at Yesterday* (Memphis: Church of God In Christ, 1995).

19. Pierre-Joseph Laurent, "Les conversions aux Assemblees de Dieu du Burkina Faso," *Journal des Africanistes* 47 (1998): 67–97; Pierre-Joseph Laurent, *Les Pentecostistes du Burkina Faso: Mariage, Pouvoir et Guerison* (Paris: Karthala, 2003); idem., "Transnationalism and Local Transformation: The Example of the Church of Assemblies of God of Burkina Faso," in *Between Babel and Pentecost*, ed. André Corten and Ruth Marshall-Fratani (Bloomington: Indiana University Press, 2001), 256–273.

20. See André Corten and Ruth Marshall-Fratani, eds., *Between Babel and Pentecost: Transnational Pentecostalism in Africa and Latin America* (Bloomington: Indiana University Press, 2001), 216–309; Ebenezer O. Adeogun, *A Transplant of the Vine: Forty Years of Foursquare History in Nigeria* (Lagos: Foursquare Gospel Church in Nigeria, 1999).

21. Adrian Hastings, *The Church in Africa, 1450–1950* (Oxford: Clarendon, 1994), 544–545.

22. Cited in Corten and Marshall-Fratani, *Between Babel and Pentecost*, 262.

23. Allan Anderson and Gerald Pillay, "The Segregated Spirit: The Pentecostals," in *Christianity in South Africa*, ed. Richard Elphinck and Rodney Davenport (Oxford: James Currey, 1997), 238; Philip L. Cook, *Zion City, Illinois: Twentieth Century Utopia* (Syracuse, N.Y.: Syracuse University Press, 1996). On Benghu, see Stanley M. Burgess, ed., *International Dictionary of Pentecostal and Charismatic Movements* (Grand Rapids, Mich.: Zondervan, 2002), 372.

24. Gerald J. Pillay, "Community Service and Conversion: Christianity among Indian South Africans," in *Christianity in South Africa*, ed. Richard Elphinck and Rodney Davenport (Oxford: James Currey, 1997), 290.

25. Ibid., 293.

26. I am grateful to Klaus Fiedler for sharing his paper "The Charismatic and Pentecostal Movements in Malawi in Cultural Perspective," *Religion in Malawi* 9 (1999): 28–38.

27. David Maxwell, "Witches, Prophets and Avenging Spirits: The Second Christian Movement in North-East Zimbabwe," *Journal of Religion in Africa* 25, no. 3 (1995): 309–339, see esp. 312. *Mhodoro spirits* were spirits of dead chiefs or big men who made their wishes known through a medium called a *svikiro*. They also possessed lions, so it was called lion spirit. *Ngozi* were spirits of people who were murdered, improperly buried, or mistreated. They afflicted members or descendants of offending families. *Shave* (pl. *mashave*) is an alien spirit, neighboring people,

whites, strangers, or certain animals that conferred some skills on its host. For instance, it can bestow skills to hunters.

28. For details, see Ben Jones, "The Church in the Village, the Village in the Church: Pentecostalism in Teso, Uganda," *Cahiers d'Etudes Africaines* 45, no. 2 (2005): 497–517; see esp. 507n17.

CHAPTER 4

1. David Barrett, "Twentieth Century Pentecostal/Charismatic Renewal in the Holy Spirit with Its Goal of World Evangelization," *International Bulletin of Missionary Research*, 12 (July 1988): 119–129.

2. Mercy Amba Oduyoye, and P. Nkemdirim, eds., *Women, Culture and Theological Education* (Enugu: SNAAP, 1998), 35; Mercy Amba Oduyoye, *Daughters of Anowa: African Women and Patriarchy* (Maryknoll: N.Y.: Orbis, 1995); Paul Gifford, *New Crusaders* (London: Pluto, 1991); and Adrian Hastings, *African Catholicism: Essays in Discovery* (London: SPCK, 1989).

3. W. J. Hollenweger, *New Wine in Old Wineskins* (Gloucester: Fellowship, 1973); *Pentecostalism between Black and White* (Belfast: Christian Journal, 1974); Kilian McDonnel, "Improbable Conversations: The International Classical Pentecostal/Roman Catholic Dialogue," *Pneuma* 17, no. 2 (1995): 163–188; Kilian McDonnel, "The Pentecostal Dimension," *Tablet* 28 (November 1992).

4. John D. Y. Peel, *Aladura* (London: Oxford University Press, 1968).

5. H. W. Turner, "Typology for African Religious Movements," *Journal of Religion in Africa* 1, no. 1 (1967): 1–34.

6. Karla Poewe, "Links and Parallels between Black and White Charismatic Churches in South Africa and the States: Potential for Cultural Transformation," *Pneuma* 10, no. 2 (1986): 141–158.

7. See the bibliography in Allan Anderson, *African Reformation* (Trenton, N.J.: Africa World, 2000), whose position appears in many articles. See also V. E W. Hayward, ed., *African Independent Church Movements* (London: Edinburgh House, 1957); Kwame Bediako, *Christianity in Africa: The Renewal of a Non-Western Religion* (Maryknoll, N.Y.: Orbis, 1995); M. L. Daneel, *The Quest for Belonging* (Gweru: Mambo, 1987); and R. I. J. Hackett, *New Religious Movements in Nigeria* (Lewiston, N.Y.: Mellen, 1987); J. B. Tinney, "The Blackness of Pentecostalism," *Pneuma* 3, no. 2 (1980), 27–36; and H. W. Turner, "Nigerian Pentecostalism," *Orita* (1971).

8. W. J. Hollenweger, *The Pentecostals* (London: Publisher, 1972), 51.

9. Allan Anderson, "Pentecostal Pneumatology and African Power Concepts: Continuity or Change," Missionalia, 19, 1(1991):65–74, see, p. 65.

10. Allan Anderson, "African Pentecostalism," *Studia Historiae Ecclesiaticae* 22, no. 1 (1996): 114–148, see esp. 121.

11. Allan Anderson, "African Independent Churches and Global Pentecostalism: Historical Connections and Common Identities," in *African Identities and World Christianity in the Twentieth Century*, ed. Klaus Koschorke (Wiesbaden: Harrassowitz, 2005): 63–76, see esp. 65, 70–71.

12. Allan Anderson and Gerald J. Pillay, "The Segregated Spirit: The Pentecostals," in *Christianity in South Africa*, ed. Richard Elphinck and Rodney Davenport (Oxford: James Currey, 1997), 233.

13. Allan Anderson, "The Newer Pentecostal and Charismatic Churches: The Shape of Future Christianity in Africa?" *Pneuma* 24, no. 2 (Fall 2002): 167–184; see esp. 169.

14. Kwabena Asamoah-Gyadu, *African Charismatics: Current Developments within Independent Indigenous Pentecostalism in Ghana* (Leiden: Brill, 2005), 20–23; and E. Kingsley Larbi, *Pentecostalism: The Eddies of Ghanaian Christianity* (Accra: CPCS, 2001).

15. Matthew Ojo, "Deeper Life Christian Ministry," *Journal of Religion in Africa* 18, no. 2 (1988): 141–162; and Allan Isaacson, *Deeper Life* (London: Hodder and Stoughton, 1990).

16. Daneel, *Quest for Belonging*, 54.

17. David Maxwell, "Witches, Prophets and Avenging Spirits," *Journal of Religion in Africa* 25, no. 3 (1995): 309–330; David Maxwell, "Historicizing Christian Independency: The Southern African Pentecostal Movement, 1908–1950," *Journal of African History* 40 (1999).

18. Maxwell, "Historicizing Christian Independency."

19. See Kalu, *Embattled Gods: Christianization of Igboland, 1841–1991*. First published by Lagos/London: Minaj, 1996; republished by Trenton, N.J.: Africa World, 2003, chap. 10.

20. Poewe, "Links and Parallels," 157.

21. Ibid.

22. Leonard Lovett, "Black Origins of the Pentecostal Movement," in *Aspects of Pentecostal-Charismatic Origins*, ed. Vinson Synan (Plainsfield, N.J.: Logos, 1975), 123–141.

23. Andrew F. Walls and Christopher Fyfe, eds., *Christianity in Africa in the 1990's* (Edinburgh: African Studies Center, University of Edinburgh, 1996), 5.

24. Ibid., 9.

25. Walter Hollenweger, "After Twenty-five Years of Research on Pentecostalism," *International Review of Missions* 75, no. 297 (1986): 3–12.

26. Daneel, "Exorcism as a Means of Combating Wizardry," *Missionalia* 18, no. 1 (1990): 220.

27. G. Oosthuizen, "African Environment: An Empirical Analysis," *African Insight* 26, no. 4 (1996): 308–324.

28. O. U. Kalu, "The Practice of Victorious Life: Pentecostal Political Theology and Practice in Nigeria, 1970–1996," *Mission: Journal of Mission Studies, University of Ottawa* 5, no. 2 (1998): 229–255.

29. Stephanie Douglas, "Bringing Order to Chaos: The Role of Typologies in the Study of African Christian Movements," *Mission: Journal of Mission Studies* 5, no. 2 (1998): 257–273.

30. Harold Turner, "Pagan Features in African Independent Churches," *Practical Anthropology* 12, no. 4 (1965): 144–151.

31. Published by Splendour Printers Enterprises, Calabar, and sponsored by Liberty Foundation Gospel Ministry, P.O. Box 3418, Calabar, Nigeria.

32. Adrian Hastings, *The Church in Africa, 1450–1950* (Oxford: Clarendon, 1994), 536–538.

33. M-L. Martin, *The Biblical Concept of Messianism* (Morija: Morija Sesetho Book Depot, 1964), 161.

34. Anderson, "Pentecostal Pneumatology," 66.

35. Rijk van Dijk, "Witchcraft and Scepticism by Proxy: Pentecostalism and Laughter in Urban Malawi," *Magical Interpretations, Material Realities: Modernity, Witchcraft and the Occult in Postcolonial Africa,* ed. Henrietta L. Moore and Todd Sanders (London: Routledge, 2001), 97–117, see esp. 101.

36. Birgit Meyer, "Christianity in Africa: From African Independent to Pentecostal-Charismatic Churches," *Annual Review of Anthropology* 33 (2004): 447–474.

37. David Maxwell, "Christianity without Frontiers: Shona Missionaries and Transnational Pentecostalism in Africa," *Christianity and the African Imagination: Essays in Honor of Adrian Hastings,* ed. David Maxwell and Ingrid Lawrie (Leiden: Brill, 2002), 295–332, esp. 295.

38. Amos Yong, *The Spirit Poured Out on All Flesh: Pentecostalism and the Possibility of Global Theology* (Grand Rapids, Mich.: Baker, 2005).

CHAPTER 5

1. Rijk van Dijk, "Young Born Again Preachers in Post-Independence Malawi," *New Dimensions in African Christianity,* ed. Paul Gifford (Nairobi: All Africa Conference of Churches, Challenge Series, 1992), 55–79, see esp. 55–56.

2. Ogbu U. Kalu, "Passive Revolution and Its Saboteurs: African Christian Initiative in the Era of Decolonization, 1955–1975," in *Mission, Nationalism, and the End of Empire,* ed. Brian Stanley (Grand Rapids, Mich.: Eerdmans, 2003), 250–277, see esp. 268.

3. This section of the paper is based on Ogbu U. Kalu, "Passive Revolution and Its Saboteurs," 250–277.

4. J. Kwabena Asamoah-Gydau, *African Charismatics: Current Developments within Independent Indigenous Pentecostalism in Ghana* (Leiden: Brill, 2005), 29.

5. Ogbu U. Kalu, *Embattled Gods: Christianization of Igboland, 1841–1991* (Lagos/London: Minaj, 1996; republished Trenton, N.J.: Africa World, 2003), chap. 10; Richard H. Burgess, "The Civil War Revival and Its Pentecostal Progeny: A Religious Movement among the Igbo People of Eastern Nigeria, 1967–2002," PhD diss., University of Birmingham, 2004; and Matthew Ojo, *The End-Time Army: Charismatic Movements in Modern Nigeria* (Trenton, N.J.: Africa World, 2006).

6. Frances Bolton, *And We Beheld His Glory* (London: Royal House Publishers, 1992); Dachi Maduoako, Irowa Edomwoynyi, Goddy Egu and Dike Mba Onu, *Flame of Fire: The Story of Scripture Union (Nigeria)* (Ibadan, Nigeria: Scripture Union (Nigeria) Press and Books Ltd., 2005).

7. Hilary Achunike, "Catholic Charismatic Movement in Igboland, 1970–1995," PhD thesis, University of Nigeria, Nsukka, 2001; see chapter 3.

8. Some of the entries in Okafor's diary can be found compiled in a good account of the those heady days by Frances Bolton, a participant. See Bolton, *And We*

Beheld His Glory (London: Royal House Publishers, 1992). This section relies much on Ogbu U. Kalu, *Embattled Gods*.

9. On the *balokole*, see Adrian Hastings, *The Church in Africa, 1450–1950* (Oxford: Clarendon, 1994), 596–600; and Ogbu U. Kalu and Graham Duncan, "*Bakuzufu*: Revival Movements and Indigenous Appropriation in African Christianity," in *African Christianity: An African Story*, ed. Ogbu U. Kalu (Pretoria: University of Pretoria, 2005), 278–307. The *balokole* anticultural belligerency turned them into martyred targets of the *Mau Mau* activists.

10. Richard Showalter served for one year in the Region Beyond Ministry, which grew out of the revival that broke among the KSCF in the 1970s, as told in *The Spiritual Awakenings in Kenya, 1970–1980: Sketches of Some Radical Believers* (Thika, Kenya: RBM, 1983). See also Peter Lowman, *The Day of His Power: A History of the International Fellowship of Evangelical Students* (Leicester: Intervarsity, 1983). On Nigeria, see Frances Bolton, *And We Beheld His Glory* (London: Publisher, 1992); Mathew Ojo, *The End-Time Army: The Charismatic Movementsl in Modern Nigeria* (Trenton, N.J.: Africa World, 2006); and Richard H. Burgess, "The Civil War Revival and Its Pentecostal Progeny: A Religious Movement among the Igbo People of Eastern Nigeria 1967–2002, PhD thesis, University of Birmingham, 2004.

11. Kyalo Nguku, "Uganda's Miracle," *Charisma* 31, no. 12 (July 2006): 36–41; and Simeon Kayiwa, *Working Miracles* (London: New Wine, 2003).

12. J. R. Mlahagwa, "Contending for the Faith: Spiritual Revival and Fellowship Church in Tanzania," in *East African Expressions of Christianity*, ed. Thomas Spear and I. N. Kimambo (Oxford: James Currey, 1999), 296–306.

13. David Maxwell, "Christianity without Frontiers: Shona Missionaries and Transnational Pentecostalism in Africa," in *Christianity and the African Imagination: Essays in Honour of Adrian Hastings*, ed. David Maxwell and Ingrid Lawrie (Leiden: Brill, 2002), 295–332, see esp. 314.

14. David Maxwell, "Witches, Prophets and Avenging Spirits," *Journal of Religion in Africa* 25, no. 3 (1995): 332.

15. David Maxwell, "Christianity without Frontiers: Shona Missionaries and Transnational Pentecostalism in Africa," in *Christianity and the African Imagination: Essays in Honor of Adrian Hastings*, ed. David Maxwell with Ingrid Lawrie (Leiden: Brill, 2002), 308.

16. Harri Englund, "The Quest for Missionaries: Transnationalism and Township Pentecostalism in Malawi," in *Between Babel and Pentecost: Transnational Pentecostalism in Africa and Latin America*, ed. André Corten and Ruth Marshall-Fratani (Bloomington: Indiana University Press, 2001), 235–254; see esp. 236

17. Ibid., 238.

CHAPTER 6

1. www.latterrainassembly.org.

2. See *The (Lagos, Nigeria) Guardian* (July 2, 2005), 24.

3. R. I. J. Hackett, "Charismatic/Pentecostal Appropriation of Media Technologies in Nigeria and Ghana," *Journal of Religion in Africa* 28, no. 3 (1998): 258–277.

4. Stewart Hoover, *Mass Media Religion: The Social Sources of the Electronic Church* (London: SAGE, 1988), 14.

5. Michael Warren, *Seeing through the Media: A Religious View of Communications and Cultural Analysis* (Harrisburg, Pa.: Trinity Press International, 1997), 106.

6. Timothy Stoneman, "Fundamentalism and Transnational Media: An Historical Perspective," paper presented at the Fundamentalism and Media Conference, University of Colorado at Boulder, October 2006, is a major study of ELWA.

7. R. E. Hiebert, D. F. Ungurait, and T. W. Bohn, *Mass Media IV: An Introduction to Modern Communication* (New York: Longman, 1985), 246.

8. Hoover, *Mass Media Religion*, 21.

9. Warren, *Seeing through The Media*, 63.

10. www.elifeonline.com.

11. *Charisma* (January 2006): 27–29.

12. Marla Frederick, *Between Sundays: Black Women and Everyday Struggles of Faith* (Berkeley and Los Angeles: University of California Press, 2003). See also Quentin J. Schultze, *Televangelism and American Culture* (Grand Rapids, Mich.: Baker, 1991); and J. Carrette and R. King, eds., *Selling Spirituality* (London: Routledge, 2005); and Martyn Percy, "The Church in the Market Place: Advertising and Religion in a Secular Age," *Journal of Contemporary Religion* 15, no. 1 (2000): 97–119, which show that much of what televangelists do in the United States and Africa (such as faith healing, miracles, and appeals for money) are banned in Great Britain by the watchdog group Code of Advertising Standards and Practice. These programs are regarded as exploiting human inadequacy and degrading the people they appeal to.

13. Kwame Bediako, "Christian Witness in the Public Sphere: Some Lessons and Residual Challenges from the Recent Political History of Ghana," in *The Changing Face of Christianity: Africa, the West and the World*, ed. Lamin Sanneh and Joel A. Carpenter (New York: Oxford University Press, 2005), 124.

14. Berit Brethauer, "Televangelism: Local and Global Dimensions," in *Religions/ Globalizations: Theories and Cases*, ed. Dwight Hopkins, Lois Lorentzen, Eduardo Mendieta, and David Batstone (Durham, N.C.: Duke University Press, 2001), 203–226, see esp. 206. Brethauer's case study of Robert Schuller's ministry in her chapter does not prove the assertion.

15. J. Kwabena. Asamoah-Gyadu "Pentecostal Media Images and Religious Globalization in Sub-Saharan Africa," in *Belief in Media: Cultural Perspectives on Media and Christianity*, ed. Peter Horsfield, Mary Hess, and Adan Medrano (Aldershot: Ashgate, 2004), 65–79, see esp. 66.

16. Asonzeh Ukah, "Seeing Is More Than Believing: Posters and Proselytization in Nigeria," in *Proselytization Revisited: Rights Talk, Free Markets and Culture Wars*, ed. R. I. J. Hackett (London: Equinox, 2006).

17. William A. Dyrness, *Visual Faith: Art, Theology and Worship in Dialogue* (Grand Rapids, Mich.: Baker, 2001), chap. 1.

18. Ukah, "Seeing Is More Than Believing," 13.

19. Matthew Ojo, *The End-Time Army: Charismatic Movements in Modern Nigeria* (Trenton, N.J.: Africa World, 2006), 263–265.

20. Ben Jones, "The Church in the Village, the Village in the Church: Pentecostalism in Teso, Uganda," *Cahiers d'Etudes Africaines* 45, no. 2 (2005): 497–517; and

R. van Dijk, "Young Born Again Preachers in Post-independence Malawi," in *New Dimensions in African Christianity*, ed. Paul Gifford (Nairobi: All African Conference of Churches, Challenge Series, 1992), 70–73.

21. Michelle Waters, "Internet Addiction Disorder and Pastoral Care," *American Journal of Pastoral Care and Counseling* 8, no. 1 (2005): 3–12.

22. Harri Englund, "The Quest for Missionaries: Transnationalism and Township Pentecostalism in Malawi," in *Between Babel and Pentecostalism*, ed. André Corten and Ruth Marshall-Fratani (Bloomington: Indiana University Press, 2001), 238.

23. Marleen de Witte, "Altar Media's Living Word: Televised Charismatic Christianity in Ghana," *Journal of Religion in Africa* 33, no. 2 (2003): 172–202; Marleen de Witte, "The Holy Spirit on Air in Ghana," *Media and Development* 52, no. 2 (2005): 22–26.

24. J. Kwabena. Asamoah-Gyadu, "Of Faith and Visual Alertness: The Message of Mediatized Religion in an African Pentecostal Context," *Material Religion*, 1, no. 3 (2005): 336–357, see esp. 341, fig. 5.

25. Birgit Meyer, "Impossible Representations: Pentecostalism, Vision, and Video Technology in Ghana," in *Religion, Media, and the Public Sphere*, ed. Birgit Meyer and Annelies Moors (Bloomington: Indiana University Press, 2006), 290–312, see esp. 300.

26. De Witte, "The Holy Spirit on Air in Ghana," 26.

27. Harri Englund, "Christian Independency and Global Membership: Pentecostal Extraversions in Malawi," *Journal of Religion in Africa* 33, no. 1 (2003): 83–111.

28. See Kwabena Asamoah-Gyadu, "Pentecostal Media Images and Religious Globalization in Sub-Saharan Africa," in *Belief in Media: Cultural Perspectives on Religion and Christianity*, ed. P. Horsfield, Mary Hess, Adan Medrano (Aldershot: Ashgate, 2004), 65–79; J. Kwabena Asamoah-Gyadu, "Unction to Function: Reinventing the *Oil of Influence* in African Pentecostalism," *Journal of Pentecostal Theology* 13, no. 2 (April 2005): 231–256; and J. Kwabena Asamoah-Gyadu, "Anointing through the Screen: Neo-Pentecostalism and Televised Christianity in Ghana," *Studies in World Christianity* 11, no. 1 (2005): 17–21.

29. Asonzeh Ukah, "Advertising God: Nigerian Christian Video-Films and the Power of Consumer Culture," *Journal of Religion in Africa* 30, no. 2 (2003): 203–231.

30. Jordan Daniel Smith, "The Arrow of God: Pentecostalism, Inequality, and the Supernatural in Southeastern Nigeria," *Africa* 71, no. 4 (2001): 587–613; and Akoko Mbe, "New Pentecostalism in the Wake of the Economic Crisis in Cameroon," *Nordic Journal of African Studies* 11, no. 3 (2002): 359–376.

31. I am grateful to Dr Rosalind Hackett of the University of Tennessee for sharing an early draft of her paper which is appearing in a collection of essays:R. I. J. Hackett, "Devil Bustin' Satellites: How Media Liberalization in Africa Generates Religious Indigenous Intolerance and Conflict," 7–8.

32. Charles Hirschkind, "Cassettes Ethics: Public Piety and Popular Media in Egypt," in *Religion, Media and the Public Sphere*, ed. Birgit Meyer and Annelies Moors (Bloomington: Indiana University Press, 2006).

33. Ghana Advertising and Media Research Foundation, *Ghana All Media and Products Survey, 2001* (Accra: Research International,2002)

34. R. I. J. Hackett, "Mediating Religion in South Africa: Balancing Air-time and Rights Claim," in *Religion, Media and The Public Sphere*, ed. Birget Meyer and Annelies Moors (Bloomington: Indiana University Press, 2006); and Robert B. Horwitz, *Communication and Democratic Reform in South Africa* (Cambridge, Mass.: Cambridge University Press, 2001).

35. Ezra Chitendo, *Singing Culture: A Study of Gospel Music in Zimbabwe* (Uppsala: The Nordic Africa Institute/Nordiska Afrikainstitutet, Research Report no.121, 2002), 14.

36. John Paul II, *Ecclesia in Africa, The Church in Africa and Its Evangelizing Mission Towards the Year 2000* (Washington, D.C.: United States Catholic Conference, 1995), 1.

37. Katrina Pype, "Dancing for God or the Devil: Pentecostal Discourse on Popular Dance in Kinshasha," *Journal of Religion in Africa* 36, nos. 3–4 (2006): 296–318. For a fuller discussion, see Ogbu U. Kalu, "Holy Praiseco: Negotiating Sacred and Popular Music and Dance in African Pentecostalism," Harvard Africa Seminar, Harvard University, Cambridge, Mass., March, 20, 2007. Forthcoming in *Pneuma*.

CHAPTER 7

1. Jack T. Thompson, "Xhosa Missionaries to Malawi: Black Europeans or African Christians?" *International Bulletin of Missionary Research* 24, no. 4 (2000): 168–171.

2. Reuben Ezemadu, *The Vision So Far: A Story of the Christian Missionary Foundation* (Ibadan: 1990), 3; and Emeka Nwankpa, *Redeeming the Land* (Accra: Achimota, 1995).

3. Steve Bruce, "The Charismatic Movement and the Secularization Thesis," *Religion* 28 (1998): 223–232.

4. From the official Web site of the RCCG, http://www.rccg.org (created and maintained by the RCCG Internet Project, Houston, Texas).

5. Beth Thavers, " Private Higher Education in Africa:Six Country Case Studies:in *African Higher Education:An International Reference Handbook*. Ed. Damtev Teferra and Philip G.Altbach (Bloomington,IN: Indiana University Press, 2003): 53–60.

6. David Oyedepo, Website of Covenant University, Ota, 2003.

7. www.daystarus.org

8. www.idahosauniversity.com

9. E. Kingsley Larbi, "African Pentecostalism in the Context of Global Pentecostal Ecumenical Fraternity: Challenges and Opportunities," *Pneuma* 24, no. 2 (Fall 2002): 138–166.

10. Darrell Guder, *The Continuing Conversion of the Church* (Grand Rapids, Mich.: Eerdmans, 2000).

11. The discussion about the indigenous African Pentecostal contribution to the evangelization of Africa has benefited from Matthew Ojo, "The Dynamics of Indigenous Charismatics Enterprises in West Africa," *Missionalia* 25, no. 4 (1997): 537–561; Matthew Ojo, "Nigerian Pentecostalism and Transnational Religious Networks in

West African Coastal Region," in *Enterprises Religieuses Transnationales en Afrique de L'Ouest*, ed. Laurent Fourchard et al. (Paris: Karthala, 2005), 395–438; and Timothy Olonade, *Battle Cry for the Nations: Rekindling the Flames of World Evangelization* (Jos: CAPRO Media, 1995).

12. See, Ogbu U Kalu, Elijah's mantle: Ministerial formation in Contemporary African Christianity" *International Review of Mission*, 94, no.373 (April, 2005): 263–277; idem, "Pentecostalism an Mission in Africa, 1970–2000" *Mission Studies*, 24 (2007):9–45.

13. Roswith Gerloff, ed., "Open Space: The African Christian Diaspora in Europe and the Quest for Human Community," *International Review of Mission* 89, no. 354 (July 2000): 273–510.

14. See www.africanmissions.org/aboutus.htm; and Afe Adogame, "A Walk for Africa: Combating the Demon of HIV/AIDS in an African Pentecostal Church: The Case of Redeemed Christian Church of God," *Scriptura: International Journal of Bible, Religion and Theology in Southern Africa* 89 (2005): 396–405.

15. Matthew Ojo, "Pentecostalism, Public Accountability and Governance in Nigeria," Pentecostal-Civil Society Dialogue on Public Accountability and Governance Conference, Lagos, October 18, 2004.

16. Peter Althouse, "Towards a Theological Understanding of Pentecostal Appeal to Experience," *Journal of Ecumenical Studies* 38, no. 4 (Fall 2001): 399–411.

17. Robert Garner, "Religion as a Source of Social Change in the New South Africa," *Journal of Religion in Africa* 30, no. 3 (2000): 310–343;idem. " The Socio-Economic Consequences of Christianity in a Black South African Suburb" University of Cambridge, PhD thesis, 1998; and Andrew F. Walls, "Africa and the Future of Christianity: A Summary and Reflection," in *Christianity in Africa in the 1990s*, ed. Christopher Fyfe and Andrew F. Walls (Edinburgh: Center for African Studies, University of Edinburgh, 1996), 146.

18. See Karla Poewe, ed., *Priority Focus: Some Needy Unreached People Groups in Nigeria* (Jos: Feyisetan, 2000).

19. Afe Adogame, "Appropriating Malachi Rhetoric in African Pentecostalism: The Case of the Redeemed Christian Church of God in Nigeria and the USA," paper delivered at the African Studies Association Conference, New Orleans, Novemeber 11–14, 2004. Paul Gifford, "A View of Ghana's New Christianity" in *The Changing Face of Christianity: Africa, the West, and the World*, ed. Lamin Sanneh and Joel A. Carpenter (New York: Oxford University Press, 2005), 89–90

20. Asonzeh Ukah, "Pastors and Profits: A Comparative Study on the Mobilisation and Organization of Money in West African Pentecostalism," paper presented at Ls Religionwissenschaft, University of Bayreuth, Germany, June 15th, 2006.

CHAPTER 8

1. Susie Cunningham Stanley, *Feminist Pillar of Fire: The Life of Alma White* (Cleveland, Tenn.: Pilgrim, 1993); Susie Cunningham Stanley, *Holy Boldness: Women Preachers' Autobiographies and Sanctified Self* (Knoxville: University of Tennessee Press, 2002).

2. Mercy Amba Oduyoye, *Daughters of Anowa: African Women and Patriarchy* (Maryknoll, N.Y.: Orbis, 1995). See a fuller treatment in Ogbu U. Kalu, *Power, Poverty and Prayer* (Frankfurt: Peter Lang, 2000), chap. 7.

3. Bolaji Olukemi Olayinka, *Female Leaders of New Generation Churches as Change Agents in Yorubaland* (PhD thesis, Obafemi Awolowo University, 2000), 137–166.

4. Ibid., 128.

5. Isabel A. Phiri, "African Women in Mission: Two Cases from Malawi," *Missionalia* 28 (2000): 267–293, see esp. 280.

6. Dorcas A. Olubanke, "The History of Good Women: Association of the Christ Apostolic Church," unpublished paper, January 2002, 8.

7. Philomena Mwaura, "A Burning Stick Plucked out of the Fire: The Story of Rev. Margaret Wanjiru of Jesus Is Alive Ministries," in *Hidden Histories of Women of Faith in Africa*, ed. Isabel Phiri and Sarojini Nadar (Pitermaritzburg: Cluster, 2002), 202–224; V. M. Mackenzie, *Not without a Struggle: Leadership Development for African American Women in Ministry* (Cleveland: United Church Press, 1996); and J. Kwabena Asamoah-Gyadu, "Fireballs in Our Midst: West Africa's Burgeoning Charismatic Churches and the Pastoral Role of Women," *Mission Studies* 15–1, no. 29 (1998): 15–31.

8. H. G. Wells, "Trinitarian Feminism: Elizabeth Johnson's Wisdom Christology," *Theology Today* 52, no. 3 (October 1995): 330–343.

9. J. C. Brown and R. Parker, "For God So Loved the World?" *Christianity, Patriarchy and Abuse: A Feminist Critique*, eds. J. C. Brown and C. R. Bohn (Cleveland: Pilgrim Press, 1989), 1–30.

10. Rosemary R. Ruether, ed., *Women Healing the Earth: Third World Women on Ecology, Feminism and Religion* (Maryknoll, N.Y.: Orbis, 1996), 161–171.

11. Elizabeth Johnson, *She Who Is: The Mystery of God in Feminist Discourse* (New York: Crossroad, 1993), 11–12.

12. Ibid., 33.

13. R. B. Hays, *The Moral Vision of the New Testament* (San Francisco: HarperSanFrancisco, 1996), 281–282.

14. Mercy A.Oduyoye and Virginia Fabella, eds., *With Passion and Compassion: Third World Women Doing Theology* (Maryknoll, N.Y.: Orbis, 1988), 14.

15. Ibid., 22. See also Elizabeth Agumba's poem "The Search for My Place in Society" in the theo-poetic section of Oduyoye, ed., *Transforming Power: Women in the Household of God* (Accra: Sam-Woode, 1997), 153–154, where one stanza reads "Nobody can send me out of the Church/For I have a message for the disciples of Christ!"

16. Ibid., 47–59.

17. I. Gebara and M. C. Bingemer, *Mary Mother of God, Mother of the Poor* (Maryknoll, N.Y.: Orbis, 1996).

18. Walter Wink, *Engaging the Powers* (Minneapolis: Fortress, 1992), 134.

19. Cheryl Bridges Johns, "Pentecostal Spirituality and Conscientization of Women," in *All Together in One Place*, ed. H. D. Hunter and P. D. Hocker (Sheffield: Sheffield Academic Press, 1993), 153–165.

20. H. Kinukawa, *Women and Jesus in Mark: A Japanese Perspective* (Maryknoll, N.Y.: Orbis, 1994).

21. I. J. Mosala, "The Implications of the Text of Esther for African Women's Struggle for Liberation in South Africa," in *Voices from the Margin: Interpreting the Bible from the Third World*, ed. R. S. Surgirtharajah (Maryknoll, N.Y.: Orbis, 1995), 168–178. See also Oduyoye, *Daughters of Anowa*, 174–175.

22. P. Turner, "The Wisdom of the Fathers and the Gospel of Christ: Some Notes on the Question of Christian Adaptation in Africa," *Journal of Religion in Africa* 4 (1971): 46–58.

23. Mercy Amba Oduyoye, "The Empowering Spirit of Religion," in *Lift Every Voice: Constructing Theology from the Underside*, ed. S. B. Thistlewaite and M. P. Engel (San Francisco: Harper, 1990), 249.

24. O. U. Kalu, "Silent Victims: Violence against Women in Tertiary Educational Institutions, Nigeria," UNIFEM-UNDP, Lagos, 1996. Musisi Kangoro echoes this in Mercy Amba Oduyoye, ed., *Transforming Power*, 18–19.

25. W. Brueggemann, *The Prophetic Imagination* (Philadelphia: Fortress, 1978), 66.

26. Walter Wink, *Engaging the Powers* (Minneapolis: Fortress, 1992), 134.

27. See J. Mbugua, ed., *Our Time Has Come: African Women Address Issues of Today* (Channel Islands, UK: Guernsey Press, 1994).

28. C. Barfoot and G. Sheppard, "Prophetic Versus Priestly Religion: The Changing Role of Women Clergy in Classical Pentecostal Churches," *Review of Religious Research* 22, no. 1 (September 1980): 2–17; and D. G. Roebuck, "Pentecostal Women in Ministry: A Review of Selected Documents," *Perspectives in Religious Studies* 16, no. 1 (1989): 29–44.

29. Margaret L. Bendroth, *Fundamentalism and Gender, 1875 to Present* (New Haven, Conn., Yale University Press, 1993).

30. Oduyoye, *Daughters of Anowa*, 11.

31. Rebecca S. Dali, *Women in Ministry with Jesus: Where Are There?* (Bukuru, Jos: Africa Christian Textbooks, 2000); and R. Marie Griffith and Barbara D. Savage, eds., *Women and Religion in the African Diaspora: Knowledge, Power and Performance* (Baltimore: Johns Hopkins University Press, 2006).

32. Helen Callaway, "Women in Yoruba Tradition and in the Cherubim and Seraphim Society," in *The History of Christianity in West Africa*, ed. Ogbu U. Kalu (London: Longman, 1980), chap. 18.

33. M. A. Oduyoye, "Spirituality of Resistance and Reconstruction" in *Women Resisting Violence: Spirituality for Life*, ed. M. Mananzana (Maryknoll, N.Y.: Orbis, 1996), 161–171.

34. Church of England Commission Report, *A Fearful Symmetry? The Complementarity of Men and Women in Ministry* (London: SPCK, 1988), 18.

35. Marie Griffith, "What Happens When Women Pray? Prayer and Paradox in Women's Aglow," Twenty-Third Annual Meeting of the Society for Pentecostal Studies, Mexico City, 1993; R. Marie Griffith, ed., *God's Daughters: Evangelical Women and the Power of Submission* (Berkeley and Los Angeles: University of California Press, 1997), chap. 6; and Evelyn Brooks Higginbotham, *Righteous Discontent: The Women's Movement in the Black Baptist Church, 1880–1920* (Cambridge, Mass.: Harvard University Press, 1993), 149.

36. Gordon Fee, *Gospel and Spirit Issues in New Testament Hermeneutics* (Peabody, Mass.: Hendricks, 1991); and Cheryl Bridges Johns, "Pentecostal Spirituality and

Conscientization of Women," in *All Together in One Place*, ed. H. D. Hunter and P. D. Hocken (Sheffield: Academic Press, 1993), 160–161.

37. L. M. Russell et al., eds., *Inheriting Our Mothers' Gardens* (Philadelphia: Westminster, 1988), 39.

CHAPTER 9

1. Stephen Ellis and Gerrie ter Haar, *Worlds of Power: Religious Thought and Political Practice in Africa* (New York: Oxford University Press, 2004), 51.

2. Adrian Hastings, *African Catholicism: Essays in Discovery* (London: SCM, 1989).

3. Birgit Meyer, "Make a Complete Break with the Past: Memory and Post-colonial Modernity in Ghanaian Pentecostalist Discourses," *Journal of Religion in Africa* 28, no. 3 (1998): 316–349, see esp. 318.

4. David Maxwell, "Witches, Prophets and Avenging Spirits," *Journal of Religion in Africa* 25, no. 3 (1995): 321–325.

5. Meyer, "Make a Complete Break with the Past." *Journal of Religion in Africa:* 28, no. 3 (1998): 319.

6. Rjik Van Djik, "Witchcraft and Scepticism by Proxy: Pentecostalism and Laughter in Urban Malawi," in *Magical Interpretations, Material Realities* eds., H. L. Moore and T. Sanders (London: Routledge, 2001), 97–117, see esp. 110.

7. J. Kwabena Asamoah-Gyadu, "To Drum or Not to Drum: Traditional Festivals, Christianity and Clashes over Religious Silence in Ghana," *Trinity Journal of Church and Theology* 15, no. 2 (July 2005): 106–116.

8. Laurenti Magesa, *African Traditional Religion: The Moral Foundations for Abundant Life* (Maryknoll, N.Y.: Orbis, 1997); Ogbu U. Kalu, "Unconquered Spiritual Gates: African Inculturation Theology Revisited," *Journal of Inculturation Theology*, Catholic Institute for West Africa, Port Harcourt 1, no. 1 (1991): 25–37; and Ogbu U. Kalu, "The Dilemma of Grassroot Inculturation of the Gospel," *Journal of Religion in Africa* 25 (February 1995): 48–72.

9. Christopher Fyfe and Andrew F. Walls, eds., *Christianity in Africa in the 1990s* (Edinburgh: Center for African Studies, University of Edinburgh, 1996), 14; and Ogbu U. Kalu, "Gospel, Culture and Mission: Revisiting an Enduring Problem," *Skrief en Kirk*, Pretoria, Jaargang 19, no. 2 (1998): 283–300.

10. Robin Horton, "African Conversion," *Africa* 41, no. 2 (1971): 87–108; Robin Horton, "African Conversion," *Africa* 45, no. 3 (1975): 219–235; and Robin Horton, "African Conversion," *Africa* 45, no. 4 (1975): 373–399.

11. M. G. Kraft, *Understanding Spiritual Powers* (Maryknoll, N.Y.: Orbis, 1995), 20; Charles H. Kraft, *Anthropology for Christian Witness* (Maryknoll, N.Y.: Orbis, 1996), 10; and Paul G. Hiebert, *Anthropological Insights for Missionaries* (Grand Rapids, Mich.: Baker, 1985), 46.

12. Ruth Marshall-Fratani, "Mediating the Global and Local in Nigerian Pentecostalism," *Journal of Religion in Africa*, 28, no. 3 (1998): 278–315, esp. 283.

13. Walter Brueggemann, *Land* (Philadelphia: Fortress, 1977), 2.

14. Walter Wink, *Naming the Powers: The Language of Power in the New Testament* (Philadelphia: Fortress, 1984), 5,15.

15. Ibid., 15.

16. Philip Jenkins, *The New Faces of Christianity: Believing the Bible in the Global South* (New York: Oxford University Press, 2006); and J. S. Mbiti, *Bible and Theology in African Christianity* (Nairobi: Oxford University Press, 1986).

17. Cheryl B. Johns, *Pentecostal Formation* (Sheffield: Academic Press, 1993), 86; Cheryl B. Johns, "Pentecostal Spirituality and Conscientization of Women" in *All Together in One Place*, H. D. Hunter and P. D. Hocken eds. (Sheffield: Sheffield Academic Press, 1993), 153–165.

18. L. R. Rambo, *Understanding Religious Conversion* (New Haven, Conn.: Yale University Press, 1993), 113–116.

19. Kwame Bediako, *Christianity in Africa: The Renewal of a Non-Western Religion* (Maryknoll, N.Y.: Orbis, 1995), 84.

CHAPTER 10

1. David Maxwell, "In Defence of African Christianity," *Journal of Religion in Africa* 33, no. 4 (2000): 464–481; Kwame Bediako, "Christian Witness in the Public Sphere: Some Lessons and Residual Challenges from the Recent Political History of Ghana," in *The Changing Face of Christianity: Africa, the West, and the World*, eds. Lamin Sanneh and Joel A. Carpenter (New York: Oxford University Press, 2005), 117–134.

2. P. Beyer, *Religion and Globalization* (London: Sage, 1994); M. Featherstone et al., eds., *Global Modernities* (London: Sage, 1993); Jeff Haynes, *Religion and Politics in Africa* (London: Zed, 1996); D. Lyon, "Glocalization and Contemporary Religion," in *A Global Faith: Essays on Evengelicalism and Globalisation*, ed. M. Hutchinson and O. U. Kalu (Sydney: CSAC, 1997), 47–68; Karla Poewe, ed., *Charismatic Christianity as a Global Culture* (Columbia: University of South Carolina Press, 1994); and R. Robertson, "Humanity, Globalization and Worldwide Religious Resurgence," *Sociological Analysis* 46, no. 3 (1985): 219–242.

3. Paul Gifford, *African Christianity: Its Public Role* (Bloomington: Indiana University Press, 1998), 322; Andrew F. Walls, "From Christendom to World Christianity: Missions and the Demographic Transformation of the Church," *Princeton Bulletin of Theology* 22, no. 3 (2001): 306–330, see esp. 306.

4. Harvey Cox, *Fire from Heaven: The Rise of Pentecostal Spirituality and the Reshaping of Religion in the Twenty-first Century* (Reading, Mass.: Addison-Wesley, 1995), 11.

5. In André Corten and Ruth Marshall-Fratani, eds., *Between Babel and Pentecost: Transnational Pentecostalism in Africa and Latin America* (Bloomington: Indiana University Press, 2001), 254.

6. Paul Gifford, *Ghana's New Christianity: Pentecostalism in a Globalizing Economy* (Bloomington: Indiana University Press, 2004).

7. Paul Gifford, "Some Recent Developments in African Christianity," *African Affairs* 93, no. 373 (1994): 513–534; Paul Gifford, "Ghana's Charismatic Churches," *Journal of Religion in Africa (JRA)* 24 (1994): 241–265; and Paul Gifford, *African Christianity*.

8. Gifford, *Ghana's New Christianity*, 140.

9. Ibid., viii–ix.

10. Ibid.

11. Ibid., ix.

12. J. Kwabena Asamoah-Gyadu, *African Charismatics: Current Development within Independent Indigenous Pentecostalism in Ghana* (Leiden: Brill, 2005).

13. Gifford, "The Complex Provenance of African Pentecostal Theology," in *Between Babel and Pentecost*, eds. André Corten and Ruth Marshall-Fratani (Bloomington: Indiana University Press, 2001), 62–79, see esp. 64.

14. Jordan D. Smith, "The Arrow of God: Pentecostalism, Inequality, and the Supernatural in Southeastern Nigeria," *Africa* 71, no. 4 (2001): 587–613.

15. Andre Droogers, "Globalisation and Pentecostal Success," in *Between Babel and Pentecost*, eds. André Corten and Ruth Marshall-Fratani (Bloomington: Indiana University Press, 2001), 41–61, see, esp. 53.

16. Gifford, *Ghana's New Christianity*, 165.

17. Ibid., 164.

18. Ibid., 172.

19. Ebere Onwudiwe, *Afro-Optimism* (New York: Praeger, 1993); Dickson Eyoh, "From Economic Crisis to Political Liberalization: Pitfalls of the New Political Sociology for Africa," *African Studies Review* 38, no. 2 (1995): 39–65.

20. *Ghana's New Christianity*, 161.

21. Information can be found at P. O. Box 5566, Aba, Abia State; e-mail: alarmncgf@yahoo.com; phone: +234-803-323-289.

22. Gifford, *Ghana's New Christianity*, 167. See Carl S. Dudley and Sally A. Johnson, *Energizing the Congregation: Images That Shape Your Church's Ministry* (Louisville: Westminster/John Knox, 1993) for different images of a congregation's interface with the public space.

23. See Stanley M. Burgess, ed., *International Dictionary of Pentecostal Charismatic Movements* (Grand Rapids, Mich.: Zondervan, 2002), 237.

24. For instance, Dag Mills publishes three ninety-day devotional booklets: *Your Quiet Time: Gethsemane; Mount Sinai; Mount Horeb* (Accra: Parchment House, 2004).

25. Smith, "The Arrow of God," 591–592; Rijk van Dijk, "Pentecostalism, Cultural Memory and the State: Contested Representations of Time in Postcolonial Malawi," in *Memory and Postcolony*, ed. Richard Webner (London: Zed, 1998), 155–181.

26. R. I. J. Hackett, *Religion in Calabar: The Religious Life and History of a Nigerian Town* (New York: Mouton de Gruyter, 1989), 164.

27. Rijk van Djik, "Witchcraft and Scepticism by Proxy: Pentecostalism and Laughter in Urban Malawi," in *Magical Interpretations, Material Realities: Modernity, Witchcraft and the Occult in Postcolonial Africa*, ed. Henrietta L. Moore and Todd Sanders (London: Routledge, 2001), 113.

28. Stephen Ellis and Gerrie ter Haar, *Worlds of Power: Religious Thought and Political Practice in Africa* (New York: Oxford University Press, 2004), chap. 4.

29. A. van Gennep, *The Rites of Passage* (Chicago: University of Chicago Press, 1960), 165; Aylward Shorter, *Songs and Symbols of Initiation* (Nairobi: Catholic Higher Institute of East Africa, 1987); and Victor Turner, *The Forest of Symbol* (Ithaca, N.Y.: Cornell University Press, 1967).

30. J. K. Olupona, "Religious Pluralism and Civil Religion in Africa," *Dialogue and Alliance* 2, no. 4 (1989): 41–48; and J. K. Olupona, *Kingship, Religion and Rituals in a Nigerian Community* (Stockholm: Almquist & Wiksell, 1991).

31. Ogbu U. Kalu, "Harsh Flutes: The Religious Dimension of the Legitimacy Crisis in Nigeria, 1993–1998," in *Nigeria in the Twentieth Century*, ed. Toyin Falola (Durham, N.C.: Carolina Academic Press, 2002), 667–685.

32. Van Djik, "Witchcraft and Scepticism by Proxy," 98.

CHAPTER 11

1. R. W. Hefner, *Conversion to Christianity: Historical and Anthropological Perspectives* (Berkeley and Los Angeles: University of California Press, 1993), 21.

2. Deidre Badejo, *Oshun: The Elegant Deity of Wealth, Power and Femininity* (Trenton, N. J.: Africa World, 1993); Ifi Amadiume, *Male Daughters Female Husbands* (London: Zed, 1985).

3. Misty Bastian, "Married in the Water: Spirit Kin and Other Afflictions of Modernity in Southeastern Nigeria," *Journal of Religion in Africa*, 27, no. 3 (May 1997): 116–134, see esp. 123.

4. H. J. Drewal, "Mami Wata Shrines: Exotica and the Constitution of Self," in *African Material Culture*, eds., M. Arnold, C. Geary, and K. Hardin (Bloomington: Indiana University Press, 1996), 308–333.

5. L. R. Rambo, *Understanding Religious Conversion* (New Haven, Conn.: Yale University Press, 1993).

6. Abner Cohen, *The Power Culture of the Elite* (Berkeley and Los Angeles: University of California Press, 1981); Paul Gifford, *Christianity in Doe's Liberia* (Cambridge: Cambridge University Press, 1993).

7. Ann Bernstein, "Flying under South Africa's Public Radar: The Growth and Impact of Pentecostals in a Developing Country," *Spirit in the World* Symposium, University of Southern California, October 4–7, 2006.

8. Emeka Nwankpa, *Redeeming the Land* (Accra: Achimota, 1995).

9. Ruth Marshall-Fratani, "Mediating the Global and Local in Nigerian Pentecostalism," *Journal of Religion in Africa*, 28, no. 3 (1998): 278–315, see esp. 306–307.

10. Kwame Bediako, *Christianity in Africa; The Renewal of a Non-Western Religion* (Maryknoll, N.Y.: Orbis, 1995), 84.

11. I. M. Enwerem, *A Dangerous Awakening: The Politicization of Religion in Nigeria* (Ibadan: IFRA, 1995).

12. Paul Gifford, *Ghana's New Christianity: Pentecostalism in a Globalizing African Economy* (Bloomington: Indiana University Press, 2004), ix.

CHAPTER 12

1. Certified True Copy, Transcript of Sharia Court of Appeal, Sokoto State (March 25, 2002): 44.

2. See www.mtrustonline.com/dailytrust/feature162003.htm.

3. Murray Last, *The Sokoto Caliphate* (London: Longmans, 1967); Mervyn Hiskett, *The Development of Islam in West Africa* (London: Longmans, 1984); and Ross Dunn,

The Adventures of Ibn Battutta (Berkeley and Los Angeles: University of California Press, 1986).

4. John Paden, *Ahmadu Bello* (Zaria: Gaskiya, 1986), 205–206.

5. John Paden, *Religion and Political Authority in Kano* (Berkeley and Los Angeles: University of California Press, 1973).

6. Allen Christelow, "Religious Protest and Dissent in Northern Nigeria," *Journal of the Institute of Muslim Minority Affairs* 6, no. 2 (1985): 375–393; Paul Lubeck, "Islamic Protest under Semi-industrial Capitalism," *Africa* 55, no. 4 (1986): 369–397; Elizabeth Isichei, "The Maitasine Rising in Nigeria, 1980–1985: A Revolt of the Disinherited," *Journal of Religion in Africa*17, no. 3 (October 1987): 194–208; M. Hiskett, "The Maitatsine Riots of Kano, 1980: An Assessment," *Journal of Religion in Africa* 17, no. 3 (1987): 209–223; and J. Takya, "The Foundations of Religious Intolerance in Nigeria," *Bulletin of Ecumenical Research* 2, no. 2 (1989): 31–41.

7. See www.oneworld.org/euconflict/sfp/part2/245.

8. Allen Christelow, "Islamic Law and Judicial Practice in Nigeria: An Historical Perspective," *Journal of Muslim Minority Affairs* 22, no. 1 (2002): 185–204.

9. Ghazali Bashri, *Nigeria and Sharia* (Leicester: The Islamic Foundation, 1994); see also www.gamji.com/sharia-conf.htm and www.sharia2001.nmonline.net.

10. Ogbu U. Kalu, "Themes in West African Church History at the Edge of the Twenty-first Century," *Missionalia* 30, no. 2 (August 2002): 235–264, esp. 237; and Charlotte and Frederick Quinn, *Pride, Faith and Fear: Islam in Sub-Saharan Africa* (Oxford: Oxford University Press, 2003), 3–32.

11. John O. Hunwick, *Sharia in Songhay: the Replies of al-Maghili to the Questions of Askia al-Hajj Muhammad* (Oxford: Oxford University Press, 1985).

12. Lamin Sanneh, *Piety and Power: Muslims and Christians in West Africa* (Maryknoll, N.Y.: Orbis, 1996).

13. Toyin Falola, *Violence in Nigeria: The Crisis of Religious Politics and Secular Ideologies* (Rochester: Rochester University Press, 1998).

14. A. R. Doi, *Non-Muslims under Sharia* (Lahore: Kazi Publications, 1990). This book grew out of a lecture he gave at Ahmadu Bello University, Zaria.

15. *New Nigerian Newspaper*, Kaduna, January 8, 2001.

16. David Laitin, *Hegemony and Culture* (Chicago: University of Chicago Press, 1986).

17. Falola, *Violence in Nigeria*, 35.

18. Charles Taylor, "On Religion and Violence," *The Arts and Science Review* (University of Toronto) 2, no. 1 (Spring 2005): 31–35.

19. Matthew Hassan Kukah, *Religion, Politics and Power in Northern Nigeria* (Ibadan, Nigeria: Spectrum, 1994).

20. Kalu, *The Scourge of the Vandals: Nature and Control of Cults in Nigerian Universities* (Nsukka: University of Nigeria Press, 2001).

21. See Stephen Ellis and Gerrie ter Haar, *Worlds of Power: Religious Thought and Political Practice in Africa* (New York: Oxford University Press, 2004).

22. Lamin Sanneh, *Piety and Power: Muslims and Christians in West Africa* (Orbis, 1996); and Lamin Sanneh, *The Crown and the Turban: Muslims and West African Pluralism* (Boulder, Colo.: Westview, 1997).

23. Bala Usman, *Manipulation of Religion in Nigeria* (Kaduna, Nigeria: Vangurd, 1987).

24. Hiskett, "The Maitatsine Riots, Kano, 1980," 209–223; and Elizabeth Isichei, "The Maitatsine Rising in Nigeria, 1980–1985," 194–208.

25. See www.gamji.com for his articles.

26. Simeon Ilesanmi, *Religious Pluralism and the Nigerian State* (Athens: Ohio University, 1997).

27. Jeff Haynes, *Religion and Politics in Africa* (London: Zed, 1996).

28. Ruth Marshall-Fratani, "Mediating the Global and the Local in Nigerian Pentecostalism," *Journal of Religion in Africa* 28, no. 3 (1998): 278–315, esp. 301.

29. Jibrin Ibrahim, "Religion and Political Turbulence in Nigeria," *Journal of African Studies* 29 (1991): 116–136.

30. Paul Gifford, *The New Crusaders: Christianity and the New Right in Southern Africa* (London: Pluto, 1991).

31. Kalu, "Sharia and Islam in Nigerian Pentecostal Rhetoric, 1970–2003," *Pneuma* 26, no. 2 (2004): 242–261.

32. I. M. Enwerem, *A Dangerous Awakening:The Politicization of Religion in Nigeria* (Ibadan: IFRA, 1995); and Afe Adogame, "Politicization of Religion and the Religionization of Politics in Nigeria," in *Religion, History, and Politics in Nigeria: Essays in Honor of Ogbu U. Kalu*, eds., Chima Korieh and Ugo Nwokeji (Lanham, Md.: University Press of America, 2005), 128–139.

33. Somini Sengupta, "Piety and Politics under a Riot-Torn Nigerian City," *New York Times*, February 21, 2003.

34. Rosalind I. J. Hackett, "Charismatic/Pentecostal Appropriation of Media Technologies in Nigeria and Ghana," *Journal of Religion in Africa* 28, no. 3 (1998): 258–277.

35. Andrew F. Walls, "Africa as the Theatre of Christian Engagement with Islam in the Nineteenth Century," *Journal of Religion in Africa* 29, no. 2 (1999): 155–174.

36. See a discussion of Johnson's *History* in John D. Y. Peel, *Religious Encounter and the Making of the Yoruba* (Bloomington: Indiana University Press, 2000): 304–309; G. T. Basden, *Niger Ibos* (1937; rep. London, Frank Cass, 1966), chap. 21; and Kristina Helgeson, "Pentecostalism as a Moral Order: Action for Israel among Pentecostals in Durban, South Africa," *Swedish Missiological Themes* 92, no. 2 (2004): 261–280.

37. See www.nigeriachristiannews@yahoogroups.com (Feb. 3, 2003).

38. Emeka Nwankpa, *Redeeming the Land* (Achimota: African Christian Publishers, 1995); Steve Okitika, *The Battle for Nations: The Ministry of Interceding for Our Nation* (Lagos: Moinab, 1996); and Kalu, "The Practice of Victorious Life: Pentecostal Political Theology in Nigeria, 1970–1996," *Mission: Journal of Mission Studies* (University of Ottawa, Canada) 5, no. 2 (1998): 229–255.

39. See www.ngrguardiannews. com /news/article23.

40. See *New Nigerian Newspaper*, no. 6812, February 6, 1986, 1.

41. Gifford, *The New Crusaders*.

CHAPTER 13

1. See Paul W. Lewis, "Reflections of a Hundred Years of Pentecostal Theology," http://www.pctii.org.cyberj/lewism.html 1/17/2003; and Philip Jenkins, *The New Faces*

of Christianity: Believing the Bible in the Global South (New York: Oxford University Press, 2006).

2. Russell P. Spittler, "Are Pentecostals and Charismatics Fundamentalists? A Review of American Uses of these Categories," in *Charismatic Christianity as a Global Culture*, ed. Karla Poewe (Columbia: University of South Carolina Press, 1994), chap. 5, see esp. 109.

3. Ibid., 108.

4. Paul Gifford, *The New Crusaders* (London: Pluto, 1991), 97.

5. Bryan Wilson, ed., *Patterns of Sectarianism* (London: Heinemann, 1967).

6. See Martyn Percy, "Fundamentalism: A Problem for Phenomenology," *Journal of Contemporary Religion* 10, no. 1 (1995): 83–91; and Stephen Hunt, "The Devil's Advocates: The Function of Demonology in the Worldview of Fundamentalist Christianity," in *Fundamentalism, Church and Society*, ed. Martyn Percy and Ian Jones (London: SPCK, 2002), 66–91.

7. M. E. Marty and R. S. Appleby, eds., *Fundamentalism Observed* (Chicago: University of Chicago Press, 1991).

8. James W. Sire, *Name the Elephant: Worldview as a Concept* (Downers Grove, Ill.: InterVarsity, 2004).

9. Mark J. Cartledge, "The Future of Glossolalia: Fundamentalist or Experiential?" *Religion* 28 (1998): 233–244; Ralph W. Hodd, Peter C. Hill, and W. Paul Williamson, *The Psychology of Religious Fundamentalism* (New York: Guilford, 2005); and Stephen Hunt, "Magical Moments: An Intellectualist Approach to the Neo-Pentecostal Faith Ministries," *Religion* 28 (1998): 271–280.

10. George Marsden, *Reforming Fundamentalism* (Grand Rapids, Mich.: Eerdmans, 1987); George Marsden, *Fundamentalism and American Culture: The Shaping of Twentieth-Century Evangelicalism* (New York, Oxford University Press, 1980), especially, chapters 12–14.

11. Hunt, "Magical Moments," 271; and Robin Horton, *Patterns of Thought in Africa and the West* (Cambridge: Cambridge University Press, 1993).

12. *Time* 168, no. 12 (September 18, 2006): 48–56; H. T. Neuman, "Cultic Origins of Word-Faith Theology within the Charismatic Movement," *Pneuma* 12, no. 1 (1990): 32–55; and Robert M. Bowman, *The Word-Faith Controversy: Understanding the Health and Wealth Gospel* (Grand Rapids, Mich.: Baker, 2001).

13. Emmanuel Kingsley Larbi, *God and the Poor* (Accra: Center for Pentecostal and Charismatic Studies, 2001).

14. Bowman, *The Word-Faith Controversy*, 227

15. E. Kingsley Larbi, "The Nature of Continuity and Discontinuity of Ghanaian Pentecostal Concept of Salvation in African Cosmology," *Asian Journal of Pentecostal Studies* 5, no. 1 (2002): 99–119; J. Kwabena Asamoah-Gyadu, *African Charismatics: Current Developments Within Independent Indigenous Pentecostalism in Ghana* (Leiden: Brill, 2005), 201–232.

16. Asamoah-Gyadu, *African Charismatics*, 141.

17. T. M. V. Berg, "Culture, Christianity and Witchcraft in a West African Context," in *The Changing Face of Christianity*, eds. L. Sanneh and J. Carpenter (New York: Oxford University Press, 2005), 45–62.

18. Asamoah-Gyadu, *African Charismatics*, 143.

19. Mercy Amba Oduyoye, *Hearing and Knowing* (Maryknoll, N.Y.: Orbis, 1986), 98; and Christian Gaba, *The Sacred Scriptures of an African People* (New York: NOK, 1974).

20. For further discussion, see Ogbu U. Kalu, "Poverty in Pre-Colonial and Colonial West Africa: Perception, Causes and Alleviation," in *Themes in West Africa's History*, ed. Emmanuel K. Akyeampong (Oxford: James Currey, 2006), 163–185.

21. Donald McGravan, *Crucial Issues in Mission Tomorrow* (Chicago: Moody, 1972), 132.

22. W. J. Hollenweger, "Healing through Prayer: Superstition or Forgotten Christian Tradition?" *Theology* 92, no. 747 (1989): 166–174, see esp. 173.

23. Laurenti Magesa, *Anatomy of Inculturation: Transforming the Church in Africa* (Maryknoll, N.Y.: Orbis, 2004), 81; and Stuart C. Bate, *Inculturation and Healing: Coping-Healing in South African Christianity* (Pietermaritzburg: Cluster, 1995). Bate's work is a plea for a holistic approach to coping-healing among the churches. He shows the strengths and weaknesses among the AICs and Pentecostals in South Africa.

24. "Divine Healing, Pentecostalism and Mission," *International Review of Mission* 93, no. 370–371 (July/October 2004): 407. The entire issue of the journal is rich with articles by prominent scholars on the subject. The Lutherans also held a conference, which is detailed in Ingo Wulfhorst, ed., *Ancestors, Spirits and Healing in Africa and Asia: A Challenge to the Church* (Geneva: LWF, 2005); and Stanley Hauerwas, *God, Medicine and Suffering* (Grand Rapids, Mich.: Eerdmans, 1990).

25. K. J. Archer, "Pentecostal Hermeneutics: Retrospect and Prospect," *Journal of Pentecostal Theology* 8 (1996): 63–81; S. A. Ellington, "Pentecostalism and the Authority of Scripture," *Journal of Pentecostal Theology* 9 (1996): 16–38; H. M. Ervin, "Hermeneutics: A Pentecostal Option, "*Pneuma* 3, no. 2 (Fall 1981); W. Iser, *The Act of Reading* (Baltimore: Johns Hopkins University Press, 1978); and C. H. Pinnock, "The Work of the Holy Spirit in Hermeneutics," *Journal of Pentecostal Theology* 2 (April 1993): 3–23.

26. Cheryl B. Johns, *Pentecostal Formation* (Sheffield: Academic Press, 1993), 86; and Steve Land, *Pentecostal Spirituality: A Passion for the Kingdom* (Sheffield: Sheffield Academic Press, 1993), chaps. 1, 4.

27. W. Brueggemann, *Texts under Negotiation: The Bible and Postmodern Imagination* (Philadelphia: Fortress, 1993), 29; and J. D. Johns, "Pentecostalism and Postmodern Worldview," *Journal of Pentecostal Theology* 7 (1995): 73–96.

28. Lewis R.Rambo, *Understanding Religious Conversion* (New Haven, Conn.: Yale University Press, 1993), 113–116.

CHAPTER 14

1. Wilbert Shenk, "Recasting Theology of Mission: Impulses from the Non-Western World," *International Bulletin of Missionary Research* 25, no. 3 (2001); Kenneth R. Ross, "Blessed Reflex: Mission as God's Spiral of Renewal," *International Bulletin of Missionary Research* 27, no. 4 (2003): 162–168; and Jehu J. Hanciles, "Migration and Mission: Some Implications for the Twenty-First Century Church," *International Bulletin of Missionary Research* 27, no. 4 (2003): 146–153.

2. Konrad Raiser, *Ecumenism in Transition: A Paradigm Shift in the Ecumenical Movement* (Geneva: WCC Publications, 1991), 54; Lesslie Newbigin, "Ecumenical Amnesia," in *International Bulletin of Missionary Research* 18, no. 1 (January 1994): 1–5; and Charles West, *The Power to Be Human* (New York: Macmillan, 1971).

3. Gaba Pastoral Letter, 7:50–51; J. Mullin, *The Catholic Church in Modern Africa* (London: Geoffrey Chapman, 1965); E. E. Uzoukwu, *Liturgy: Truly Christian, Truly African* (Eldoret: Gaba, 1982); and F. K. Lumbala, *Celebrating Jesus in Africa: Liturgy and Inculturation* (Maryknoll, N.Y.: Orbis, 1998).

4. K. Carroll, *Yoruba Religious Art* (London: Geoffrey Chapman, 1967); and R. I. J. Hackett, *Art and Religion in Africa* (London: Cassell, 1996).

5. Ogbu U. Kalu, *Divided People of God: Church Union Movement in Nigeria, 1867–1967* (New York: NOK, 1978); Ogbu U. Kalu, "Church Unity and Religious Change in Africa," in *Christianity in Independent Africa*, ed. Edward Fashole-Luke (London: Rex Collings, 1979), 164–175.

6. J. Mugambi, J. Mutiso-Mbinda, and J. Vollbrecht, *Ecumenical Initiatives in Eastern Africa* (Nairobi: AACC/AMCEA Joint Research Project, 1992).

7. J. V. Taylor, "Selfhood: Presence or Personae?" in *The Church Crossing Frontiers: Essays on the Nature of Mission. In Honour of Bengt Sundkler* (Uppsala: Studia Missionalia Uppsaliensia 11, 1969), 171–176. See esp. contributions by Lars Thurnberg, 209–225, and Lesslie Newbigin, 245–265.

8. J. C. McKenna, *Finding a Social Voice: The Church and Marxism in Africa* (New York: Fordham University Press, 1997).

9. Eliott Kendall, *The End of an Era* (London: SCM, 1978), 85; Ogbu U. Kalu, "Church, Mission and Moratorium," in *The History of Christianity in West Africa*, ed. Ogbu U. Kalu (London: Longman, 1980), 365–374; Ogbu U. Kalu, "Not Just New Relationship but a Renewed Body," *International Review of Mission* 64 (April 1975): 143–148; and Ogbu U. Kalu, "Passive Revolution and Its Saboteurs:African Christian Initiative in the Era of Decolonization" in *Mission, Nationalism and the End of Empire: Ed Brian Stanley* (Grand Rapids, Mich.: Eerdmans, 2003), 250–277; T. A Beetham, *Christianity and the New Africa* (London: Pall Mall, 1967).

10. Marika Sherwood, *Pastor Daniels Ekarte and the African Churches Mission* (London: Savannah, 1994). Another Nigerian, Ernest Akin, ran the Wesleyan African Mission located in Templar Hall as a combined church and small loans scheme for destitute Africans in Liverpool, while the Methodist African and West Indian Mission Religious and Social Institute also operated for a short period. Both institutions disappeared by 1948.

11. Afe Adogame, "A Home Away from Home: The Proliferation of Celestial Church of Christ in Diaspora-Europe," *Exchange* 27, no. 2 (1998): 141–160.

12. Steve S. C. Moon, "The Recent Korean Missionary Movement: A Record of Growth," *International Bulletin of Missionary Research* 27, no. 1 (2003): 11–16; and Robert Coote, "Shifts in the North American Protestant Full-time Missionary Community," *International Bulletin of Missionary Research* 29, no. 1 (2005): 12–13.

13. Callum Brown, *The Death of Christian Britain* (London: Routledge, 2001).

14. Paul T. Zeleza, "Contemporary African Migrations in a Global Context," *African Issues* 30, no. 1 (2002): 9–14.

15. See "African Scholars and the African Humanities: A Symposium," African Studies Program, Northwestern University, Evanston, Ill., June 3, 2004.

16. See http://mondediplo.com/maps/.

17. See http://news.bbc.co.uk/1/hi/world/africa/3568329.stm.

18. M. Splindler, "The Impossible Quest for a General Theory of the Diaspora," *Exchange* 27, no. 1 (1998); Roswith Gerloff, "Pentecostals in the African Diaspora," in *Pentecostals after a Century*, eds. Allan H. Anderson and Walter J. Hollenweger (Sheffield: Sheffield Academic Press, 1999), 67–86; and G. ter Haar, *African Christians in Europe* (Nairobi: Acton, 2001): 118–135. Ter Haar discusses the terminology and its difficulties.

19. Afe Adogame, "The Quest for Space in the Global Spiritual Marketplace: African Religions in Europe," *International Review of Mission* 89, no. 354 (2000): 400–409.

20. See a collection of essays in Afe Adogame and Cordula Weisskoppel, eds., *Religion in the Context of African Migration* (Bayreuth: Bayreuth African Studies 75, 2005).

21. Kevin Ward, "Ugandan Christian Communities in Britain," *International Review of Missions* 89, no. 354 (July 2000): 320–328.

22. Galia Sabar and Shlomit Kanari, "I'm Singing My Way Up: The Significance of Music among African Christian Immigrants in Israel," *Studies in World Christianity* 12, no. 2 (2006): 101–125.

23. Rijk van Dijk, "From Camp to Encompassment: Discourses of Transubjectivity in Ghanaian Pentecostal Diaspora," *Journal of Religion in Africa* 27, no 2 (May 1997): 135–159, see esp. 149; and G. Ter Haar, "Strangers in the Promised Land: African Christians in Europe," *Exchange* 24, no. 1 (1995): 1–33.

24. Andrew Walls, *The Missionary Movement Christian History: Studies in the Transmission of the Faith* (Maryknoll, N.Y.: Orbis, 1996), 258–259.

25. Roswith Gerloff, ed., "Open Space: The African Christian Diaspora in Europe and the Quest for Human Community," *International Review of Mission* 89, no. 354 (July 2000). The entire issue of the journal is devoted to papers from various conferences on the theme.

26. Alasdair Crockett and David Voas, "Generations of Decline: Religious Change inTwentieth-Century Britain," *Journal for the Scientific Study of Religion* 45, no. 4 (December 2006): 567–584.

27. E. W. Blyden, *Christianity, Islam and the Negro Race* (London: W. B. Whittingham, 1888), 143; and Hollis. R Lynch, *Edward Wilmot Blyden: Pan-Negro Patriot, 1832–1912* (London: Oxford University Press, 1967), 147.

Selected Bibliography

Achunike, Hilary. "Catholic Charismatic Movement in Igboland, 1970–1995." PhD thesis, University of Nigeria, Nsukka, 2001.

Adeogun, Ebenezer O. *A Transplant of the Vine: Forty Years of Foursquare History in Nigeria.* Lagos: Foursquare Gospel Church in Nigeria, 1999.

Adogame, Afe. "African Communities in Diaspora." In *African Christianity: An African Story,* ed. Ogbu U. Kalu. Pretoria: University of Pretoria, 2005, 494–514.

———. "Appropriating Malachi Rhetoric in African Pentecostalism: The Case of the Redeemed Christian Church of God in Nigeria and the USA." Paper delivered at the African Studies Association Conference, New Orleans, November 11–14, 2004.

———. "To Be or Not to Be: Politics of Belonging and African Christian Communities in Germany." In *Religion in the Context of African Migration,* ed. Afe Adogame and Cordula Weisskoeppel. Bayreuth: Bayreuth African Studies Series, no.75, (2005), 1–22.

———. "A Home Away from Home: The Proliferation of Celestial Church of Christ in Diaspora-Europe." *Exchange* 27, no. 2 (1998): 141–160.

———. "Locating Religion in the Context of African Migration." In *Religion in the Context of African Migration,* ed. Afe Adogame and Cordula Weisskoeppel. Bayreuth: Bayreuth African Studies Series, no.75, (2005):1–22.

———. "Mission from Africa: The Case of the Celestial Church of Christ in Europe. *Zeitschrift fur Missionwissenschaft und Religionwissenschaft* 84, no. 1 (2000): 29–44.

———. "Politicization of Religion and the Religionization of Politics in Nigeria." In *Religion, History, and Politics in Nigeria: Essays in Honor of Ogbu U. Kalu,* ed. Chima Korieh and Ugo Nwokeji. Lanham, Md.: University Press of America, 2005, 128–139.

———. "The Quest for Space in the Global Spiritual Marketplace: African Religions in Europe." *International Review of Mission* 89, no. 354 (2000): 400–409.

———. "Traversing Local-Global Religious Terrain: African New Religious Movements in Europe." *Zeitschrift für Religionwissenschaft* 10 (2002): 33–49.

———. "A Walk for Africa: Combating the Demon of HIV/AIDS in an African Pentecostal Church: The Case of Redeemed Christian Church of God." *Scriptura: International Journal of Bible, Religion and Theology in Southern Africa* 89 (2005): 396–405.

Adogame, Afe, and Wolfang Weiss. "The Interplay of Religion and Law in Germany." *Revue Pro Religionistiku* 8, no. 1 (2000): 41–64.

Adogame, Afe, and Cordula Weisskoppel, eds., *Religion in the Context of African Migration.* Bayreuth: Bayreuth African Studies 75, 2005.

Afigbo, Adiele E. *Ropes of Sand: Studies in Igbo History and Culture.* Lagos: Oxford University Press, 1981.

Akutto, F. W. B. *The Indigenization of Christianity: A Study in Ghanaian Pentecostalism.* Oxford: Oxford University Press, 1975.

Althouse, Peter. "Towards a Theological Understanding of Pentecostal Appeal to Experience." *Journal of Ecumenical Studies* 38, no. 4 (Fall 2001): 399–411.

Amadiume, Ifi. *Male Daughters Female Husbands.* London: Zed, 1985.

Anderson, Allan. "African Independent Churches and Global Pentecostalism: Historical Connections and Common Identities." In *African Identities and World Christianity in the Twentieth Century,* ed. Klaus Koschorke. Wiesbaden: Harrassowitz, 2005, 63–76.

———. "African Pentecostalism." *Studia Historiae Ecclesiaticae* 22, no. 1 (1996): 114–148.

———. "The Contextual Pentecostal Theology of David Yonggi Cho." *Asian Journal of Pentecostal Studies,* 7, no. 1 (2004)

———. "The Dubious Legacy of Charles Parham: Racism and Cultural Insensitivities among Pentecostals." *Pneuma* 27, no. 1 (2005): 51–64.

———. *An Introduction to Pentecostalism: Global Charismatic Christianity.* Cambridge: Cambridge University Press, 2004.

———. *Moya: The Holy Spirit in an African Context* Pretoria: University of South Africa Press, 1991.

———. "Pentecostal Approaches to Faith and Healing." *International Review of Mission* 91, no. 363 (October 2002): 523–534.

———. "The Prosperity Message in the Eschatology of Some Charismatic Churches." *Missionalia* 15, no. 2 (1987): 72–83.

———. *Zion and Pentecost: The Spirituality and Experiences of Pentecostal and Zionist/ Apostolic Churches in South Africa.* Pretoria: University of South Africa Press, 2000.

———. *African Reformation.* Trenton, N.J.: Africa World Press, 2000.

———. "The New Jerusalem: The Role of the Azusa Street Revival in the Global Expansion of Pentecostalism" Paper delivered at the 35th Annual Meeting of the Society for Pentecostal Studies, Pasadena, CA., March 23–25, 2006.

———. "The Newer Pentecostal and Charismatic Churches: The Shape of Future Christianity in Africa?" *Pneuma: The Journal of the Society for Pentecostal Studies* 24, no. 2 (Fall 2002): 167–184.

Anderson, Allan and Pillay, Gerald, J. "The Segregated Spirit: The Pentecostals." In *Christianity in South Africa*, ed. Richard Elphinck and Rodney Davenport. Oxford: James Currey, 1997, 227–241.

Andersson, Efraim. *Messianic Popular Movements in the Lower Congo*. Uppsala: Studia Ethnographica Upsaliensia, 1958.

Archer, K. J. "Pentecostal Hermeneutics: Retrospect and Prospect." *Journal of Pentecostal Theology* 8 (1996): 63–81.

Asahu-Ejere, Kingsley. *The Kingdom of God and Healing Exorcism*. Frankfurt: Peter Lang, 2003.

Asamoah-Gyadu, J. Kwabena. *African Charismatics: Current Developments Within Independent Indigenous Pentecostalism in Ghana*. Leiden: Brill, 2005.

———. "An African Pentecostal on Mission in Eastern Europe: The Church of the Embassy of God in the Ukraine." *Pneuma* 27, no. 2 (2005): 297–321.

———. "Anointing through the Screen: Neo-Pentecostalism and Televised Christianity in Ghana." *Studies in World Christianity* 11, no. 1 (2005): 1–28.

———. "Blowing the Cover: Media Projections of Religious Functionaries/Specialists in an African Context." *Legon Journal of the Humanities: University of Ghana* 14 (2003): 1–20.

———. "Born of Water and the Spirit: Pentecostal/Charismatic Christianity in Africa." In *African Christianity: An African Story*, ed. Ogbu U. Kalu. Pretoria: University of Pretoria Press, 2005, 389–409.

———. "Faith Healing and Mission: Reflections on a Consultative Process." *International Review of Mission* 95, nos. 370/371 (July/October 2004): 372–378.

———. "Fireballs in our Midst: West Africa's Burgeoning Charismatic Churches and the Pastoral Role of Women." *Mission Studies* 15-1, no. 29 (1998): 15–31.

———. " 'God's End-time Militia': Ecclesiology in Ghana's Charismatic Ministries." *Journal of African Christian Thought* 7, no. 1 (2004): 31–37.

———. "Half a Century of Touching Lives: Nigerian Charismatic Personalities and African (Ghanaian) Christianity, 1953–2003." In *Religion, History and Politics in Nigeria: Essays in Honour of Ogbu U. Kalu*, ed. Chima J. Korieh and G. Ugo Nwokeji. Lanham, Md.: University Press of America, 2005, 230–245.

———. "Listening with African Ears: Reflections on the 2005 World Mission Conference." *International Review of Mission* 94, no. 374 (July 2005): 343–353.

———. "Media and Fundamentalism: Re-shaping Sub-Saharan African Christianity." *Media and Development: Journal of the World Association for Christian Communication* LII, no. 2 (2005): 17–21.

———. "Mission to Set the Captives Free: Healing, Deliverance, and Generational Curses in Ghanaian Pentecostalism." *International Review of Mission* 93, nos. 370–371 (July/October 2004): 389–406.

———. "Missionaries without Robes: Lay Charismatic Fellowships and the Evangelization of Ghana." *Pneuma: The Journal of the Society for Pentecostal Studies* 19, no. 2 (1997): 167–188.

———. "Of Faith and Visual Alertness: The Message of Mediatized Religion in an African Pentecostal Context." *Material Religion* 1, no. 3 (2005): 336–357.

———. "Of Sour Grapes and Children's Teeth: Inherited Guilt, Human Rights, and Processes of Restoration in Ghanaian Pentecostalism." *Exchange: Journal of Ecumenical and Missiological Research* 33, no. 4 (2004): 334–353.

———. "Pentecostal Media Images and Religious Globalization in Sub-Saharan Africa." In *Belief in Media: Cultural Perspectives on Media and Christianity*, ed. Peter Horsfield, Mary Hess, and Adan Medrano. Aldershot: Ashgate, 2004: 65–79.

———. "Pentecostalism and the Missiological Significance of Religious Experience: The Case of Ghana's Church of Pentecost." *Trinity Journal of Church and Theology* 12, nos. 1, 2 (2002): 30–57.

———. "Pentecostalism in Africa and the Changing Face of Christianity: Pentecostal/Charismatic Renewal in Ghana." *Mission Studies* 19–2, no. 38 (2002): 14–39.

———. "Salvation in Independent Churches and Charismatic Ministries in Ghana." *Trinity Journal of Church and Theology* 2, no. 2 (1992): 84–98.

———. "The Church in the African State: The Pentecostal/Charismatic Experience in Ghana." *Journal of African Christian Thought* 6, no. 1 (1998): 51–57.

———. "To Drum or Not to Drum: Traditional Festivals, Christianity and Clashes over Religious Silence in Ghana." *Trinity Journal of Church and Theology* 15, no. 2 (July 2005): 106–116.

———. "Unction to Function: Reinventing the *Oil of Influence* in African Pentecostalism." *Journal of Pentecostal Theology* 13, no. 2 (April 2005): 231–256.

———. "Vigil and Its Implications for Religion, Evil and Public Space." *Journal of Religion in Africa* 35, no. 1 (2005): 93–117.

Atiemo, Abamfo O. *The Rise of Charismatic Movement in the Mainline Churches in Ghana*. Accra: Asempa, 1993.

———. "Singing with Understanding: The Story of Gospel Music in Ghana." *Studies in World Christianity* 12, no. 2 (2006): 142–163.

Ayandele, Emmanuel A. *Holy Johnson*. London: Frank Cass, 1971.

Ayegboyin, Deji I. "A Rethinking of Prosperity Teaching in the New Pentecostal Churches in Nigeria." *Black Theology: An International Journal* 4, no. 1 (2006): 70–86.

Badejo, Deidre. *Oshun: The Elegant Deity of Wealth, Power and Femininity*. Trenton, N. J.: Africa World, 1993.

Baeta, C. G. *Prophetism in Ghana*. London: SCM, 1962.

Barfoot, C., and G. Sheppard. "Prophetic Versus Priestly Religion: The Changing Role of Women Clergy in Classical Pentecostal Churches." *Review of Religious Research* 22, no. 1 (September 1980): 2–17.

Barnes, Michael H., ed. *Theology and the Social Sciences*. Maryknoll, N.Y.: Orbis, 2001.

Barrett, David. "Twentieth Century Pentecostal/Charismatic Renewal in the Holy Spirit with Its Goal of World Evangelization." *International Bulletin of Missionary Research* 12 (July 1988): 119–129.

Bartholomew, Richard. "Publishing, Celebrity and the Globalisation of Conservative Protestantism." *Journal of Contemporary Religion* 21, no. 1 (2006): 1–14.

Bastian, Misty. "Married in the Water: Spirit Kin and Other Afflictions of Modernity in Southeastern Nigeria." *Journal of Religion in Africa* 27, no. 3 (May 1997): 116–134.

Bate, Stuart C. *Inculturation and Healing: Coping-Healing in South African Christianity.* Pietermaritzburg: Cluster, 1995.

Bashri, Ghazali. *Nigeria and Sharia.* Leicester,: The Islamic Foundation, 1994.

Bediako, Kwame. "Christian Witness in the Public Sphere: Some Lessons and Residual Challenges from the Recent Political History of Ghana." In *The Changing Face of Christianity: Africa, the West, and the World,* ed. Lamin Sanneh and Joel A. Carpenter. New York: Oxford University Press, 2005, 117–134.

———. *Christianity in Africa: The Renewal of a Non-Western Religion.* Maryknoll, N.Y.: Orbis, 1995.

———. *Theology and Identity: The Impact of Culture upon Christian Thought in the Second Century and Modern Africa.* Oxford: Regnum, 1992.

Berg, T. M. V. "Culture, Christianity and Witchcraft in a West African Context." In *The Changing Face of Christianity,* ed. L. Sanneh and J. Carpenter. New York: Oxford University Press, 2005, 45–62.

Bernstein, Ann. "Flying under South Africa's Public Radar: The Growth and Impact of Pentecostals in a Developing Country." A paper presented at the "Spirit in the World" Symposium, University of Southern California, October 4–7, 2006.

Bevans, Stephen. "Unraveling a 'Complex Reality': Six Elements of Mission." *International Bulletin of Missionary Research* 27, no. 2 (April 2003): 50–53.

Bevans, Stephen, and Roger Schroeder, eds. *Mission for the Twenty-First Century.* Chicago: Chicago Center for Global Ministries Publications, 2001.

Beyer, P. *Religion and Globalization.* London: Sage, 1994.

Bibby, Reginald W. *Restless God: The Renaissance of Religion in Canada.* Don Mills: Ontario: Stoddart, 2002.

Blumhofer, Edith. *Restoring the Faith: The Assemblies of God, Pentecostalism, and American Culture.* Chicago: University of Illinois Press, 1993.

Blyden, E. W. *Christianity, Islam and the Negro Race.* London: W. B. Whittingham, 1888.

Bolton, Frances. *And We Beheld His Glory.* London: Royal House Publishers, 1992.

Boo-Wong, Yoo. *Korean Pentecostalism: Its History and Theology.* New York: Peter Lang, 1988.

Bowman, Robert M. *The Word-Faith Controversy: Understanding the Health and Wealth Gospel.* Grand Rapids, Mich.: Baker, 2001.

Brethauer, Berit. "Televangelism: Local and Global Dimensions." In *Religions/ Globalizations: Theories and Cases,* eds. Dwight Hopkins, Lois Lorentzen, Eduardo Mendieta, and David Batstone. Durham, N.C.: Duke University Press, 2001, 203–226.

Brouwer, Steve, Paul Gifford, and Susan Rose. *Exporting the American Gospel: Global Christian Fundamentalism.* New York: Routledge, 1996.

Brown, Callum. *The Death of Christian Britain.* London: Routledge, 2001.

Bruce, Steve. "The Charismatic Movement and the Secularization Thesis." *Religion* 28 (1998): 223–232.

Brueggemann, W. *Texts under Negotiation: The Bible and Postmodern Imagination.* Philadelphia: Fortress, 1993.

Brueggemann, Walter. *Land.* Philadelphia: Fortress, 1977.

———. *The Prophetic Imagination.* Philadelphia: Fortress, 1978.

Burgess, G. "The Calcutta Revival of 1907." *Asian Journal of Pentecostal Studies (AJPS)* 6, no. 1 (2003): 123–143.

———. "Latter Rain Falling in the East." *Church History* 68 (September 1999): 648–665.

Burgess, Richard H. "The Civil War Revival and Its Pentecostal Progeny: A Religious Movement among the Igbo People of Eastern Nigeria 1967–2002." PhD diss., University of Birmingham, 2004.

Burgess, Stanley M., ed. *International Dictionary of Pentecostal and Charismatic Movements.* Grand Rapids, Mich.: Zondervan, 2002.

———. "Pentecostal of India." *Asian Journal of Pentecostal Studies (AJPS)* 4, no. 1 (2001): 85–98.

Burpeau, Kemp P. *God's Showman: A Historical Study of John G. Lake and South African/American Pentecostalism.* Oslo: Refleks, 2004.

Callaway, Helen. "Women in Yoruba Tradition and in the Cherubim and Seraphim Society." In *The History of Christianity in West Africa*, ed. Ogbu U. Kalu. London: Longman, 1980, chap. 18.

Carrette, J., and R. King, eds. *Selling Spirituality.* London: Routledge, 2005.

Carroll, K. *Yoruba Religious Art.* London: Geoffrey Chapman, 1967.

Cartledge, Mark J. "The Future of Glossolalia: Fundamentalist or Experiential?" *Religion* 28 (1998): 233–244.

Chafer, Tony, ed. *Promoting the Colonial Idea: Propaganda and Visions of Empire in France.* New York: Palgrave, 2002.

Chirenje, J. Mutero. *Ethiopianism and African Americans in South Africa, 1883–1916.* Baton Rouge: Louisiana State University Press, 1987.

Chitendo, Ezra. "The Insider/Outsider Problem in Research on Religion and Migration." In *Religion in the Context of Migration*, ed. A. Adogame and C. Weisskoppel. Bayreuth: Bayreuth African Studies 75, (2005), 79–94.

———. *Singing Culture: A Study of Gospel Music in Zimbabwe.* Uppsala: Nordiska Afrikainstitutet, research report no. 121, 2002.

Christellow, Allen. "Islamic Law and Judicial Practice in Nigeria: An Historical Perspective." *Journal of Muslim Minority Affairs* 22, no. 1 (2002): 185–204.

———. "Religious Protest and Dissent in Northern Nigeria." *Journal of the Institute of Muslim Minority Affairs* 6, no. 2 (1985): 375–393.

Cohen, Abner. *The Power Culture of the Elite.* Berkeley and Los Angeles: University of California Press, 1981.

Coleman, Simon. "Charismatic Christianity and the Dilemma of Globalization." *Religion* 28 (1998): 245–256.

Cook, Philip L. *Zion City, Illinois: Twentieth Century Utopia.* Syracuse, N.Y.: Syracuse University Press, 1996.

Coote, Robert. "Shifts in the North American Protestant Full-time Missionary Community." *International Bulletin of Missionary Research* 29, no. 1 (2005): 12–13.

Copeland, David. "The Urbanization of Popular African Music: Some Theoretical Observations," *Popular Music* 2 (1982): 113–130.

Corten, André, and Ruth Marshall-Fratani, eds. *Between Babel and Pentecost: Transnational Pentecostalism in Africa and Latin America.* Bloomington: Indiana University Press, 2001.

Cox, Harvey. *Fire from Heaven: The Rise of Pentecostal Spirituality and the Reshaping of Religion in the Twenty-First Century.* Reading, Mass.: Addison-Wesley, 1995.

Creech, Joe. "Visions of Glory: The Place of the Azusa Street Revival in Pentecostal History." *Church History* 65 (1996): 405–424.

Christelow, A. "Islamic Law and Judicial Practice in Nigeria: An Historical Perspective." *Journal of Muslim Minority Affairs* 22, no. 1 (2002): 185–204.

Christelow, Allen. "Religious Protest and Dissent in Northern Nigeria." *Journal of the Institute of Muslim Minority Affairs* 6, no. 2 (1985): 375–393.

Crockett, Alasdair, and David Voas. "Generations of Decline: Religious Change inTwentieth-Century Britain." *Journal for the Scientific Study of Religion* 45, no. 4 (December 2006): 567–584.

Dali, Rebecca S. *Women in Ministry with Jesus: Where Are There?* Bukuru, Jos: Africa Christian Textbooks, 2000.

Daneel, M. L. *African Earthkeepers: Wholistic Interfaith Mission.* Maryknoll, N.Y.: Orbis, 2001.

———. "Exorcism as a Means of Combating Wizardry." *Missionalia* 18, no. 1 (1990): 220–247.

———. *The Quest for Belonging.* Gweru: Mambo, 1987.

Danfulani, Umar H. D. "Exorcising Witchcraft: The Return of the Gods in NRMs on the Jos Plateau." *African Affairs* 98, no. 391 (April 1999): 167–193.

Dayton, Donald. *Theological Roots of Pentecostalism.* Metuchen, N. J.: Scarecrow, 1987.

De Craemer, Willy. *The Jamma and Church: A Bantu Catholic Movement in Zaire.* Oxford: Clarendon, 1977.

Denny, Elder J. W. *A Nostalgic Look at Yesterday.* Memphis: COGIC, 1995.

De Witte, Marleen. "Altar Media's Living Word: Televised Charismatic Christianity in Ghana." *Journal of Religion in Africa* 33, no. 2 (2003): 172–202.

———. "The Holy Spirit on Air in Ghana." *Media and Development* 52, no. 2 (2005): 22–26.

Dickson, Kwesi. *Theology in Africa.* (Maryknoll, N. Y.: Orbis, 1984).

Doi, A. R. *Non-Muslims under Sharia.* Lahore: Kazi Publications, 1990.

Douglas, Stephanie. "Bringing Order to Chaos: The Role of Typologies in the Study of African Christian Movements." *Mission: Journal of Mission Studies* 5, no. 2 (1998): 257–273.

Drewal, H. J. "Mami Wata Shrines: Exotica and the Constitution of Self." *African Material Culture,* eds. M. Arnold, C. Geary, and K. Hardin. Bloomington: Indiana University Press, 1996, 308–333.

Drooges, Andre. "Globalisation and Pentecostal Success." In *Between Babel and Pentecost,* eds. André Corten and Ruth Marshall-Fratani. Bloomington: Indiana University Press, 2001, 41–61.

Dudley, Carl S., and Sally A. Johnson. *Energizing the Congregation: Images That Shape Your Church's Ministry.* Louisville: Westminster/John Knox, 1993.

Dunn, Ross. *The Adventures of Ibn Battutta.* Berkeley, and Los Angeles: University of California Press, 1986.

Dyrness, William A. *Visual Faith: Art, Theology and Worship in Dialogue.* Grand Rapids, Mich.: Baker, 2001.

Ekeh, P. P. *Colonialism and Social Structure.* Ibadan: University of Ibadan Press, 1983.

Ellington, S. A. "Pentecostalism and the Authority of Scripture." *Journal of Pentecostal Theology* 9 (1996): 16–38.

Ellis, Stephen, and Gerrie ter Haar. *Worlds of Power: Religious Thought and Political Practice in Africa*. New York: Oxford University Press, 2004.

Elphinck, Richard, and Rodney Davenport, eds. *Christianity in South Africa*. Oxford: James Currey, 1997.

Engelke, Matthew. "Discontinuity and the Discourse of Conversion." *Journal of Religion in Africa* 34, no. 1 (2004): 82–109.

Englund, Harri. "Christian Independency and Global Membership: Pentecostal Extraversions in Malawi." *Journal of Religion in Africa* 33, no. 1 (2003): 83–111.

———. "The Quest for Missionaries: Transnationalism and Township Pentecostalism in Malawi." In *Between Babel and Pentecostalism*, ed. André Corten and Ruth Marshall-Fratani Bloomington: Indiana University Press, 2001, 235–254.

Enwerem, I. M. *A Dangerous Awakening: The Politicization of Religion in Nigeria*. Ibadan: IFRA, 1995.

Ervin, H. M. "Hermeneutics: A Pentecostal Option." *Pneuma* 3, no. 2 (Fall 1981).

Eyoh, Dickson. "From Economic Crisis to Political Liberalization: Pitfalls of the New Political Sociology for Africa." *African Studies Review* 38, no. 2 (1995): 39–65.

Ezemadu, Reuben. *The Vision So Far: A Story of the Christian Missionary Foundation*. Ibadan, 1990.

Falola, Toyin. *Violence in Nigeria: The Crisis of Religious Politics and Secular Ideologies*. Rochester: Rochester University Press, 1998.

Faupel, D. William. *The Everlasting Gospel: The Significance of Eschatology in the Development of Pentecostal Thought*. Sheffield: Sheffield Academic Press, 1996.

Featherstone, M. et al., eds., *Global Modernities*. London: Sage, 1993.

Fee, Gordon. *Gospel and Spirit Issues in New Testament Hermeneutics* (Peabody, Mass.: Hendricks, 1991.

Fee, Gordon. "Towards a Pauline Theology of Glossolalia." In *Pentecostalism in Context*, eds. W. Ma and R. P. Menzies. Sheffield: Academic Press, 1997, 24–37.

Ferdinando, Keith. *The Triumph of Christ in African Perspective*. Carlisle: Paternoster, 1999.

Ferguson, James. *Expectation of Modernity: Myths and Meanings of Urban Life in the Zambian Copperfield*. Berkeley and Los Angeles: University of California Press, 1999.

Fiedler, Klaus. "The Charismatic and Pentecostal Movements in Malawi in Cultural Perspective." *Religion in Malawi* 9 (1999): 28–38.

Frederick, Marla. *Between Sundays: Black Women and Everyday Struggles of Faith*. Berkeley and Los Angeles: University of California Press, 2003.

Freston, Paul. "Evangelicals and Politics: A Comparison between Africa and Latin America." *Journal of Contemporary Religion* 13, no. 1 (1998): 37–49.

———. *Evangelicals and Politics in Asia, Africa and Latin America*. Cambridge: Cambridge University Press, 2001.

Fyfe, Christopher, and Andrew F. Walls, eds., *Christianity in Africa in the 1990s*. Edinburgh: Center for African Studies, University of Edinburgh, 1996.

Gaba, Christian. *The Sacred Scriptures of an African People.* New York: NOK, 1974.

Garner, Robert. "Religion as a Source of Social Change in the New South Africa." *Journal of Religion in Africa* 30, no. 3 (2000): 310–343.

George, A. C. "Pentecostal Beginnings in Travancore." *Asian Journal of Pentecostal Studies (AJPS)* 4, no. 2 (2001): 215–237.

Gerloff, Roswith, ed. "Open Space: The African Christian Diaspora in Europe and the Quest for Human Community." *International Review of Mission* 89, no. 354 (July 2000)

———. "Pentecostals in the African Diaspora." In *Pentecostals After a Century*, ed. Allan H. Anderson and Walter J. Hollenweger. Sheffield: Sheffield Academic Press, 1999, 67–86.

Gifford, Paul. "Africa Shall Be Saved: An Appraisal of Reinhard Bonkke's Pan African Crusade." *Journal of Religion in Africa* 17 (1987): 63–92.

———. *African Christianity: Its Public Role.* Bloomington: Indiana University Press, 1998.

———. "A View of Ghana's New Christianity." In *The Changing Face of Christianity: Africa, the West, and the World*, ed. Lamin Sanneh and Joel A. Carpenter. New York: Oxford University Press, 2005, 81–96.

———. "Chiluba's Christian Nation: Christianity as a Factor in Zambian Politics, 1991–1996." *Journal of Contemporary Religion* 13, no. 3 (1998): 363–381.

———. *Christianity in Doe's Liberia.* Cambridge: Cambridge University Press, 1993.

———. "The Complex Provenance of African Pentecostal Theology." In *Between Babel and Pentecost*, ed. André Corten and Ruth Marshall-Fratani. Bloomington: Indiana University Press, 2001, 62–79.

———. "Ghana's Charismatic Churches." *Journal of Religion in Africa* 24 (1994): 241–265.

———. *Ghana's New Christianity: Pentecostalism in a Globalizing African Economy.* Bloomington: Indiana University Press, 2004.

———. *New Crusaders: Christianity and the New Right in Southern Africa.* London, Pluto, 1991.

———, ed. *New Dimensions in African Christianity.* Nairobi: AACC, 1992.

———. "Some Recent Developments in African Christianity." *African Affairs* 93, no. 373 (1994): 513–534.

Githieya, Francis K. *The Freedom of the Spirit: African Indigenous Churches in Kenya.* Atlanta: Scholars Press, 1997.

Goff, J. R., and G. Wacker, eds. *Portraits of a Generation: Early Pentecostal Leaders.* Fayetteville: University of Arkansas Press, 2002, 87–104, 123–142.

Greene, Herman L. *UPCAG-The First 90 Years, 1919–1945.* Sussex, N. J.: Geda, 2005.

Griffith, Marie. "What Happens When Women Pray? Prayer and Paradox in Women's Aglow." A paper presented at the Twenty-Third Annual Meeting of the Society for Pentecostal Studies, Mexico City, March, 15,1993.

Griffith, R. Marie. *God's Daughters: Evangelical Women and the Power of Submission.* Berkeley and Los Angeles: University of California Press, 1997.

Griffith, R. Marie, and Barbara D. Savage, eds., *Women and Religion in the African Diaspora: Knowledge, Power and Performance.* Baltimore: Johns Hopkins University Press, 2006.

Guder, Darrell. *The Continuing Conversion of the Church*. Grand Rapids, Mich.: Eerdmans, 2000.

Gundani, Paul. "Independent Prophets and the Quest for Wholeness/Healing." *Studia Historicae Ecclesiasticae* 24, no. 1 (1998): 1–16.

Hackett, R. I. J. *Art and Religion in Africa*. London: Cassell, 1996.

———. "Charismatic/Pentecostal Appropriation of Media Technologies in Nigeria and Ghana." *Journal of Religion in Africa* 28, no. 3 (1998): 258–277.

———. "Mediating Religion in South Africa: Balancing Air-Time and Rights Claim." In *Religion, Media, and the Public Sphere*, eds. Birgit Meyer and Annelies Moors. Bloomington: Indiana University Press, 2006.

———. "New Directions for African and Asian Charismatics." *Pneuma* 18, no. 1 (1996): 67–77.

———. *New Religious Movements in Nigeria*. Lewiston, N. Y.: Mellen, 1987.

———. *Religion in Calabar: The Religious Life and History of a Nigerian Town*. New York: Mouton de Gruyter, 1989.

———. "The Prosperity Gospel in West Africa." In *Religion and the Transformation of Capitalism*, ed. R. Roberts. London: Routledge, 1995, 199–214.

Hanciles, Jehu. *Euthanasia of Mission: Autonomy of an African Church in a Colonial Context*. Westport, Conn: Praeger, 2002.

———. "Migration and Mission: Some Implications for the Twenty-First Century Church." *International Bulletin of Missionary Research* 27, no. 4 (2003): 146–153.

Hastings, Adrian. *African Catholicism: Essays in Discovery*. London: SPCK, 1989.

———. *The Church in Africa, 1450–1950*. Oxford: Clarendon, 1994.

Hauerwas, Stanley. *God, Medicine and Suffering*. Grand Rapids, Mich.: Eerdmans, 1990.

Hawn, C. Michael. *Gather into One: Praying and Singing Globally*. Grand Rapids, Mich.: Eerdmans, 2003, 104–188.

Hays, R. B. *The Moral Vision of the New Testament*. San Francisco: HarperSanFrancisco, 1996.

Haynes, Jeff. *Religion and Politics in Africa*. London: Zed, 1996.

Hayward, V. E W., ed. *African Independent Church Movements*. London: Edinburgh House, 1957.

Hefner, R. W. *Conversion to Christianity: Historical and Anthropological Perspectives*. Berkeley and Los Angeles: University of California Press, 1993.

Helgeson, Kristina. "Pentecostalism as a Moral Order: Action for Israel among Pentecostals in Durban, South Africa." *Swedish Missiological Themes* 92, no. 2 (2004): 261–280.

Hiebert, Paul G. *Anthropological Insights for Missionaries*. Grand Rapids, Mich.: Baker, 1985.

Hiebert, R. E., D. F. Ungurait, and T. W. Bohn. *Mass Media IV: An Introduction to Modern Communication*. New York: Longman, 1985.

Higginbotham, Evelyn Brooks. *Righteous Discontent: The Women's Movement in the Black Baptist Church, 1880–1920*. Cambridge, Mass.: Harvard University Press, 1993.

Hirschkind, Charles. "Cassettes Ethics: Public Piety and Popular Media in Egypt." In *Religion, Media and the Public Sphere*, ed. Birgit Meyer and Annelies Moors. Bloomington: Indiana University Press, 2006.

Hiskett, M. "The Maitatsine Riots of Kano, 1980: An Assessment." *Journal of Religion in Africa* 17, no. 3 (1987): 209–223.

Hiskett, Mervyn. *The Development of Islam in West Africa*. London: Longmans, 1984.

Hock, Klaus. "Jesus Power-Super Power: On the Interaction between Christian Fundamentalism and New Religious Movements in Africa." *Mission Studies* 12, no. 1 (1995): 56–70.

Hocken, Peter D. "A Charismatic View on the Distinctiveness of Pentecostalism." In *Pentecostalism in Context: Essays in Honor of William W. Menzies*, ed. Wonsuk Ma and Robert P. Menzies. Sheffield: Sheffield Academic Press, 1997, 103.

Hollenweger, W. J. "After Twenty-Five Years of Research on Pentecostalism." *International Review of Missions* 75, no. 297 (1986): 3–12.

———. "Healing through Prayer: Superstition or Forgotten Christian Tradition?" *Theology* 92, no. 747 (1989): 166–174.

———. *New Wine in Old Wineskins*. Gloucester: Fellowship, 1973.

———. *Pentecostalism between Black and White*. Belfast: Christian Journals, 1974.

———. *The Pentecostals*. London: SCM Press, 1972.

Hodd, Ralph W., Peter C. Hill, W. Paul Williamson. *The Psychology of Religious Fundamentalism*. New York: Guilford, 2005.

Hoover, Stewart. *Mass Media Religion: The Social Sources of the Electronic Church*. London: SAGE, 1988.

Horn, J. Nico. "The Experience of the Spirit of Apartheid: Recovery of the Black Roots of Pentecostalism for South African Theology." In *Experiences of the Spirit*, ed. Jan A. B. Jongeneel. Frankfurt: Peter Lang, 1989: 117–140.

Horton, Robin. "African Conversion." *Africa* 41, no. 2 (1971): 87–108.

———. "African Conversion." *Africa* 45, no. 3 (1975): 219–235.

———. "African Conversion." *Africa* 45, no. 4 (1975): 373–399.

———. *Patterns of Thought in Africa and the West*. Cambridge: Cambridge University Press, 1993.

Horwitz, Robert B. *Communication and Democratic Reform in South Africa*. Cambridge, Mass.: Cambridge University Press, 2001.

Hunt, Stephen. "The Devil's Advocates: The Function of Demonology in the Worldview of Fundamentalist Christianity." In *Fundamentalism, Church and Society*, eds. Martyn Percy and Ian Jones. London: SPCK, 2002, 66–91.

———. "Magical Moments: An Intellectualist Approach to the Neo-Pentecostal Faith Ministries." *Religion* 28 (1998): 271–280.

Hunwick, John O. *Sharia in Songhay: The Replies of al-Maghili to the Questions of Askia al-Hajj Muhammad*. Oxford: Oxford University Press, 1985.

Ibe, Basil O. *The Ultimate Christian Generation: The Emergence of the Prophetic Company*. Lagos: Rehoboth, 2001.

Ibrahim, Jibrin. "Religion and Political Turbulence in Nigeria." *Journal of African Studies* 29 (1991).

Ihejirika, Walter "Media and Fundamentalism in Nigeria." *Media and Development* 52, no. 2 (2005): 38–43.

Emeka, Paul, " Benson Idahosa Factor in Nigerian Pentecostalism," PhD thesis, University of Nigeria, Nsukka, 2001.

Ilesanmi, Simeon. *Religious Pluralism and the Nigerian State*. Athens: Ohio University, 1997.

Irvin, Dale. "Ecumenical Dislodgings," *Mission Studies* 22, no. 2 (2005): 187–205.

———. "Pentecostal Historiography and Global Christianity: Rethinking the Question of Origin," *Pneuma* 27, no. 1 (2005): 35–50.

Isaacson, Allan. *Deeper Life*. London: Hodder and Stoughton, 1990.

Iser, W. *The Act of Reading*. Baltimore: Johns Hopkins University Press, 1978.

Isichei, Elizabeth. "The Maitasine Rising in Nigeria, 1980–1985: A Revolt of the Disinherited." *Journal of Religion in Africa*17, no. 3 (October 1987): 194–208.

Jenkins, Philip. *The New Faces of Christianity: Believing the Bible in the Global South*. New York: Oxford University Press, 2006.

———. *The Next Christendom: The Coming of Global Christianity*. New York: Oxford University Press, 2002.

Johns, Cheryl B. *Pentecostal Formation*. Sheffield: Academic Press, 1993.

Johns, Cheryl Bridges. "Pentecostal Spirituality and Conscientization of Women." In *All Together in One Place*, ed. H. D. Hunter and P. D. Hocken. Sheffield: Sheffield Academic Press, 1993, 153–165.

Johns, J. D. "Pentecostalism and Postmodern Worldview." *Journal of Pentecostal Theology* 7 (1995): 73–96.

Johnson, Elizabeth. *She Who Is: The Mystery of God in Feminist Discourse*. New York: Crossroad, 1993.

Jones, Ben. "The Church in the Village, the Village in the Church: Pentecostalism in Teso, Uganda." *Cahiers d'Etudes Africaines* 45, no. 2 (2005): 497–517.

Kalu, Ogbu U. "Church, Mission and Moratorium." In *The History of Christianity in West Africa*, ed. Ogbu U. Kalu. London: Longman, 1980, 365–374.

———. "Church Unity and Religious Change in Africa." In *Christianity in Independent Africa*, ed. Edward Fashole-Luke London: Rex Collings, 1979.

———. "The Dilemma of Grassroot Inculturation of the Gospel." *Journal of Religion in Africa* 25 (February 1995): 48–72.

———. *Divided People of God: Church Union Movement in Nigeria, 1867–1967* (New York: NOK, 1978.

———. "Doing Mission through the Post Office: The Naked Faith People of Igboland, 1920–1960." *Neue Zeitschrift fur Missionwissenschaft* 54, no. 4 (2000): 263–280.

———. "Elijah's Mantle: Ministerial Formation in Contemporary African Christianity." *International Review of Missions* 94, no. 373 (April 2005): 263–277.

———. *Embattled Gods: Christianization of Igboland, 1841–1991*. Trenton, N. J.: Africa World Press, 2003.

———. "Ethiopianism and the Roots of Modern African Christianity." In *Cambridge History of Christianity: World Christianities, c. 1815–c. 1914*, ed. Sheridan Gilley and Brian Stanley. Cambridge: Cambridge University Press, 2005, 8:576–592.

———. "Globecalisation and Religion: The Pentecostal Model in Africa." In *Uniquely African?* eds. J. L. Cox and G. ter Haar. Trenton, N.J.: Africa World, 2003, 215–240.

———. "Gospel, Culture and Mission: Revisiting an Enduring Problem." *Skrief en Kirk*, Pretoria, Jaargang 19, no. 2 (1998): 283–300.

————. "Harsh Flutes: The Religious Dimension of the Legitimacy Crisis in Nigeria, 1993–1998." In *Nigeria in the Twentieth Century*, ed. Toyin Falola. Durham, N.C.: Carolina Academic Press, 2002, 667–685.

————. "Holy Praiseco: Negotiating Sacred and Popular Music and Dance in African Pentecostalism." Harvard Africa Seminar, Harvard University, March, 20, 2007. Forthcoming in *Pneuma*.

Kalu, Ogbu U. "Not Just New Relationship but a Renewed Body." *International Review of Mission* 64 (April 1975): 143–148.

————. "Passive Revolution and Its Saboteurs: African Christian Initiative in the Era of Decolonization, 1955–1975." In *Mission, Nationalism, and the End of Empire*, ed. Brian Stanley. Grand Rapids, Mich.: Eerdmans, 2003, 250–277.

————. "Poverty in Pre-colonial and Colonial West Africa: Perception, Causes and Alleviation." In *Themes in West Africa's History*, ed. Emmanuel K. Akyeampong. Oxford: James Currey, 2006, 163–185.

————. *Power, Poverty, and Prayer*. Frankfurt: Peter Lang, 2000.

————. "The Practice of Victorious Life: Pentecostal Political Theology and Practice in Nigeria, 1970–1996." *Mission: Journal of Mission Studies, University of Ottawa* 5, no. 2 (1998): 229–255.

————. *The Scourge of the Vandals: Nature and Control of Cults in Nigerian Universities*. Nsukka: University of Nigeria Press, 2001.

————. "Sharia and Islam in Nigerian Pentecostal Rhetoric, 1970–2003." *Pneuma* 26, no. 2 (2004): 242–261.

————. "Themes in West African Church History at the Edge of the Twenty-First Century." *Missionalia*, 30, no. 2 (August 2002): 235–264.

————. "Unconquered Spiritual Gates: African Inculturation Theology Revisited." *Journal of Inculturation Theology*, Catholic Institute for West Africa, Port Harcourt 1, no. 1 (1991): 25–37.

————. "Waves from the Rivers: The Spread of the Garrick Braide Movement in Igboland, 1918–1939." *Journal of the Historical Society of Nigeria* 8, no. 4 (June 1977): 95–110.

Kalu, Ogbu U., and Graham Duncan. "*Bakuzufu*: Revival Movements and Indigenous Appropriation in African Christianity." In *African Christianity: An African Story*, ed. Ogbu U. Kalu (Pretoria: University of Pretoria, 2005), 278–307.

Karkkainen, Veli-Matti. *Pneumatology: The Holy Spirit in Ecumenical, International, and Contextual Perspective*. Grand Rapids, Mich.: Baker, 2002.

Kasiera, E. Musembe. "Development of Pentecostal Christianity in Western Kenya." PhD thesis, University of Aberdeen, 1981.

————. "The Foundation and Development of Nyang'ori Mission, 1909–1924." seminar paper, Department of Philosophy and Religious Studies, University of Nairobi, Feb. 20, 1980.

Kay, William. *Pentecostal Britain*. Carlisle: Paternoster, 2000.

Kayiwa, Simeon. *Working Miracles*. London: New Wine, 2003.

Kendall, Eliott. *The End of an Era*. London: SPCK, 1978.

Kinukawa, H. *Women and Jesus in Mark: A Japanese Perspective*. Maryknoll, N.Y.: Orbis, 1994.

Kraft, Charles. *Anthropology for Christian Witness*. Maryknoll, N.Y.: Orbis, 1996.

————. *Appropriate Christianity*. Pasadena, Calif.: Wm. Carey Library, 2005.

Kraft, M. G. *Understanding Spiritual Powers*. Maryknoll, N.Y.: Orbis, 1995.

Kukah, Matthew Hassan. *Religion, Politics and Power in Northern Nigeria*. Ibadan, Nigeria: Spectrum, 1994.

Lagerwerf, Leny. "Leadership Training in an African Independent Churches—Working with Whites." *Exchange* 23, no. 3 (Dec ember 1994): 54–56.

Laitin, David. *Hegemony and Culture*. Chicago: University of Chicago Press, 1986.

Land, Steve. *Pentecostal Spirituality: A Passion for the Kingdom*. Sheffield: Sheffield Academic Press, 1993.

Larbi, E. Kinsgley. "African Pentecostalism in the Context of Global Pentecostal Ecumenical Fraternity: Challenges and Opportunities." *Pneuma* 24, no. 2 (Fall 2002): 138–166.

————. *Eddies of Ghanaian Pentecostalism*. Accra: CPCS, 2001.

————. *God and the Poor*. Accra: Center for Pentecostal Charismatic Studies, 2001.

————. "The Nature of Continuity and Discontinuity of Ghanaian Pentecostal Concept of Salvation in African Cosmology." *Asian Journal of Pentecostal Studies (AJPS)* 5, no. 1 (2002): 99–119.

Last, Murray. *The Sokoto Caliphate*. London: Longmans, 1967.

Laurent, Pierre-Joseph. "Les conversions aux Assemblees de Dieu du Burkina Faso." *Journal des Africanistes* 47 (1998): 67–97.

————. *Les Pentecostistes du Burkina Faso: Mariage, Pouvoir et Guerison*. Paris: Karthala, 2003.

————. "Transnationalism and Local Transformation: The Example of the Church of Assemblies of God of Burkina Faso." In *Between Babel and Pentecost*, ed. André Corten and Ruth Marshall-Fratani. Bloomington: Indiana University Press, 2001, 256–273.

Leonard, Christine. *A Giant in Ghana: The Story of James McKeown and the Church of the Pentecost*. Chicester: New Wine Ministries, 1989.

Liandon, Roberts. *John G. Lake: The Complete Collection of His Life and Teachings*. Laguna Hills, Calif.: Roberts Liandon Ministries, 1999.

Linden, Ian. *Catholics, Peasants and Chewa Resistance in Nyasaland, 1889–1939*. Berkeley and Los Angeles: University of California Press, 1974.

Lonsdale, J. M. "European Attitudes and African Pressures: Missions and Government in Kenya between the Wars." In *Hadith 2*, ed. B. A. Ogot. Nairobi: East Africa Publishing House, 1975, 229–242.

Lovett, Leonard. "Black Origins of the Pentecostal Movement." In *Aspects of Pentecostal-Charismatic Origins*, ed. Vinson Synan. Plainsfield, N. J.: Logos, 1975, 123–141.

Lowman, Peter. *The Day of His Power: A History of the International Fellowship of Evangelical Students*. Leicester: Intervarsity, 1983.

Lubeck, Paul. "Islamic Protest under Semi-industrial Capitalism." *Africa* 55, no. 4 (1986): 369–397.

Ludwig, Frieder. "Elijah II: Radicalisation and Consolidation of the Garrick Braide Movement, 1915–1918." *Journal of Religion in Africa* 22, no. 4 (1993): 298–315.

Lugwuana, L. "Medicine, Spiritual Healing and African Response." *Africa Theological Journal* 23, no. 1 (2000): 17–32.

Lumbala, F. K. *Celebrating Jesus in Africa: Liturgy and Inculturation*. Maryknoll, N.Y.: Orbis, 1998.

Lynch, Hollis R. *Edward Wilmot Blyden*. New York: Oxford University Press, 1967.

Lyon, D. "Glocalization and Contemporary Religion." In *A Global Faith: Essays on Evengelicalism and Globalisation*, ed. M. Hutchinson and O. U. Kalu. Sydney: CSAC, 1997, 47–68.

Mabogunje, Akin. *Urbanisation in Nigeria*. London: Oxford University Press, 1968.

Macchia, Frank. "Tongues as a Sign: Towards a Sacramental Understanding of Pentecostal Experience." *Pneuma* 5 (1993): 61–76.

Mackenzie, V. M. *Not without a Struggle: Leadership Development for African American Women in Ministry*. Cleveland: United Church Press, 1996.

Magesa, Laurenti. *African Traditional Religion: The Moral Foundations for Abundant Life*. Maryknoll, N.Y.: Orbis, 1997.

———. *Anatomy of Inculturation: Transforming the Church in Africa*. Maryknoll, N.Y.: Orbis, 2004.

Marshall-Fratani, Ruth. "Mediating the Global and the Local in Nigerian Pentecostalism." *Journal of Religion in Africa* 28, no. 3 (1998): 278–315.

———. "Pentecostalism in Southern Nigeria: An Overview." In *New Dimensions in African Christianity*, ed. Paul Gifford. Nairobi: All Africa Council of Churches, 1992, 7–32.

———. "Power in the Name of Jesus: Social Transformation and Pentecostalism in Western Nigeria Revisited." In *Legitimacy and State in Twentieth Century Africa*, ed. T. O. Ranger and Olufemi Vaughan. London: Macmillan, 1993, 213–246.

Martin, David. "The Global Expansion of Radical Primitive Christianity." *Princeton Seminary Bulletin* 26, no. 1 (2005): 111–122.

Martin, David. *Pentecostalism: The World Their Parish*. Oxford: Blackwell, 1990.

Martin, M-L. *The Biblical Concept of Messianism*. Morija: Morija Sesetho Book Depot, 1964.

Marty, M. E., and R. S. Appleby, eds., *Fundamentalism Observed*. Chicago: University of Chicago Press, 1991.

Maxwell, David. *African Gift of the Spirit: Pentecostalism and the Rise of a Zimbabwean Transnational Religious Movement*. Oxford: James Currey, 2006.

———. "African Gifts of the Spirit: Fundamentalism and the Rise of the Born Again Movement." In *Fundamentalism, Church and Society*, ed. Martyn Percy. London: SPCK, 2001.

———. "Catch the Cockerel before Dawn: Pentecostalism and Politics in Postcolonial Zimbabwe." *Africa* 70 (2000): 249–277.

———. "Christianity without Frontiers: Shona Missionaries and Transnational Pentecostalism in Africa." In *Christianity and the African Imagination: Essays in Honor of Adrian Hastings*, ed. David Maxwell and Ingrid Lawrie. Leiden: Brill, 2002, 295–332.

———. "Delivered from the Spirit of Poverty: Pentecostalism, Prosperity and Modernity in Zimbabwe." *Journal of Religion in Africa* 28, no. 3 (1998): 350–373.

———. The Durawall of Faith: Pentecostal Spirituality in Neo-Liberal Zimbabwe." *Journal of Religion in Africa* 35, no. 1 (2005): 4–32.

———. "Historicizing Christian Independency: The Southern African Pentecostal Movement, 1908–1950." *Journal of African History* 40 (1999).

———. "In Defence of African Christianity." *Journal of Religion in Africa* 33, no. 4 (2000): 464–481.

———."Witches, Prophets and Avenging Spirits." *Journal of Religion in Africa* 25, no. 3 (1995): 309–339.

Mbe, Akoko. "New Pentecostalism in the Wake of the Economic Crisis in Cameroon." *Nordic Journal of African Studies* 11, no. 3 (2002): 359–376.

Mbiti, John S. *Bible and Theology in African Christianity*. Nairobi: Oxford University Press, 1986.

———. "Christianity and the Traditional Religions of Africa." *International Review of Missions* 59, no. 236 (1970): 430–441.

———. *Prayers of African Religion*. London: SPCK, 1975.

McDonnel, Kilian. "Improbable Conversations: The International Classical Pentecostal/Roman Catholic Dialogue." *Pneuma* 17, no. 2 (1995): 163–188.

———. "The Pentecostal Dimension." *Tablet* 28 (November 1992).

McGravan, Donald. *Crucial Issues in Mission Tomorrow*. Chicago: Moody, 1972.

McIntosh, Janet. "Going Bush: Black Magic, White Ambivalence and Boundaries of Belief in Postcolonial Kenya." *Journal of Religion in Africa* 36, no. 3 (2006): 254–295.

McKenna, J. C. *Finding a Social Voice: The Church and Marxism in Africa*. New York: Fordham University Press, 1997.

McLung, L. Grant. " 'Try to Get People Saved': Revisiting the Paradigm of an Urgent Pentecostal Missiology." In *The Globalization of Pentecostalism: A Religion Made to Travel*, ed. Murray Dempster, Byron Klaus, Douglas Peterson. Oxford: Regnum, 1999, 30–51.

Meyer, Birgit. "Christianity in Africa: From African Independent to Pentecostal-Charismatic Churches." *Annual Review of Anthropology* 33 (2004): 447–474.

———. "If You Are a Devil, You Are a Witch, and If You Are a Witch, You Are a Devil: The Integration of Pagan Ideas into the Conceptual Universe of Ewe Christians in Southeastern Ghana." *Journal of Religion in Africa* 22 (1992): 98–132.

———. "Impossible Representations: Pentecostalism, Vision, and Video Technology in Ghana." In *Religion, Media, and the Public Sphere*, ed. Birgit Meyer and Annelies Moors. Bloomington: Indiana University Press, 2006, 290–312.

———. " 'Make a Complete Break with the Past': Memory and Postcolonial Modernity in Ghanaian Pentecostalist Discourses." *Journal of Religion in Africa* 28, no. 3 (1998): 316–349.

———. *Translating the Devil: Religion and Modernity among the Ewe in Ghana*. Trenton, N. J.: Africa World, 1999.

Milingo, Emmanuel. *The World in Between: Christian Healing and the Struggle for Spiritual Survival*. London: Hurst, 1984.

Mlahagwa, J. R. "Contending for the Faith: Spiritual Revival and Fellowship Church in Tanzania." In *East African Expressions of Christianity*, ed. Thomas Spear and I. N. Kimambo (Oxford: James Currey, 1999): 296–306.

Moon, Steve S. C. "The Recent Korean Missionary Movement: A Record of Growth." *International Bulletin of Missionary Research* 27, no. 1 (2003): 11–16.

Moran, S. E., and L. Schlemmer. *Faith for Fearful*. Durban: Center for Applied Social Sciences, University of Natal, 1984.

Mosala, I. J. "The Implications of the Text of Esther for African Women's Struggle for Liberation in South Africa." In *Voices from the Margin: Interpreting the Bible from the Third World*, ed. R. S. Surgirtharajah. Maryknoll, N.Y.: Orbis, 1995, 168–178.

Mugambi, J., J. Mutiso-Mbinda, and J. Vollbrecht. *Ecumenical Initiatives in Eastern Africa*. Nairobi: AACC/AMCEA Joint Research Project, 1992.

Mullin, Joseph, *The Catholic Church in Modern Africa: A Pastoral Theology*. London, Geoffrey Chapman, 1965.

Mundadan, Mathias. "The Changing Task of Christian History." In *Enlarging the Story: Perspectives on Writing World Christian History*, ed. W. R. Shenk. Maryknoll, N.Y.: Orbis, 2002, 22–53, see esp. 23.

Mwaura, Philomena N. "A Burning Stick Plucked Out of the Fire: The Story of Rev. Margaret Wanjiru of Jesus Is Alive Ministries." In *Hidden Histories of Women of Faith in Africa*, ed. Isabel Phiri and Sarojini Nadar. Pitermaritzburg: Cluster, 2002, 202–224.

―――. "Nigerian Missionary Enterprises in Kenya." *Religion, History and Politics in Nigeria: Essays in Honor of Ogbu U. Kalu*, ed. Chima J. Korieh and G. Ugo Nwokeji. Lanham, Md.: University Press of America, 2005, 246–264.

Nadler, Lawrence B., Courtright, Jeffrey L., and Nadler, Marjorie K., "Why Do People Give Money to Televangelists?: A Pentecostal Development Explanation." *Journal of Communication and Religion* 19, no. 2 (September 1996): 47–58.

Ndubuisi, Luke. *Pauline Concept of Charisma in 1 Corinthians 12*. Frankfurt: Peter Lang, 2003.

Neuman, H. T. "Cultic Origins of Word-Faith Theology within the Charismatic Movement." *Pneuma* 12, no. 1 (1990): 32–55.

Newbigin, Lesslie. "Ecumenical Amnesia." In *International Bulletin of Missionary Research* 18, no. 1 (January 1994): 1–5.

Nguku, Kyalo. "Uganda's Miracle." *Charisma* 31, no. 12 (July 2006): 36–41.

Nketia, J. H. Kwabena. *The Music of Africa*. New York: Norton, 1974.

Nwankpa, Emeka. *Redeeming the Land*. Achimota, Ghana: African Christian Publishers 1995.

Nyamnjoh, Francis. *Africa's Media: Democracy and the Politics of Belonging*. London: Zed, 2005.

Oduyoye, Mercy Amba. *Daughters of Anowa: African Women and Patriarchy*. Maryknoll, N.Y.: Orbis, 1995.

―――. "The Empowering Spirit of Religion." In *Lift Every Voice*: Constructing Christian Theology from the Underside ed. S. B. Thistlewaite and M. P. Engel. San Francisco: Harper, 1990.

―――. *Hearing and Knowing*. Maryknoll, N.Y.: Orbis, 1986.

―――, ed., *Transforming Power: Women in the Household of God*. Accra: Sam-Woode, 1997.

Oduyoye, Mercy Amba, and P. Nkemdirim, eds. *Women, Culture and Theological Education*. Enugu: SNAAP, 1998.

Ojo, Matthew. "Deeper Life Christian Ministry." *Journal of Religion in Africa* 18, no. 2 (1988): 141–162.

————. "The Dynamics of Indigenous Charismatic Enterprises in West Africa." *Missionalia* 25, no. 4 (1997): 537–561.

————. *The End-Time Army: Charismatic Movements in Modern Nigeria*. Trenton, N.J.: Africa World, 2006.

————. "Nigerian Pentecostalism and Transnational Religious Networks in the West African Coastal Region." In *Enterprises Religieuses Transnationales en Afrique de L'Ouest*, ed. Laurent Fourchard et al. Paris: Karthala, 2005, 395–438.

————. "Pentecostalism, Public Accountability and Governance in Nigeria." Pentecostal-Civil Society Dialogue on Public Accountability and Governance Conference, Lagos, Nigeria, October 18, 2004.

————. "Religion, Public Space and the Press in Contemporary Nigeria." In *Christianity and Social Change in Africa*, ed. Toyin Falola. Durham, N.C.: Carolina Academic Press, 2005, 233–250.

Okitika, Steve. *The Battle for Nations: The Ministry of Interceding for Our Nation*. Lagos, Moinab, 1996.

Olonade, Timothy. *Battle Cry for the Nations: Rekindling the Flames of World Evangelization*. Jos: CAPRO Media, 1995.

Olanyinka, Bolaji Olukemi. *Female Leaders of New Generation Churches as Change Agents in Yorubaland*. PhD thesis, Obafemi Awolowo University, 2000.

Olubanke, Dorcas A. "The History of Good Women: Association of the Christ Apostolic Church," unpublished paper, January 2002.

Olupona, J. K. *Kingship, Religion and Rituals in a Nigerian Community*. Stockholm: Almquist & Wiksell, 1991.

————. "Religious Pluralism and Civil Religion in Africa." *Dialogue and Alliance* 2, no. 4 (1989): 41–48.

Omenyo, Cephas N. "Charismatic Churches in Ghana and Contextualization." *Exchange: Journal of Missiological and Ecumenical Research* 31 (2002): 252–277.

————. "The Charismatic Renewal Movement in Ghana." *Pneuma: The Journal of the Society for Pentecostal Studies* 16 (1994): 169–185.

————. "Charismatization of Mainline Churches in Ghana." In *Charismatic Renewal in Africa: A Challenge for African Christianity*, ed. Mika Vahakangas and Andrew A. Kyomo. Nairobi: Acton, 2003, 5–26.

————. "Essential Aspects of African Ecclesiology: The Case of the African Independent Churches." *Pneuma: The Journal of the Society for Pentecostal Studies* 22 (2000): 231–248.

————. "From the Fringes to the Centre: Pentecostalization of the Mainline Churches in Ghana." *Exchange: Journal of Missiological and Ecumenical Research* 34 (2005): 39–60.

————. "Neur Wein in alten scläuchen? Charismatische Erneuerung in den gefestgten Kirchen Ghanas." *Information brief* 4 (2000): 16–21.

————. *Pentecost outside Pentecostalism: A Study of the Development of Charismatic Renewal in the Mainline Church in Ghana*. Zoetermeer, Netherlands: Boekencentrum, 2002.

———. "Work of the Spirit in Proclamation and the Manifestation of Charisms of the Spirit within the Church—A Reformed Perspective." *Trinity Journal of Church and Theology* 10, nos. 1, 2 (2000): 19–32.

Omenyo, Cephas, and David Choi. "Korean Missionary Enterprise in West Africa, 1979–1999." *Exchange* 29, no. 3 (2000): 213–229.

Onwudiwe, Ebere. *Afro-Optimism*. New York: Praeger, 1993.

Onyinah, Opoku. "Contemporary Witchdemonology Africa." *International Review of Mission* 93, nos. 370–371 (July/October 2004): 330–345.

———. "Pentecostalism and the African Diaspora." *Pneuma* 26, no. 2 (Fall 2004): 216–241.

Oosthuizen, G. "African Environment: An Empirical Analysis." *African Insight* 26, no. 4 (1996): 308–324.

Otabil, Mensah. *Beyond the Rivers of Ethiopia: A Biblical Revelation on God's Purpose for the Black Race*. Accra: Altar International, 1992.

———. *Enjoying the Blessings of Abraham*. Accra: Altar International, 1992.

Paden, John. *Ahmadu Bello*. Zaria: Gaskiya Press, 1986, 205–206.

———. *Religion and Political Authority in Kano*. Berkeley, and Los Angeles: University of California Press, 1973.

Peel, John D. Y. *Aladura*. London: Oxford University Press, 1968.

———. *Religious Encounter and the Making of the Yoruba*. Bloomington: Indiana University, 2000.

Percy, Martyn. "Fundamentalism: A Problem for Phenomenology." *Journal of Contemporary Religion* 10, no. 1 (1995): 83–91.

———. "The Church in the Market Place: Advertising and Religion in a Secular Age." *Journal of Contemporary Religion* 15, no. 1 (2000): 97–119.

Phiri, Isabel A. "African Women in Mission: Two Cases from Malawi." *Missionalia* 28 (2000): 267–293.

Pillay, Gerald J. "Community Service and Conversion: Christianity among Indian South Africans." In *Christianity in South Africa*, ed. Richard Elphinck and Rodney Davenport. Oxford: James Currey, 1997, 286–296.

Pinnock, C. H. "The Work of the Holy Spirit in Hermeneutics." *Journal of Pentecostal Theology* 2 (April 1993): 3–23.

Pleas, Charles H. P. *Fifty Years' Achievement, from 1905–1956: A Period in History of the Church of God in Christ* Memphis: Church of God in Christ, 1956.

Poewe, Karla, ed. *Charismatic Christianity as a Global Culture*. Columbia: University of South Carolina Press, 1994.

———. "Links and Parallels between Black and White Charismatic Churches in South Africa and the States: Potential for Cultural Transformation." *Pneuma* 10, no. 2 (1986): 141–158.

Priority Focus: Some Needy Unreached People Groups in Nigeria. Jos: Feyisetan, 2000.

Pype, Katrina. "Dancing for God or the Devil: Pentecostal Discourse on Popular Dance in Kinshasha." *Journal of Religion in Africa* 36, no. 3 (2006): 296–318.

Quinn, Charlotte, and Frederick Quinn. *Pride, Faith and Fear: Islam in Sub-Saharan Africa*. Oxford: Oxford University Press, 2003.

Raiser, Konrad. *Ecumenism in Transition: A Paradigm Shift in the Ecumenical Movement.* Geneva: WCC Publications, 1991.

Rambo, Lewis R. *Understanding Religious Conversion.* New Haven, Conn.: Yale University Press, 1993.

Randall, Ian. *Evangelical Experiences: A Study in the Spirituality of English Evangelicals, 1918–1931.* Carlisle: Paternoster, 1999.

Rasmussen, Ane Marie Bak. *Modern African Spirituality: The Independent Holy Spirit Churches in East Africa, 1902–1976.* London: British Academic Press, 1996.

Reed, Michael. *Strategic Level Warfare: A Modern Mythology?* Fairfax, Va.: Xulon, 2002.

Robbins, Catherine. "Tukutendereza: A Study of Social Change and Withdrawal in the Balokole Revival of Uganda." PhD thesis, Columbia University, New York, 1975.

Roberstson, R. "Humanity, Globalization and Worldwide Religious Resurgence." *Sociological Analysis* 46, no. 3 (1985): 219–242.

Roebuck, D. G. "Pentecostal Women in Ministry: A Review of Selected Documents." *Perspectives in Religious Studies* 16, no. 1 (1989): 29–44.

Rommen, Edward, ed. *Spiritual Power and Missions: Raising the Issues.* Pasadena, Calif.: Wm. Carey Library, 1995.

Ross, Kenneth R. "Blessed Reflex: Mission as God's Spiral of Renewal." *International Bulletin of Missionary Research* 27, no. 4 (2003): 162–168.

Russell, L. M. et al., eds., *Inheriting Our Mothers' Gardens.* Philadelphia: Westminster, 1988.

Saayman, William A. "Some Reflections on the Development of the Pentecostal Mission Model in South Africa." *Missionalia* 21, no. 1 (1993).

Sabar, Galia. "The African Christian Diaspora in the Holy Land." In *Religion in the Context of Migration,* ed. A. Adogame and C. Weisskoppel. Bayreuth: Bayreuth African Studies 75, 2005), 155–190.

———. "African Christianity in the Jewish State: Adaptation, Accommodation and Legitimization of Migrant Workers' Churches, 1990–2003." *Journal of Religion in Africa* 34, no. 4 (2004): 407–437.

Sabar, Galia, and Shlomat Kanari. "I'm Singing My Way Up: The Significance of Music amongst African Migrants in Israel." *Studies in World Christianity* 12, no. 2 (2006): 101–125.

Samita, Z. W. "The African Church of the Holy Spirit: Origins and Advent in Kabra Division, Kamenga District." *TransAfrican Journal of History* 25 (1996): 123–145.

Sanneh, Lamin. *The Crown and the Turban: Muslims and West African Pluralism.* Boulder, Colo.: Westview, 1997.

———. *Piety and Power: Muslims and Christians in West Africa.* Maryknoll, N.Y.: Orbis, 1996.

———. *Whose Religion Is Christianity?* Grand Rapids, Mich.: Eerdmans, 2003.

Sanneh, Lamin. *Abolitionists Abroad: American Blacks and the Making of Modern West Africa.* Cambridge, Mass.: Harvard University Press, 1999.

———, and Joel Carpenter. *The Changing Face of Christianity: Africa, the West, and the World.* New York: Oxford University Press, 2005.

———. *Translating the Message: Missionary Impact on Culture.* Maryknoll, N.Y.: Orbis, 1989.

Schultze, Quentin J. *Televangelism and American Culture*. Grand Rapids, Mich.: Baker, 1991.

Shank, David. "The Prophet Harris: A Historiographical and Bibliographical Survey." *Journal of Religion* 14, no. 2 (1983).

Shenk, W., ed., *Enlarging the Story: Perspectives on Writing World Christian History*. Maryknoll, N.Y.: Orbis, 2002.

Shenk, Wilbert. "Recasting Theology of Mission: Impulses from the Non-Western World." *International Bulletin of Missionary Research* 25, no. 3 (2001).

Sherwood, Marika. *Pastor Daniels Ekarte and the African Churches Mission*. London: Savannah, 1994.

Shorter, Aylward. *Jesus as the Witchdoctor*. Maryknoll, N.Y.: Orbis, 1985.

———. *Songs and Symbols of Initiation*. Nairobi: Catholic Higher Institute of East Africa, 1987.

Shorter, Aylward, and Joseph Njiru. *New Religious Movements in Africa*. Nairobi: Paulines Publications Africa, 2001.

Showalter, Richard. *The Spiritual Awakenings in Kenya, 1970–1980: Sketches of Some Radical Believers*. Thika, Kenya: RBM, 1983.

Simon, Benjamin. "African Christians in the German-speaking Diaspora of Europe." *Exchange* 31, no. 1 (2002): 21–35.

Simpson, Anthony. *"Half-London" in Zambia: Contested Identities in a Catholic Mission School*. Edinburgh: Edinburgh University Press, 2003.

Sire, James W. *Name the Elephant: Worldview as a Concept*. Downers Grove, Ill.: InterVarsity, 2004.

Smith, Jordan Daniel. "The Arrow of God: Pentecostalism, Inequality, and the Supernatural in Southeastern Nigeria." *Africa* 71, no. 4 (2001): 587–613.

Spittler, Russell P. "Are Pentecostals and Charismatics Fundamentalists? A Review of American Uses of These Categories." In *Charismatic Christianity as a Global Culture*, ed. Karla Poewe. Columbia: University of South Carolina Press, 1994, chap. 5.

Splindler, M. "The Impossible Quest for a General Theory of the Diaspora." *Exchange* 27, no. 1 (1998).

Stanley, Susie Cunningham. *Feminist Pillar of Fire: The Life of Alma White*. Cleveland, Tenn.: Pilgrim, 1993.

———. *Holy Boldness: Women Preachers' Autobiographies and Sanctified Self*. Knoxville: University of Tennessee Press, 2002.

Stewart, Ignatius. "Churches as a Stock of Social Capital for Promoting Development in Western Cape Communities." *Journal of Religion in Africa* 36, no. 3 (2006): 346–378.

Stoneman, Timothy. "Fundamentalism and Transnational Media: An Historical Perspective." A paper presented at the Fundamentalism and Media Conference, University of Colorado at Boulder, October, 9–12, 2006.

———. "Preparing the Soil for Global Revival; Station HCJB's Radio Circle, 1949–1959." *Church History* 76, no. 1 (March 2007): 114–155.

Sundberg, Carl. *Conversion and Contextual Conceptions of Christ*. Studia Missionalia Svecana 81. Uppsala: Swedish Institute of Missionary Research, 2000.

Takya, J. "The Foundations of Religious Intolerance in Nigeria." *Bulletin of Ecumenical Research* 2, no. 2 (1989): 31–41.

Tasie, G. O. M. *Thoughts and Voices of an African Church: Christ Army Church, Nigeria.* Jos: Connack Nigeria, 1997.

Taylor, Charles. "On Religion and Violence." *The Arts and Science Review* (University of Toronto) 2, no. 1 (Spring 2005): 31–35.

Taylor, J. V. "Selfhood: Presence or Personae?" In *The Church Crossing Frontiers: Essays on the Nature of Mission. In Honour of Bengt Sundkler.* Uppsala: Studia Missionalia Uppsaliensia 11 (1969): 171–176.

Temu, A. J. *British Protestant Missions.* London: Longman, 1972.

Ter Haar, Gerrie. *African Christians in Europe.* Nairobi: Acton, 2001.

———. *Halfway to Paradise: African Christians in Europe.* Cardiff: Cardiff Academic Press, 1998.

———. *Spirit of Africa: The Healing Ministry of Archbishop Milingo of Zambia.* London: Hurst, 1992.

———. "Standing Up for Jesus: A Survey of New Developments in Christianity in Ghana." *Exchange* 23, no. 3 (1994): 221–240.

———. "Strangers in the Promised Land: African Christians in Europe." *Exchange* 24, no. 1 (1995): 1–33.

———. "A Wondrous God: Miracles in Contemporary Africa." *African Affairs* 102 (2001): 409–428.

Thompson, Glen. "Transported Away: The Spirituality and Piety of Charismatic Christianity in South Africa, 1976–1994." *Journal of Theology for Southern Africa* 11 (2004): 128–145.

Thompson, Jack T. "Xhosa Missionaries to Malawi: Black Europeans or African Christians?" *International Bulletin of Missionary Research* 24, no. 4 (2000): 168–171.

Tinney, J. B. "The Blackness of Pentecostalism." *Pneuma* 3, no. 2 (1980): 27–36.

Turner, H. W. "Nigerian Pentecostalism." *Orita, University of Ibadan,* (1971): 7–15.

———. "Typology for African Religious Movements." *Journal of Religion in Africa* 1, no. 1 (1967): 1–34.

——— "Pagan Features in African Independent Churches." *Practical Anthropology* 12, no. 4 (1965): 144–151.

Turner, P. "The Wisdom of the Fathers and the Gospel of Christ: Some Notes on the Question of Christian Adaptation in Africa." *Journal of Religion in Africa* 4 (1971): 46–58.

Victor Turner. *The Forest of Symbol.* Ithaca, N.Y.: Cornell University Press, 1967.

Uchegbulam, Victor. *Transforming the Local Church into an Apostolic and Prophetic Praying Church.* Lagos: Rehoboth, 2002.

Ukah, Asonzeh. "Advertising God: Nigerian Christian Video-Films and the Power of Consumer Culture." *Journal of Religion in Africa* 30, no. 2 (2003): 203–231.

———. "Mobilities, Migration and Multiplication: The Expansion of the Religious Field of the Redeemed Christian Church of God, Nigeria." In *Religion in the Context of African Migration,* ed. A. Adogame and C. Weisskoppel. Bayreuth: Bayreuth African Studies 75, 2005, 317–342.

————. "Pastors and Profits: A Comparative Study on the Mobilisation and Organization of Money in West African Pentecostalism." Paper presented at Ls Religionwissenschaft, University of Bayreuth, Germany, June 15, 2006.

————. "Religion and Mass Media: A Sociological Perspective." MA thesis, University of Ibadan, 1997.

————. "Seeing Is More Than Believing: Posters and Proselytization in Nigeria." In *Proselytization Revisited: Rights Talk, Free Markets and Culture Wars*, ed. R. I. J. Hackett. London: Equinox, 2006.

————. "Those Who Trade with God Never Lose: The Economics of Pentecostal Activism in Nigeria." *Christianity and Social Change in Africa: Essays in Honor of JDY Peel*, ed. Toyin Falola. Durham, N.C.: Carolina Academic Press, 2005, 253–274.

Ukpabio, Helen. *The Seat of Satan Exposed*. Calabar, Nigeria: Splendour Printers Enterprises, 1992.

Usman, Bala. *Manipulation of Religion in Nigeria*. Kaduna, Nigeria: Vanguard, 1987.

Uzoukwu, E. E. *Liturgy: Truly Christian, Truly African*. Eldoret: Gaba, 1982.

Van Gennep, A. *The Rites of Passage*. Chicago: University of Chicago Press, 1960.

Vahakangas, Mika, and Andrew Kyomo, eds. *Charismatic Renewal in Africa: A Challenge for African Christianity*. Nairobi: Acton, 2003.

Van Djik, Rijk. "From Camp to Encompassment: Discourses of Transubjectivity in Ghanaian Pentecostal Diaspora." *Journal of Religion in Africa* 27, no. 2 (May 1997): 135–159.

————. "Pentecostalism, Cultural Memory and the State: Contested Representations of Time in Postcolonial Malawi." In *Memory and Postcolony*, ed. Richard Webner. London: Zed, 1998, 155–181.

————. "Witchcraft and Scepticism by Proxy: Pentecostalism and Laughter in Urban Malawi." In *Magical Interpretations, Material Realities: Modernity, Witchcraft and the Occult in Postcolonial Africa*, ed. Henrietta L. Moore and Todd Sanders. London: Routledge, 2001, 97–117.

————. "Young Born Again Preachers in Post-independence Malawi." In *New Dimensions in African Christianity*, ed. Paul Gifford. Nairobi: All Africa Conference of Churches, Challenge Series, 1992, 55–79.

Wacker, Grant. *Heaven Below: Early Pentecostals and American Culture*. Cambridge, Mass.: Harvard University Press, 2001.

Wagner, C. Peter. *Breaking Strongholds in Your City*. Ventura, Calif.: Regal, 1993.

Walls, A.F. *The Missionary Movement Christian History: Studies in the Transmission of the Faith*. Maryknoll, N.Y.: Orbis, 1996.

————. "Africa and the Future of Christianity: A Summary and Reflection." In *Christianity in Africa in the 1990s*, ed. Christopher Fyfe and Andrew F. Walls. Edinburgh: Center for African Studies, University of Edinburgh, 1996.

————. "Africa as the Theatre of Christian Engagement with Islam in the Nineteenth Century." *Journal of Religion in Africa* 29, no. 2 (1999): 155–174.

————. *The Cross-Cultural Process in Christian History*. Maryknoll, N.Y.: Orbis, 2000.

————. "From Christendom to World Christianity: Missions and the Demographic Transformation of the Church." *Princeton Bulletin of Theology* 22, no. 3 (2001): 306–330.

Walls, Andrew F., and Christopher Fyfe, eds. *Christianity in Africa in the 1990s.* Edinburgh: African Studies Center, University of Edinburgh, 1996.

Ward, Kevin. "Obedient Rebels: The Relationship between the Early *Balokole* and the Church of Uganda." *Journal of Religion in Africa* 19, no. 3 (1989).

———. "Tukutenderaza Yesu: The Balokole Revival Movement in Uganda." In *From Mission to Church*, ed. Zablon Nthamburi. Nairobi: Acton, 1991. 113–144.

———. "Ugandan Christian Communities in Britain." *International Review of Missions* 89, no. 354 (July 2000): 320–328.

Warren, Max. *Revival: An Inquiry.* London: SCM, 1954.

Warren, Michael. *Seeing through the Media: A Religious View of Communications and Cultural Analysis.* Harrisburg, Penn.: Trinity Press International, 1997.

Waters, Michelle. "Internet Addiction Disorder and Pastoral Care." *American Journal of Pastoral Care and Counseling* 8, no. 1 (2005): 3–12.

Webster, J. B. *The African Churches among the Yoruba, 1888–1922.* Oxford: Clarendon, 1964.

Wells, H. G. "Trinitarian Feminism: Elizabeth Johnson's Wisdom Christology." In *Theology Today* 52, no. 3 (October 1995): 330–343.

West, Charles. *The Power to Be Human.* New York: Macmillan, 1971.

Wilmore, Gyraud. *Black Religion and Black Radicalism.* Maryknoll, N.Y.: Orbis, 1998, chap. 10.

Wilshade, R. L. *Sectarianism in South Nyasaland.* London: Oxford University Press, 1965.

Wilson, Bryan, ed., *Patterns of Sectarianism.* London: Heinemann, 1967.

Wink, Walter. *Engaging the Powers.* Minneapolis: Fortress, 1992.

———. *Naming the Powers: The Language of Power in the New Testament.* Philadelphia: Fortress, 1984.

Wold, J. C. *God's Impatience in Liberia.* Grand Rapids, Mich.: Eerdmans, 1968.

Wulfhorst, Ingo, ed. *Ancestors, Spirits and Healing in Africa and Asia: A Challenge to the Church.* Geneva: LWF, 2005.

Yong, Amos. *Beyond the Impasse: Towards a Pneumatological Theology of Religions.* Grand Rapids, Mich.: Baker Academics, 2003.

———. *The Spirit Poured Out on All Flesh: Pentecostalism and the Possibility of Global Theology.* Grand Rapids, Mich.: Baker, 2005.

Yoo, Boo-Wong. *Korean Pentecostalism: Its History and Theology.* New York: Peter Lang, 1988.

Young-Hoon, Lee. "Korean Pentecost: The Great Revival of 1907." *Asian Journal of Pentecostal Studies (AJPS)* 4, no. 1 (January 2001): 73–83.

Zeleza, Paul T. "Contemporary African Migrations in a Global Context." *African Issues* 30, no. 1 (2002): 9–14.

Index